“This timely contribution addresses a hot topic in American public discourse. The volume encourages its readers to think with a wide selection of Christian and Jewish interpreters from different centuries about each one of the Ten Commandments. Doing so enables readers to engage with the chain of interpreters and participate in the conversation. The book shows that the wide variety of possible interpretations, many of which are related to the times and social groups of the interpreters, is not a hindrance to understanding but rather an essential part of an ongoing process of reading and applying the commandments in various contexts. This volume will be particularly helpful for learning groups, for individuals seeking to deepen their understanding of the Ten Commandments, and as a textbook or key resource for undergraduate courses on the reception history of the commandments.”

—Ehud Ben Zvi
professor emeritus of history, classics, and religion,
University of Alberta

“Sara Koenig’s new book on the Ten Commandments is an eminently readable and entirely fascinating tour of the Decalogue and its almost stupefying range of interpretation throughout the ages. Not afraid to offer something of a ‘scrapbook’ that focuses in especially on themes, Koenig’s selection is nevertheless remarkably thorough in scope even as she pays close attention to the smallest of exegetical details. This will be the first book I consult on the meaning(s) of the Ten Commandments in the history of reception.”

—Brent A. Strawn
D. Moody Smith Distinguished Professor of Old Testament
and Professor of Law, Duke University

“Koenig’s illumination of the Ten Commandments through their history of reception across thousands of years, covering a wide array of cultural contexts and media, offers readers a rich, nuanced exploration of these unimaginably generative texts. By examining how each commandment has been interpreted and applied across different religious traditions and historical contexts, Koenig reveals their remarkable adaptability and enduring relevance. This scholarly yet accessible work demonstrates how these ancient principles continue to shape our world today, and invites readers to engage thoughtfully with their own understanding of the Ten Commandments. This is an instant classic for anyone interested in biblical interpretation, religious history, and ethical reflection.”

—Brennan Breed
associate professor of Old Testament, Columbia Theological Seminary

"In this tour de force, Koenig offers a close reading of the Ten Commandments and surveys their reception and interpretation across history. This book is an essential and timely resource for those interested in the complex nature of the commandments' reception along with their value for readers today."

—Jenny Matheny
associate professor of Christian Scriptures,
George W. Truett Theological Seminary

"Once again, Sara Koenig presents her readers with a treasure trove of insights into an Old Testament text's reception history within the Jewish and Christian traditions. Sifting a mountain of potentially relevant literature, Koenig's lucid, charitable, and well-paced prose provides just the right balance of scholarly depth and digestibility. For anyone who aims to interpret the Ten Commandments in a fresh context, this worthy volume proves an enriching investment whose dividends are guaranteed."

—Daniel J. D. Stulac
assistant professor of the Old Testament,
Briercrest College

"Sara Koenig has dug deeply into the reception history of the Decalogue. This wide-ranging exploration of Jewish and Christian interpretation of the commandments is a rich and inspiring feast for both scholarly and lay readers."

—J. Richard Middleton
professor emeritus of biblical worldview and exegesis,
Northeastern Seminary at Roberts Wesleyan University

The Ten Commandments *through the* Ages

Sara M. Koenig

William B. Eerdmans Publishing Company
Grand Rapids, Michigan

Wm. B. Eerdmans Publishing Co.
2006 44th Street SE, Grand Rapids, MI 49508
www.eerdmans.com

Published 2025
Printed in the United States of America

31 30 29 28 27 26 25 1 2 3 4 5 6 7

ISBN 978-0-8028-8212-7

Library of Congress Cataloging-in-Publication Data

A catalog record for this book is available from the Library of Congress.

To Bob Drovdahl,

for teaching me as well as learning with me

CONTENTS

INTRODUCTION

My university was given a Torah scroll by benefactors who wanted students to be able to learn from interacting with the physical scroll, so I frequently take students to the library to view the scroll. Each time, our librarian opens the scroll to Deuteronomy 5 so that students can see how the text of the Ten Com-

Torah scroll

mandments is visually distinct from the rest of the writing. The surrounding verses and chapters fill the columns of the scroll, but the prohibitions—the Hebrew לא, *l'* ("not")—are on the far left side of a column and the object of the prohibitions on the far right side, with a great deal of blank space between the words. The unique visual layout for the Ten Commandments in the Torah scroll indicates how, amid the hundreds of laws in the Bible, the Ten Commandments stand out.

Exactly why these stand out could be explained by a number of reasons. They are the first laws thundered down from God to Moses on Mount Sinai in Exodus 20 and foundational for many of the laws that follow in the book of the covenant. Repetition indicates significance in Hebrew texts, and the Ten Commandments get repeated almost verbatim in Deuteronomy 5. Jesus identifies the two greatest laws as (1) love God and (2) love neighbor (Matt 26:36–40; Mark 12:28–31; Luke 10:25–28), and while those come from Deut 6:5 and Lev 19:18, many use those two great laws as a heuristic for categorizing the Ten Commandments.[1] That is, how we can love God gets explained in the first few of the Ten Commandments: by not worshiping other gods, by not using God's name in an improper way, by observing a Sabbath. We can love our neighbors by not murdering them, not bearing false witness against them, not coveting what they have. Additionally, many have seen the Ten Commandments reiterated and echoed throughout the Bible: in the holiness code set forth in

1. Dale Allison describes the Christian tradition's understanding of the two great commandments as a summary of the Decalogue as "incessant." It appears in Irenaeus, in the fourth-century *Apostolic Constitutions* (2:36); in the writings of Rabanus Maurus (776–856), Thomas Aquinas (1225–1274), and John Calvin (1509–1564); in the *Heidelberg Catechism* (1562) and the *Westminster Confession* (1646–1647); in the commentaries of Matthew Poole (1624–1679) and Cornelius à Lapide (1562–1637); in the works of Matthew Henry (1662–1714) and Jonathan Edwards (1703–1758); in the systematic theologies of Thomas Watson (1692) and John Gill (1769–1770); in the 1928 and 1945 *Book of Common Prayer*; and in the current *Catechism of the Catholic Church*. Dale C. Allison, "The History of the Interpretation of Matthew: Lessons Learned," *In die Skriflig/In Luce Verbi* 49 (2015): https://tinyurl.com/2ptp4hex. The Greek Didache, ca. 70–150 CE, identifies two ways in the world, one of death and the other of life. The way of life includes loving God and neighbor, along with following the golden rule. Explanations for how to love one's neighbor include the second half of the Decalogue along with other commandments such as "do not equivocate . . . you shall not hate anyone." Huub van De Sandt and David Flusser observe that the double love commandment is thought of as covering the entire Torah. *The Didache: Its Jewish Sources and Its Place in Early Judaism and Christianity* (Minneapolis: Fortress, 2002), 162. Similarly, Saadiah Gaon classified the whole 613 mitzvot under one or another of the Ten Commandments in *Siddur R. Saadiah Gaon*. According to the Talmud, "Hananiah the nephew of R. Joshua says: Between each pair of Commandments were inscribed the letters of the Torah" (*Sotah* 8:3).

Leviticus 19, in the description of the one who can ascend God's holy mountain in Psalm 15, and even as the organizing structure for books of the Bible.[2]

For the purposes of this book, I suggest that the Ten Commandments stand out because of their brevity, which invites us into the act of interpretation and allows us to apply them in flexible ways to our particular situations. That is, because they are so brief—in Hebrew, several commandments consist of only two words—there are a number of possible ways to understand and follow them. Moshe Greenberg explains: "The Decalogue is outstanding for its scope and its suggestiveness: its terms are general and even ambiguous; it does not prescribe penalties (which would have defined and limited the scope of each Commandment); it invites explication, clarification, or even expansion."[3]

In other words, the Ten Commandments have such a broad scope because as they are stated in Exodus 20 and Deuteronomy 5, they are so brief and general. It turns out that, for example, there are many possible ways for a person to "honor [their] father and mother." For some, it might look like patience with an elderly parent. For others, it could involve refusing to fight

2. Andrew Hill and John Walton, for example, suggest that Deut 6–26 is structured under the Ten Commandments, in *A Survey of the Old Testament* (Grand Rapids: Zondervan Academic, 2009). They argue that after the Decalogue is given in Deut 5, the remainder of the book contains explanations of how to live them out in relation to God and people. David Noel Freedman proposed that the structure of Exodus through 2 Kings reflects the violation of the first nine commandments, in *The Nine Commandments: Uncovering a Hidden Pattern of Crime and Punishment in the Hebrew Bible* (New York: Doubleday, 2000). But, Daniel Block criticizes Freedman, writing, "To make this work he uses data extremely selectively and is forced to rearrange the commands on stealing (Josh 7), murder (Judg 19), and adultery (2 Sam 11–12) on the basis of Jeremiah 7:9." "The Decalogue in the Hebrew Scriptures," in *The Decalogue through the Centuries: From the Hebrew Scriptures to Benedict XVI*, ed. Jeffrey P. Greenman and Timothy Larsen (Louisville: Westminster John Knox, 2012), 22. Moreover, Block is wary of those who see the Ten Commandments where they may not be explicitly present. Against Weinfeld's suggestion that Lev 19 references the Ten Commandments, Block writes, "It may just as well have been based on a general awareness of the importance of these three commands for maintaining a covenantal culture." Block, "The Decalogue in the Hebrew Scriptures," 21.

3. Moshe Greenberg, "The Decalogue Tradition Critically Examined," in *The Ten Commandments in History and Tradition*, ed. Ben-Zion Segal, English version ed. Gershon Levi (Jerusalem: Magnes, 1990), 116–17. Daniel Block similarly affirms the general nature of the Ten Commandments as follows: "The surrounding narrative (cf. 19:4–6), the form of the Decalogue, and the nature of the ten terms demonstrate that this document functions, not as a legal code, but as a statement of covenantal policy, as guidance for life, creating an ideal rather than decreeing law. The Commandments are so general as to be virtually unenforceable through the judicial system. Their intention is to create a framework and ethos within which Israelites were to live." Block, "The Decalogue in the Hebrew Scriptures," 5.

with a narcissistic parent who blames you for their own actions. Because of their form, the Ten Commandments have been identified as "apodictic" commandments, absolute commands often with an assumed penalty of death. This type of commandment is contrasted with "casuistic," or case laws, based on precedents and often presented in an if/then form.[4] I suggest that as they have been interpreted throughout history and in the lived experience of those who seek to follow them, the Ten Commandments are casuistic. If your mother is experiencing memory loss, then you can honor her by listening to her repeat her stories without interrupting. If your father is a narcissist, you can honor him by maintaining boundaries in your relationship. The Ten Commandments are not casuistic in the sense that they provide us the cases; rather, their literary structure invites us to bring our particular cases into conversation with the brevity of what is being commanded.

This book will utilize the approach of reception history to explore the various ways people throughout time have interpreted and applied the Ten Commandments. Eric Ziolkowski explains reception history using an analogy from American football: he notes that the task of the "receiver" is to catch the ball and then move it further down the field.[5] Though a receiver may have a number of routes available, any given receiver will only move the ball in one particular way during one particular play of one particular game.[6] Just so, in principle a (brief) biblical text could be interpreted in a variety of ways, but as a text gets "caught" in a particular place and in a particular time by a particular community or individual, its meaning will become set and defined in that place and by that interpreter. When we take a broad historical view, such as is afforded to us by reception history, we can see that there is no single interpretation of a given commandment. Another way to say this is that the Ten Commandments are not only brief but abstract. The abstract principle of honoring parents needs to be made concrete in the real context of a family. To return to the metaphor of American football, the principle of the game is to

4. This division follows the one set forth by Albrecht Alt's 1934 article, "Die Ursprünge des israelitischen Rechts," later published in English as "The Origins of Israelite Law," in *Essays on Old Testament History and Religion*, trans. R. A. Wilson (Garden City, NY: Doubleday, 1967), 101–71.

5. Eric Ziolkowski, "Webinar: Exploring the Bible and Its Impact with EBR Online," June 24, 2020.

6. Brennan Breed discusses principles of reception history for biblical studies, drawing in particular on French philosopher Giles Deleuze's idea that a text could have various potential meanings, but only one meaning is made actual at a given time. Breed, *Nomadic Text: A Theory of Biblical Reception History* (Bloomington: Indiana University Press, 2014), 119–24.

move the ball down the field, but that remains an abstract ideal until it happens in a concrete way in a specific game.

Reception history arises within the biblical canon itself, which has collected a variety of possible understandings of what it might mean to honor one's parents: in Exod 21:15, we read, "one who hits his mother or father will surely die," and in Exod 21:17, "one who curses his mother or father will surely die." These two verses clarify that physical violence or cruel words against parents would be ways to dishonor them; they also present this as a legal absolute, spelling out the capital punishment of death for the offender. In contrast, in the commandment itself, there is no penalty but a benefit for honoring parents: "so that your days will be long in the land that the LORD your God has given to you" (Exod 20:12). Of course, biblical law is not the only place to learn more about honoring a parent. As readers continue through the Bible, they encounter stories about a righteous king like Asa, who does not follow the path of his unrighteous biological father Abijah but instead "did what was right in the sight of the LORD, as his father David did" (1 Kgs 15:11).[7] They read Jesus's admonition, "If anyone comes to me and does not hate father and mother, wife and children, brothers and sisters—yes, even their own life—such a person cannot be my disciple" (Luke 14:26). And they read Paul's explanation that to honor a parent is to "obey" (Eph 6:1). Read together, all these receptions provide texture and nuance to how someone can honor a parent. And those are just a few examples from the Bible, not including how this commandment was taught by medieval rabbis, catechized by Protestants and Catholics, or explained in popular and even secular culture. Biblical studies as a field sometimes confines itself to the historical and social world of the biblical text, not relating to later developments. Reception history, however, observes a text's meaning and application throughout history, up through and into the reader's world.

In the chapters that follow, I will demonstrate how each commandment has been received in given times and places. This reception history will not—and frankly, cannot—be exhaustive. Instead, it will represent a collection of possibilities for understanding and applying each commandment. It will not follow a simple diachronic method that begins in the ancient world of the biblical text and moves through time to today. Instead, it will identify broad themes in the reception of each commandment and give examples of receptions across history that interpret the commandment in similar ways; a twenty-

7. And there are countless examples of unrighteous kings who do not follow in their father's example, or the example of the prototypical faithful kingly ancestor, David.

first-century pop song may be placed in conversation with an eleventh-century commentary. New Testament scholar Rachel Nicholls criticizes biblical reception histories that resemble a "scrapbook,"[8] displaying what the author found interesting, meaningful, or memorable. I contend, however, that there is something valuable in gathering and organizing together material that is interesting but also informative and even invitational. That is, I hope that readers of this book will be invited and encouraged to consider how they might receive and follow the Ten Commandments today.

Why Ten?

More than ten total things are commanded in Exod 20:1–17 and Deut 5:6–21: just in Exod 20:4–5, a person is forbidden from (1) making an idol, (2) bowing down to an idol, and/or (3) serving that idol. Maimonides explained that there are thirteen different things being commanded in Exod 20:2–17 and one additional in Deut 5:6–21; Martin Buber discusses how there are twenty-three;[9] and in a 1772 synagogue in Cavaillon, France, on the inner side of the doors of the holy ark, twelve—not ten—commandments are listed.[10] The reason why Jews and Christians come up with the number ten is based on Exod 34:28, which quantifies them as "the ten words" (cf. also Deut 4:13). While there is agreement on the total number, ten, different communities assign different numbers to the various commandments. The Jewish "first word" is what some Christians understand to be the prologue: "I am the LORD your God, who brought you out of the land of Egypt, out of the house of slavery." Some combine the command not to have any other gods and not to make or worship idols into a single command. Others make two distinct commandments

8. Rachel Nicholls, *Walking on the Water: Reading Mt. 14:22–23 in the Light of Its* Wirkungsgeschichte (Leiden: Brill, 2008), 26.

9. Martin Buber, *Moses: The Revelation and the Covenant* (New York: Harper and Row, 1958), 132.

10. Gad B. Sarfatti, "The Tablets of the Law as a Symbol of Judaism," in *The Ten Commandments in History and Tradition*, ed. Ben-Zion Segal, English version ed. Gershon Levi (Jerusalem: Magnes, 1990), 414. Karlheinz Rabast proposed that the Decalogue was originally a dodecalogue, as follows: (1) YHWH your God, (2) no other god, (3) no image, (4) don't worship them (god and image), (5) don't misuse my name, (6) don't do any work on the Sabbath, (7) don't curse your father and mother, (8) don't kill a man in his person, (9) don't commit adultery with the wife of your neighbor, (10) don't steal a man or a woman, (11) don't be a false witness against your neighbor, (12) don't covet the property of your neighbor. *Das Apodiktische Recht im Deuteronomium und im Heiligkeitsgesetz* (Berlin: Heimatdienstverlag, 1949), 35–36.

against coveting: the commandment not to covet a neighbor's wife is separate from the commandment not to covet other things belonging to a neighbor. For example, see the following chart:

Content	Jewish	Roman Catholic, Lutheran	Eastern Orthodox, most Protestants
"I am the LORD your God" (Exod 20:2; Deut 5:6)	1	1	prologue
"no other gods" (Exod 20:3; Deut 5:7)	2	1	1
"no idols" (Exod 20:4–6; Deut 5:8–10)	2	1	2
"name of the LORD" (Exod 20:7; Deut 5:11)	3	2	3
"Sabbath" (Exod 20:8–11; Deut 5:12–15)	4	3	4
"honor father and mother" (Exod 20:12; Deut 5:16)	5	4	5
"don't murder" (Exod 20:13; Deut 5:17)	6	5	6
"don't commit adultery" (Exod 20:14; Deut 5:18)	7	6	7
"don't steal" (Exod 20: 15; Deut 5:19)	8	7	8
"don't bear false witness" (Exod 20:16; Deut 5:20)	9	8	9
"don't covet your neighbor's wife" (Exod 20:17; Deut 5:21)	10	9	10
"don't covet your neighbor's property" (Exod 20:17; Deut 5:21)	10	10	10

With the number ten (mostly) agreed upon, there are various possibilities assigned to its significance. Eduard Nielsen notes how "ten" is a typological number in the Torah: genealogies in Gen 5 and 11 (and also in Ruth 4) are structured by ten generations; for ten righteous people in Sodom, God would have spared the city (Gen 18:32); the number ten appears several places in the design of the Tabernacle (ten curtains [Exod 26:1]); ten-cubit-long frames (Exod 26:16); the west end of the courtyard is to have ten posts and ten bases (Exod 27:12); and a "tenth" of one's possessions is what is to be given to God as a tithe (Gen 28:22).[11] Genesis Rabbah states in references to the ten times God "said" in Genesis 1, "With ten utterances the world was created,"[12] and several Jewish commentaries make connections between God's ten words at creation and God's ten words in the Decalogue. For example, a midrash explains:

> "I am the Lord, thy God," corresponds to the first word at the creation: "Let there be light," for God is the eternal light. The second commandment: "Thou shalt have no strange gods before me," corresponds to the second word: "Let there be a firmament in the midst of the waters, and let it divide the waters from the waters." For God said: "Choose between Me and the idols; between Me, the fountain of living waters, and the idols, the stagnant waters." The third commandment: "Thou shalt not take the name of thy God in vain," corresponds to the word: "Let the waters be gathered together," for as little as water can be gathered in a cracked vessel, so can a man maintain his possessions which he has obtained through false oaths. The fourth commandment: "Remember to keep the Sabbath holy," corresponds to the word: "Let the earth bring forth grass," for he who truly observes the Sabbath will receive good things from God without having to labor for them, just as the earth produces grass that need not be sown. For at the creation of man it was God's intention that he be free from sin, immortal, and capable of supporting himself by the products of the soil without toil. The fifth commandment: "Honor thy father and thy mother," corresponds to the word: "Let there be lights in the firmament of the heaven," for God said to man: "I gave thee two lights, thy father and thy mother, treat them with care." The

11. Eduard Nielsen, *The Ten Commandments in New Perspective* (Naperville, IL: Alec R. Allenson, 1968), 6–10.

12. Midrash Rabbah, Gen 17:1; cf. Pirkei D'Rabbi Eliezer 3; Pirkei Avot 5:1; Megillah 21b:9; Avot D'Rabbi Natan 31:2; Derekh Chayim 5:15:6, etc.

> sixth commandment: "Thou shalt not kill," corresponds to the word: "Let the waters bring forth abundantly the moving creature," for God said: "Be not like the fish, among whom the great swallow the small." The seventh commandment: "Thou shalt not commit adultery," corresponds to the word: "Let the earth bring forth the living creature after his kind," for God said: "I chose for thee a spouse, abide with her." The eighth commandment: "Thou shalt not steal," corresponds to the word: "Behold, I have given you every herb-bearing seed," for none, said God, should touch his neighbor's goods, but only that which grows free as the grass, which is the common property of all. The ninth commandment: "Thou shalt not bear false witness against thy neighbor," corresponds to the word: "Let us make man in our image." Thou, like thy neighbor, art made in My image, hence bear not false witness against thy neighbor. The tenth commandment: "Thou shalt not covet the wife of thy neighbor," corresponds to the tenth word of the creation: "It is not good for man to be alone," for God said: "I created thee a spouse, let each keep to his spouse, and let not one among ye covet his neighbor's wife."[13]

Another connection is made between the Ten Commandments and God's instructions to Moses that the Israelites pay a half-shekel during the census so that no plague would come upon them (Exod 30:11–16). Because a half-shekel weighed ten *gera*, Rabbi Joshua b. Rabbi Nehemiah said in the name of Rabbi Yochanan b. Zakai: "Because the Israelites transgressed the Decalogue, each of them must give ten gera."[14] Lamentations Rabbah uses the number ten to explain that those in exile abandoned the Decalogue, because the numerical value of the Hebrew word בָּדָד, *bādād* ("alone") is ten.[15] In reference to Lam 1:1, which reads "Alas, she sits alone," the commentary in Lamentations Rabbah explains, "Alone from those who abide by the Decalogue, which you abandoned."[16]

Several Christian writers related the Ten Commandments to the ten plagues in Exodus, beginning with Augustine, who influenced eighth-century Benedictine Rabanus Maurus. Maurus's work was then adapted by twelfth-

13. Louis Ginzberg and David Stern, *Legends of the Jews*, trans. Henrietta Szold and Paul Radin (Philadelphia: The Jewish Publication Society, 2003), 1:610.

14. Pesikta de-Rav Kahana.

15. ב equals 2 and ד equals 4, so the consonants added together equal 10. The vowel points are not included in the numerical value of a word.

16. Sefaria, citing *The Sefaria Midrash Rabbah*, 2022, https://tinyurl.com/mw7hhek5.

century English archbishop Stephen Langton in his commentary on Exodus, and twelfth-century French theologian William of Auxerre subsequently reworked Langton's comments into his own writing. For example, William writes that the third plague of gnats signifies the small but constant irritation of worldly cares, which can be cured by the third commandment to keep a Sabbath day, in which one can rest from those cares.[17] Athanasius offered another, different allegorical interpretation, suggesting that David's ten-stringed harp alluded to the Ten Commandments.[18]

Lesley J. Smith discusses how for medieval interpreters the number ten was as much ideological as it was numerical, an understanding that may filter into other possible ways to understand ten:[19] it consists of seven (the biblical number for perfection or completion) plus three (a holy number). Or, humans have ten fingers and ten toes; in fact, counting on one's fingers is utilized as a mnemonic tool to teach children about the commandments. The number ten is an important integer in counting, a number to which people frequently round up, and the basis of the decimal system. Journalist Ira Glass muses, "There's 10 of them, you know, so it's enough that you feel like you're getting a comprehensive view. And yet at the same time, it's just 10, right?

17. Lesley J. Smith, *The Ten Commandments: Interpreting the Bible in the Medieval World* (Leiden: Brill, 2014), 62.

18. Martin van Schaik, *The Harp in the Middle Ages: The Symbolism of a Musical Instrument* (Amsterdam: Rodopi, 2005), 81 and 156.

19. As an example, Philo Judaeus wrote, "Here our admiration is at once aroused by their number, which is neither more nor less than is the supremely perfect, Ten. Ten contains all different kinds of numbers, even as 2, odd as 3, and even-odd as 6, and all ratios, whether of a number to its multiples or fractional, when a number is either increased or diminished by some part of itself. So too it contains all the analogies or progressions, the arithmetical where each term in the series is greater than the one below and less than the one above by the same amount, as for example 1 2 3; the geometrical where the ratio of the second to the first term is the same as that of the third to the second, as with 1 2 4, and this is seen whether the ratio is double or treble or any multiple, or again fractional as 3 to 2, 4 to 3, and the like; once more the harmonic in which the middle term exceeds and is exceeded by the extremes on either side by the same fraction, as is the case with 3, 4, 6. Ten also contains the properties observed in triangles quadrilaterals and other polygons, and also those of the concords, the fourth, fifth, octave and double octave intervals, where the ratios are respectively 1⅓, i.e., 4: 3, 1½, i.e., 3: 2, doubled, i.e., 2: 1, fourfold, i.e., 8: 2. Consequently it seems to me that those who first gave names to things did reasonably, wise men that they were in giving it the name of decad, as being the dechad, or receiver, because it receives and has made room for every kind of number and numerical ratio and progressions, and also concords and harmonies." Smith, *The Ten Commandments*, 38.

10—manageable. Not too overwhelming. Sure, I could do 10. 10? Sure."[20] But in comedian George Carlin's irreverent sketch on the Ten Commandments, he questions the number, saying: "Why ten? Why not nine, or eleven? I'll tell you why. Because ten sounds important. Ten sounds official. . . . Ten is the basis for the decimal system; it's a decade. It's a psychologically satisfying number: the top ten; the ten most wanted; the ten best-dressed. So deciding on Ten Commandments was clearly a marketing decision." [21]

One need not agree with Carlin's conclusion to notice how a list of "ten" communicates something authoritative, even today. The characters Aaron Burr and Alexander Hamilton sing about the ten duel commandments in Lin-Manuel Miranda's musical *Hamilton*. There are "Ten Commandments of" all sorts of things: the civil rights movement, con men, gold miners, electric guitars, electrical safety, online safety, tractor safety, parenting, pizza, punk.[22] Cartoonist Roz Chast drew "The Ten Passive Aggressive Commandments" for the *New Yorker*. And three years into his hosting of *Late Night with David Letterman*, the comedian began including a "Top Ten List" on his show, a bit that continued until he left the show. Benedictine Sister of Erie, Pennsylvania, Joan

20. Ira Glass, host, *This American Life*, podcast, episode 332, "The Ten Commandments," May 4, 2007, https://tinyurl.com/5ah9j5dm.

21. Carlin ultimately suggests that only two are necessary in his own "revised list of the Two Commandments: First: Thou shalt always be honest and faithful. . . . And second: Thou shalt try real hard not to kill anyone, unless, of course, they pray to a different invisible man than the one you pray to. Two is all you need folks. Moses could have carried them down the hill in his pocket," https://tinyurl.com/2hy6urjs.

22. Civil rights movement: Michael Curry, *Love Is the Way: Holding On to Hope in Troubling Times* (New York: Avery, 2020), 91; con men: *CBS News*, *Money Watch*, "The Ten Commandments for Con Men," by Geoffery James, March 7, 2011, https://tinyurl.com/49kakunx; gold miners: Museum of San Francisco, "The Miner's Ten Commandments," February 8, 2000, https://tinyurl.com/28mm2z27; electric guitars: Musicacademy, "The 10 Commandments of Electrical Guitar, https://tinyurl.com/2d72ybv8; electrical safety: Auburn University, citing *Orbit*, the journal of the Rutherford High Energy Laboratory, Didcot, England, January 31, 1965, https://tinyurl.com/6wkfnxh3; online safety: Taha Khalid, "The Ten Commandments of Online Safety," *Cyberspace* (blog), CCSI, https://tinyurl.com/4w9yr6cc; tractor safety: Kubota, "The Ten Commandments of Tractor Safety," which has been received and restated in several state governmental websites, such as a "farm safety" site for the states of Georgia, Maine, and Missouri, https://tinyurl.com/mr22zfna; parenting: "The Ten Commandments of Parenting," *Wise Family Wellness* (blog), August 22, 2018, https://tinyurl.com/ypmfak7b; pizza: "The Ten Commandments of Pizza," *Pizza Cowboy* (blog), https://tinyurl.com/mw6br8a4; punk: Bono, *Surrender: 40 Songs, One Story* (New York: Alfred A. Knopf, 2022), 85.

Chittister wrote "Ten Commandments for a Pandemic Moment in American History" in 2020; based on the biblical Ten Commandments, these included, in reference to "honor your father and mother": "Remember to honor both sides of the aisle—Republican and Democrat," and in reference to "you shall not kill": "Remember: Thou shalt not kill with partisanship the American spirit of differences."[23] In the field of biblical studies, Robert Alter offers a list of "Ten Commandments for Translators"[24] and Kristin Swenson has "Ten Commandments for Reading and/or Using the Bible."[25]

In 1989, Ted Turner said the Ten Commandments were out of date in a nuclear age and offered as an alternative his "Ten Voluntary Initiatives," which included "pledges" such as the one to "use as little toxic chemicals, pesticides and other poisons as possible"; "promises" such as the one "to contribute to those less fortunate than myself to help them become self-sufficient and enjoy the benefits of a decent life, including clean air and water, adequate food, health care, housing, education and individual rights"; and "supports," such as support of "the total elimination of all nuclear, chemical and biological weapons, and, in time, the total elimination of all weapons of mass destruc-

23. Joan Chittister, "Ten Commandments for a Pandemic Moment in American History," *National Catholic Reporter*, July 9, 2020, https://tinyurl.com/ubyth7s2.

24. Stephanie Bastek, "The Ten Commandments of Bible Translation," *The American Scholar*, April 19, 2019, https://tinyurl.com/5xh5kcnw.

25. Swenson's "Ten Commandments for Reading and Using the Bible" map onto the commandments themselves. She writes:

> 1. Thou shalt not make the Bible God (// Thou shalt have no other gods before me) 2. Thou shalt not worship the object itself (// Thou shalt not make for thyself an idol) 3. Thou shalt not presume that any given translation is the text itself (// Thou shalt not take the name of the LORD in vain) 4. Mind the gap(s) (// Remember the Sabbath day and keep it holy) 5. Honor the knowledge and wisdom of your predecessors (// Honor thy father and mother) 6. Thou shalt not use the Bible for character assassination (// Thou shalt not kill) 7. Thou shalt not forsake wisdom to embrace careless interpretations (// Thou shalt not commit adultery) "Don't be seduced by the superficial, easy, or simplistic." 8. Thou shalt not take biblical texts out of context (// Thou shalt not steal) 9. Thou shalt not presume to issue divine judgment of others (// Thou shalt not bear false witness against your neighbor) 10. Thou shalt not desire a different Bible than the one you have, no matter how exasperating it can be sometimes (// Thou shalt not covet your neighbor's wife or anything that belongs to your neighbor).

A Most Peculiar Book: The Inherent Strangeness of the Bible (New York: Oxford Academic, 2021), https://doi.org/10.1093/oso/9780190651732.003.0012.

tion."[26] Similar to Turner, Christopher Hitchens in 2010 criticized the "old" Ten Commandments, suggesting that it was time to "take up the revisionist chisel" to "the original stone version that badly needs a rewrite." He proposed "Ten New Commandments" for the 21st century.[27] Another version of "Ten Commandments for the Modern Era" was offered in 2015, updated in 2016, by Kylie Barton, a journalist for the *Huffington Post*. She introduces her list by writing, "By now, we all know that murder is wrong, theft is seriously frowned upon, cheating is repugnant, and that we should be kind to our parents. The old religious based 10 commandments are now firmly rooted in our minds, so it's about time we had some new ones relevant to the more secular society we have become."[28]

For the four hundredth anniversary of the King James Bible in 2011, the University of York in the UK organized a competition for children ages five to sixteen to create "Ten Commandments for the 21st Century" (otherwise known as 10C for 21C).[29] These three new sets of commandments—or "initiatives"—each include environmental concerns, putting limits on technology, and a concern for generosity in interpersonal relationships. While I might quibble with Barton's assertion that the "old" Ten Commandments are "firmly rooted in our minds," there does seem to be a general consensus that a list of ten is helpful for how to live and behave.

26. Charles Trueheart, "Ted Turner Updates Moses: Cable Mogul Delivers 'Ten Initiatives,'" *Washington Post*, October 30, 1989, https://tinyurl.com/y3xpcp7c.

27. Christopher Hitchens and Jacques del Conte, "The New Commandments," *Vanity Fair*, March 4, 2010, https://tinyurl.com/ycyp2dkh. Hitchens's commandments are

> I: Do not condemn people on the basis of their ethnicity or color.; II: Do not ever use people as private property.; III: Despise those who use violence or the threat of it in sexual relations.; IV: Hide your face and weep if you dare to harm a child.; V: Do not condemn people for their inborn nature.; VI: Be aware that you too are an animal and dependent on the web of nature, and think and act accordingly.; VII: Do not imagine that you can escape judgment if you rob people with a false prospectus rather than with a knife.; VIII: Turn off that fucking cell phone.; IX: Denounce all jihadists and crusaders for what they are: psychopathic criminals with ugly delusions.; X: Be willing to renounce any god or any religion if any holy commandments should contradict any of the above.

28. Kylie Barton, "10 Commandments for the Modern Era," *HuffPost*, December 21, 2006, https://tinyurl.com/2h2kbj58. Barton's list includes the commandment to "live sustainably," which is similar to one of Turner's initiatives. She also forbids "bigotry" and encourages people to "limit screen time," both of which are similar to Hitchens's.

29. University of York, "Youngsters' Modern Take on the Ten Commandments," July 15, 2011, https://tinyurl.com/upp54vfh.

Another numerical issue related to the Ten Commandments is how they get divided, especially among the two tablets mentioned in Exod 32:15. Both commentaries and visual art testify to various possibilities. Augustine wrote that when the first tablet consists of three commandments (and the second tablet consists of seven), "the mystery of the Trinity more clearly shines forth."[30] In other words, Augustine prefers to divide into three and seven to emphasize the Christian triune God. John Calvin argues for four commandments on the first tablet, and six on the second one.[31] Those who divide them into five and five include Josephus, Origen, and medieval Torah scholar Ramban.[32] Jewish midrashim emphasize the correspondence between the first five and the last five, as follows:

> The first commandment: "I am the Lord, thy God," corresponds to the sixth: "Thou shalt not kill," for the murderer slays the image of God. The second: "Thou shalt have no strange gods before me," corresponds to the seventh: "Thou shalt not commit adultery," for conjugal faithlessness is as grave a sin as idolatry, which is faithlessness to God. The third command-

30. Augustine, "Sermon 33: On What Is Written in the Psalm: *O God, I Will Sing You a New Song*," in *The Works of Saint Augustine*, vol. 3.2, *Sermons*, ed. John E. Rotelle, trans. Edmund Hill (Brooklyn, NY: New City Press, 1990), 155.

31. Calvin explains, "Those who so divide them as to give three precepts to the First Table and relegate the remaining seven to the Second, erase from the number the commandment concerning images, or at least hide it under the First. There is no doubt that the Lord gave it a distinct place as a commandment, yet they absurdly tear in two the Tenth Commandment about not coveting the possessions of one's neighbor. Besides, their division of the commandments was unknown in a purer age, as we shall soon see. Others, with us, count four articles in the First Table, but in place of the First Commandment, they put a promise without a Commandment. But I, unless convinced only by the clearest contrary evidence, take the ten words mentioned by Moses to be the Ten Commandments; and they seem to me to be arranged in quite the most beautiful order. Granting them their opinion, I shall follow what seems more probable to me, namely, that what they take as the First Commandment should occupy the place of the preface to the whole law. Then the commandments follow, four to the First Table, six to the Second." *Institutes of the Christian Religion*, ed. John T. McNeill, trans. and indexed by Ford Lewis Battles (Philadelphia: The Westminster Press, 1960), 1:378.

32. On Exod 20:13, Ramban writes, "Thus, of the Ten Commandments, there are five which refer to the glory of the Creator and five are for the welfare of man, for [the fifth commandment], *Honor thy father*, is for the glory of G-d, since it is for the glory of the Creator that He commanded that one honor one's father who is a partner in the formation of the child. Five commandments thus remain for the needs and welfare of man." Sefaria, citing *The Contemporary Torah*, ed. David E. S. Stein et al. (Philadelphia: Jewish Publication Society, 2006), https://tinyurl.com/mr3fxmnd.

> ment: "Thou shalt not take the name of the Lord in vain," corresponds to the eighth: "Thou shalt not steal," for theft leads to a false oath. The fourth commandment: "Remember the Sabbath day, to keep it holy," corresponds to the ninth: "Thou shalt not bear false witness against thy neighbor," for he who bears false witness against his neighbor commits as grave a sin as if he had borne false witness against God, saying that He had not created the world in six days and rested on the seventh, the Sabbath. The fifth commandment: "Honor thy father and thy mother," corresponds to the tenth: "Covet not thy neighbor's wife," for one who indulges this lust produces children who will not honor their true father, but will consider a stranger their father.[33]

Thomas Torrance writes, "there is, therefore, an appropriateness in thus dividing the Ten Words [into five and five], as they represent, in two perfect halves, the beautiful poise and symmetry of our moral and religious obligations."[34]

Reinhard Kratz divides the Ten Commandments on the basis of first- and third-person references to God, thus grouping the first two commandments (Exod 20:2–6) into a section that emphasizes God's exclusive claim on God's people, and the final eight (Exod 20:7–17) further subdivided, with two dealing with sacred matters and six dealing with secular ones.[35] Rabbi Lord Jonathan Sacks suggests reading the ten in three sets of three, thereby highlighting the uniqueness of the final commandment about coveting. Sacks explains,

> The first three (one God, no other God, do not take God's name in vain) are about God, the Author and Authority of the laws. The second set (keep Shabbat, honour parents, do not murder) are about createdness. Shabbat reminds us of the birth of the universe. Our parents brought us into being. Murder is forbidden because we are all created in God's image (Gen. 9:6). The third three (don't commit adultery, don't steal, don't bear false witness) are about the basic institutions of society: the sanctity of marriage, the integrity of private property, and the administration of justice.[36]

33. Ginzberg and Stern, *Legends of the Jews*, 1:609.

34. Thomas Torrance, *The Beatitudes and the Decalogue* (London: Skeffington and Son, 1992), 27.

35. Reinhard Kratz, "Der Dekalog im Exodusbuch," *VT* 44 (1994): 207–14.

36. "To Thank before We Think," *Covenant & Conversation* (blog), *Jonathan Sacks: The Rabbi Sacks Legacy*, https://tinyurl.com/3dfsm5cu.

Hebrew Bibles have the commandments against murder, stealing, adultery, and testifying falsely against a neighbor in a single verse—Exod 20:13—following the Masoretic notation. By contrast, the LXX gives each commandment its own verse, as do English Bibles. Their presentation in a single verse in Hebrew, what Aviya Kushner describes as "yoked together . . . crammed into one line,"[37] suggests an interrelatedness between those commandments that may be less evident when they each have their own verse.[38] Gad B. Sarfatti traces the visual representation of the Ten Commandments in Jewish and Christian art, noting that while a number of pieces of art depict Moses receiving a scroll from God, beginning in the fourth century the Ten Commandments were depicted on two rectangular tablets—Moses often holding one in each hand—and then in the sixth century, those were replaced with tablets with rounded tops. [39] Even today, the Jewish military chaplain's insignia consists of two rounded tablets with a star of David on top and the Hebrew numbers from one to ten, five on each tablet.

John Wesley excoriates those in his day who have focused their religion on duty toward humans and have neglected a love of God. He specifically names "the great triumvirate, Rousseau, Voltaire and David Hume" and criticizes them for having "hereby willfully and designedly put asunder what God has joined, the duties of the first and second table. It is separating the love of our neighbor from the love of God."[40] Wesley's reference to the two tables is,

37. Aviya Kushner, *The Grammar of God: A Journey into the Words and Worlds of the Bible* (New York: Spiegel & Grau, 2015), 128.

38. For example, Rashi asks what they have in common, and concludes that perhaps they are linked because they were all punishable by death, though Rashi does not discuss the prohibition against false testimony. Sefaria, citing "Rashi on Exodus 20:13," M. Rosenbaum and A. M. Silbermann, London, 1929–34, https://tinyurl.com/skh7ur3v.

39. Sarfatti explains, "up to the end of the Middle Ages, Jews did *not* use the Tablets as a symbol, and did not even depict them in drawings . . . the symbols in use in [antiquity] were the menorah, the censer, the Ark of the Covenant, the *megillah*, lulav, etrog and shofar—that is, objects seen and used by Jews regularly in ritual, or objects from the days of the Sanctuary that were still alive in the memory of the people. But who had seen the Tablets of the Law? The Holy Ark had not been extant in the Second Temple; and even in the First Temple the Tablets were enclosed within the Holy Ark and no one dared look at them. Furthermore, since it was forbidden to copy the form of any of the ritual objects of the Temple [Maimonides, *Mishneh Torah*, book VIII, 7:10], it is unlikely that anyone even thought of making a likeness of the Tablets, whose sacredness far exceeded that of any other object." Sarfatti, "The Tablets as Symbol of Judaism," 385.

40. John Wesley, "The Unity of the Divine Being," Sermon 114 in *The Works of John Wesley*, ed. Albert C. Outler (Nashville: Abingdon, 1987), 69. D. Stephen Long points out how these same arguments are made in a less polemic way by Henri de Lubac in *The Drama of*

of course, in connection with that Christian tendency to see in the ten the commandments to love God (and that, contained in the first five), and to love others (listed in the latter five). Wesley also echoes, in the eighteenth century, what Irenaeus affirmed at the end of the second century, when he said that when the Israelites received the Ten Commandments, the purpose was "to enjoin love of God and to teach just dealings with our neighbor."[41]

The order of the Ten Commandments is also understood as significant.[42] As Wesley's comments above indicate, many believe that one can only love neighbor if one has begun with love of God. Aquinas writes, "Although, by way of the senses, we have more knowledge of our neighbor than of God, yet the love of God is the basis of the love of our neighbor, as will be shown later. And therefore the commandments that direct us to God are rightly placed first."[43] Nahum Sarna points out that the Ten Commandments "opens with 'the LORD your God' and closes with 'your neighbor.'"[44] With the Jewish "first word" as "I am the LORD your God who brought you out of slavery," several Jewish commentators suggest that knowing the identity of that God is first, and necessary, in order to obey and love that God. As will be discussed in the first chapter, specifically knowing God's salvific act of freeing God's people from slavery is foundational for knowing the character of God and trusting God.

Others suggest that the order of the commandments that have to do with human relationships are in order of significance: that is, murder is "worse" than "theft," and so precedes it in the list of things forbidden.[45] In the Maso-

---

Atheist Humanism, and Charles Taylor in *A Secular Age*, that "exclusive humanism—love of neighbor—cut off from something beyond itself, fails finally to serve humanism itself." "John Wesley," in *The Decalogue through the Centuries: From the Hebrew Scriptures to Benedict XVI*, ed. Jeffrey P. Greenman and Timothy Larsen (Louisville: Westminster John Knox, 2012), 170.

41. Irenaeus, *Against Heresies* 4.16.3.

42. In the pilot episode from the TV show *The West Wing*, members of the religious right are arguing with the president's staff about the Commandments and incorrectly identify "the first commandment" as "you shall honor your father and mother." President Jed Bartlett appears on screen, saying that the first one is "I am the LORD your God, thou shalt worship no other god before me."

43. Thomas Aquinas, *Summa Theologica*, I-II, Q. 100, Art. 6, ad. 1, https://tinyurl.com/25ezxwfj.

44. Nahum Sarna, *The JPS Torah Commentary: Exodus* (Philadelphia: Jewish Publication Society, 2003), 108. By contrast, Emmett Fox wrote, "It does not matter in what order you put them. One does not have to take the Ten Commandments chronologically because actually they are not quite in logical order." *The Ten Commandments: The Master Key to Life* (New York: Harper and Row, 1953), 36.

45. Aquinas, for example, wrote, "we see the order determined by gravity of sins. It is, indeed, worse, and more repugnant to reason, to sin by deed than in speech, and in speech

retic Text of Exodus and Deuteronomy, the ordering is the same, but LXX has in Exodus the order "adultery, theft, murder" and "adultery, murder, theft" for Deuteronomy.[46] The Nash Papyrus, a document discovered at the turn of the twentieth century that contains the Shema from Deuteronomy 6 as well as a version of the Ten Commandments, also has the order "adultery, murder, theft."[47] But if reception history is our primary methodology, it is hard to sustain an argument that the commandments that come later are somehow lesser than those that appear earlier in the list: some interpreter argues that every commandment is "the" most important commandment out of the Ten. For example, Ephraim Radner suggests that the name commandment is at the center of every act humans do,[48] Aquinas writes that no sin is as dangerous as stealing, and R. Joshua the son of Hanina teaches that keeping the Sabbath is "equal to the entire law" (Midrash Tanchuma, Ki Tisa 33:6).

Exodus and Deuteronomy Variations

While the Ten Commandments appear in both Exodus and Deuteronomy, there are more than twenty differences between the two. These differences range from small things like the connecting Hebrew particle וְ, *wə* ("and") at the beginning of the word,[49] to more substantial differences, such as the rationale given for keeping the Sabbath. Even that small detail of a single Hebrew consonant is considered important; for example, in the commandment to not covet, instead of reading the list of things as separate or distinct, the "and" suggests something inclusive or additional about it. That is, you ought not covet your neighbor's house *and* your neighbor's field.

---

than in thought. And among sins of act, murder, which takes away an existing life, is worse than adultery, which jeopardizes the security of the child to be born; and adultery worse than theft, which is concerned with external goods." Aquinas, *Summa Theologica*, I-II, Q. 100, Art. 6, co., https://tinyurl.com/25ezxwfj.

46. F. H. Woods and B. J. Roberts think that the last may be original because it's borne out by Luke 18:20; Rom 13:9, Nash papyrus, and Philo. Stamm, *The Ten Commandments in Recent Research*, 22.

47. F. C. Burkitt, "The Hebrew Papyrus of the Ten Commandments," *JQR* (1903): 395–408.

48. Ephraim Radner, "Taking the Lord's Name in Vain," in *I Am the LORD Your God: Christian Reflections on the Ten Commandments*, ed. Carl E. Braaten and Christopher R. Seitz (Grand Rapids: Eerdmans, 2005), 82.

49. This occurs seven times in Deut 5, while it does not exist in Exod 20. Stamm, *The Ten Commandments*, 14.

Because Deuteronomy's version of the Ten Commandments is longer than that found in Exodus, Stamm argues that it comes later, reflecting "modernizing tendencies. . . . The additions in Deut. 5 . . . betray a desire for more precision in content and greater rhetorical fullness."[50] German scholars Frank-Lothar Hossfeld and Bernhard Lang both argue, by contrast, that the Deuteronomy version is original and was incorporated into the Sinai narrative by a postexilic redactor.[51] Eleventh-century Jewish scholar Ibn Ezra wrote that the Ten Commandments in Exodus contained God's precise words, "with no additions or deletions," but that Moses rephrased them in Deuteronomy, adding, "The practice of wise people in any language is that they preserve the meaning and are unconcerned about changes in wording as long as the meaning stays the same."[52] Ibn Ezra's comment is somewhat unorthodox; because I believe changes in wording do affect meaning, I will point out variations between Exodus and Deuteronomy in the commandments in subsequent chapters.

Negatives and Positives

The rhetoric of the Ten Commandments as mostly negative prohibitions—"you shall not"—has been both praised and criticized. George Mendenhall points out how negative commandments would allow more self-determination and more freedom to semi-nomads recently freed from slavery than positive commands would.[53] By contrast, an example of seeing the negatives as, well, negative, can be seen in William Blake's poem "The Garden of Love," which describes a chapel built in the middle of said garden.

50. Stamm, *The Ten Commandments*, 15.

51. In David L. Baker, *The Decalogue: Living as the People of God* (Downers Grove, IL: InterVarsity Press Academic, 2017), 14–15; Baker's own view is that Exodus is earlier.

52. Martin Lockshin refers to Ibn Ezra's comment as a "non-explanation," writing, "Notably, ibn Ezra's Torah commentary has remained popular, even venerated, over the centuries. Apparently traditional Judaism tolerates exegetical variety, at least to some extent, even ibn Ezra's type of exegesis that potentially undermines basic principles of the midrashic method." Martin Lockshin, "Two Versions of the Decalogue: Ibn Ezra's Non-Explanation," TheTorah.com, 2019, https://tinyurl.com/ywzvjjmd.

53. George Mendenhall, "Ancient Oriental and Biblical Law," *Biblical Archeology* 17 (1954): 30.

And the gates of this Chapel were shut
And 'Thou Shalt Not' writ over the door
So I turn'd to the Garden of Love
That so many sweet flowers bore
And I saw it was filled with graves
And tomb-stones where flowers should be
And Priests in black gowns, were walking their rounds
And binding with briars, my joys and desires.[54]

Blake's larger critique of organized religion, with death where flowers should be and priests who stifle "joys and desires," relates some of that harsh repressiveness to the negative, "thou shalt not," which dissuades the speaker in the poem from even entering the chapel. Perhaps the very language of "not" leads to a view that the law is restrictive and adverse.[55]

Many receptions, however, understand that the negative implies something positive. James Durham writes, "every Commandment doth both enjoyn and forbid."[56] Bonaventure asserts, "When God prohibits something in any commandment, he commands its opposite; and conversely, when God commands something, he prohibits its opposite," giving the example that in the commandment about honoring parents, dishonoring them is prohibited, whereas in the commandment prohibiting adultery, chastity is commanded.[57] Similarly, Puritan Lancelot Andrewes wrote that while the Ten Commandments "are for the most part of them negative; whence we note the confirmation of the rule of extension to include the affirmative, for *qui prohibit impedimentum praecipit adjumentum*, 'he that forbiddeth what hindereth doth command what furthereth.'"[58]

54. Poet Allen Ginsberg of "Howl" fame sang a version of this poem, among other Blake poems, in his 1969 album, *Songs of Innocence and Experience.*

55. There is a long anti-Jewish history of reading law as repressive, restrictive, negative, and even harmful. Often this includes contrasting the Old Testament law with a New Testament grace, or even contrasting the Old Testament God of wrath with the loving second person of the Trinity, Jesus.

56. James Durham, *The Law Unsealed, or, a practical exposition of the Ten Commandments. With a resolution of several momentous questions and cases of conscience.* In the digital collection Early English Books Online, https://tinyurl.com/phfsuw6v, 6.

57. Bonaventure, *St. Bonaventure's Collations on the Ten Commandments*, trans. Paul J. Spaeth (New York: Franciscan Institute, 1995), 97.

58. Lancelot Andrewes, *A Pattern of Catechistical Doctrine and Other Minor Works* (Oxford: John Henry Parker, 1846; New York: AMS, 1967), 81.

Luther and Calvin each discuss the positive formulations implied in the negative commandments. In John Wesley's Sermon 25, on the Sermon on the Mount, he describes every commandment as "a covered promise,"[59] and Presbyterian pastor Earl Palmer said that each of the Ten Commandments implies a "grand positive."[60] A website titled "10 Love Commandments" explains how each of the Ten Commandments "has a don't and a do side, covering all thoughts, words, and deeds": so, the commandment that states "don't take God's name in vain" also means, "do glorify God's name—bless, sing to the Lord, control your tongue."[61] Not only have the Ten Commandments themselves been understood to imply positive actions, they also have been read as positive insights into the nature of God: that is, the commandment forbids killing because God is a God of life who gives life and preserves life.[62] We are forbidden from false testimony against a neighbor because God is a God of Truth, or as Calvin put it, "since God (who is truth) abhors a lie, we must practice truth without deceit toward one another."[63]

Walter Harrelson writes about how the negative formulation helps "to underscore kinds of action that would mean the ruin of human life in community,"[64] arguing that these are more powerful than lists of what should or must be done. Harrelson also asserts that the prohibitions in the Decalogue provide freedom from legalism: "Legalism arises when the requirements of God are made too specific, when they are related too directly to the concrete requirements of life, when life begins to be too tightly hedged about by Torah. . . . A free and sovereign God demonstrates his love and grace and lays down that pattern of human activity that is ruled out in principle, inviting his

59. ResourceUMC, "John Wesley Sermons: Sermon 25—Upon Our Lords Sermon on the Mount 5," https://tinyurl.com/2p95shjd.

60. Earl Palmer, "You Shall Not Kill," *Preaching Today*, July 2020, https://tinyurl.com/4tp95ped.

61. TenLoveCommandments.com, https://tinyurl.com/469cdb6w.

62. Cf. Walter Harrelson, *The Ten Commandments and Human Rights* (Philadelphia: Fortress, 1980), 115. Eugenia Gamble writes in reference to the commandment against murder, "God is one who holds life and death and who values all life." *Words of Love: A Healing Journey with the Ten Commandments* (Louisville: Westminster John Knox, 2022), 204.

63. Calvin, *Institutes*, 1, 411.

64. Harrelson, *The Ten Commandments*, 112. He continues, "The prohibitions must have a character different from that of curse ritual or treaty or code of law that contains the specification of punishment to follow upon stated misdeeds. What is needed is a set of prohibitions that cover wide areas of human conduct, sum these up, and laconically state that they are not to be done."

people freely to come to terms with life under these constraints. . . . Let the pattern of positive law develop too richly and profusely, uncontrolled by the basic prohibitions, and freedom and joy in God are endangered."[65]

The negative formulation gives clear boundaries about what is forbidden without legislating what "should" be done. The "shalt nots" express the outer limits, but there is room for freedom and even creativity within the bounds of the limits.

Unique or Not?

Some receptions of the Ten Commandments praise their uniqueness,[66] while, as mentioned in the opening paragraphs of this introduction, others note how similar they are to other biblical texts, especially Exod 34:11–26; Deut 27:15–26; Ezek 18:5–9; Hos 4:2; Jer 7:9; and Ps 15. A midrash on Leviticus 19 connects each Commandment with a corresponding verse in that chapter, as follows:

> In the Commandments it is written (in Exod. 20:2 = Deut. 5:6): I < AM > THE LORD YOUR GOD; and here (in Lev. 19:2): I < AM > THE LORD YOUR GOD.
>
> In the Commandments it is written (in Exod. 20:3 = Deut. 5:7): YOU SHALL HAVE NO < OTHER GODS BESIDE ME >; and here (in Lev. 19:4): DO NOT TURN UNTO IDOLS.
>
> In the Commandments it is written (in Exod. 20:7 = Deut. 5:11): YOU SHALL NOT TAKE < THE NAME OF THE LORD YOUR GOD IN VAIN >; and here (in Lev. 19:12): YOU SHALL NOT SWEAR FALSELY BY MY NAME.
>
> In the Commandments it is written (in Exod. 20:8; cf. Deut. 5:12): REMEMBER [THE SABBATH DAY]; and here it is written (in Lev. 19:3): YOU SHALL KEEP MY SABBATHS.
>
> In the Commandments it is written (in Exod. 20:12 = Deut. 5:16): HONOR YOUR FATHER AND YOUR MOTHER; and here it is written (in Lev. 19:3, cont.): YOU EACH SHALL FEAR HIS MOTHER AND HIS FATHER.

65. Harrelson, "Karl Barth on the Decalogue," *Sciences Religieuses* 6 (1976–77): 239.

66. E.g., Earl Palmer, *Old Law New Life: The Ten Commandments and New Testament Faith* (Nashville: Abingdon, 1984), 21.

> In the Commandments it is written (in Exod. 20:13 = Deut. 5:17): YOU SHALL NOT MURDER; and here it is written (in Lev. 19:16): YOU SHALL NOT STAND OVER THE BLOOD OF YOUR NEIGHBOR.
>
> In the Commandments it is written (in Exod. 20:13 [14] = Deut. 5:17 [18]): YOU SHALL NOT COMMIT ADULTERY; and here it is written (in Lev. 19:2): YOU SHALL BE HOLY.
>
> In the Commandments it is written (in Exod. 20:13 [15] = Deut. 5:17 [20]): YOU SHALL NOT STEAL; and here it is written (in Lev. 19:11): YOU SHALL NOT STEAL.
>
> In the Commandments it is written (in Exod. 20:13 [16] = Deut. 5:17): YOU SHALL NOT BEAR < FALSE WITNESS AGAINST YOUR NEIGHBOR >; and here it is written (in Lev. 19:16): YOU SHALL NOT GO AROUND AS A SLANDERER AMONG YOUR PEOPLE.
>
> In the Commandments it is written (in Exod. 20:14 [17] = Deut. 5:18 [21]): YOU SHALL NOT COVET; and here it is written (in Lev. 19:13): YOU SHALL NOT OPPRESS YOUR NEIGHBOR, AND YOU SHALL NOT ROB HIM.[67]

Daniel Block is representative of many scholars who conclude that the Ten Commandments represent the general framework for covenantal living, such that the ideas—of sole fidelity to God, of treating others in the community in particular ways—get repeated in these different sections of the Old Testament.[68] Craig Evans notes how, in the New Testament, the commandments up through Sabbath are not explicitly quoted, but presupposed, whereas Jesus quotes from "honor your father and mother" through "you shall not testify falsely against a neighbor" and Paul quotes from commandments 5–10.[69]

The Ten Commandments share similarities with other ancient West Asian legal codes, such as the Sumerian "Instructions of Shuruppak," which contain warnings about stealing, killing, and adultery.[70] The "Protestation of Guiltlessness of the Dead" in the Egyptian *Book of the Dead* has clauses with sim-

67. Midrash Tanchuma Buber, Kedoshim 3:2.

68. Daniel I. Block, "The Decalogue in the Hebrew Scriptures," in *The Decalogue through the Centuries: From the Hebrew Scriptures to Benedict XVI*, ed. Jeffrey P. Greenman and Timothy Larsen (Louisville: Westminster John Knox, 2012), 19–21.

69. Craig A. Evans, "The Decalogue in the New Testament," in *The Decalogue through the Centuries: From the Hebrew Scriptures to Benedict XVI*, ed. Jeffrey P. Greenman and Timothy Larsen (Louisville: Westminster John Knox, 2012), 38.

70. William W. Hallo, *The Context of Scripture: Canonical Compositions from the Biblical World* (Leiden: Brill, 2002), 1:176.

ilar content to the commandments, including "I have not stolen; I have not been covetous; I have not killed men; I have not lied; I have not committed adultery."[71] Karel van der Toorn points out how the social ethics found in the commandments starting with "honor your father and mother" through "do not testify against your neighbor as a false witness" can be found in Mesopotamian laws.[72] The Ten Grave Precepts in Buddhism also bear strong similarities to the social ethics in the Ten Commandments; among other things, they affirm not killing, not stealing, not misusing sex, and not speaking falsely.[73]

Philip Turner writes that while modernity tended to believe in some sort of universal moral law, postmodernity rejects such universality, looking instead to "communities of discourse, each with its own take on the world." Turner explains that to discuss the Ten Commandments in the Church in postmodernity,

> I must, at the outset, place them within an interpretive community, and so within the life of the church rather than within the life of humankind as such. The problem is that, though I want to do that, I do not want to do that alone. That is, I do not want to introduce the Ten Commandments as simply a Christian or a Jewish thing. Neither, however, do I wish to introduce them simply as a generally negotiable form of moral wisdom. In respect to the decalogue, I want to have my cake and eat it too. I want them to inscribe God's will for humankind as such, and I want them to have a special significance within the common life of both Judaism and the church.[74]

The methodology of reception history affords the "both/and" instead of insisting on the "either/or," so perhaps Turner can have what he wants. Or perhaps William P. Brown's argument that the Ten Commandments have "a resonant uniqueness" [75] is more precise; it accurately describes how there is some-

71. Hallo, *The Context of Scripture*, 2:12.

72. Karel van der Toorn, *Sin and Sanction in Israel and Mesopotamia: A Comparative Study* (Assen: Van Gorcum, 1985), 13–20.

73. The language is, "I vow not to kill; I vow not to take what is not given, I vow not to misuse sexuality, I vow to refrain from false speech, I vow not to slander." San Francisco Zen Center, "The Sixteen Bodhisattva Precepts," https://tinyurl.com/yznxmjhn.

74. Philip Turner, "The Ten Commandments in the Church in a Postmodern World," in *I Am the LORD Your God: Christian Reflections on the Ten Commandments*, ed. Carl E. Braaten and Christopher R. Seitz (Grand Rapids: Eerdmans, 2005), 5.

75. William P. Brown, *The Ten Commandments: The Reciprocity of Faithfulness* (Louisville: Westminster John Knox, 2004), 2–3.

thing distinct about the form and setting for the Ten Commandments but that their content resonates deeply in other texts and even in other societies.

Display of the Ten Commandments in the United States

For at least four decades in the United States, people have debated the appropriateness of displaying the Ten Commandments in courtrooms and other federal buildings. Those in favor of such display tend to emphasize the "resonance"—to borrow Brown's term mentioned above—of the commandments for social ethics, especially the commandments to not kill and steal. Others in favor of their display emphasize the "Christian" aspect of the "Judeo-Christian" principles from the founding of the United States, as is evidenced by the fact that none of the proposed displays follow the Jewish numbering of the Ten Commandments. In fact, that there is not widespread agreement even among Christians about how to number the Ten Commandments is one argument against their display. Another reason why people oppose their display is that several of the Ten Commandments explicitly deal with ways to worship God,[76] and to show that in public governmental buildings would seem to be contrary to the principles of religious freedom also present among the founders of the country.

In 1980, the Supreme Court invalidated a Kentucky statute requiring the posting of the Ten Commandments in every public classroom in the state, reasoning that the "avowed" secular purpose was not sufficient because "the Ten Commandments are undeniably a sacred text in the Jewish and Christian faiths, and no legislative recitation of a supposed secular purpose can blind us to that fact."[77] But beginning in the 1990s, numerous cases were litigated about public display of the Ten Commandments. Jay A. Sekulow and Francis J. Manion write, "from about 1997 on, hardly a month went by without a decision

76. For example, Nancy Duff writes, "While one could possibly give a secular interpretation of the last six commandments for honoring parents and prohibiting stealing, lying, killing, and coveting, a secular interpretation *cannot* be given to the first four. . . . These commandments are without question *religious* in nature; no secular interpretation can uncover their meaning." "The Old Testament in Public: The Ten Commandments, Evolution, and Sabbath Closing Laws," in *The Cambridge Companion to the Hebrew Bible/Old Testament*, ed. Stephen B. Chapman and Marvin A. Sweeney (Cambridge: Cambridge University Press, 2016), 451.

77. Supreme Court of the United States. *U.S. Reports: Stone v. Graham*, 449 U.S. 39, 1980. Periodical, https://www.loc.gov/item/usrep449039/.

being issued by either a district court or court of appeals on the constitutionality of some Ten Commandments display somewhere in the nation."[78] Two notable examples are, first, in 2001, when Chief Justice Roy Moore of Alabama installed a large granite monument of the Ten Commandments (with quotations from the Declaration of Independence and "The Star-Spangled Banner" around the pedestal) in the state's court building in Montgomery. In 2003, the Alabama Court of the Judiciary—an ethics panel made up of leading judges, lawyers, and elected officials—ordered the monument removed and terminated Moore's term in office.[79] Second, in 2006, Republican Congressman Lynn Westmoreland of Georgia was the cosponsor of a bill that would require the Ten Commandments be displayed in the US House of Representatives and the US Senate. When Westmoreland appeared on *The Stephen Colbert Show* that year, the host Stephen Colbert, himself a practicing Roman Catholic, asked him to name the Ten Commandments. Westmoreland listed three—don't murder, don't lie, don't steal—before admitting that he could not name them all.[80] If this cringeworthy segment deservedly got laughs, it also exposed how for many Americans arguing that the Ten Commandments need to be publicly displayed, the commandments about how to treat other people are primary, and those about God seem of lesser significance.

Debates and legislation about the Ten Commandments in public settings in the United States continue: in April 2023 in Texas, a bill that would require the Ten Commandments to be posted in public school classrooms passed the Texas Senate and was placed on the General Texas State Calendar in May.[81] Critics of this 2023 bill (SB 1515) call it an example of Christian nationalism.[82] And in June 2024, Louisiana Governor Jeff Landry signed legislation to man-

78. Jay A. Sekulow and Francis J. Manion, "The Supreme Court and the Ten Commandments: Compounding the Establishment Clause Confusion," *William & Mary Bill of Rights Journal* 33 (2005), https://tinyurl.com/5f4663xs.

79. Steven Wilf, "The Ten Commandments and the Problem of Legal Transplants in Contemporary America," in *The Decalogue and Its Cultural Influence*, ed. Dominik Markl (Sheffield: Sheffield Phoenix, 2013), 359.

80. Though Westmoreland was derided for his "hypocrisy" and ignorance in not being able to list all Ten, he is certainly not alone in that. Pulitzer Prize–winning editorial cartoonist David Horsey's cartoon of September 6, 2003—the same year when a federal court ordered the removal of a 5,280-pound granite monument to the Ten Commandments from the rotunda of Alabama's judicial building because it was a violation of the First Amendment—features a series of people who offer answers like "Thou shalt obey your teacher."

81. Texas legislature, SB 1515, 2023, https://tinyurl.com/ereshhej.

82. Paul Waldman, "The Texas Legislature Explores New Frontiers of Christian Nationalism," *Washington Post*, May 9, 2023, https://tinyurl.com/3ent5k5x.

date the display of the Ten Commandments in every public classroom in the state. Timothy S. Hogue observes that these sorts of legal cases enshrine the Ten Commandments as "an American monument in a civil context."[83] Steven Wilf suggests that when a Decalogue monument is placed in a legal location like a courthouse, "it suddenly, strikingly transplants a set of ancient laws into America's legal landscape. The particular word-text has been effaced and the iconic text—the tablets as symbol—has taken its place with its message of a stolid, unchanging compass for moral law in a time of declining public and private moral values."[84] Monuments and displays can represent an ideology of laws "set in stone," a kind of gravitas that may be as or more important than the content of the laws.

A different sort of public display of the Ten Commandments can be found in the town of Murphy, North Carolina. Within the biblical theme park "Fields of the Wood" is the World's Largest Ten Commandments: two tablets are set into a hill with concrete letters that are five feet in height and four feet wide, spelling out the commandments using King James's language. The two tablets are three hundred feet from side to side, and purportedly, they are visible from five thousand feet in the air. The park and the Ten Commandments display were created in 1943 by A. J. Tomlinson, general overseer of the Church of God/ Church of God of Prophecy; the park also contains a baptismal pool, a replica of Jesus's burial tomb, and a path for prayer with monuments inscribed with a variety of biblical verses.[85] Timothy Beal notes how the dramatic size of the words of the commandments makes them difficult to read. He writes, "The intent here seems to be to elicit a religious experience of awe in the face of a sacred law that is *overwhelmingly, ineffably huge* in a most literal way."[86]

Ten Commandments in Popular Culture

The World's Largest Ten Commandments skirt the line between public display and popular culture, and indeed, the Ten Commandments have appeared in popular culture in a variety of ways. Cecil B. DeMille's 1956 movie *The Ten Commandments* was really about the life of Moses, though it ended with

83. Timothy Hogue, *The Ten Commandments: Monuments of Memory, Belief, and Interpretation* (Cambridge: Cambridge University Press, 2023), 7.

84. Wilf, "The Problem of Legal Transplants in Contemporary America," 369.

85. Church of God of Prophecy, "Our Story," https://tinyurl.com/5n6s8jt7.

86. Timothy K. Beal, *Roadside Religion: In Search of the Sacred, the Strange, and the Substance of Faith* (Boston: Beacon Press, 2006), 111.

Charlton Heston carrying two tablets, with the commandments inscribed in paleo-Hebrew.[87] DeMille's movie inspired *Les Dix Commandements*, a 2000 French-language musical comedy written by Élie Chouraqui and Pascal Obispo, which was subsequently adapted into a less comedic version in *Ten Commandments: The Musical*; it debuted in Hollywood, California, in 2004 with Val Kilmer playing the role of Moses. The musicals both include a song about the Ten Commandments toward the end. In 2007, David Wain's indie comedy movie *The Ten* sought to spoof each commandment in a series of interrelated vignettes, with mixed reviews.[88]

A more highly acclaimed film adaptation of the Ten Commandments is Polish filmmaker Krzysztof Kieślowski's 1989 Polish miniseries *Dekalog*. Set in a high-rise condominium complex in Warsaw, each of Kieślowski's ten one-hour films examines one of the commandments set in late 1980s Poland, where life is complex and good moral choices are somewhat ambiguous. Kieślowski explained in an interview, "What fascinates me about the Commandments is that we all agree that they are just and appropriate, but at the same time, we violate them every day. They interest me because they allow me to examine the moral ambivalence of human beings."[89] *Dekalog* presents the Ten Commandments as interrelated: Lloyd Baugh explains, "in *Two*, the name of God is honored by renewed fidelity in marriage and by respect for the life of an unborn child; in *Three*, the Holy Day of Christmas is sanctified not so much by the protagonist's pro forma presence at Mass, but by his decision to remain faithful to his wife; though *Six* does consider impure acts as immoral, its pri-

87. There is a similar image in the 1998 DreamWorks animated movie *The Prince of Egypt*. While many saw DeMille's film as iconic, reviewer R. Evett wrote the following: "For a film on the ten commandments, this is a splendid demonstration of how to violate the first three. In making the Almighty talk as if He were at the bottom of a well, and by showing Him as a sort of suburban show-off and spoilsport, determined to toss off miracles as if they were parlor tricks, DeMille has given us a vision of God so shocking in its naivete that even an atheist must blanch at the idea of disbelieving in anything so inconsequential." "There Was a Young Fellow from Goshen," *New Republic* 135, no. 24 (1956): 20; referenced in Melanie J. Wright, *Moses in America: The Cultural Uses of Biblical Narrative* (Oxford: Oxford University Press, 2003), 119.

88. According to the website Rotten Tomatoes, audiences gave "The Ten" a rating of 2.8 out of 5, and critics a 4.9 out of 10, https://tinyurl.com/veyx8zbh.

89. Lloyd Baugh, "The Reception of the Decalogue in Film: Krzysztof Kieślowski's *Decalogue*," in *The Decalogue and Its Cultural Influence*, ed. Dominik Markl (Sheffield: Sheffield Phoenix, 2013), 344.

mary focus is a story of the redemptive power of love."[90] Though Kieślowski does represent sinfulness as a nearly universal human existential situation, with most protagonists in the films guilty of violating a commandment in a serious way, in all except for the film *Seven*, they overcome their sinfulness and make good and moral choices.[91]

The Ten Commandments are also received as novels: in Scott Shepherd's 2021 murder mystery, *The Last Commandment*, a serial killer murders victims who he believes have violated each of the commandments: the first victim is an Oxford don who specializes in Greek mythology and thus supports "other gods." Second is a sculptor creating images of archangels. The third victim is the lead singer for a band called The Blasphemers whose name, if not music, blasphemes God's name, and the fourth is a priest who works on the Sabbath day. The killer continues through nine total victims—the ninth is a journalist who bears false witness—and the final intended victim is one who had "coveted" the killer's girlfriend.[92]

Austrian-American publisher and Hollywood producer Armin L. Robinson commissioned and published ten novellas in 1945 as a response to Hitler's Nazi Germany. In the preface to the book, titled *The Ten Commandments: Ten Short Novels of Hitler's War against the Moral Code*, Robinson explains that he felt obliged to pursue the project after hearing about Hitler's comments about the Decalogue: purportedly, Hitler had declared that the Nazi movement would fight against God and God's commandments, as discussed in the following chapter. The first novella, titled "The Tables of the Law," was written by Thomas Mann as a dramatic retelling of Moses's story; after the golden calf, Moses says, "I know well and God knows beforehand that His commandments will not be kept, that there will be transgressions against His words always and everywhere." Gerhard Lauer describes how Judge Ulrich Meinerzhagen quoted that sentence from Mann during the 2005 trial in Germany of Ernst Zündel, a notorious Holocaust denier. Lauer writes, "It is not enough to know the Ten Commandments, it is more important to rewrite them, maybe rewrite them better. And that is exactly what Judge Meinerzhagen did, when he quoted from

90. Baugh, "The Reception of the Decalogue in Film," 345. In fact, Baugh identifies the primacy of love as the first of four moral principles for Kieślowski; the others are: (1) the primacy of the physical and moral life of the child, the right of the child to be born, to live, to be protected, to be free; (2) the sacrality of human life in general; and (3) the moral commitment of husband and wife to the sacrality of marriage.

91. Baugh, "The Reception of the Decalogue in Film," 349.

92. Scott Shepherd, *The Last Commandment* (New York: Mysterious Press, 2021).

Mann's story: he told the story again. Through such retelling, the Decalogue stays alive."[93]

Use and Usefulness

A passage in the Talmud (Sota 5a) describes Mount Sinai as neither the highest nor lowest mountain in the region, but a medium-sized one, symbolizing that the Ten Commandments are addressed to the average person. According to David Hazony, this means that the Ten Commandments do not set forth impossibly high standards but are meant for real human beings with all their faults and failings, who can nevertheless improve themselves and the world around them when they seek to follow them.[94] Certainly, the Ten Commandments throughout the ages have been used in Jewish and Christian worship: chanted on the Jewish festival *Shavuot* as part of covenant renewal, recited in synagogues,[95] utilized in Christian services of Holy Communion in prayers of confession,[96] and forming the backbone of many Christian catechisms, such as Luther's Shorter and Longer Catechisms. Luther's use of the Ten Commandments deserves some attention, especially given his tendency to speak harshly against the law and even Judaism. Luther emphasized the importance of the Ten Commandments especially for the young, but also praised them as the complete guide for human life. In the Book of Concord 361 he wrote: "Anyone who knows the Ten Commandments perfectly knows the entire scriptures. In all affairs and circumstances he can counsel, help, comfort, judge and make decisions in both spiritual and temporal matters. He is qualified to sit in judg-

93. Gerhard Lauer, "The Law and the Artist in the Age of Extremes: On Thomas Mann's *Das Gesetz*," in *The Decalogue and Its Cultural Influence*, ed. Dominik Markl (Sheffield: Sheffield Phoenix, 2013), 330.

94. David Hazony, *The Ten Commandments: How Our Most Ancient Moral Text Can Renew Modern Life* (New York: Scribner, 2010), 38.

95. Though, as discussed below, recitation of the Ten Commandments in public Jewish worship was halted.

96. Cranmer's 1552 Prayer Book Service of Holy Communion instructed that after the collect for the day, "Then shall the Priest rehearse distinctly all the Ten Commandments: and the people kneeling, shall after every Commandment ask God's mercy for their transgression of the same, after this sort. . . . 'Lord, have mercy upon us, and incline our hearts to keep this law.'" Jeffrey P. Greenman, "Lancelot Andrewes," in *The Decalogue through the Centuries: From the Hebrew Scriptures to Benedict XVI*, ed. Jeffrey P. Greenman and Timothy Larsen (Louisville: Westminster John Knox, 2012), 151–52.

ment upon all doctrines, estates, persons, laws, and everything else in the world."[97] Luther even put the Ten Commandments to song, which is translated into the English in the hymn, "These Are the Holy Ten Commandments."[98]

Luther was by no means the only one to use the Ten Commandments for catechesis: Cardinal Robert Bellarmine's 1614 Small Catechism included them in response to the statement, "Let us now come to that which we must do to love God and our neighbor. Tell me the Ten Commandments."[99] In Great Britain between 1603 and 1622, at least nineteen editions of John Dod and Robert Cleaver's catechism were published under the short title, *A plain and familiar exposition of the ten commandments*; the longer title was *Ten Commandments with a methodicall short Catechisme, containing briefly all the principall grounds of Christian Religion.*[100] More systematic dissemination of the Decalogue took place during the first years of Queen Elizabeth I throughout the mid-eighteenth century. Historian Ian Green writes, "literally millions of copies of the Decalogue were published from the 1560s to the mid-eighteenth century in hundreds of editions of the Book of Common Prayer, *The ABC with the Catechisme*, and *The Primer and Catechisme*, for use with literate and illiterate adults and children in church, school, and home."[101]

97. Similarly, in "A Brief Explanation of the Ten Commandments, the Creed, and the Lord's Prayer," Luther wrote that these three were required to be learned and known by the ordinary Christian who cannot read the Scriptures, "For these three contain fully and completely everything that is in the Scriptures, everything that ever should be preached, and everything that a Christian needs to know, all put so briefly and so plainly that no one can make complaint or excuse, saying that what he needs for his salvation is too long or too hard to remember."

98. Lyrics translated into English include, "Thou shalt give love and honor due/To father, and to mother too/And help them when their strength decays/So shalt thou have length of days." The Free Lutheran Chorale-Book, "These Are the Holy Ten Commands," https://tinyurl.com/4j2ea4ax.

99. Bellarmine's catechism was reworked for Roman Catholics in North America by a council in Baltimore in 1855, known as "A Catechism of Christian Doctrine, Prepared and Enjoined by Order of the Third Council of Baltimore," or more simply, "The Baltimore Catechism." This too was revised and replaced in 2004 by the United States Catholic Catechism for Adults. All of these catechisms contain the Ten Commandments.

100. Ruth Bottigheimer, *The Bible for Children: From the Age of Gutenberg to the Present* (New Haven: Yale University Press, 2014), 225n15. The Ten Commandments appear in poem form in the English thirteenth-century Kildare Manuscript, as well as in a fourteenth-century piece, "Prick of Conscience," https://tinyurl.com/4zws4psz.

101. Ian Green, "The Dissemination of the Decalogue in English and Lay Responses to Its Promotion in Early Modern English Protestantism," in *The Decalogue and Its Cultural*

The Ten Commandments are also contained in the Reformed Heidelberg and Westminster and Baptist Catechisms. The Ten Commandments appeared in catechisms across the Americas used by missionaries attempting to teach faith to converts: Luis Resines writes that for missionaries in the Caribbean and Mexico during the sixteenth century, "the Decalogue was essential to the presentation of the Christian faith. It is not enough to speak only of what we must believe (dogma, the Creed), but of what we need to do, and that leads directly to the Decalogue. All catechisms talk about it and include it among their statements."[102]

In the 1552 *Book of Common Prayer*, the liturgy for the communion service included the priest rehearsing each of the Ten Commandments, and the people kneeling were to ask God's mercy for their transgression by responding, "Lord, have mercy upon us, and incline our hearts to keep this law."[103] The Talmud explains that priests in the Temple used to read aloud the Ten Commandments during daily prayers before the Shema (from Deut 6:4–9), but eventually recitation of the Ten Commandments was abolished "because of the arguments of the heretics" (Berachot 12a:4–8). These "heretics" wrongly said that only the Ten Commandments came from God and not the rest of the Torah; so the Ten Commandments were left out of the service lest the heretics argue that Jews needed to observe nothing else. Evidence suggests that Jews in Egypt in the tenth to twelfth centuries would read the Ten Commandments after services,[104] and Rabbi Joseph Karo teaches that a person may recite them in private daily, just not in public worship (Shulchan Arukh, Orach Chayim 1:5).

Certainly, the Ten Commandments have been *used* in worship and catechesis; they are also particularly *useful* in those applications because they are brief, as was mentioned earlier. But that brevity allows for flexibility in interpretation and allows people to apply them in particular ways to particular

Influence, ed. Dominik Markl (Sheffield: Sheffield Phoenix, 2013), 180. Janice Surlin's 2016 Jewish children's book, *The Greatest Ten*, is not a formal catechism but seeks to teach children the Ten Commandments to the tune of the song "This Old Man." The commandments about murder and adultery are reworded in age-appropriate ways, with the following words, or lyrics: "Do not harm anyone, God says this must not be done; if you know a person is doing something bad, tell your teacher, Mom or Dad. . . . When you love someone who cares about and loves you too, How you act is the only way for your love to show, and be loyal, God says so." Janice Surlin, *The Greatest Ten* (Columbia, SC: Hummingbird Jewel Press, 2016).

102. Luis Resines, "American Catechisms of the Sixteenth Century," in *The Decalogue and Its Cultural Influence*, ed. Dominik Markl (Sheffield: Sheffield Phoenix, 2013), 233.

103. Green, "The Dissemination of the Decalogue," 179.

104. Jacob Mann, *The Jews in Egypt and in Palestine under the Fatimid Caliphs* (Oxford: Oxford University Press, 1920), 221.

times and settings. Andrewes drew on the fact that the commandments occur in the second person singular form to say, "we learn that they appertain to all alike; that they must be particularly applied."[105] Ephraim Urbach wrote, "Actually, the urge to find brief formulations for the guidance of people in ordering their lives is a general one. Those who ask for such formulations want short, concentrated answers. Certain passages in the Bible, in which some scholars have thought to find decalogues or mini decalogues, are really nothing more than attempts to satisfy this demand – to answer the question: 'How shall I order my life?'"[106]

The brevity of the Ten Commandments is a feature and not a flaw of their form, as they allow for a greater variety of possibilities in how a person interprets and applies them. Urbach goes on to say that listing out guidance for life in a brief formulation is not meant to "minimize the observance of the detailed mitzvot in which the general principles find expression."[107] In other words, the brief—and general—formulae get expressed in maximal ways of observance as members in the community seek to live them out.

Not everyone views the "general" as positive. In reference to seeing the Ten Commandments as fitting under the general principles to love God and love neighbor, Dale Allison writes, "Maybe our post-Kantian preference for general principles over concrete imperatives disinclines us to relate the generalisations

105. Andrewes, *A Pattern of Catechistical Doctrine*, 81. While the commandments are in the second person singular "you," because it takes the form of the Hebrew *masculine* singular, feminist critiques are concerned that women are not included. Cf. Judith Plaskow, *Standing Again at Sinai: Judaism from a Feminist Perspective* (New York: HarperCollins, 1991), 25; Athalya Brenner, "An Afterword: The Decalogue—Am I an Addressee?," in *A Feminist Companion to Exodus—Deuteronomy*, ed. Athalya Brenner (Sheffield: Sheffield Academic Press, 1994), 255–58; David J. A. Clines, "The Ten Commandments: Reading from Left to Right," in *Interested Parties: The Ideology of Writers and Readers of the Hebrew Bible*, ed. David J. A. Clines (Sheffield: Sheffield Phoenix, 2009): 33–35. Certainly the original setting is exclusive to the men, though as Breed reminds us with his metaphor, texts are like nomads in reception history: they have an original context, but they move out of that into new settings and applications.

106. Ephraim E. Urbach, "The Role of the Ten Commandments in Jewish Worship," in *The Ten Commandments in History and Tradition*, ed. Ben-Zion Segal, English version ed. Gershon Levi (Jerusalem: Magnes, 1990), 174. Bono, the lead singer of the band U2, described the Ten Commandments as giving the people of God "clarity on how best to live." *Surrender: 40 Songs, One Story* (New York: Alfred A. Knopf, 2022), 511. If this is a general desire—how to live life well, how to order one's life—it seems especially urgent in this time in human history, with our ecological and geopolitical global instability, as well as the awareness post-pandemic of the fragility of human life and health.

107. Urbach, "The Role of the Ten Commandments," 175.

about God and neighbour to the more specific imperatives in the Decalogue. The double commandment to love is certainly easier to bend to our purposes than the ten commandments."[108]

One could criticize my language of "flexibility" in interpretation and application of the Ten Commandments as bending them to my own purposes, and I recognize the whiff of relativism in such language or practice. But rather than preferring the general over the concrete, my belief is that we can and should apply the Ten Commandments in concrete and specific ways to our concrete and specific lives and contexts, such that they become more useful. Again, if honoring parents can only happen in one specific, concrete way, it becomes far less useful for the real lives of real people who have specific and different relationships with their parents than is true for other real people and their specific parents. If my football receiver only moves the ball down the field every time by going up through the center, the route becomes stale and unproductive, and my team will not succeed. But there are playbooks for how to receive and move the ball well, just as there are examples in the text and throughout history of how to live out the Ten Commandments in productive, even life-giving ways. To perhaps risk pushing the football metaphor too far, reception history can also invite a level of participation and even "play." There can be value and even enjoyment in watching how others have received the Ten Commandments, but reception history welcomes anyone to engage, joining into that history of interpretation and application.

Additionally, the language in the Ten Commandments provides constraints on relativism, especially in its term "neighbor," which suggests that to follow the commandments is never a solitary, privatized endeavor but is always best done in community. Certainly, for the people of ancient Israel, the sphere of private moral concern is always connected (even in some small way) with the embodied communal life.[109] Wendell Berry suggests that "the present condition of most Americans" tends toward what journalist Paul Tenny described as "a collection of unrelated individuals whose interactions are mediated through various shallow and transactional mechanisms, where common ground with a neighbor can only, at best, be found in the most banal of trivialities." Berry sees the Ten Commandments (and the four gospels) as

108. Allison, "The History of Interpretation of Matthew," 6.

109. David Bently Hart expressed this idea by writing, "There's no such thing as that sphere of private moral concern separated entirely from the embodied communal life of people of Israel." David Bentley Hart, host, *PloughCast*, episode 67, "David Bentley Hart and the Worship of Mammon," August 15, 2023, https://tinyurl.com/2ea5d488.

providing an alternative vision to this tendency, one that gives instructions for "heavenly and neighborly love."[110]

Conclusion

The Ten Commandments get described through many metaphors. Hungarian pastor József Farkas writes, "The Ten Commandments are not a collection of medical prescriptions: 'Do this, and you will be healed; and you will be all right.' No, the Ten Commandments are rather a *compass* which shows the direction in which we must seek salvation."[111] Zora Neal Hurston uses the metaphor of a compass slightly differently, writing, "Moses lifted the freshly chiseled tablets of stone in his hands and gazed down the mountain to where Israel waited in the valley. He knew a great exultation. Now men could be free because they could govern themselves. They had something of the essence of divinity expressed in order. They had the chart and compass of behavior."[112] Journalist Chris Hedges compares the Ten Commandments to guideposts or even a lighthouse, writing, "They are our protection against the siren calls of glory, wealth and power that will ultimately dash us against the rocks."[113]

To return to the idea that the Ten Commandments contain an invitation, in 2009, in honor of the five hundredth anniversary of Calvin's birth, Romanian sculptor Liviu Mocan created a monument, which he titled "The Invitation/Decalogue." It consists of ten golden pillars around fifteen feet high, set in a circle, with a small seat cut into each one where a visitor can sit; the sculpture was intended to be interactive. The pillars are described as "resembling human fingers" with two sides: "a smooth, contoured side facing towards the centre . . . the other side, facing outwards, forms a sharp, unyielding blade."[114] Marsh Moyle notes that while the pillars appear threatening on the outside, they create a protective ring around the inner space where the "fingers" feel inviting.

110. Wendell Berry, *The Need to Be Whole: Patriotism and the History of Prejudice* (Berkeley: Shoemaker and Company, 2022), 147.

111. József Farkas, *Bench Marks*, trans. John R. Bodo (Richmond: John Knox, 1969), 111.

112. Zora Neale Hurston, *Moses, Man of the Mountain* (New York: Harper Perennial, 1991), 233.

113. Chris Hedges, *Losing Moses on the Freeway: The Ten Commandments in America* (New York: Free Press, 2005), 175.

114. Liviu Mocan, "The Invitation/Decalogue," https://tinyurl.com/54kyn8ae.

Moyle comments that, inside the circle, there is freedom to trust, freedom from behaviors—like murder or lying—that would destroy love and freedom: the space provided by the Ten Commandments represents a better country, a better place where we are invited to enter, where we are invited to live.[115]

115. Marsh Moyle, *Rumors of a Better Country: Searching for Trust and Community in a Time of Moral Outrage* (London: Inter-Varsity Press, 2023), 8–11. Other artistic receptions of the Ten Commandments highlight different aspects of meaning. Israeli artist Yossi Rosenstein created six paintings in his "Commandments" series in 1995, several of which have large candles in the image, https://tinyurl.com/2pye57tw. American artist Keith Haring created a set of ten large—approximately 25 feet high by 17.5 feet wide—paintings on site at the Contemporary Art Museum in Bordeaux, France in 1985. Sylvie Couderc, "The Ten Commandments: An Interview," The Keith Haring Foundation, 1985, https://tinyurl.com/6ncx39c4. Dutch artist Anneke Kaai has a series of twelve abstract paintings: the first represents what she describes as the "context" for the commandments (what others describe as the "prologue," or what Jews understand to be the first word) and the subsequent ten paintings in the series are for each one of the Ten Commandments. The final painting is titled "Christ Is the Fulfillment of the Law"; Kaai explains that it "expresses gratitude to Jesus Christ who came to fulfill the Law." Artist Anne Kekaai, "The Ten Commandments (12x)," https://tinyurl.com/5n75tpzy.

1

"I Am the LORD Your God"

While Christians treat Exod 20:2 as a preamble or introductory preface to the Ten Commandments, in Jewish enumerations this statement about God's redemptive act is considered the first commandment. In fact, twelfth-century Jewish philosopher Maimonides places this as the very first of the 248 positive commandments, explaining that what is being commanded in Exod 20:2 is to know that there is a God. What follows, in Maimonides's ordering, is, next, to believe in God's unity (cf. Deut 6:4), then, to love God (Deut 6:5), and then, to fear God (Deut 6:13).[1]

Because there is no imperative contained in the phrase "I am the LORD your God," some emphasize that it is the first "word," rather than the first "commandment." This correlates with Exod 34:28, which gives the number "ten"; they are literally *ʿăśeret hadĕbārîm*, "the ten words." But Maimonides is not the only one to refer to this as a commandment; in response to the question, "How can we understand this utterance as a 'commandment'? In what way does it represent an order to the listener?" the twelfth- to thirteenth-century European commentary Da'at Zekenim answers that the statement "I am the LORD your God" implies to the listener that they are to accept God's identity and existence as a fact.[2] Thus, the commandment to know that there is a God is not direct but implied.

1. Sefaria, citing "Sefer HaMitzvot, Positive Commandments 1:1," Sefaria Edition 2021, trans. Rabbi Francis Nataf, https://tinyurl.com/ycxunwue.

2. Sefaria, citing *The Contemporary Torah*, ed. David E. S. Stein et al. (Philadelphia: Jewish Publication Society, 2006), https://tinyurl.com/5yvpt7kn. The commentary goes on to explain that what follows from accepting God's identity and existence is knowing that there is a system of reward and punishment that God is capable of meting out because God is creator. "It follows from accepting this as a fact that there is a system of reward and punishment for your actions, as He is capable of meting out reward and punishment as a result of being the Creator. Rabbi Tanchuma adds that this obligation of yours is the direct result of your having been allowed to see Him revealing Himself as a mighty warrior at the

Who Brought You Out of the Land of Egypt, Out of the House of Slavery

If the first phrase in Exod 20:2 implies a command to believe in God's existence, the second half of the verse details a particular and significant action of this God. The statement that God brought the Israelites out of the land of Egypt is repeated almost one hundred times throughout the Old Testament. In Deuteronomy's version of the Sabbath commandment, this is the explanation given for keeping the Sabbath, to remember that they were slaves in Egypt, and God brought them out (Deut 5:15). When Moses instructs the people about the festival of unleavened bread, he admonishes them to remember that God brought them from the land of Egypt, from the house of slavery (Exod 13:3); they are to tell their children who ask about the meaning of the festival that God brought them out of Egypt (Exod 13:14). God's action—of bringing them out of Egypt—is the motivating reason to remember the LORD in Deut 6:12 and 8:14; the reason for fidelity to God in Deut 13:5, 10 and Josh 24:17; and included in prophetic admonitions to the people in Jer 34:13; Mic 6:4; and Amos 2:10. This action has implications for the Israelites' identity, as in Lev 26:13 when the people are told that they were brought out of Egypt so that they would no longer be slaves. It also has implications for God's identity according to Lev 22:32–33, when God explains that God "brought you out of the land of Egypt to be your God." The action even reverberates beyond God's relationship with Israel; as Ezek 20:9 explains, the surrounding nations were able to see and know God because God brought the Israelites out of Egypt.

In reference to Exod 20:2, Rashi explains, "That act of bringing you out is alone of sufficient importance that you should subject yourselves to Me."[3] The Passover song *Dayenu*, "It Would Have Been Enough," seems to echo Rashi's sentiment. The lyrics begin with "if he had brought us out of Egypt, it would have been enough," but as the song continues, each stanza builds on the previous one, listing the increasingly amazing actions God did on behalf of Israel.[4]

sea of reeds, when He saved you miraculously and meted out punishment to your pursuers. At the same time, He appeared to you in the guise of a merciful God at Mount Sinai. Do not make the mistake of thinking that the Power that addressed you at Mount Sinai, is a different Power than the One which dealt with the Egyptians. You have merely witnessed God manifesting Himself as possessing multiple attributes. The word אנכי is best translated as 'I and no one else.'"

3. Sefaria, citing "Rashi on Exodus 20:2:1," M. Rosenbaum and A. M. Silbermann, London, 1929–34, https://tinyurl.com/4j3zvvp3.

4. The lyrics continue, "If he had brought us out and not defeated their gods, it would

The first, and foundational, of God's mighty acts in the song is bringing the Israelites out from Egypt, from the house of slavery.

Another example of this idea can be found in a midrash on Exod 20:2, which states,

> Why were the ten commandments not stated at the beginning of the Torah? An analogy: A man enters a province and says (to the inhabitants): I will rule over you. They respond: Did you do anything for us that you would rule over us? Whereupon he builds the (city) wall for them, provides water for them, wages war for them, and then says: I will rule over you—whereupon they respond: Yes! Yes! Thus, the Lord took Israel out of Egypt, split the sea for them, brought down manna for them, raised the well for them, brought in quail for them, waged war with Amalek for them, and then said to them: I will rule over you—whereupon they responded: Yes! Yes![5]

The reference to liberation "from the house of slavery" occurs less frequently than "out of Egypt," but they are always linked: in addition to the beginning of the Ten Commandments (Exod 20:2 and Deut 5:6), this appears in Exod 13:3, 14; Deut 6:12; 7:8; 8:14; 13:6[5], 11[10]; Josh 24:17; Judg 6:8; Jer 34:13; and Mic 6:4. As Origen put it, "The first word of God's commandments bears on freedom."[6] Unsurprisingly, the story of God liberating God's people from bondage in slavery was especially important to African American slaves. Allen Dwight Callahan explains that for slaves in America, "The Exodus was the Bible's narrative argument that God was opposed to American slavery and would return a catastrophic judgment against the nation as he had against ancient Egypt. The Exodus signified God's will that African Americans too would no longer be sold as bondspeople, that they too would go free."[7]

Rhondda Robinson Thomas traces the reception history of Exodus in Afro-Atlantic literature and identifies Phyllis Wheatley's 1774 "Letter to Reverend Samson Occum" as the earliest published piece of writing to in-

---

have been enough; if he had defeated their gods and not killed their firstborn, it would have been enough."

5. Sefaria, citing "Mekhilta DeRabbi Yishmael, Tractate Bachodesh 5:1–3 Mechilta," trans. Rabbi Shraga Silverstein, https://tinyurl.com/3a4c3a86.

6. Origen, *Homilies on Genesis and Exodus*, trans. Ronald E. Heine (Washington, DC: Catholic University of America Press, 1982), 317.

7. Allen Dwight Callahan, *The Talking Book: African Americans and the Bible* (New Haven: Yale University Press, 2006), 83.

corporate the exodus narrative into a critique of American slavery. At the time, the colonists often characterized themselves as Israelites breaking free from bondage from an English "Pharaoh." In the letter, Wheatley—a former slave—highlights the hypocrisy of those colonists who demand liberty while enslaving Africans.[8] Court documents related to the 1822 execution of Denmark Vesey—a free man of African descent found guilty of plotting what could have been the largest insurrection with enslaved persons—describe how "Vesey read to us from the Bible, how the Children of Israel were delivered out of Egypt from bondage."[9]

In African American use of the exodus, the connection between deliverance from slavery and the law at Sinai was seldom acknowledged. The Spiritual "Didn't Old Pharaoh Get Lost" contains a rare reference to Sinai with the lyrics, "And the Lord spoke to Moses / From Sinai's smoking top / Saying 'Moses, lead the people / Till I shall bid you stop.'" In reference to this song, Callahan notes, "There is no mention of the law, not even the Ten Commandments. . . . Not Ten Commandments but one: keep moving."[10] Likely, the law was less useful than the narrative. But the biblical summaries themselves connect the law, specifically the Ten Commandments, with the story of God's deliverance from slavery. Esau McCaulley writes, "In a sense the question behind all questions for the Black Christians is this one. Did God intend our freedom?"[11] McCaulley goes on to explain that the exodus narrative definitively affirms that God "is a God who hears the sufferings of an enslaved people and rescues them. . . . This rescue becomes a part of his résumé."[12]

Rashi gives another explanation as to why God would describe Godself as the one who delivered them from Egypt:

8. Rhondda Robinson Thomas, *Claiming Exodus: A Cultural History of Afro-Atlantic Identity, 1774–1903* (Waco, TX: Baylor University Press, 2013), 10. That both colonists and slaves see themselves as God's people, the Israelites in the exodus, is striking. Similarly, "persecuted Afrikaners saw themselves as the oppressed people of God whose oppressors were the French and the British. They wandered in the 'wilderness' till they reached the 'Promised Land' in South Africa." Patrick Kofi Amissah, *The Prophetic Voice of Amos on Contemporary Social Justice* (Leiden: Brill, 2023), 19.

9. Jeremy Schipper, *Denmark Vesey's Bible: The Thwarted Revolt That Put Slavery and Scripture on Trial* (Princeton: Princeton University Press, 2022), 3.

10. Callahan, *The Talking Book*, 102.

11. Esau McCaulley, *Reading While Black: African American Biblical Interpretation as an Exercise in Hope* (Downers Grove, IL: IVP Press, 2020), 139.

12. McCaulley, *Reading While Black*, 143.

> Because He had revealed Himself to them at the Red Sea as a mighty man of war and here He revealed Himself as a grey-beard filled with compassion, as it is stated in connection with the Giving of the Law, (Exodus 24:10) "and there was under His feet as it were a brick-work of sapphire," which is explained to mean that this (the brick-work) was before Him at the time of their bondage; "and there was as the essence of heaven" (i.e. joy and gladness) when they had been delivered, thus the Divine Glory changed according to circumstances,—therefore He stated here: Since I change, appearing in various forms, do not say, "There are two divine Beings"; it is I Who brought you forth from Egypt and Who appeared to you at the Sea. (cf. Mekhilta d'Rabbi Yishmael 20:2:2)

Rashi's explanation here offers several intriguing possibilities: that God would change, that God would appear in different forms, or even that God's compassion is connected to giving the law. Of course, such a positive view of the law is common in Jewish writings and beliefs, such as in Sabbath prayers and throughout Psalm 119.[13]

Patrick D. Miller suggests that God's act of redemption from slavery in Egypt is so fundamental to understanding God that it ought to be added to the first article of the Apostles' and the Nicene-Constantinopolitan Creed. Miller's concern with what he called "an overly compact and thus deficient first article" led him to propose a revision, which would read, "I believe in God the Father Almighty, Creator of heaven and earth, who delivered Israel from Egyptian bondage." Miller acknowledges that many other things could be added but argues that God's action on behalf of Israel in Egypt is "the defining moment for Israel" and in this action, "one sees that the Maker of heaven and earth is bent toward the weak and the oppressed, toward those who are in bondage and dying."[14] Miller goes on to connect God the Father's act of redemption in Egypt with God the Son's act of redemption on the cross, arguing that the addition to the first article would therefore strengthen Christian understanding of the persons and work of the Trinity. In Miller's words, "The Son thus continues the saving and freeing work of the Father revealed paradigmatically in the Exodus. The ongoing work

13. Clark Williamson notes "the Christian tradition's predominantly pejorative treatment of 'law.'" *A Guest in the House of Israel: Post-Holocaust Church Theology* (Louisville: Westminster John Knox, 1993), 24. Such a negative view of the law in Christianity in part is based on reading certain New Testament texts without attentiveness to the Jewish contexts of Jesus and Paul.

14. Patrick D. Miller, "Rethinking the First Article of the Creed," *Theology Today* 61 (2005): 503–4.

of God to release humankind from those chains that bind and destroy life is a central feature of the Christian claim. That divine work includes release from the bondage of sin but also, at least eschatologically, from all forms of destruction and bondage, including suffering and death. The one who delivered Israel from death also delivered Jesus from death, and therein lies our hope."[15]

Though it is unlikely that any ecumenical council would decide to add a clause to the creeds anytime soon, Miller's proposal points to the foundational nature of God's redeeming Israel from slavery in Egypt. Miller also seems to indicate that remembering God's act in Exodus could lead to remembering (all) other redemptive acts God has done and continues to do for God's people.

Christopher J. H. Wright suggests that each of the Ten Commandments can be understood as responsibilities given to God's people in order to preserve the rights and freedoms gained by the exodus. For example, because God freed them from unremitting forced labor under Pharaoh, they must preserve the right of regular Sabbath rest for everyone in their society, as the Sabbath command insists. Because God freed them from the infanticide practiced by the Egyptians, they must respect life, as the commandment against murder makes clear.[16]

In a conversation during the eleventh century, Rabbi Judah Halevi asks his friend Ibn Ezra why in the Ten Commandments does God not introduce Godself as the God who created the heavens and the earth.[17] Ibn Ezra answers that people who believe in God have different levels of faith, and for people who have studied the sciences and seen God's work in creation, the brief statement "I am the LORD" would encompass God's creative acts, so to specify "who made heaven and earth" would be superfluous. But more simple people—Ibn Ezra refers to them as "nonintelligent" because those are the people who need proof of God's existence—can remember how when God brought people out of Egypt, all the people present saw God's miracles. Thus, God included the phrase "who brought you out of the land of Egypt" to recall the specific acts of God made visible to the wise and unwise and would also give those simple people answers for heretics who might challenge their faith.[18]

15. Miller, "Rethinking," 506.

16. Christopher J. Wright, *Old Testament Ethics for the People of God* (Downers Grove, IL: InterVarsity Press, 2004), 262.

17. Judah Halevi, *The Kuzari (Kitab Al Khazari): An Argument for the Faith of Israel*, trans. Hartwig Hirschfeld (New York: Schocken Books, 1964), 25. Rabbi Jonathan Sacks suggests that Halevi's question is because he is "reacting against the neo-Aristotelianism that he saw creeping into Judaism." *The Great Partnership: Science, Religion, and the Search for Meaning* (New York: Schocken, 2011), 65.

18. The "non-intelligent" person has to be shown tangible proof of God's existence.

Where to Place the "Am"?

The first clause of Exod 20:2 has no verb in Hebrew, and therefore it is possible to place the verb "to be" in two places: after "I," so that the verse reads "I am the LORD, your God who brought you out of the land of Egypt," or after God's name, so, "I, the LORD, am your God who brought you out of the land of Egypt."[19]

The first is how the Septuagint and Vulgate translate the Hebrew and seems to emphasize self-introduction. Walther Zimmerli explains that this translation suggests, "The most important element here is the disclosure of Yahweh's personal name, a name containing the full richness and honor of the One naming himself."[20] Not only is there a God who exists but that God self-identifies by the name LORD. Dennis J. McCarthy notes differences between Exod 20:2 and the historical prologues in ancient Western Asian treaties. In Exodus, the LORD uses the first person, but in other treaties the sovereign speaks in the third person. In those non-biblical treaties, the historical events are introduced by a clause beginning with "when," but in Exodus, "the following clause is not the impersonal when but who. It is less concerned with what happened than with who did it. . . . The purpose . . . is not so much motivation as identification."[21]

The second emphasizes the relationship, that the LORD is the personal God of the Israelites: "your God." Zimmerli explains that in this translation—"I, YHWH, am your God"—there are both a gracious element of con-

---

Ibn Ezra here takes issue with a contemporary, Rabbi Judah Ha-Levi, who felt that philosophical proof of God's existence is insufficient for a truly spiritual life. See book 1 of the Kuzari. Aviva Kushner also references this conversation when discussing the Ten Commandments in *The Grammar of God: A Journey into the Words and Worlds of the Bible* (New York: Spiegel & Grau, 2015), 126–27.

19. Another option is to make the connection with the verb in Exod 20:3, "Besides me, Yahweh your God, who brought you out of the land of Egypt, you shall have no other gods." Johann Jacob Stamm, with M. E. Andrew, *The Ten Commandments in Recent Research* (London: SCM, 1967), 76.

20. Walther Zimmerli, *I Am Yahweh*, trans. Douglas W. Stott, ed. Walter Brueggemann (Atlanta: John Knox, 1982), 1–2.

21. Dennis J. McCarthy, SJ, *Treaty and Covenant: A Study in Form in the Ancient Oriental Documents and in the Old Testament* (Rome: Biblical Institute Press, 1981), 251. Timothy S. Hogue's study on Levantine "I Am" monuments, which "first appeared during the Late Bronze Age in North Syria [e.g., statue of Idrimi of Alalaḫ]," demonstrates how those monuments typically were inscribed with the first-person pronoun followed by the agent's name, genealogy, and titles. *The Ten Commandments: Monuments of Memory, Belief, and Interpretation* (Cambridge: Cambridge University Press, 2023), 28–29.

cern as well as an element of demand and an exclusive claim. This phrase contains the covenant promise for God to be in relationship with and the only God for the people.[22] In a similar vein to Zimmerli, Walter Harrelson writes that the claim in Exod 20:2 is "not a mere monism, for the one who places the demand is Yahweh the deliverer from bondage, the one who marks oppression and will not forever endure it."[23]

Emphasis on God's disclosure of the name YHWH begs a follow-up question: Who is this YHWH? Long before German scholarly source criticism sought to distinguish the identity and characterization of YHWH from the more generic "Elohim," third-century Rabbi Abba bar Mamal taught that

> The Holy One . . . said to Moses: You seek to know My name? I am named according to My actions. At [different] times I am named God Almighty [El Shaddai], [Lord of] Hosts [Tzevaot], God [Elohim], the Lord [Y-H-V-H]. When I judge creatures, I am called Elohim. When I wage war against the wicked, I am called Tzevaot. When I abide a person's sins, I am called El Shaddai. When I have mercy on my world I am called Y-H-V-H, as Y-H-V-H is nothing other than the attribute of mercy, as it is stated: "Y-H-V-H, Y-H-V-H, merciful and gracious God" (Exodus 34:6). That is, "I will be what I will be," I am named based on My actions. (Midrash Rabbah Exodus 3:6)

Theodore J. Lewis notes how in texts and iconography, YHWH is characterized in distinct ways: as the Divine Warrior and the Family God, as king and judge, and as the Holy One. YHWH's holiness is often made evident in acts of power, particularly on behalf of the disadvantaged. For example, Lewis discusses how Hannah's song in 1 Samuel 2 describes that "Yahweh is a holy and knowing God who reverses fortunes, especially on behalf of the disadvantaged (the weak, the hungry, the barren, the poor, and the needy; 1 Sam 2:4–8). Such divine care for the underprivileged echoes what we saw with Yahweh as the ideal judge, and here too the poet praises him as magistrate of the ends of the earth (*yhwh yādîn ʾapsê ʾāreṣ*; 1 Sam 2:10)."[24] Martin Buber suggests that

22. Zimmerli, *I Am Yahweh*, 2. Zimmerli notes how even though this statement is a syntactically independent nominal clause, it alludes to the next commandment to not have any other gods.

23. Walter Harrelson, *The Ten Commandments and Human Rights* (Philadelphia: Fortress, 1980), 60.

24. Theodore J. Lewis, *The Origin and Character of God: Ancient Israelite Religion through the Lens of Divinity* (Oxford: Oxford University Press, 2020), 589.

the name YHWH could possibly be "in some degree only an extension of the word *hu*, meaning he . . . the one, the Unnameable" but then argues that God in Exodus is not seeking to be unnamed or unknown. Instead, God's identification as YHWH means "I am and remain present. . . . I again and again stand by those whom I have befriended, and I would have you know indeed that I befriend you."[25] Buber also, elsewhere, in his characteristic language, emphasizes the personal nature of the Ten Commandments by saying, "The Ten Commandments are not part of an impersonal codex governing an association of men. They were uttered by an *I* and addressed to a *Thou*."[26] Certainly Exod 20:2 will echo in the commandment about lifting up the (specific) name of YHWH (Exod 20:7).

Exodus 20:2 in Catechisms

The brief story that God brought Israel out of the land of Egypt is absent in Luther's larger catechism, which simply begins with the commandment "Do not have any gods before me." In the Westminster Larger Catechism, the verse is identified—and discussed—as "the preface to the Ten Commandments." Question and answer 101 in the Westminster Catechism explains that "as with Israel of old," so today God is in covenant with all God's people, and as God delivered Israel from slavery in Egypt, "so he delivereth us from our spiritual thraldom; and therefore we are bound to take him for our God alone, and to keep all his commandments."[27] Calvin writes, "Whether you make the first sentence a part of the First Commandment or read it separately makes no difference to me, provided you do not deny to me that it is a sort of preface to the whole law."[28] The 1997 Catechism of the Catholic Church teaches that "the

25. Martin Buber, *Moses: The Revelation and the Covenant* (New York: Harper and Row, 1958), 50–51.

26. Martin Buber, "What Are We to Do about the Ten Commandments?," in *On the Bible: Eighteen Studies*, ed. Nahum N. Glatzer (Syracuse: Syracuse University Press, 2000), 118.

27. John Wesley's "Explanatory Notes" to the Ten Commandments similarly connect God's deliverance from slavery then to deliverance from spiritual bondage today: "[God] had brought them out of the land of Egypt—Therefore they were bound in gratitude to obey him, because he had brought them out of a grievous slavery into a glorious liberty. By redeeming them, he acquired a farther right to rule them; they owed their service to him, to whom they owed their freedom. And thus, Christ, having rescued us out of the bondage of sin, is entitled to the best service we can do him." https://tinyurl.com/452hsf2u.

28. John Calvin, *Institutes of the Christian Religion*, ed. John T. McNeill, trans. and indexed by Ford Lewis Battles (Philadelphia: Westminster, 1960), 379.

first of the 'ten words' recalls that God loved his people first"[29] and though it includes Exod 20:2 as part of the first commandment, section 2084 affirms that "God makes himself known by recalling his all-powerful, loving, and liberating action in the history of the one he addresses."[30]

The Priority of Grace to Law

Karl Barth writes about law as "the form of the Gospel" and described Exod 20:2 as demonstrating "the priority of grace to law."[31] While this is clearly Christian language, the sentiment runs throughout receptions of the Decalogue. For example, twentieth-century Hungarian pastor József Farkas accuses Christians of not taking seriously "the start" of the Ten Commandments, which makes it clear that God first did something and only after asked for a response from people. Farkas writes that, though many people do interpret the Ten Commandments as God cracking a whip "ten times so that the human rabble might behave themselves," his interpretation is that because of God's love, God "addresses us, talks with us, and gives us revelation, guidance, direction, help. The giving of the Ten Commandments, these ten helps, is one expression of God's helpful love."[32] Farkas's description of God cracking a whip is similar to a statement supposedly made by Adolf Hitler, as reported by Hermann Rauschning, a former Nazi party member who became a critic of the regime. According to Rauschning, Hitler said, "Ah, the God of the deserts, that crazed, stupid, vengeful Asiatic despot with his powers to make laws! That slavekeeper's whip! That devilish 'Thou shalt, thou shalt!' And that stupid 'Thou shalt not.' It's got to get out of our blood, that curse from Mount Sinai!"[33] Though both share the metaphor of a whip, the descriptions of God from Hitler and Farkas couldn't be more different. For Hitler, the laws are a curse, but for Farkas they are an expression of love. For Hitler, the law comes from despotic power. Farkas emphasizes that God first acted on behalf of Israel in Exod 20:2 and then out of love and care gave "these ten helps" to God's people.

29. *Catechism of the Catholic Church*, §2061, https://tinyurl.com/yck4rj5y.

30. *Catechism of the Catholic Church*, §2084, https://tinyurl.com/4p79yjf6.

31. Karl Barth, *Church Dogmatics*, III.4, ed. G. W. Bromiley and T. F. Torrance (Edinburgh: T&T Clark, 1961), 205.

32. József Farkas, *Bench Marks*, trans. John R. Bodo (Richmond, VA: John Knox, 1969), 78.

33. Herman Rauschning, "Preface: A Conversation with Hitler," in Armin Robinson, *The Ten Commandments: Ten Short Novels of Hitler's War against the Moral Code* (New York: Simon & Schuster, 1944), xii.

David Hazony reads Exod 20:2 not as a prologue but as the first commandment and suggested it is less a description of God and more a message about who humans can be and about what humans are capable of. He writes, "just as God is at heart a redeemer, so too are we, each of us, potential redeemers."[34]

Conclusion

American philosopher Allan Bloom tells a story in his 1987 *The Closing of the American Mind* about one of his teachers who "wrote a Ten Commandments for Americans that began, 'I am the Lord thy God who brought thee out of the house of the European tyrants into my own land, America: Relax!'"[35] Bloom's teacher's rewriting of Exod 20:2 is an interesting example of the value of reception history writ large. It illustrates how ancient language and concepts are reworked into updated settings and contexts. The "house of slavery" in Egypt gets changed into "the house of European tyrants." Bloom's teacher adds the idea that America is God's own land, a thought that was replete among the colonists who settled America, and perhaps was reassuring in the late 1980s, at the end of the twentieth century. But, as diachronic reception history allows us to look back at how texts were received in the past, it also affords the opportunity to admit that such a reception rings more dissonantly in 2024 with the rise of Christian nationalism. Additionally, Bloom's teacher's reception does not consider the perspective of Indigenous Americans. The flexibility of the biblical text—for better or for worse—and our desire to make the text useful, helpful, and applicable in our own settings and times will continue through the ages and in various receptions of all the remaining commandments.

34. David Hazony, *The Ten Commandments: How Our Most Ancient Moral Text Can Renew Modern Life* (New York: Scribner, 2010), 42.

35. Alan Bloom, *The Closing of the American Mind* (New York: Simon & Schuster, 1988), 227.

2

"No Other Gods, No Idols"

Reception history demonstrates how Exod 20:3–6 has been understood in two ways: both as a single commandment and also separated into two distinct commandments. In fact, as discussed in the introductory chapter, the enumeration of these into "ten" differs because of how these verses get divided. The single commandment instructs exclusive faithfulness to God: not worshiping any other god or thing, loving only God and keeping God's commandments. When the verses are separated out into two commandments, the first is found in Exod 20:3, which states, "You shall not have any other gods besides or before me." The second, distinct commandment starts in Exod 20:4, forbidding the creation of any image. When these are received as separate commandments, the first one already covers the idea of exclusive worship of one God, so the second one forbids making any image of that God. The Talmud, Augustine, Roman Catholics, and Lutherans combine them into a single commandment, whereas Philo, Eastern Orthodoxy, and Reformed Christianity separate them into two distinct commandments. Jonathan Willis criticizes what he identifies as "the problem" with combining them: "It made of the First Commandment a loose, baggy monster, comprising the full text of Exodus 20:1–6."[1] When they are separated, receptions in particular of Exod 20:4–6—the commandment to not have idols—tend to be polemical, describing the actions in a way that the person doing the action would not recognize, as when Protestants critique "idolatry" in Roman Catholic worship. The word "idol" becomes a heavy hitter in this sort of polemic. Classics scholar Mary Beard's language about historical iconoclasm is apt: "It was always easy enough to deplore idolatry, harder to agree what counts as such."[2] This chapter will cover receptions of Exod 20:3–6,

1. Jonathan Willis, *The Reformation of the Decalogue: Religious Identity and the Ten Commandments in England, c. 1485–1625* (Cambridge: Cambridge University Press, 2017), 29.

2. Mary Beard, *How Do We Look: The Body, the Divine, and the Question of Civilisation* (New York: Liveright, 2018), 177.

illustrating what is at stake in interpreting them together, as well as discussing how they are received when they are separated.

Gods and Idols in Exodus 32

Just over ten chapters after the commandments in Exod 20, the biblical canon seems to conflate gods and idols in the story of the golden calf. The text refers to "the great sin" of the people (Exod 32:30) in singular form: it could be identified as their worship of a golden calf instead of God, identifying the calf as the one who brought them out of Egypt and worshiping the calf in place of God. Alternatively, the great sin could be that the people and Aaron are worshiping the LORD, imagined and formed as a golden calf. They are faithful to the first commandment—no other gods—but their desire to see God in a physical form led them to create a calf as a representation of God. Supporting the idea of the golden calf as an image of God, Stephen Fowl writes, "The calf as idol is not a turning away from the one true God to worship other gods; it is the people's illegitimate attempt to shape, control, and limit the one true God; to make, in effect, a new, more manageable and domesticated version of the LORD."[3]

Similarly, Brevard Childs explains that God is not being replaced by the calf but represented.[4] Contemporary visual artist Scott Erickson's image "Golden Calf" includes his brief commentary, which echoes Fowl's idea of wanting to shape and control God. Erickson writes, "For thousands of years, the same story over and over, is substituting that which I can control, for that which invites me to have faith, that it's not all up to me."[5]

Erickson's calf stands on a pedestal that has the letters "CTRL" on it, a reference to the abbreviation for "control" on a computer keyboard. Another example of wanting to control—rather than be controlled by—one's god is found in the song "A Golden Calf" in a musical retelling of the exodus story for children called "Are We There Yet?" The lyrics include the refrain, "Gimme, gimmie, gimme what I want / don't tell me what to do / Moses' God says 'thou shalt not,' / our god just says 'moo.'"[6] These lyrics, however, also blur the distinction between an image of God and another god: the children sing about how they

3. Stephen E. Fowl, *Idolatry* (Waco, TX: Baylor University Press, 2019), 15.

4. Brevard Childs, *The Book of Exodus: A Critical, Theological Commentary* (Philadelphia: Westminster, 1974), 567.

5. Scott Erickson (@scottthepainter), May 10, 2024, https://tinyurl.com/2s42pten.

6. Tom S. Long and Allen Pote, *Are We There Yet?* (Carol Stream, IL: Hope, 2005), https://tinyurl.com/ymkfaybb.

want a god who will simply give them what they want, instead of "Moses' God" who gives them commandments and expects them to keep them.

Exodus 32 is a chapter with a complicated history of editing and revision, and the words and phrases in the narrative have been mustered as evidence for both possible receptions of the calf: as another god or as a manifestation of God. The Hebrew word *elohim* can be translated as "gods," as in foreign gods, not the LORD. In this understanding, when the people ask Aaron to make them "*elohim*" they are asking to worship something different from the LORD. The plural verb in Exod 32:1 "gods who will go [plural] before us" and the plural demonstrative in 32:4—"these are your gods," not "this is your [singular] god"—also seems to indicate multiple foreign gods. Rabbi Simeon ben Ioḥai accounts for the plurals by teaching that Aaron did not make just one calf but thirteen: one for everyone and one each for the rest of the twelve tribes (j. Sanh 10:2:3).

The word *elohim* is also translated and used as a proper name, "God." So, instead of asking for a different god, it could be that the people are asking Aaron to create for them a material form of God, though again, the plural demonstrative and verb might suggest the alternate explanation. Yet Aaron's declaration in Exod 32:5, "Tomorrow will be a festival to the LORD," can be understood as his belief that the people are going to worship the LORD or perhaps as his attempt to steer the worship into a more orthodox direction.

The complex content of Exodus 32 also gets explained as the product of different editors of the chapter. Because Jeroboam in 1 Kgs 12:28 says the same phrase as the Israelites in Exod 32:12—"these are your gods who brought you out of Egypt"—several biblical scholars suggest that Exodus 32 was added later to the text by a Deuteronomic editor who wanted to emphasize Jeroboam's problematic policy; this would also explain the plural verb and demonstrative, because Jeroboam made two separate calves: one for Bethel and one for Dan (1 Kgs 12:29).[7] Youn Ho Chung asserts that the Elohist understands the sin of the calf as breaking the commandment to not have other gods, while the Deuteronomistic editor understood it to infringe on the commandment to not make an image of God.[8] Patrick Miller, who treats Exod 20:3–5 as two distinct commandments, acknowledges the difficulty in separating the worship of other gods from the worship of images of God. Miller writes, "The story of the golden calf tells us that the First with the Second commandment, forming the principal commandment, was the first to go under."[9] Admittedly, Miller's

7. Childs, *Exodus*, 566.

8. Youn Ho Chung, *The Sin of the Calf: The Rise of the Bible's Negative Attitude toward the Golden Calf* (New York: Continuum; T&T Clark International, 2010), 97–107.

9. Patrick D. Miller, *The Ten Commandments* (Louisville: Westminster John Knox, 2009), 55.

quote is itself complicated, but his language of "the principal commandment" as a single commandment seems to combine the two.

Two recent versions of a metallic statue in the United States caught the attention of journalists who compared them to the golden calf in Exodus 32. In February 2021, at the Conservative Political Action Conference, a golden-colored statue of Donald Trump was presented to conference attendees. Zack Beauchamp, a senior correspondent at Vox, writes, "In theory, the voters in 2020 could have been the party's Moses, the loss of the White House and the Senate their bitter ashwater. And yet, here they are, still building idols of a false god."[10] In 2022, the cryptocurrency company Elon GOAT Token commissioned a statue with Elon Musk's head atop the body of a goat—to reflect the acronym Greatest of All Time—riding a rocket that shot live flames and delivered it to Tesla's Gigafactory in Austin, Texas. The statue cost $600,000 to create and is more than thirty feet long and twenty feet tall. The company's founders, Ashley Sansalone and Cory Strawbridge, explain that they created the "monument" to honor Musk's accomplishments and contributions to cryptocurrency; the rocket and flames were to indicate Musk's involvement in SpaceX. Mira Fox, writing for the Jewish newsletter *Forward*, suggests, "Perhaps Sansalone, and Musk's other acolytes need to brush up on the story of false idols. They might sacrifice themselves on the altar of Musk, but he can't reward their worship. He is, after all, a false idol."[11]

Gods and Idols in Isaiah

Isaiah 40–46 reiterates over and over again that the LORD is God, and there are no other gods;[12] John Calvin explains that Isaiah is the "most emphatic" of all the prophets on the subject.[13] The LORD's identity as God, of course, echoes back to the prologue to the Ten Commandments, and the crux of the commandments in Exod 20:3–4 seems to be that YHWH is the only God for

10. Zack Beauchamp, "This Golden Statue of Trump at CPAC Is a Perfect Metaphor for the State of the GOP," *Vox*, February 26, 2021, https://tinyurl.com/2semtaku.

11. Mira Fox, "Move over Golden Calf—Meet Elon Musk's Golden Goat," *Forward*, November 18, 2022, https://tinyurl.com/yz6by2v6.

12. Isa 41:10; 43:3; 48:17 reiterates "I am your God"; 43:11 proclaims, "I am the LORD, besides me there is no savior," while 43:13; 44:6; 45:5–6; and 45:14 have God saying, "besides me there is no other/no God." Isa 45:18 declares, "he is God, there is no other," and Isa 45:21 repeats, "there is no other god." Isa 43:9–10 emphasizes, "no god was formed before me"; 43:12 has God saying, "I saved you and not some foreign god," and Isa 44:9–20, "tell about all who make idols are nothing." Isa 46:6–7 gives the specific example of someone making a god from gold and silver but concludes, "this god cannot answer, or save."

13. Calvin, *Institutes*, 101.

God's people. But the language of Isaiah can be understood both as saying that there is no other god, in that no other god exists, as well as saying that there is no other god like the LORD. Isaiah, like the prologue to the Ten Commandments, also emphasizes knowing who this God is and what this God has done. God is the one who created, who saves, who redeems, who carries. In contrast to the LORD who carries, these other gods weigh the people down and are a burden to the people (Isa 46:1–4). In contrast to the God who declares the former things and the things yet to come, these gods do nothing (Isa 41:24). Isaiah, like other prophets, not only inveighs against the other gods but also against those people who are foolish enough to form and shape a thing and identify it as a "god." Here, too, there is a blurring of distinctions between gods and idols that are fashioned out of material substances. Similar themes occur in Wisdom of Solomon 15, with descriptions of the foolish workers who count it a glorious thing to mold counterfeit gods (Wis 15:8–13) and the foolish enemies of God's people who thought that these idols of other nations were gods (Wis 15:14–17).

No Other Gods

Exod 20:3, the verse that contains the commandment not to have other gods, also includes the phrase *'l pny*, alternatively translated "before me"[14] (KJV, NASB, NIV, ESV), "besides me" (Christian Standard Bible, New American Bible), "in my sight" (Tyndale, Coverdale 1535), "except me" (CEB), and "to my face" (Smith's Literal Translation). When it is understood as "no other gods before me," there seems to be an emphasis on order, that God is to be put first, and no other god should be placed before God. Stamm notes that this phrase carries a hostile undertone in Gen 16:12, describing Ishmael's adversarial stance over and against his brothers, and in Deut 21:16, describing a potential and unsanctioned preference for a son of an unloved wife in an inheritance.[15] W. F. Albright explained that the sense was "you shall not prefer other gods to me."[16] When the phrase is understood as "no other gods besides [or except] me," it raises the question of what is a god; Luther defines a god as "that from which we are to expect all good and to which we are to take refuge in all distress."[17]

14. As in Exod 20:20, the fear is put "before you" so you won't sin; or Exod 33:19, "goodness pass before you."

15. JPS translates the phrase in Deut 21:16 as "in disregard of."

16. W. F. Albright, *From the Stone Age to Christianity: Christian Monotheism and the Historical Process* (Baltimore: Johns Hopkins University Press, 1940), 297.

17. Martin Luther, *Luther's Large Catechism with Study Questions*, ed. F. Samuel Janzow (St. Louis: Concordia, 1978), 13.

Henning Graf Reventlow suggested that Exod 20:3 be read not as an exhortation but as an assertion, "This point is the victory of YHWH over the foreign gods, which can only be proclaimed and not demanded."[18] Following Reventlow, Walter Brueggemann writes that the commandment is a victory cry, "There will be no other gods . . . because I have come and defeated the other gods."[19] Marsh Moyle describes the phrase as an invitation to intimacy with God. Moyle suggests that if God were an actor speaking on stage this line would not be delivered by a shaking fist or a wagging finger, but rather God would deliver these words in a kind and inviting tone.[20]

The biblical prophets, in particular, do refer to other gods in polemic terms. During Elijah's showdown with the prophets of Baal in 1 Kings 18, he mocks both those prophets and their "other god," urging those prophets to shout louder because maybe their god is deep in thought, busy, traveling, or sleeping (1 Kgs 18:27). Ultimately, all the people confess in 1 Kgs 18:39 that the LORD is God. Similar mocking language appears in Isa 41:21–24, when the LORD asks other gods to do something to prove that they are gods but concludes that they are nothing and their work is empty.

Who Are the Other Gods?

Several other gods are named in the Old Testament as Baal, Asherah, Bel, Nebo, and Molech, among others, with particular durability to Baal. Luther—who combines Exod 20:3–6 into a single first commandment and thereby refers to gods and idols interchangeably—identified Mammon, or money and possessions, as "the most common idol on earth,"[21] but Luther also describes the self as a potential god, explaining that when a person seeks help, consolation and salvation in one's own works, that can lead to elevating and regarding oneself as god.[22] Aquinas identifies the other gods through people's worship, saying

18. Henning Graf Reventlow, *Gebot und Predigt im Dekalog* (Gütersloh: Gütersloher Verlagshaus Gerd Mohn, 1962), 26–28.

19. Walter Brueggemann, *The Creative Word: Canon as a Model for Biblical Education* (Philadelphia: Fortress, 1982), 36.

20. Moyle imagines God as an actor on a stage wondering about the tone of the commandment, writing, "Should the actor wag a finger or shake a fist? Is he saying, 'Don't you *dare* have any other gods before me'? Should the tone be kind and inviting?" *Rumors of a Better Country: Searching for Trust and Community in a Time of Moral Outrage* (London: Inter-Varsity Press, 2023), 59.

21. Luther, *Large Catechism*, 14.

22. Luther does admit that his teaching here is so subtle that it "is not for young pupils." *Large Catechism*, 16.

that some people worship demons, some worship "lower elements" such as fire or wind, and some worship other humans.[23] To return to Luther's definition, anything in which a person could expect good and in which someone could take refuge could potentially become a god. Timothy Keller echoes Luther's idea by emphasizing how the things that are good in life—one's relationships or even one's ministry—can become what he calls a "counterfeit god." Keller explains, "The greater the good, the more likely we are to expect that it can satisfy our deepest needs and hopes. Anything can serve as a counterfeit god, especially the best things in life."[24]

Contemporary author Neil Gaiman, in his novel *American Gods*, identifies these new gods in America as "gods of credit card and freeway, of Internet and telephone, of radio and hospital and television, gods of plastic and of beeper and of neon";[25] "of computers and telephones";[26] of media;[27] of railroads, airplanes, and cars.[28] Gaiman includes descriptions of the things sacrificed to these American gods. After hearing the television describe itself as "the all-seeing eye . . . the boob tube . . . I'm the little shrine the family gathers to adore. . . . The TV's the altar. I'm what people are sacrificing to," one character asks another, "What do they sacrifice?" The answer is, "Their time, mostly. . . . Sometimes each other."[29] Gaiman also describes the car gods as "a powerful, serious faced contingent, with blood on their black gloves and on their chrome teeth: recipients of human sacrifice on a scale undreamed-of since the Aztecs."[30]

Philosopher David Bentley Hart suggests that because many people today believe in nothing, what gets predominantly worshiped is nothingness. He writes that unlike other "gods" in the past, the god of "nothingness" is elusive and protean, and, "whether he manifests himself in some demonic titanism of the will, like the mass delirium of the Third Reich, or simply in the mesmeric

23. Thomas Aquinas, *The Commandments of God: Conferences on the Two Precepts of Charity and the Ten Commandments*, trans. Laurence Shapcote, OP, with an introduction by Thomas Gilby, OP (London: Burns, Oates & Washbourne, 1937), 27–29.

24. Timothy Keller, *Counterfeit Gods: The Empty Promises of Money, Sex, and Power, and the Only Hope That Matters* (New York: Penguin Random House, 2009), xix.

25. Neil Gaiman, *American Gods: A Novel* (New York: William Morrow, 2001), 137–38.

26. Gaiman, *American Gods*, 395.

27. Gaiman, *American Gods*, 431.

28. Gaiman, *American Gods*, 537.

29. Gaiman, *American Gods*, 175.

30. Gaiman, *American Gods*, 537. Keller writes, "We may not actually burn incense to Artemis, but when money and career are raised to cosmic proportions, we perform a kind of child sacrifice, neglecting family and community to achieve a higher place in business and gain more wealth and prestige." *Counterfeit Gods*, xiv.

banality of consumer culture, his throne has been set in the very hearts of those he enslaves. And it is this god, I think, against whom the first commandment calls us now to struggle."[31]

In the 1950s, American author Joy Davidman wrote as follows about people worshiping various things:

> I worship a fishtail Cadillac convertible, brother. All my days I give it offerings of oil and polish. Hours of my time are devoted to its ritual; and it brings me luck in all my undertakings; and it establishes me among my fellows as a success in life. . . . I worship my house beautiful, sister. Long and loving meditations have I spent on it; the chairs contrast with the rug, the curtains harmonize with the woodwork, all of it is perfect and holy. The ash trays are in exactly the right place, and should some blasphemer drop ashes on the floor, I nearly die of shock. I live only for the service of my house, and it rewards me with the envy of my sisters, who must rise up and call me blessed. Lest my children profane the holiness of my house with dirt and noise, I drive them out of doors.[32]

Davidman begins and ends her paragraph about these people worshiping their "fishtail Cadillac convertible" and their "house beautiful" with the question, "What shape is your idol?" Davidman's language, once again, illustrates the collapse of the distinction between a god and an idol.

No Idols

And yet, an idol can be distinguished from a rival god in two ways: first, as something shaped, formed, or created by humans; and second, as a visual, physical, or mental image of God. The Hebrew word translated as "idol" is *pesel*, which comes from the verb to "hew, or hew into shape," so another translation for "idol" could be "hewn thing." In the Old Testament, these idols are hewn from stone, wood, or metal. As mentioned above, Isaiah and the Wisdom of Solomon criticize those people who take clay or wood and shape them into something to

31. David Bentley Hart, "God or Nothingness," in *I Am the LORD Your God: Christian Reflections on the Ten Commandments*, ed. Carl E. Braaten and Christopher R. Seitz (Grand Rapids: Eerdmans, 2005), 58–59.

32. Joy Davidman, *Smoke on the Mountain: An Interpretation of the Ten Commandments* (Philadelphia: Westminster Press, 1954), 30.

worship. Additionally, Deut 4:15 underscores that because the Israelites saw no shape when God spoke to them out of the fire at Horeb, they were not to make an idol—*pesel*—for themselves in any likeness of any man or woman, any beast on earth, any winged bird that flies, any creature that creeps, or any fish in the waters below the earth (4:16–18). Gad Sarfatti discusses the distinction between "having" another god, as is indicated by the verb in Exod 20:3,[33] and "making" that other god, as Exod 20:4 literally says, "you shall not *make* for yourself a hewn thing." An idol can be received in the sense that someone can be given an idol by another person, but as the texts describe—and critique—the shaping, forming, and crafting of the idol, the process seems to be as significant as the final product.

If the sense of the verb *ʿaśah* ("to make") and the noun *pesel* ("idol") is more about making by cutting or carving something physical, it does not prohibit the idea that we can "make" mental or philosophical creations. For example, sociologist Andrew L. Whitehead's book *American Idolatry* identifies Christian nationalism as a current manifestation of idolatry in the United States.[34] David Hazony defines an idol as anything we can focus on and worship that distracts us from God; his examples include a person, something natural like the sun or moon, or something we create ourselves such as a statue, institution, a job, a flag, or an idea.[35] Eugenia Ann Gamble writes that an idol can be anything: "Habits, compulsions, addictions, ways of doing things, timelines, goals, our self-image, or our inner critic . . . our own hurts, wounds, fears, or the distorted stories we tell," suggesting that those stories we tell about ourselves are perhaps "the most potent idols of all."[36] Bernd Wannenwetsch argues that covetousness, as "an essential phenomenon of modern-day capitalism," reflects the core of idolatry for many today.[37]

The sheer variety of examples of idols throughout reception history sup-

33. The Hebrew verb is literally "to be," so a wooden translation would be something like "there shall not be for you another God." Gad B. Sarfatti, "The Tablets of the Law as a Symbol of Judaism," in *The Ten Commandments in History and Tradition*, ed. Ben-Zion Segal, English version ed. Gershon Levi (Jerusalem: Magnes, 1990), 414–17.

34. Andrew L. Whitehead, *American Idolatry: How Christian Nationalism Betrays the Gospel and Threatens the Church* (Grand Rapids: Brazos, 2023). Whitehead also argues that this Christian nationalism—a type of idolatry—is itself bolstered by three other idols: fear, power, and violence. Stephen Fowl also identified a connection between "whiteness" in the United States and idolatry, as well as noting how fear often led to various types of idolatry, such as in Isa 28–31. Fowl, *Idolatry*, 126–29.

35. David Hazony, *The Ten Commandments: How Our Most Ancient Moral Text Can Renew Modern Life* (New York: Scribner, 2010), 50.

36. Eugenia Ann Gamble, *Words of Love: A Healing Journey with the Ten Commandments* (Louisville: Westminster John Knox, 2022), 34.

37. Bernd Wannenwetch, "The Desire of Desire: Commandment and Idolatry in Late

ports John M. G. Barclay's comment that idolatry is "a portmanteau word into which many different concepts can conveniently be packed."[38] Halbertal and Margalit quantify those different concepts into four main categories. First is to see idolatry as rebellion against God by choosing to follow another god; the prophets illustrate this through the metaphor of marriage and adultery. This category would relate to the collapsing of Exod 20:3 and 20:4 into a single commandment, where to practice idolatry is to worship another god. Halbertal and Margalit's second category is to see idolatry as error, as the wrong representation of the true God. Third is to understand idolatry as worshiping either an aspect of God, or an intermediary of God, instead of God. And fourth is captured by the Hebrew phrase *avodah zarah*, which is the title of an entire Talmud tractate. The phrase translates literally as "strange worship" (cf. Numbers 10) and emphasizes the "strangeness" of worshiping another god or worshiping God in strange or incorrect ways.[39] Nathan MacDonald uses the story of the golden calf in Exodus 32 to illustrate how idolatry can be understood alternatively as illegitimate representation or political rebellion—two of Halbertal and Margalit's categories—but also parody, false imagination, greed, and folly.[40] In relation to idolatry as greed, Patrick Miller notes the economic dimensions in the prohibitions against creating a god out of silver or gold in Exod 20:23, which is contrasted with God's altar being made only out of earth in Exod 20:24. Miller suggests that, therefore, making idols "is seen to be tied to an economic situation of wealth and affluence."[41] Greed and idolatry are also connected in Eph 5:3–5 and Col 3:5, with "thanksgiving" identified as the disposition and practice that can counter idolatry as greed.[42]

Capitalist Societies," in *Idolatry: False Worship in the Bible, Early Judaism and Christianity*, ed. Stephen C. Barton (New York: Continuum, 2007), 316.

38. John M. G. Barclay, "Snarling Sweetly: Josephus on Images and Idolatry," in *Idolatry: False Worship in the Bible, Early Judaism, and Christianity*, ed. Stephen C. Barton (London: T&T Clark, 2007), 73.

39. Moshe Halbertal and Avishai Margalit, *Idolatry*, trans. Naomi Goldblum (Cambridge, MA: Harvard University Press, 1992), 240. Halbertal and Margalit also explain that these four approaches constitute four different sets of oppositions: (1) the opposition of other gods to God; (2) the opposition of the false and mistaken god to the true and right God, that is an opposition between imagination and reason; (3) the opposition between an aspect of God or an intermediary power and the supreme God; (4) the opposition of an alien/strange worship of God to the right worship of God. *Idolatry*, 241.

40. Nathan MacDonald, "Recasting the Golden Calf: The Imaginative Potential of the Old Testament's Portrayal of Idolatry," in *Idolatry: False Worship in the Bible, Early Judaism and Christianity*, ed. Stephen C. Barton (New York: Continuum, 2007), 22–39.

41. Miller, *The Ten Commandments*, 56–57.

42. Fowl, *Idolatry*, 72–73.

Idol Making

John Calvin wrote in reference to Acts 28:6, "Every one of us, even from his mother's womb, is a master craftsman of idols."[43] Elsewhere, he referred to human nature as "a perpetual factory of idols,"[44] and several different receptions offer explanations as to what motivates this factory. Daniel Stulac writes that attraction to idolatry is never intellectual, but rather, "idols appeal to the gut, to the appetites, to the affections."[45] Stulac also explains idolatry as appealing to a human's desire for a predictable, transactional scheme of relationship with a god. He writes, "Abject dependence on God is just so insulting, isn't it? But of course idols never deliver what they promise, for they remain only blocks of wood and stone."[46]

In a similar vein—and seeming to separate out the commandment from no other gods to making an image of God—French philosopher and sociologist Jacques Ellul mused:

> Idols are indispensable for mankind. We need to see things represented and make the powers enter our domain of reality. It is a sort of kidnapping. False gods are powers of all sorts that human beings discern in the world. The Bible clearly distinguishes these from the idol, which is the visualization of these powers and mysterious forces. Things that can be seen and grasped are certain and at our disposition. It is fundamentally unacceptable for us to be at the disposition of these gods ourselves, and unable to have power over them. Prayer or offering cannot satisfy, since they provide no sure domination. If, on the contrary, a person makes his own image and can certify that it is the deity, he is no longer afraid. Idols quiet our fears.[47]

43. John Calvin, *Commentary on the Acts of the Apostles*, vol. 2, ed. Henry Beveridge, trans. Christopher Fetherstone, https://tinyurl.com/4zjhazxz.

44. Calvin, *Institutes*, 108. Fowl notes that Calvin's assumption that idolatry is the default condition of all humans doesn't make a distinction between Christians and non-Christians, nor does it account for growth in holiness. Fowl writes, "The claim that the human heart is a perpetual idol factory does not account for believers whose hearts must be in some ways transformed from their unbelieving state. There must, at least in principle, if not always in practice, be a difference from those baptized into the death and resurrection of Christ, whose hearts are, over time, and in the light of specific dispositions, gradually distracted away from the single-minded love of God and neighbor." Fowl, *Idolatry*, 125.

45. Daniel J. D. Stulac, *Gift of the Grotesque: A Christological Companion to the Book of Judges* (Eugene, OR: Cascade, 2022), 6.

46. Stulac, *Gift of the Grotesque*, 48–49.

47. Jacques Ellul, *Humiliation of the Word* (Grand Rapids: Eerdmans, 1985), 86–87.

Whitehead notes that "identifying idols tends to make people angry";[48] again, Whitehead's main argument is that White Christian nationalism is the dominant idolatry currently in the United States. In 2005, journalist Chris Hedges wrote, "America's most pervasive idolatry is the idolatry of the self," giving the examples of the entertainment industry, the self-help industry, plastic surgeons, fashion mavens, and "those who promise quick and easy ways to become rich and powerful" as evidence for his claim.[49]

Fowl asserts that it is never the immediate intention of a person of faith to practice idolatry, that no one would wake up and declare, "Today I will worship a false god!" Instead, Fowl sees idolatry as the result of a series of small, gradual, and incremental moves that misdirect the person away from God and toward something else that is not God.[50] Calvin suggests that what motivates idolatry is the desire to harness divine power through visual representations.[51] Calvin does not mince words about the "brute stupidity" of those who worship idols,[52] describing the human mind that does so as "stuffed . . . with presumptuous rashness . . . labors under dullness . . . is sunk in the grossest ignorance."[53] And yet, Calvin also writes that humans are not so foolish as to believe that they have created a deity out of wood and stone; they understand that God is something more, but these physical forms and images of God begin to represent God for them.[54]

In fact, there does not seem to be a consensus in reception history whether or not those who worship idols genuinely believe that the created thing is divine. David L. Baker lists Hebrew words other than *pesel* used for "idol" and notes the derogatory connotations of them as follows. Baker explains that *gillul* (Jer 50:2; Ezek 6:4–13; 22:3–4) "is probably a play on the word for dung (*gél*), implying that idols are disgusting"; *'elîl* (Isa 2:8, 18, 20; 10:10–11; Hab 2:18) "literally means 'worthless thing'"; "*shiqquts* . . . (Ezek 5:11; 7:20; 20:7–8) derives from a Hebrew root associated with unclean animals"; *to'éva* (Isa 44:19; Jer 16:18; Ezek 5:9, 11) "refers to something that is utterly unacceptable for the people of God"; *shékér* "('deception,' 'falsehood') and *hével* ('futility,' 'vanity')

48. Whitehead, *American Idolatry*, 39.

49. Chris Hedges, *Losing Moses on the Freeway: The Ten Commandments in America* (New York: Free Press, 2005), 161.

50. Fowl, *Idolatry*, 3–4.

51. Calvin, *Institutes*, 109; cf. Carlos M. N. Eire, *War against the Idols: The Reformation of Worship from Erasmus to Calvin* (London: Cambridge University Press, 1986), 217.

52. Calvin, *Institutes*, 100.

53. Calvin, *Institutes*, 108.

54. Calvin, *Institutes*, 109–10.

suggest that workmen who make these worthless things are deceiving those who worship them (e.g. Jer 10:14–15)."[55]

In a Jewish legend about Abraham and his father Teraḥ, Rabbi Ḥiyya, grandson of Rav Ada of Yafo, explained that Teraḥ both worshiped and sold idols. When Teraḥ went away, he installed Abraham as salesperson in his place. One time when a man came to buy something, Abraham asked his age, and when finding out that the man was sixty years old, Abraham said, "Woe to this man who is sixty years old and seeks to prostrate himself before something that is one day old." Out of shame, the potential buyer left. Another time a woman came in with a dish of fine flour and asked Abraham to offer it to the idols. Abraham shattered all of them but one with a club and then placed the club in the hand of the remaining largest idol. When Teraḥ returned, he asked Abraham what happened. Abraham told his father that the woman came and asked him to offer the flour to the gods, and when Abraham did so, the idols started arguing among themselves about who would get to eat first, until the big idol got up, took the club, and shattered the rest of them. Teraḥ asked Abraham, "Are you mocking me? Are they sentient at all?" Thus, Abraham provoked his father to admit that the idols had no power to think, feel, or act in any way (Genesis Rabbah 38.15).[56]

Iconoclasm

While Abraham was the legendary first person to destroy idols, he was certainly not the last.[57] In the year 726 CE, the emperor of the capital of the Byzantine

55. David L. Baker, *The Decalogue: Living as the People of God* (Downers Grove, IL: InterVarsity Press, 2017), 57.

56. Other legends about Abraham describe him as only ten days old when he realized that other created things are not God. "When the sun sank, and the stars came forth, he said, 'These are the gods!' But the dawn came, and the stars could be seen no longer, and then he said, 'I will not pay worship to these, for they are no gods.' Thereupon the sun came forth, and he spoke, 'This is my god, him will I extol.' But again the sun set, and he said, 'He is no god,' and beholding the moon, he called her his god to whom he would pay Divine homage. Then the moon was obscured, and he cried out: 'This, too, is no god! There is One who sets them all in motion.'" Louis Ginzberg and David Stern, *Legends of the Jews*, trans. Henrietta Szold and Paul Radin (Philadelphia: Jewish Publication Society, 2003), 1:170.

57. In the reboot of *Battlestar Galactica* from 2004 to 2009, in the episode titled "Escape Velocity," the character Gaius Baltar smashes idols representing the "Lords of Kobol" worshiped by the polytheists in their society. Shayna Sheinfeld discusses this in her article, "The Old Gods Are Fighting Back: Mono- and Polytheistic Tensions in Battlestar Galactica and Jewish Biblical Interpretation," *Journal for Interdisciplinary Biblical Studies* 3 (summer 2021): 1–19.

empire purportedly ordered an image of Jesus to be removed from the facade of his imperial palace. The removal of that painting represented the beginning of an official ban on images of the divine that lasted for over a century. Mary Beard explains, "Lurid stories were spread about the evil of the iconoclasts, which went so far as to suggest that the wickedness of those who destroyed images of Jesus was second only to those who crucified Jesus in the first place. As usual in history, we have very little from the losers'—that is the iconoclasts'—side, although we can make a good guess at what their arguments would have been (the Second Commandment would have been a start)."[58] Beard may be too modest; while acknowledging that there are limited sources from the iconoclasts, Vladimir Baranov points out how Origen's teachings about God as spirit may have inspired iconoclasts to object to images of God.[59] In fact, as Baranov demonstrates, both sides in the Byzantine iconoclastic controversy accepted the authority of the commandment, but they interpreted it in radically different ways.[60]

Iconoclasm resurged in the sixteenth through seventeenth centuries, when the Protestant Reformers viewed the Roman Catholic use of religious images in worship as "idolatrous icons," or other "excesses." Both Luther, in his catechisms, and Calvin, in his *Institutes*, rail against the "papists" for ignoring the commandment prohibiting images in worship. In the sixteenth century in Switzerland, reformer Andreas Karlstadt used the Decalogue to argue that this commandment was as morally important as the commandment to not kill.[61] Karlstadt led the charge—literally—against the Roman Catholic places of worship, where the Protestants destroyed statues, stained glass windows, etc. In England, the destruction wrought by the seventeenth-century Protestant iconoclasts is still visible at the Ely Cathedral. Beard acknowledges that while what happened there is "one of the most mythologized and probably highly embellished incidents,"[62] the story is that on January 9, 1644, Thomas Cromwell marched into the cathedral and told the priest conducting the evening service to stop; in the following days, Cromwell "either actively encouraged or did nothing to stop his troops, who made their way through the vestry and cloisters, smashing the place."[63] In particular, the "Lady Chapel" at Ely, which

58. Beard, *How Do We Look*, 180–81.

59. Vladimir A. Baranov, "Origen and the Iconoclastic Controversy," in *Origen and the Alexandrian Tradition: Papers of the 8th International Origen Congress, Pisa, 27–31 August 2001*, ed. L. Perrone (Leuven: Leuven University Press, 2003), 1045.

60. Baranov, "Origen and the Iconoclastic Controversy," 1051.

61. Eire, *War Against the Idols*, 58.

62. Beard, *How Do We Look*, 183.

63. Beard, *How Do We Look*, 183.

was dedicated to Mary, still bears signs of destruction. Instead of the original stained glass, which was smashed by reformers, the windows are now simply clear glass. Sculptures of saints, kings and prophets, and even scenes from the life of Mary were also destroyed by either removing the entire sculpture or destroying the head or hands and leaving the body in place. Beard muses about the figures who are still present at Ely—without their heads or hands—as follows: "It is almost as if they have been turned into a different kind of image in their own right. The statues now standing proud, bearing the scars of their mutilation, have become a visual narrative of religious conflict."[64]

One argument utilized in sixteenth-century iconoclastic literature is that physical images cannot represent God because God—who is infinite and spiritual—cannot be represented in material form. To do so would lead people to believe that God is a material being. As Christoph Markschies explains, "A widely held assumption exists within the monotheism central to both the Jewish and Christian Bible that the divine is completely transcendent. The key evidence readily resorted to is the prohibition against graven images from the Ten Commandments."[65] According to Maimonides, for example, anthropomorphism regarding God is a great error, whether that be expressed in the perception that God has a body or even attributing emotions to God.[66] But Markschies draws on Benjamin Sommer's work to explain that the assumption that God is utterly transcendent is one-sided, if not false, and even if the commandment against hewn images prohibits worship of a depiction of God's body, it would be premature to conclude that God does not possess a body.[67] In his exploration of biblical texts and Jewish tradition, Sommer asserts at the outset of his writing, "The God of the Hebrew Bible has a body."[68] While, as Markschies notes, Exod 20:4–6 is silent as to whether or not God takes on corporeal form, Christian belief in Jesus's incarnation is a tenet of Christian faith that is proclaimed loudly and clearly and may give further texture to debates about this point.

As so often happens in the Bible, various passages speak differently about how much (or little) visual and material images are to be used to worship God. Certainly, the instructions for the Tabernacle—which comprise a good third of the entire book of Exodus—explain how the physical and material world

64. Beard, *How Do We Look*, 184–86.

65. Christoph Markschies, *God's Body: Jewish, Christian, and Pagan Images of God*, trans. Alexander Johannes Edmonds (Waco, TX: Baylor University Press, 2019), 20.

66. Maimonides, *Guide of the Perplexed*, 1:36.

67. Markschies, *God's Body*, 20.

68. Benjamin D. Sommer, *The Bodies of God and the World of Ancient Israel* (Cambridge: Cambridge University Press, 2009), 1.

is to be used in creating the space for the Israelites in the wilderness to meet with and worship God. Fowl points out how, in Deut 6:8–9, God's people's use of words as signs on people, houses, and public buildings is a crucial practice in remembering God.[69] And the ornate accoutrements created to furnish the Temple (1 Kgs 7:13–51) indicate that beautiful physical items were a part of orthodox worship in ancient Israel. But also, several passages warn of how tools for worship become themselves objects of worship. Again, the golden calves—in Exodus 32 as well as in 1 Kgs 12:28–30—could have been intended as representations of the LORD. Ephods, both Gideon's ephod in Judges 8 and Micah's ephod in Judges 17, were part of the priestly garments but "became a snare" to Gideon and his family (Judg 8:27) and were among the evidence of the moral and theological decline that occurred when "Israel had no king" (Judg 17:6), the repeated statement that appears for the first time in the verse immediately following the description of Micah making his ephod and an idol in Judg 17:5.[70] The rabbis made the connection between the instructions to the priest on the day of Yom Kippur to only wear garments of white instead of the typical ornate priestly clothing and the possibility of misguided worship. Rabbi Simon said in the name of Rabbi Yehoshua that the high priest was forbidden from entering the Holy of Holies wearing garments of gold "to avoid feeding arguments to Satan, who might say, 'Yesterday they worshipped gods of gold, and today they want to serve you in garments of gold?'" (Leviticus Rabba 21:10).

As with all of the Ten Commandments, the commandment forbidding making idols is not the final word on the amount of austerity (or physical beauty) in orthodox worship. In the centuries following the iconoclasm of the Protestant Reformation, many places of worship have embraced beautiful art, while other people seem to prefer worshiping in plain and even stark spaces. Davidman identified a particular type of idolatry, which she titled "churchianity." She wrote,

69. Fowl, *Idolatry*, 125.

70. Stuart Weeks writes, "Perhaps because this prohibition assumes that such images are usually the product of rival religions, not Yahwism, or perhaps because his redaction of Judges does not take a 'light-touch' approach, the Deuteronomistic Historian does not labor this point, or even question Micah's unorthodox establishment of his own sanctuary. Instead he is content just to make his standard, wry comment on the period, that 'In those days there was no king in Israel, everyone did what seemed right to them (17:6).' "Recasting the Golden Calf: The Imaginative Potential of the Old Testament's Portrayal of Idolatry," in *Idolatry: False Worship in the Bible, Early Judaism, and Christianity*, ed. Stephen C. Barton (London: T&T Clark, 2007), 7. Interestingly, the Talmud explains that Micah was not counted among the wicked because he had been generous to travelers, offering them his bread. Nedarim 25a, Megillah 13a, Sanhedrin 103b.

> The seventeenth century Puritans saw that a beautiful church and a beautiful ritual could easily become idols, and hoped to avoid the danger by making ritual and church as bare and ugly as they could. But almost at once there arose new Baalim: church organization, church discipline, or even the Bible itself, read assiduously morning and night and seldom understood at all. Men thought they were bringing their children to Christ by forcing them to sit still, white and frightened, listening to the edifying tale of how Joshua slaughtered babies or Elisha sent she-bears to eat up bad little boys.[71]

Davidman's description of "churchianity" indicates how it is not simply physical or material depictions that can lead into idolatry.

Do Not Bow Down or Worship

Exodus 20:4 clearly forbids bowing down before and/or worshiping any image in the form of anything in heaven above or on the earth beneath or in the waters below. Eastern Orthodox and Roman Catholic Christians make a clear distinction between veneration of icons and saints, and the worship of those icons and people, though the distinction continues to seem to get lost on many Protestants today. Baker, dividing Exod 20:3–6 into two commandments, explains that while the first commandment warns not to worship other gods, the second commandment tells how to worship God.[72] In David Foster Wallace's 2005 commencement speech at Kenyon College, he opines that "in the day-to-day trenches of adult life, there is actually no such thing as atheism. There is no such thing as not worshipping. Everybody worships. The only choice we get is what to worship."[73] Though Foster Wallace's language may depart from formal religious words, and certainly departs from exclusive Judeo-Christian teachings, his sentiment echoes many other receptions of Exod 20:3–6 as they warn against the dangers of idolatry, saying, "And the compelling reason for maybe choosing some sort of god or spiritual-type thing to worship—be it JC or Allah, be it YHWH or the Wiccan Mother Goddess, or the Four Noble Truths, or some inviolable set of ethical principles—is that pretty much anything else you worship will eat you alive."[74] Foster Wallace went on to explain

71. Davidman, *Smoke on the Mountain*, 38.

72. Baker, *The Decalogue*, 50.

73. David Foster Wallace, "This Is Water," Kenyon College commencement address, 2005, https://tinyurl.com/2pscah2d.

74. Foster Wallace, "This Is Water."

that when one who worships money—Luther's primary idol—or things will never feel as if they have enough; one who worships one's own body and beauty will always feel ugly; one who worships power will feel weak and afraid; and one who worships one's intellect will feel stupid and always on the verge of being exposed as a fraud. Worshiping the right thing, Foster Wallace explains, will lead to freedom: a statement that resonates with God's identity as the one who brought the people out of slavery.

A Jealous God, Punishing and Showing Mercy

Calvin commented on the explanatory clause in Exod 20:5 that God is a jealous God, referring to it as a "warning" and a "threat" that "ought to be of no little avail in shaking off our sloth."[75] Some Jewish sources, however, wonder why God would need to be jealous. When General Agrippa asked Rabban Gamliel why God would be jealous, for if the other gods were not real, why would God pay them any attention at all, the rabbi responded with a parable that resonates with Halbertal and Margalit's identification of idolatry and marital unfaithfulness. Gamliel explained that if a man takes a second wife who is superior to the first, the first wife will understand. But if the second wife is inferior, the first will rightly be infuriated that her husband would lessen his devotion to her for an unworthy woman. When a philosopher asked why God simply did not destroy idols, Gamliel answered that people do not worship only idols but also worship the sun, moon, and stars. Rabban Gamliel asked the philosopher, "Should God destroy the entirety of creation on account of such foolishness?"[76] Another midrash has Rachel speaking to God during the exile, telling God about the night when Jacob was supposed to marry Rachel. Rachel said,

> "I hid under the bed where he was lying with my sister, and he would speak to her and she would be silent, and I would answer everything he said so that he would not recognize my sister's voice, and thus I did this for kindness of her. I was not jealous of her and I did not permit her to be humiliated. And if I, who am only flesh and blood, dust and ashes, was not jealous of my co-wife and did not permit her to be shamed and humiliated, then You, O Living King, why are You jealous of idols that have no reality, and why have you exiled my children and allowed them

75. Calvin, *Institutes*, 384.

76. Rachel S. Mikva, *Broken Tablets: Restoring the Ten Commandments and Ourselves* (Woodstock, VT: Jewish Lights, 1999), 17.

> to be killed by the sword?" . . . Immediately God's pity was stirred and he said, "For you, Rachel, I will return the Israelites to their place." (Petihkta, Eikhah Rabbah 21)

Calvin does explain how God's jealousy and punishment described in Exod 20:5 are not inconsistent with divine justice and references Ezek 18:20 when God declares that God will not punish children for the sins of their parents.[77] A Jewish legend explains that when Moses heard that God would visit upon the descendants the sins of their fathers, "only if the consecutive generations were one after another sinful, he cast himself upon the ground and thanked God for it; for he knew it never occurred among Israel that three consecutive generations were sinful."[78] Calvin also thoroughly explains God's promise of mercy for thousands in Exod 20:6, noting how God limits punishment to a few generations but extends the riches of mercy to exponentially more.[79]

Positive Formulation

As with all the commandments that are worded negatively, receptions of Exod 20:3–6 explain the positive directives that are implied. British Puritan Lancelot Andrewes explains the first commandment as containing three affirmations: "We must have a God; Him for our God; Him alone, and none else."[80] Davidman similarly explains that the commandment to not have other gods must include God's commandment "Thou shalt have me."[81] Gerhard Von Rad writes that because no image could represent God, the Israelites were encouraged to understand God's character and purpose by remembering their shared history with God. Thus, the command to not create an image encourages choosing God, remembering what God has done, and worshiping God properly, which includes imaging and imagining God in ways that are theologically orthodox and humble.[82] C. S. Lewis writes in *The Screwtape Letters* that

77. Calvin, *Institutes*, 385.

78. Ginzberg and Stern, *Legends of the Jews*, 1:605.

79. Calvin, *Institutes*, 387–88.

80. Lancelot Andrewes, *A Pattern of Catechistical Doctrine and Other Minor Works* (Oxford: John Henry Parker, 1846; AMS: New York, 1967), 82. Whitehead writes that he hopes readers of his book would "commit to the ongoing work of turning from the idols of white Christian nationalism and receive Christ Jesus as Lord." *American Idolatry*, 189.

81. Davidman, *Smoke on the Mountain*, 23.

82. Gerhard Von Rad, *Old Testament Theology*, trans. D. M. G. Stalker (New York: Harper & Row, 1962), 1:212–19. Von Rad often discusses how the history was neatly contained in the

while many humans pray to a "composite object" they have created of God, proper prayer to God could be addressed, "Not to what I think thou art but to what thou knowest thyself to be."[83] In a different letter written to his fictional friend Malcolm, Lewis writes: "The prayer preceding all prayer is 'May it be the real I who speaks. May it be the real Thou that I speak to.' . . . [God] must constantly work as the iconoclast. Every idea of Him we form, He must in mercy shatter."[84] In other words, these commandments positively encourage intellectual and theological humility, admitting that any human conception of God cannot encompass God.

Additionally, many receptions of the commandment forbidding making an image understand that humans, who are created in God's image, are to represent God in the world. Calvin puts it in a pithy way: "Israel is to make no image of the Lord, but is to be such an image of God in the world."[85] Harrelson asserts,

> The second commandment is more violated by what we fail to do than by what we do. We fail to claim our place as human beings, charged to be a representation of the cause and the claim of God on earth . . . committed to let the peoples of earth know what it means to live consciously as those created in God's image and likeness. Our temptation is not to identify the creature with the Creator, to claim a kind of power for our representation of God on earth that should not be claimed for any created thing. Our greater temptation is to miss the corollary of the second commandment: that God will have only one kind of representation on earth, one that is close to his very nature and power—human beings made in his image, and a community called out to embody this vocation before the nations of earth.[86]

József Farkas extends the meaning of the second commandment as it relates to humans, by saying that people who create for themselves a "fixed image" of another person are breaking the commandment. He counsels, "So don't make yourself any such likenesses of anyone, but choose the more difficult task. Say, 'I don't know. I will watch you. I want to see what you develop into.'"[87]

---

credo in Deut 26:5–10, which extended back to Abraham—the wandering Aramean who was the father of the Israelites—but also extended to God's setting the Israelites free from slavery, as Exod 20:2 reiterates.

83. C. S. Lewis, *The Screwtape Letters* (New York: Collier Books, 1982), 22.

84. Lewis, *Letters to Malcolm: Chiefly on Prayer* (New York: Harcourt, Brace & World, Inc. 1964), 82.

85. Calvin, *Institutes*, 101.

86. Harrelson, *The Ten Commandments*, 67.

87. József Farkas, *Bench Marks*, trans. John R. Bodo (Richmond, VA: John Knox, 1969), 39.

Conclusion

Many receptions of the Ten Commandments spend more time explaining Exod 20:3–6 than any other commandment. For example, Lancelot Andrewes spends sixty-two pages discussing these, and only nine pages on the commandment forbidding misuse of God's name; for Andrewes, these commandments relate to far-reaching topics such as knowledge, faith, fear, humility, hope, and prayer.[88] Though William Whatley titled his book *A pithie, short, and Methodicall opening of the Ten commandements*, he also allots sixty-two pages to these and discusses the name commandment over twenty-one pages.[89] The sheer volume of material on other gods and idols suggests that these commandments have been elevated throughout reception history. And yet, the brief and somewhat enigmatic statement that concludes the first letter of John may also signify that there is something relatively self-explanatory in saying "Little children, keep yourself from idols" (1 John 5:21). What it looks like to have other gods and idols and who those other gods or idols are may shift and change in reception history, and still there is something enduring about the commandments and how they can be applied.

88. Andrewes, *A Pattern of Catechistical Doctrine*, 81–143.

89. William Whatley, *A pithie, short, and methodicall opening of the Ten commandements* (London: Printed by John Haviland for Thomas Pauier and Leonard Greene, 1622), https://tinyurl.com/yc58ervc.

3

"God's Name"

Nancy Fuchs-Kreimer describes her experience of being devastated at the funeral of her great-uncle Al, who was survived by his wife and two teenage children, when "the freelance rabbi hired by the funeral home for the occasion . . . provided a clumsy compendium of 'it's all for the best,' promises of the afterlife, and 'it could have been worse.' . . . Such *vain* comfort. How dare the rabbi bring God into all this sadness and in such a patently unbelievable fashion? I had come to the conclusion that God is the sum of all that is good and wondrous in the world; now God's name was being misused for what I believed to be false consolation. This, I concluded, is what it means to take God's name in vain."[1]

This commandment has been simplified into the statement "don't swear." While that is not outside the scope of what is forbidden, it does not capture all the possible implications for what is being commanded. The text of Exod 20:7 is a relatively long commandment and, as with the commandment forbidding image making, includes an explanatory clause introduced by the Hebrew word *kî*, translated as "for," or "because."[2] Someone could take God's name in vain by saying, "oh my God!" not as a prayer but simply as a punctuation, which would be like swearing, but the dense language in the commandment suggests something more complicated and even something more specific, as Fuchs-Kreimer's example indicates. In fact, this commandment has been explained in over twenty different ways throughout reception history; Carmen Imes

1. Nancy Fuchs-Kreimer, "Thou Shalt Not Take the Name," in *Broken Tablets: Restoring the Ten Commandments and Ourselves*, ed. Rachel S. Mikva (Woodstock, VT: Jewish Lights, 1999), 32–33.

2. Patrick D. Miller contrasts the sanction in the commandment about image making with the sanction contained here: he describes the sanction in Exod 20:5–6 as "general," but the sanction in the commandment about the name is "direct," with the judgment "directly related to the prohibition." *The Ten Commandments* (Louisville: Westminster John Knox, 2009), 81.

notes that the number of potential meanings is more than twice the number of lexemes in the commandment itself.[3] But as with the other commandments, this is not a liability but a feature. John I. Durham writes that the language of the name commandment was "deliberately chosen to permit a wide range of application, covering every dimension of the misuse of Yahweh's name."[4]

A relatively literal translation would be "You shall not lift/bear the name of YHWH your God for falsehood/emptiness, because YHWH will not hold guiltless the one who lifts/bears his name for falsehood/emptiness." As that translation indicates, two of the Hebrew words signify different possible meanings: (1) *nś'*, translated either as "lift up," "bear," or "take," and (2) *šw'*, translated as either "false" or "empty." Many receptions understand the first word as an elliptical way to refer to speech, so ways of talking about God's name are prohibited, though some receptions understand this as prohibiting a more literal or symbolic action. The second word is variously understood as prohibiting use of God's name for bad or malicious actions; in vain, thoughtless, or profane ways; falsely or for falsehood such as specifically in situations of perjury or false witness; or some combination of the previous three.[5] And though, by comparison, the phrase "the name of YHWH" is fairly direct, it also has been understood and applied differently by those who seek to obey this commandment.

Speech or Action? Translations of *ns'*

By far the majority of receptions understand this commandment to refer to one's speech, where to "take" God's name is to speak it in a certain way. The Aramaic translation of Exod 20:7 in Targum Onqelos (ca. 50–150 CE) uses the

3. Carmen Joy Imes, *Bearing YHWH's Name at Sinai: A Reexamination of the Name Command of the Decalogue* (University Park, PA: Eisenbrauns, 2018), 7. There are seventeen words in Exod 20:7, but because words are repeated, there are only ten lexemes, and Imes counts at least twenty-three distinct meanings proposed.

4. John I. Durham, *Exodus* (Grand Rapids: Zondervan Academic, 1990), 288.

5. F. J. Coffin suggested that variations in meanings of this commandment can be traced to translations of the Hebrew word *šw'*, which he classifies into four categories: (1) bad or malicious, which purportedly relates to the Arabic word *såa* meaning "bad" or the Ethiopic *såa*, so the commandment prohibits using God's name for a bad or malicious purpose; (2) in vain, thoughtless, profanely, as in the LXX, Samaritan Pentateuch, and Vulgate; (3) falsely or for falsehood including specific commands against perjury or false swearing, as in Graecus Venetus, Syriac, Targum, Arabic, De Wette; and (4) as a combination of (2) and (3), as in the Talmud, Philo, Josephus, Luther, and Calvin. Coffin, "The Third Commandment," *JBL* 19 (1900): 168.

verb *ymy* ("to say, swear"). Seventeenth-century Puritan theologian Thomas Watson asserted that this commandment does have to do with one's speech, proclaiming that "the tongue is the prime offender" of this commandment.[6] Watson's enumeration of the various types of speech included irreverence, hypocrisy, profanity, false worship, unbelieving prayer, the use of Scripture by wicked people, oaths (either excessive, unnecessary, vile, or false), false authorization, unseemly speech, rash vows, speaking evil of God, and making promises one does not intend to keep.[7] So, pretty much any sort of speech could break this commandment. Contemporary author Jonathan Merritt specifies it slightly in his book, writing, "Words are too powerful to use carelessly, especially when you're speaking God."[8]

Timothy Hogue suggests that an early version of the commandment read "You shall not maliciously erase the name of Yahweh your God, for Yahweh will not acquit the one who erases his name maliciously."[9] Based on the usage of the word *ns'* in Ps 116:13, "I will lift up the cup of salvation," Hogue suggests "a physical act rather than a mode of speaking is envisioned by the name commandment in the Decalogue" and that what was forbidden was the act of lifting the name of YHWH off of monuments by erasing this, though this meaning was lost in later receptions and replaced with a metaphoric understanding of speaking the name.[10]

The verb more frequently refers to an action of lifting up or carrying. Instead of the verb *ns'*, the Aramaic Targum Neofiti uses the word *nsb*, "to lift up, take, carry, or bear." After carefully and thoroughly examining the use of the words in the Hebrew, Imes concludes that this word is best translated as "bear," "carry," or possibly "receive," explaining that the word *ns'* "never refers to speech without some explicit contextual clues."[11] Imes draws on priestly imagery such as in Exod 28:12 and 28:29, where Aaron as the high priest is commanded to "bear" the "names" of each tribe on his shoulders and breastplate as a memorial to the LORD, and Num 6:27, where God explains that the priests "will place my name on the Israelites, and I will bless them." Imes suggests that

6. Thomas Watson, *Body of Divinity: Contained in Sermons upon the Assembly's Catechism* (Grand Rapids: Baker, 1979), 36.

7. Watson, *Body of Divinity*, 36.

8. Jonathan Merritt, *Learning to Speak God from Scratch: Why Sacred Words Are Vanishing—and How We Can Revive Them* (New York: Convergent, 2018), 46.

9. Timothy S. Hogue, *The Ten Commandments: Monuments of Memory, Belief, and Interpretation* (Cambridge: Cambridge University Press, 2023), 77.

10. Hogue, *The Ten Commandments*, 90.

11. Imes, *Bearing YHWH's Name*, 100.

this imagery provides an interpretive key for the name commandment: that God's chosen and elect have God's name upon them because God has claimed them as God's own, and they are to "bear" God's name through their obedience to God's covenant stipulations, through righteous conduct and character.[12]

Religious Abuse and God's Reputation

If Israel's identity as a people is bound up with the name of YHWH and YHWH's claim upon them, they can do damage to God's reputation through a range of behaviors.[13] Ephraim Radner understands the name commandment as getting at "the very center of *every act* we do and at its motivation in the human heart" but especially when the motivations are connected with religious goals.[14] Walter Harrelson, in fact, rewords this commandment as "do not use the power of religion to harm others."[15] He explains:

> When religion is turned perversely against the very means that it uses to bring blessing, then the springs are poisoned and little can be done. How massive is the damage that has been done by those who have lifted up God's name for mischief. Thousands and thousands struggle for health in mental institutions trying to undo, with professional help, the damage done by those who have driven them into psychosis by the warnings of eternal damnation. Unloved in this world by family and friends, as they believe, they have concluded that God too will not love them, cannot love them, until they do what the religious practitioner demands they do. God, too, may then be identified as a deceiver and destroyer. These

12. Imes, *Bearing YHWH's Name*, 181. For a related but slightly different argument, Alice Mandell discusses how the inscriptions on Aaron's priestly uniform suggest that Aaron's very body operates as a ritual vessel in the tabernacle, dedicating the people to God to be holy. Alice Mandell, "Aaron's Body as a Ritual Vessel in the Exodus Tabernacle Building Narrative," in *New Perspectives on Ritual in the Biblical World*, ed. Laura Quick and Melissa Ramos (London: T&T Clark, 2022), 159–81.

13. Imes, *Bearing YHWH's Name*, 87.

14. Ephraim Radner, "Taking the Lord's Name in Vain," in *I Am the LORD Your God: Christian Reflections on the Ten Commandments*, ed. Carl E. Braaten and Christopher R. Seitz (Grand Rapids: Eerdmans, 2005), 80 (emphasis mine).

15. Walter Harrelson, *The Ten Commandments and Human Rights* (Philadelphia: Fortress, 1980), 194.

more subtle ways of abusing the power of God are far more destructive, I believe, than those prevalent in ancient societies.[16]

Russell Moore, the editor in chief for *Christianity Today*, wrote that the Southern Baptist Convention Executive Committee's complicity in covering up sexual abuse was in violation of the commandment for proper use of the name of God, saying, "Sexual abuse, in any context and by any institution, is a grave atrocity. It's worse when this horror is committed—or covered up—by leveraging personal or institutional trust. But using the very name of Jesus to carry out such wickedness against those he loves and values is a special evil."[17]

Moore has equated the "name of Jesus" with the name of the LORD, something that Christians do throughout the reception of this commandment. But with all the potential biblical texts one could draw on to castigate the church for covering up sexual abuse,[18] Moore—himself an ordained Baptist minister who served as president of the Ethics & Religious Liberty Commission of the Southern Baptist Convention from 2013 to 2021—appeals to the commandment about using God's name to do so.

Twentieth-century Hungarian pastor József Farkas writes that he interprets this commandment as addressed primarily to "us praying, preaching, witnessing, churchly people."[19] Imes takes a similar stance, arguing that the commandment "cannot be considered a universal prohibition; people outside the covenant do not bear his name. It is specifically applicable to his covenant people."[20] Thomas Torrance applies the commandment to God's people but extends its meaning, explaining, "Most people assume that it refers to a verbal profanation of the name of God. But this is incorrect, for it covers the whole range of religious life. It means: Thou shalt not spend thy life in vain—thou shalt not be called the people of Jehovah without fulfilling the purpose for which He made and sanctified you."[21] In these receptions, the commandment

16. Harrelson, *The Ten Commandments*, 76.

17. Russell Moore, "Abuse and the Third Commandment," *Christianity Today* 66 (July/August 2022): 36.

18. For example, one might appeal to Ezek 34, which describes the bad shepherds who feed themselves (on the sheep!) instead of protecting them, or Jesus's harsh warning for anyone who harms a little one who trusts in him (Matt 18:6).

19. József Farkas, *Bench Marks*, trans. John R. Bodo (Richmond, VA: John Knox, 1969), 47.

20. Imes, *Bearing YHWH's Name*, 122.

21. Thomas Torrance, *The Beatitudes and the Decalogue* (London: Skeffington and Son, 1992), 71.

is less about the words used and more about actions committed or omitted by people who identify themselves in relationship to God.

Oaths

Many receptions affirm that the particular, primary, and precise application of the commandment has to do with oaths. For example, Calvin wrote, "The commandment has particular reference to the oath, wherein the perverse abuse of the Lord's name is in the highest degree detestable, that thereby we may be better frightened away altogether from all profaning of it (cf. Deut 5:11)."[22] Calvin included several pages on the various types of oaths one could take, including the oath as confession to God, the false oath as a desecration of God's name, the idle oath, and the extrajudicial oath.[23] Biblical scholar Patrick D. Miller affirmed that oath taking is a primary issue for this commandment,[24] and Aquinas explained that the commandment "precisely prohibits oath taking."[25] Yet all three of these interpreters acknowledge that the commandment is not limited to oaths. Calvin wrote that the commandment is ultimately about "hallowing the majesty of God's name,"[26] and Miller wrote that, given the many places in the Bible where people do swear an oath by God's name, there is more to the commandment than simply forbidding oaths.[27] Though Aquinas began his discussion on the meaning of the commandment with a focus on oath taking, he applied this commandment to a broad sweep of doctrinal exposition, explaining that "every misuse of God's name is thereby prohibited."[28]

22. John Calvin, *Institutes of the Christian Religion*, ed. John T. McNeill, trans. and indexed by Ford Lewis Battles (Philadelphia: Westminster, 1960), 1:388–89.

23. Calvin, *Institutes*, 389–93.

24. Miller, *The Ten Commandments*, 93.

25. Aquinas, *Summa Theologica*, I-II, Q. 100, Art. 5, ad. 3, https://tinyurl.com/awp6brr8.

26. Calvin, *Institutes*, 394.

27. Miller gives several examples, including Deut 6:13, which affirms, "The LORD your God you shall fear, and him you shall serve; and by his name alone you shall swear." Rahab and the spies in Josh 2 swear oaths to each other by the LORD, and the covenantal relationship between Jonathan and David is undergirded by the oaths they make to one another in 1 Sam 20 in God's name. Miller, *The Ten Commandments*, 94–95.

28. Aquinas, *Summa Theologica*, II-II, Q. 122, Art. 3, ad. 2, https://tinyurl.com/24w2bhkv. In the reverse order of Calvin, Miller, and Aquinas, Lancelot Andrewes starts his commentary on this commandment by stating that "the end of this commandment is the praise of God . . ." but then focuses on oath taking. Andrewes, *A Pattern of Catechistical Doctrine and Other Minor Works* (Oxford: John Henry Parker, 1846; AMS, New York, 1967), 231.

Radner suggests that the elaborate interpretive focus on oath taking as the core of this commandment was a late development in the church, appearing in the high middle ages and continuing through the early modern era.[29] Yet, there are analogies from ancient western Asia, such as in the Dingir.šà.dib.ba incantations, which confess, "My God, I did not know how severe your punishment is. I frivolously uttered a solemn oath by your name. Like the one who frivolously uttered a solemn oath by his god. As from one who frivolously uttered an oath by his god."[30]

Imes identifies four types of oaths forbidden to one of God's people, all four of which would violate the commandment: (1) oaths sworn falsely by affirming an untruth, by disavowing a truth, by failing to keep a promise either not to do something or to do something; (2) oaths sworn unnecessarily by affirming an obvious truth, by swearing habitually; (3) oaths sworn with evil intent to trick, to do evil, or selfishly; and (4) oaths sworn by a false god.[31] Rashi affirms that the commandment prohibits both idle or reckless oaths and false or untrue oaths.[32] But by contrast, Coffin identified three classes of permissible oaths in the Old Testament: (1) a covenant ratified by an oath, such as in Gen 26:31; 31:53; 1 Sam 20:17; 2 Kgs 11:4); (2) an appeal to God in attestation of the truth of a statement, such as in Gen 24:7; 50:25; Exod 22:11; Josh 9:18; and (3) the judicial oath, for which Coffin gives no examples.[33] Seventeenth-century British philosopher John Locke would seem to agree with the second of Coffin's types; in his *A Letter Concerning Toleration*, he wondered how one could trust the word of an atheist for whom the name of God could not certify an oath.[34]

Empty or False? Translations of *šw'*

As mentioned above, the Hebrew word *šw'* can be translated as either "false" or "empty," and the choice of how to understand it leads to other implications for

29. Radner identifies the emergence of this focus with Peter Lombard in the twelfth century when canon law became its own discipline. Radner, "Taking the Lord's Name in Vain," 81–83.

30. W. G. Lambert, "Dingir.šà.dib.ba Incantations," *JNES* 33 (1974): 297.

31. Imes, *Bearing YHWH's Name*, 8.

32. Sefaria, citing *The Contemporary Torah*, ed. David E. S. Stein et al. (Philadelphia: Jewish Publication Society, 2006), https://tinyurl.com/5ysuybkc.

33. Coffin, "The Third Commandment," 184. Further discussion about "swearing by the name of the LORD" will follow below.

34. In Radner, "Taking the LORD's Name in Vain," 212.

this commandment. F. J. Coffin classified translations of *šw'* into four general categories.[35] The first is to translate it as "bad" or "malicious," which purportedly relates to the Arabic word *sắa* meaning "bad" or the Ethiopic *sảa* and suggests prohibiting using God's name for a bad or malicious purpose.[36] Coffin understands Emil Kautzsch and J. P. Lange as interpreting the commandment in this way, saying that Lange makes the commandment a prohibition of the malicious use of the divine name. "The right apprehension of the name is presupposed, but the correctness of the apprehension is hypocritically employed by the transgressor in the interest of selfish-ness and vice."[37] Lange uses the German word *freventlich*, which can be translated as "sacrilegious, criminal, outrageous, wanton, wicked, or impious." Even if linguistic connections are thin, this understanding is robust in reception history as can be seen in the examples above of God's reputation, or those below of using God's name for political or personal gain.

A second way to translate *šw'* is "in vain, thoughtless, profanely," as happens with the LXX *epi mataiō*, Vulgate, "in vanum." This translation also suggests "empty" or "ineffective." Imes explains, "A claim to covenantal membership without faithfulness to covenant stipulations was 'empty.'"[38] Rachel S. Mikva explains that "vanity" would include any superfluous use of God's name[39] and references the Talmudic teaching that to recite an unnecessary blessing would be a violation of the name command (b. Ber 33a:35). The Talmud also appeals to this commandment when instructing those making an offering to the Lord. They are not to say, "To the Lord a burnt offering or . . . to the Lord a peace offering," but instead, the one making the offering should identify the offering first and only then say that the offering is being made to the Lord. The reason is that "if one first says: To the Lord, perhaps he will change his mind and not complete the sentence in order to avoid consecrating the offering, and he will have uttered the name of God in vain" (b. Ned 10b:1).

A third way *šw'* is translated is as "falsely" or "for falsehood," as in Syriac "mendacio" (in Walton's Latin Polyglot) and by De Wette as "Unwarheit" "untruth, falsehood." Coffin relates this to stipulations against perjury or false swearing. In Job 31:5, the word *šw'* appears in parallel with *mirmah* ("false"). Deuteronomy's version of the commandment about not witnessing falsely

35. F. J. Coffin, "The Third Commandment," *JBL* 19 (1900): 168.

36. Harrelson writes, "Rather than being an expression for emptiness or insubstantiality, the term carries with it active power for harm." *The Ten Commandments*, 73.

37. Coffin, "The Third Commandment," 168.

38. Imes, *Bearing YHWH's Name*, 105.

39. Rachel S. Mikva, *Broken Tablets: Restoring the Ten Commandments and Ourselves* (Woodstock, VT: Jewish Lights, 1999), 27.

against a neighbor uses this word *šw'* to describe the nature of the witness, but in Exod 16, the word *šqr* is used, which more properly means "lying."[40]

Coffin's fourth classification is a combination of the second and third, to understand the word as both referring to empty or superfluous use of God's name and using it falsely or in a lying manner. Targum Onqelos represents this, as the first occurrence of *šw'* in the verse ("you shall not lift up God's name") is *mgv*, which means "for nothing, in vain," and the second one ("for the LORD will not hold guiltless the one who lifts up God's name") as *šqr*, "lie, falsehood." As Calvin discusses the name commandment, he explains that it prohibits false swearing and should be applied to all occasions when God's name is mentioned, prohibiting any light or frivolous use of God's name.[41] Martin Luther translates *šw'* in Exod 20:7 with the German word "missbrauchen," literally "misuse," which could include using God's name in a frivolous way or falsely. Illustrated Bibles of the Ten Commandments have as their example of breaking this commandment the story in Lev 24, where the man blasphemes and curses.

Religion and Politics

In 1941, British author and philosopher C. S. Lewis published an essay titled "Meditation on the Third Commandment." Nowhere in the piece is the commandment about God's name either mentioned or quoted; rather, Lewis's goal was to forestall the creation of a political "Christian Party" in England. Lewis's essay began with a definition of politics as the means to achieve societal ends. He asserted that most political parties could agree on desirable ends such as security and a living wage, and what distinguished one party from another was how to achieve those ends. Then, Lewis asserted that because Christians can and do disagree about such means, no Christian party would be politically successful, nor genuinely Christian. Either the party would be too small to be politically effective and be "tempted to accept help from unbelievers who profess themselves quite openly to be the enemies of God"[42] or it would be falsely claiming to represent all Christians. Lewis wrote, "Whatever it calls itself, it will represent, not Christendom, but a part of Christendom. . . . By

40. The distinction between "false" and "lying" will be discussed again, in relationship to the commandment forbidding false witness against a neighbor.

41. Calvin, *Institutes*, 388–89.

42. C. S. Lewis, "Meditations on the Third Commandment," in *God in the Dock: Essays on Theology and Ethics*, ed. Walter Hooper (Grand Rapids: Eerdmans, 1970), 197.

the mere act of calling itself the Christian Party it implicitly accuses all Christians who do not join it of apostasy and betrayal."[43] In 2000, American legal scholar Stephen Carter wrote a book titled *God's Name in Vain* about religion and politics in the United States, paying special attention to the rise of the Moral Majority and the Christian Coalition. More than two decades after the publication of Carter's book, there seems to be no end to American politicians appealing to God and God's name in their political discourse and aspirations. Carter explains that Lewis's essay inspired his title and then writes, "The discovery of what the Third Commandment actually says I leave, as Lewis did, as an exercise for the reader."[44] So while neither Lewis's essay nor Carter's book specifically references or discusses the commandment, both allude to how referring to a political party or interest group as "Christian" could violate it.

Farkas was more direct when he wrote about Billy Graham's support for the war in Vietnam, writing:

> When a Christian evangelist speaks of bombings and mass murder as a "crusade" for the defense of Christian civilization, we are in the presence of a grievous transgression against the commandment "You shall not take the name of the Lord in vain." The least the evangelist could do would be to say, "Our Christianity is impotent; we don't understand what is going on in the world; we have no word from the Lord." But let him not set forth his own philosophy as it if were the word of God! Billy Graham could have said, "I don't understand what is going on in the world"; and believe me, this might frequently be the most honest form of Christian witness—to admit that we do not know what God wants nor what we must do.[45]

Patrick Miller notes how the invocation of God's name by oath "can be a way of wielding political power for personal ends and goals by putting a divine imprimatur on the ruler's plans and decisions."[46] In the narrative about the succession to David's throne, seven times someone swears an oath in the name of the LORD (1 Kgs 1:13, 17, 29, 30; 2:8, 23, 42). Brevard Childs observed that when David on his deathbed references his previous oath that he swore by the LORD to not kill Shimei (1 Kgs 2:8), David also clearly intimates that Solomon should kill Shimei. Childs writes, "Although strictly speaking the oath

43. Lewis, "Meditations," 198.

44. Stephen L. Carter, *God's Name in Vain: The Wrongs and Rights of Religion in Politics* (New York: Basic Books, 2000), 8.

45. Farkas, *Bench Marks*, 49.

46. Miller, *The Ten Commandments*, 100.

is not broken, David resorts to a form of deception to execute his vengeance against Shimei . . . the reader is left to ponder whether God's name has not, in fact, been dishonored by such human casuistry."[47] In 1 Kgs 2:23–24, Solomon invokes God's name to justify his decision to kill his brother Adonijah, the main rival to Solomon for their father's throne.[48] Farkas wrote, "Whenever we attempt to dominate our fellowmen and use the name of God to buttress our claim upon them, we are in effect breaking the third commandment."[49] And while the examples above are in political situations, twentieth-century Christian author Joy Davidman wrote that the commandment about God's name is broken whenever it is used for selfish ends, even in situations such as "getting our own way in a family quarrel."[50]

Specific Name

The wording of the commandment in Exodus and Deuteronomy specifies that the name to be used rightly is the name YHWH, which appears from the beginning of the Yahwistic story in Gen 2:4b, but Gen 4:26 notes that "at that time people began to invoke the name of YHWH." God reveals this name to Moses in response to Moses's question of what he should tell the Israelites if they ask him the name of this God (Exod 3:13–16).[51] In the priestly account in Exod 6:2–8, God reiterates that God's name is YHWH, and this name is bound up with God's identity. Miller writes that in Exod 6:7 when God says, "you shall know that I am YHWH," the implication is that they will come to know who YHWH is and what this name connotes because of the events that are to come.[52] God further explicates the name and identity YHWH in Exod 34:6–7 when God proclaims the name "YHWH," saying, "gracious and merciful, slow to anger, abounding in steadfast love and faithfulness, maintaining steadfast love for the thousandth generation, forgiving iniquity and transgression and sin, yet by no means clearing the guilty, but visiting the iniquity of the parents

47. Brevard Childs, *Old Testament Theology in a Canonical Context* (Minneapolis: Augsburg Fortress, 1990), 69.

48. Miller, *The Ten Commandments*, 100.

49. Farkas, *Bench Marks*, 48.

50. Davidman, *Smoke on the Mountain: An Interpretation of the Ten Commandments* (Philadelphia: Westminster, 1954), 48.

51. Different proposals are discussed in Brevard Childs, *The Book of Exodus: A Critical, Theological Commentary* (Philadelphia: Westminster Press, 1974), 52–53.

52. Miller, *The Ten Commandments*, 75.

upon the children and the children's children, to the third and the fourth generation." This "YHWH creed" appears in various ways and in different details throughout the Old Testament (Num 14:18; Nah 1:3; Ps 86:15; 103:8; 145:8; Neh 9:17, 31; Jon 4:2)[53] and echoes the rationale given in the commandment not to make idols in Exod 20:5–6.

Miller suggests that in the book of Deuteronomy and the Deuteronomistic History the name of God becomes "a kind of theologoumenon, a manifestation of the presence of God."[54] For example, in Deut 12:5, 21; and 14:24, the place of worship is described as a place where YHWH will choose to put his name or cause his name to dwell. In Solomon's prayer at the dedication of the temple, he makes six separate references to building a house "for the name of the LORD" (1 Kgs 8:16, 17, 18, 19, 20, 44) and also quotes the LORD as saying "my name will be there" in the temple (1 Kgs 8:29). Miller writes, "There is a sense that the God who dwells in heaven but cannot be contained even there is present in the temple in and through the divine name."[55] In the book of Ezekiel, God speaks about doing things for the sake of God's name (Ezek 20:9, 14, 22, 44; 36:22).

In many receptions through history, the name commandment is about prohibiting misuse of the particular name YHWH. For example, Philo understood Lev 24:16, which warns against blaspheming the name, as a prohibition against pronouncing the Tetragrammaton.[56]

There are various—and competing—instructions on the use of the name YHWH in the Talmud. According to Mishnah Yoma 6:2, only the high priest would use the name on the Day of Atonement. According to b. Sot 7:6, when a priest speaks the benediction from Num 6:24–26 in the temple, he should speak the name YHWH, but in the country the priest should use the name "Adonai." The Mishnah contains the teaching that the sages advocated that people use God's name to greet one another, indicating that there was no prohibition against pronouncing the Name (Berakhot 9:5). B. Kid 71a 10 records a debate between rabbis about the frequency of teaching students how to pro-

53. Amy Erickson, *Jonah: Introduction and Commentary* (Grand Rapids: Eerdmans, 2021), 391.

54. Miller, *The Ten Commandments*, 78. Cf. Tryggve Mettinger, who references Exod 33:18–23 as follows: "Moses is not allowed to behold God's 'glory' nor is he allowed to glimpse God's face. But he does hear! And what he hears is clearly stated: He hears God pronounce God's name, YHWH for him. "When God Pronounces His Name (*šēm*), the divine presence is made manifest (v. 19, cf. 34:5–6)," in *In Search of God: The Meaning and Message of the Everlasting Names*, trans. Frederick H. Cryer (Philadelphia: Fortress, 1988), 9.

55. Miller, *The Ten Commandments*, 79.

56. Philo, *On the Life of Moses*, 2:114, 206.

nounce correctly the four-letter name of God. One rabbi says that this should happen only once every seven years, but another says it should take place twice every seven years.[57] In b. Pes 50a: 19, Rav Naḥman bar Yitzḥak said that even though God's name is written with the letters *yod* and *heh*, in this world, it should be read as "Adonai," but in the "World-to-Come," it will be different: then and there, God's name will be written and read aloud as YHWH.

Faithful Jews today are often reluctant to pronounce and even write God's name because of a concern that it would be violating the commandment about the name.[58] This is why I have chosen to spell out the four letters of God's name instead of writing it out with vowels. Others will substitute "Adonai," or "Lord," or even "Ha-Shem"; some write the name as "G*d" in order to honor it. American rock band Vampire Weekend's 2013 album, *Modern Vampires of the City*, included a song titled "Ya Hey," which seems to be a pun on the name YHWH but is not vocalized because Jewish lead singer Ezra Koenig is respecting the Jewish tradition to not pronounce the name.[59] The song even uses digital voice modulation for "Ya Hey"; the chorus includes the lyric "You won't even say your name / only 'I am who I am,'" which is a reference to Exod 3:14.

Power in the Name

Jewish legends attest to the power in God's name; according to one, God gave Methuselah permission "to write the Ineffable Name upon his sword, wherewith he slew ninety-four myriads of the demons in a minute" until the firstborn demon entreated him to desist and gave Methuselah the names of the rest of the demons and thus power to bind them in iron fetters.[60] Another legend explains that the same name was on Aaron's staff and it was the name that caused the staff's blossoming and bearing of ripe almonds in Num 17:8.[61]

57. The tractate continues, explaining, "Rav Naḥman bar Yitzḥak says: It stands to reason in accordance with the one who says that they transmit it once every seven years, as it is written: 'This is My name forever [le'olam]' (Exodus 3:15), which is written so that it can be read le'alem, to hide. This indicates that the Divine Name must remain hidden" (b. Kid 71a 10).

58. In his Arukh ha-Shulhan (ḤM 27:3), Jehiel Michael Epstein criticizes the practice of writing a divine name even in vernacular, calling it an "exceedingly grave offense."

59. By contrast, the rock band U2, whose members are Christian, composed the song "Yahweh" for their 2004 album *How to Dismantle an Atomic Bomb* and repeatedly vocalize the name in the song.

60. Louis Ginzberg and David Stern, *Legends of the Jews* (Philadelphia: Jewish Publication Society, 2003), 1:131.

61. Ginzberg and Stern, *Legends of the Jews*, 1:730.

Because God's name has such power, other legends tell about drastic consequences when God's name gets misused. Watson—the seventeenth-century Puritan theologian—wrote about the Arian bishop Olympias who "reproached and blasphemed the sacred Trinity; whereupon he was suddenly struck with three flashes of lightning, which burned him to death"; and Felix, an officer of Julian, "sarcastically seeing the holy vessels which were used in the sacrament said in scorn of Christ, 'See what precious vessels the Son of Mary is served withal.' Soon after, he was taken with vomiting of blood from his blasphemous mouth, of which he died."[62]

For Watson, both Olympias and Felix were examples of how God will punish in this life those who blaspheme God's name. Another Jewish legend, worth quoting in full, explains:

> Swearing falsely has terrible consequences not only for the one who does it but it endangers all the world. For when God created the world, He laid over the abyss a shard, on which is engraved the Ineffable Name, that the abyss may not burst forth and destroy the world. But as often as one swears falsely in God's name, the letters of the Ineffable Name fly away, and as there is then nothing to restrain the abyss, the waters burst forth from it to destroy the world. This would surely come to pass, if God did not send the angel Ya'asriel, who has charge of the seventy pencils, to engrave anew the Ineffable Name on the shard.[63]

The New Testament attests to the power in Jesus's name in several places: Jesus's followers are given power to drive out demons (Matt 7:22; Mark 9:38–39; Luke 9:49; 10:17; Acts 19:13) and heal (Acts 3:6, 16; 4:7) through Jesus's name. In John's gospel, Jesus encourages the disciples to ask "in Jesus' name" so that they will receive their request (John 14:13–14; 15:16; 16:23–24). The letter to the Philippians, after describing Jesus's kenosis and obedience to death on the cross, declares that God gave Jesus "the name that is above every other name" and that "at the name of Jesus every knee will bow in heaven and on earth and under the earth" (Phil 2:9–10).

Luther teaches that to "always have God's name on our lips" prevents the devil from harming us, explaining: "We should also constantly urge and encourage children to honor God's name and to have it constantly on their lips

62. Watson, *Body of Divinity*, 288.

63. Ginzberg and Stern, *Legends of the Jews*, 1:605–6.

no matter what they meet up with in their experience. . . . This is also a blessed, useful practice, and a powerfully effective one, against the devil, who is always lurking around trying to bring us into sin and shame, misery and trouble. He has a very strong distaste for the name of God and cannot stay around long where anyone utters and calls upon God's name from the heart."[64]

Positive Use of God's Name

As the example from Luther's catechism above indicates, concerns about misusing God's name must be balanced by receptions that affirm the importance of positive use of God's name. Miller comments, "The community that avoids misuse of the name by empty and false uses does not avoid the use of the name of God. On the contrary, it cries out the name, and it sings out the name."[65] Many biblical psalms describe people asking for deliverance and forgiveness for the sake of God's name (e.g., Ps 23:3; 79:9); the psalms also include God's people calling "on the name of the LORD" (e.g., Ps. 116:4; cf. Lam 3:55). Coffin explains, "Calling upon the name of a god implies allegiance to that god, trust and faith in his power. If Israel was to grow more loyal to Yahweh, it was only to be realized by the sole invoking of his name in time of need."[66]

Bonaventure writes that this commandment teaches that "we can use the name of God without taking it in vain, in three ways: in actions, in promises, and in speech."[67] Davidman writes, "One stranger way of misusing the name of God is the modern trick of not using it at all. Many, though their hearts may ache for a faith, have so many painful associations connected with the very *word* 'God' that they cannot bear the sound of it. . . . Thus a necessary corollary of the Third Commandment must be: Thou shalt take the name of the Lord thy God in earnest!"[68] So, for Davidman, in addition to speaking and using God's name—rather than not using it—the commandment also encourages people to use God's name with fervor, sincerity, and conviction.

64. Martin Luther, *Luther's Large Catechism with Study Questions*, ed. F. Samuel Janzow (St. Louis: Concordia, 1978), 23–24.

65. Miller, *The Ten Commandments*, 111.

66. Coffin, "The Third Commandment," 178.

67. Bonaventure, *St. Bonaventure's Collations on the Ten Commandments*, trans. Paul J. Spaeth (New York: Franciscan Institute, 1995), 55.

68. Davidman, *Smoke on the Mountain*, 47–48.

Conclusion

Thus, receptions of the name commandment include not only whether or not God's name is used but how. Again, Fuchs-Kreimer's feeling that there was a misuse of God's name at her great-uncle's funeral points to the idea that there is a proper use of God's name: to rightly and truthfully bring comfort and succor instead of false consolation. This idea also relates to Imes's understanding that to bear God's name involves living rightly as God instructs, so that God's people can represent God well in the world.

4

"Sabbath"

Few if any of the college students I teach know about "blue laws" in the United States, those laws prohibiting work, travel, or commerce on Sundays. (They are also, more obviously, known as "Sunday Closing Laws"; the other moniker may come from the supposed tradition that Puritans in New England bound their religious laws in blue books.)[1] I suspect this is less about my students' general lack of knowledge or education about history and is more about how hard it is for them to conceive of a day when work wouldn't happen or when they couldn't go to a restaurant or store. After all, most can click on a button anytime to purchase something. Even though some American states still forbid the purchase of alcohol on Sundays, for example, and car dealerships are closed on Sundays in Illinois, since the 1950s the legislation surrounding observing the Christian Sabbath as a day of rest has been slowly and steadily overturned. More details about these blue laws, as well as reasons for their removal, will be discussed below, but they are a fascinating reception of the commandment about Sabbath in the United States. Blue laws touch on questions such as which of the days of the week should be observed, which activities could be engaged in and which must be avoided, and how "work" relates to production, commerce, and capitalism. Moreover, when Sabbath was no longer legislated by civic authorities—or even socially encouraged by one's community—it became more personal and individualized. Throughout this book, I hope to demonstrate how reception history of the Ten Commandments does encourage application of these laws in someone's life in a personal way, yet something is lost when it is entirely up to the individual to practice and live out these laws.

1. Or, the color blue was associated with colonial laws, in contrast with the red emblem of British royalty. Or, the term "blue" was used in the vernacular of the times to refer to Puritanism itself. Essentially, there is no consensus about the origin of the term.

CHAPTER 4

The Sabbath in the Commandments

Remember and Observe

The commandment differs in Exodus and Deuteronomy in three ways: the verbs used, the addition of the phrase "as the LORD your God commanded you" in Deuteronomy, and the motivations. In reference to the verbs, Exodus commands, "*Remember* the Sabbath day, to keep it holy" (Exod 20:8); in Deuteronomy, it's "*Observe* the Sabbath day, to keep it holy." A Jewish teaching holds that God spoke both words—"remember" and "observe"—with one utterance;[2] this idea comes from Ps 62:12[11], which says, "One thing God spoke, two things we heard" (Mekhilta d'Rabbi Yishmael 20:8:1). The hymn *Lekhah Dodi* (Come, my beloved), which is sung in synagogues on Friday nights to welcome the Sabbath, affirms this idea with the following lyrics:

> "Observe" and "remember" in one utterance
> the one and unique God made us hear
> The LORD is one and his name is one
> for renown, for splendour, and for praise.

Jon Levenson notes how, by including words from Deut 6:4, "the LORD is one," and Zech 14:9, "on that day the LORD shall be one and his name one," the song's composer Solomon Alkabetz, a sixteenth-century Kabbalist, links the "miraculous oneness of the two variant openings of the fourth commandment to the at least equally miraculous—in fact unparalleled—oneness of the God who issued the command."[3]

In reference to the variation in words between Exodus and Deuteronomy, Ramban wrote, "But I wonder! If *remember* and *observe* were both said by the Almighty, why were they not [both] written in the first Tablets? It is possible that in both the first and second Tablets, [only] *remember* was written, and Moses explained to Israel that *observe* was [also] said with it. This is indeed the true intent [of the saying of the Rabbis that '*remember* and *observe*' were both spoken with one utterance]."[4]

2. Both Rashi and Ramban explain this: Sefaria, citing "Rashi on Exodus 20:8:1," M. Rosenbaum and A. M. Silbermann, London, 1929–34, https://tinyurl.com/9k24e774; Sefaria, citing "Ramban on Exodus 20:8:1," Charles B. Chavel. Shilo, 1971–76, https://tinyurl.com/2uhp383b.

3. Jon Levenson, *Israel's Day of Light and Joy: The Origin, Development, and Enduring Meaning of the Jewish Sabbath* (University Park, PA: Eisenbrauns, 2024), 81.

4. Sefaria, citing "Ramban on Exodus 20:8:1," Charles B. Chavel, Shilo, 1971–76, https://tinyurl.com/2uhp383b.

Both words, "remember" (*zākôr*) and "observe" (*šāmôr*), occur in the Hebrew grammatical form of an infinitive absolute, which can function as an imperative, and this is how most English translations render them. Drawing on the work of Hebraists Paul Joüon and Takamitsu Muraoka, however, T. Desmond Alexander explains that this form is "equivalent to an injunctive future rather than to an imperative" and so has the sense of "you shall . . ." or "you must. . . ."[5] An infinitive can be translated with a sense that the action is ongoing, which is how Chizkuni, a Jewish commentator in thirteenth-century France, explained possible meanings of the word; that this ongoing "remembering" should mean that the Sabbath day is present in one's thinking throughout the week. This could happen through referring to every day by its proximity to the previous Sabbath, saying, "the first day after the Sabbath, the second day after the sabbath, etc." Remembering could also look like daily awareness of when the last Sabbath occurred and when the next one would take place. Chizkuni offered another possible meaning, that "remembering" is about reminding the listener of the first time they heard about the Sabbath when they were in the wilderness.[6] Several biblical scholars similarly suggest that the word "remember" indicates that the Israelites are already familiar with the idea of the seventh day as a day of rest, from God's provision of twice enough manna on the day before the Sabbath day in Exod 16:22–30.[7] Nahum Sarna noted that in Exodus, the law about the seventh day of the week begins with the seventh letter of the Hebrew alphabet, ז, *z*.[8] Rashi offers a very practical reception of the word "remember," saying, "if, for example, you come across a nice article of food during the week, put it by for the Sabbath."[9] Several teachings in the Talmud affirm that to "remember" is something positive, connected with feasting and celebrating. Rachel S. Mikva explains, "The Talmud teaches that *zachor* [remember, in Exodus] reminds us to celebrate the positive, such as fine food and Torah study, and *shamor* [keep, in Deuteronomy] charges us to guard against violating the 'do not's.' The spirit of Shabbat is lost if we take

5. T. Desmond Alexander, *Exodus* (Downers Grove, IL: IVP Academic, 2017), 389.

6. Sefaria, citing Chizkuni, "Exodus 20:8:1," trans. and annotated by Eliyahu Munk, https://tinyurl.com/yu744t8b.

7. For representative interpretations, see Alexander, *Exodus*, 411; and Brevard Childs, *The Book of Exodus: A Critical, Theological Commentary* (Philadelphia: Westminster, 1974), 416.

8. Nahum M. Sarna, *The JPS Torah Commentary: Exodus* (Philadelphia: Jewish Publication Society, 2003), 112.

9. Rashi referenced the Talmud tractate Beitzah, which includes the example of Shammai the Elder, who would always set aside the choice food for Shabbat, always leaving the best quality of food for the Sabbath, such that it was said, "all his days he would eat in honor of Shabbat" (b. Beitzah 16a:4), Sefaria, "Rashi on Exodus," 20:8:1," M. Rosenbaum and A. M. Silbermann, London, 1929–34, https://tinyurl.com/9k24e774.

from it only a series of restrictions and forget to rejoice. It is also lost if we fail to see the holiness of committing to certain limits."[10]

Though the word "remember" (*zkr*) does not introduce the Sabbath commandment in Deut 5:12, it does occur to introduce Deuteronomy's rationale for the Sabbath day in 5:15, "remember that you were slaves in Egypt." Patrick Miller explains that the structure of the Exodus form of the commandment is as follows:

> Remember the creating work of God and the rest of God; from that memory you are to rest and sanctify a day. Remembering the Lord's work of creation that ended in a day of rest will lead you to keep a day of rest and to set it apart to the Lord. The Deuteronomic structure works differently. . . . In terms of the logic, it is not remember to keep but the reverse: Keep the Sabbath, and by so doing two purposes will be accomplished. You will remember the redemptive work of God on your behalf, and you will provide rest for the slaves under your control. So in the case of Exodus, the community is called to remember and to obey out of that memory; in the Deuteronomic form, the community obeys to keep alive the memory of redemption and to bring about the provision of rest from toil for all members of the community.[11]

Keep It Holy

Both versions of the commandment include that the "remembering" and "observing" of the Sabbath is to "keep it holy." Many receptions link this to God's action in Gen 2:3 of blessing the seventh day and making it holy. Abraham Heschel emphasizes how unique it is to consider holiness in relationship to time and not to a physical space. He explains that many other religions connect the idea of holiness to space, such as in a temple, or even in nature, but Sabbath is about holiness in time.[12] Martin Luther teaches, "The day as such requires no sanctifying, for it was created holy in itself. But God wants it to be holy for you. It is through you that it becomes holy or unholy depending on whether

10. Rachel S. Mikva, *Broken Tablets: Restoring the Ten Commandments and Ourselves* (Woodstock, VT: Jewish Lights, 1999), 44.

11. Patrick D. Miller, *Deuteronomy: Interpretation; A Bible Commentary for Teaching and Preaching* (Louisville: Westminster John Knox, 2011), 80.

12. Abraham Joshua Heschel, *The Sabbath* (New York: Farrer, Straus and Giroux, 2005), 79–83.

what you do on that day is holy or unholy."[13] Joy Davidman has specific instructions to answer the question of how someone can make a day holy. She explains that it includes stopping work, which she defines as "stopping all the pursuits we engage in for necessity not for pleasure, all our struggles with the world conceived as an enemy that is trying to starve us to death"; by looking at the world and seeing its goodness; by participating in "all its good and friendly and loving activities, and rejoicing in them. And, above all, by looking beyond the world to the Love that sustains it."[14] Luther advocates reserving the Sabbath day for "holy words, holy works, and holy living," perhaps allowing different things on other days of the week, but Davidman's instructions seem to be worth practicing daily. Of course, because the word "holy" means "set apart," Luther's advice about doing things—or not doing things—in a manner that is distinct from the other days of the week seems to follow the idea of Sabbath as holy.

Sabbath Motivations

Another difference between Exodus and Deuteronomy, as mentioned above, is the reason for keeping the Sabbath. Exodus references God's creation in Genesis 1, saying, "For in six days God created the heavens, earth, sea, and all that is in them, but rested the seventh day; therefore the Lord blessed the Sabbath day and made it holy" (Exod 20:11). Deuteronomy motivates by recalling God's deliverance from slavery in Exodus, saying, "Remember that you were a slave in the land of Egypt, and the Lord your God brought you out from there with a mighty hand and an outstretched arm; therefore the Lord your God commanded you to keep the Sabbath day" (Deut 5:15). These "differences" need not be in opposition to one another; as Levenson comments, "Israel comfortably accepted both a cosmological and a historical etiology of the Sabbath: the latter is both a mimetic reenactment of the creator God's primordial rest and an enduring memorial to Israel's relief from slavery after the exodus. There is no indication of a tension between cosmology and history in this instance. The two could coexist nicely, for they reinforce each other: history concretizes cosmology, and cosmology lifts history above the level of the mundane."[15]

13. Martin Luther, *Luther's Large Catechism with Study Questions*, ed. F. Samuel Janzow (St. Louis: Concordia, 1978), 26.

14. Joy Davidman, *Smoke on the Mountain: An Interpretation of the Ten Commandments* (Philadelphia: Westminster, 1954), 58.

15. Jon Levenson, *Creation and the Persistence of Evil: The Jewish Drama of Divine Omnipotence* (Princeton: Princeton University Press, 1988), 82.

In fact, both are included in the version of Deuteronomy from the Dead Sea Scrolls; scroll 4Q41 tacks on the reminder of creation at the end of Deut 5:15 so that it reads, "You shall remember that you were a servant in the land of Egypt, and Yahweh your God brought you out of there by a mighty hand and by an outstretched arm. Therefore Yahweh your God commanded you to keep the Sabbath day, to sanctify it, because in six days Yahweh made the heavens and the earth, the sea and all which is in them, and he rested on the seventh day. Therefore, Yahweh blessed the seventh day to sanctify it."

Certainly God's act of creating and God's work in the exodus are both valuable motivations for keeping the Sabbath, but there are also distinct gains from each.

Sabbath and Creation

Focusing on creation as a motivation for keeping Sabbath highlights how, because God stopped work, humans can and should also stop their work. After all, humans are created in God's image and can do what God did. However, though they bear God's image, humans are not God, and the work done by humans is not the sort of universe-sustaining work that God does. While Exod 20:9 proclaims, "Six days you shall labor and do all your work," the Mekhilta notes that it is not possible for a human to complete all work in six days; only God could do that. Thus, the meaning of Exod 20:9 is that humans are to rest on the Sabbath as if all their work was done, or rest from even the thought of working.[16]

While almost every English translation of Gen 2:2 explains that God "rested" on the seventh day,[17] Levenson points out how according to the Hebrew verb in Gen 2:2, God does not "rest," but rather, "stops."[18] This is significant for Levenson because the noun "Sabbath" (*šabbāt)* seems to derive from the verb *šabat*, which means "cease, come to an end."[19] Some receptions are uncomfortable with the idea that God would "need" to rest. For example, seventeenth-century British commentator Matthew Henry proclaims, "God did

16. Cf. Heschel, *The Sabbath*, 32.

17. Some exceptions include the Good News translation and the International Standard Version, which say, "God stopped working."

18. Levenson explains that even though one may reasonably infer a connection between stopping and resting, the lexical evidence still matters. *Israel's Day of Light and Joy*, 92.

19. Levenson, *Israel's Day of Light and Joy*, 19–23.

not rest as one weary, but as one well pleased."[20] Carmen Imes writes, "It's not that God is tired and needs a nap which is why God rests, but rather, God can sit back and enjoy the fruit of God's success, like a king who rests after enemies have been defeated and the realm is at peace."[21] Several scholars affirm that the idea of God "resting" is associated with God's enthronement as king; for example, God says about Zion, "This is my resting place forever and ever; here I will sit enthroned" (Ps 132:14).[22] Rest and enthronement get connected in other ancient southwest Asian texts such as the Ugaritic Baal Cycle, when, after Baal is victorious in battle, he is enthroned, and a palace is built where he can feast and celebrate (KTU 1.3). Thus, Sabbath is to be celebrated in honor of creation, when God was victorious over cosmological forces, the ultimate king.

Exodus 20:11 connects God's stopping work on the seventh day with God's blessing of the Sabbath. A midrash explains that God blessed the day because the day did not have a partner: Sunday has Monday as its partner, Tuesday has Wednesday, Thursday has Friday, but Sabbath has no corresponding day. Rabbi Shimon ben Yoḥai taught that the Sabbath then said to God, "'Master of the universe, all of them [the other days] have partners, but I do not have a partner.' The Holy One blessed be He said to it: 'The congregation of Israel is your partner'" (Bereshit Rabbah 11:8). Rashi explained that God blessed the Sabbath through the miracle of manna in Exodus 16, but in contrast, Rashbam understood God's blessing as a summary statement; that God did not do something additional and special to make the Sabbath blessed. Instead, Rashbam wrote that God blessed the Sabbath day because, "By the time the sabbath arrived, God had already created food and everything else that humans need. So the sabbath was blessed with all good things."[23]

Environmentalism is another implication of the focus on creation as motivation for Sabbath keeping. Norman Wirzba explains that the Sabbath completes creation and is also intended for the whole of creation.[24] He titles a chapter in his book, "Sabbath Environmentalism," drawing not only on the ref-

20. Matthew Henry, *Commentary on the Whole Bible*, vol. 1 (Old Tappan, NJ: Fleming H. Revell, 1970).

21. Carmen Joy Imes, *Bearing God's Name: Why Sinai Still Matters* (Downers Grove, IL: IVP Academic, 2019), 54.

22. Cf. Delbert Hillers, "Ritual Progression of the Ark and Ps 132," *CBQ* 30 (January 1968): 48–55.

23. Martin Lockshin, *Rashbam's Commentary on Exodus: An Annotated Translation* (Atlanta: Scholars Press, 1997), 217.

24. Norman Wirzba, *Living the Sabbath: Discovering the Rhythms of Rest and Delight* (Grand Rapids: Brazos, 2006), 142.

erence to creation in Exod 20:11 but also the inclusion of animals in Exod 20:10 and Deuteronomy 14 and other texts that encourage a rest for the entire land such as Exod 23:10–11 and Lev 25:1–7. American author and environmentalist Wendell Berry claims, "The intended instruction of the sabbath day is that, while we rest, God's six days of Creation continue. All that we primarily depend upon, the world and its plentitude of good things, does not depend upon us—although, because of our ability to desecrate and destroy it, its good care and preservation does depend upon us."[25]

Sabbath and Liberation

Focusing on the exodus as a motivation for keeping Sabbath highlights that God is a God who redeems and sets people free from slavery. As chapter 2 discusses, this is the first "Word" in Judaism, that God brought God's people out of the land of Egypt, out of the house of slavery (Exod 20:2; Deut 5:6). God is the ultimate "master" of God's people,[26] but God is good and loving and even commands the people serving God to rest. God's people are not required continually to work, strive, or prove themselves; they are not enslaved to Pharaoh or to others. Walter Brueggemann writes in his book *Sabbath as Resistance* about how the act of observing Sabbath is an act of resistance against forces that seek to define the world and people through a lens of commerce. He writes, "It is resistance because it is a visible insistence that our lives are not defined by the production and consumption of commodity goods."[27] But according to Brueggemann, Sabbath is not only resistance; it also provides an alternative, which is "the awareness and practice of the claim that we are situated on the receiving end of the gifts of God."[28] A. J. Swoboda acknowledges that the title of his book, *Subversive Sabbath*, "reflects a tone similar to" Brueggemann's book[29] and explains that the Sabbath is subversive because it "will be challenging for anyone to live out in our busy, frenetic world. Sabbath goes

25. Wendell Berry, *The Need to Be Whole: Patriotism and the History of Prejudice* (Berkeley: Shoemaker and Company, 2022), 140.

26. Cf. God's language that Pharaoh should let God's people go in order that they may "serve" God.

27. Walter Brueggemann, *Sabbath as Resistance: Saying No to the Culture of Now* (Louisville: Westminster John Knox, 2014), xiii–xiv.

28. Brueggemann, *Sabbath as Resistance*, xiv.

29. A. J. Swoboda, *Subversive Sabbath: The Surprising Power of Rest in a Nonstop World* (Grand Rapids: Brazos, 2018), 11n3.

against the very structure and system of the world we have constructed. . . . The Sabbath is subversive, countering so many of the deathly ways we have felt at home in."[30]

Though Tricia Hersey's book *Rest Is Resistance: A Manifesto* does not include the word "Sabbath" in the title unlike Brueggemann and Swoboda, her argument is similar to theirs, if even more pointed. On her Instagram page, "The Nap Ministry," Hersey explained, "The purpose of a Sabbath and rest is to save us. To proclaim enough has been done and to uplift [that] there isn't any more needed to be worthy of care, rest, and connection."[31] Hersey, also known as "the Nap Bishop," founded the ministry in 2016. While a graduate student at Emory University, she worked as an archivist in the library and read testimonies written by enslaved people in the United States, coming to the realization that they were treated as "human machines." Their stories helped her realize that the brutal origins of American capitalism, when people were forced to work to exhaustion, are still operative today. The Nap Ministry's web page proclaims, "We believe rest is a form of resistance and name sleep deprivation as a racial and social justice issue."[32] Hersey writes about how, though she hears from people that institutions and governments ought to make it easier to rest, the framework of the "Rest Is Resistance" movement is different, because "we are resting regardless of what any of these systems are doing. We are not waiting. We are not asking permission."[33] Hersey encourages people to uncouple their sense of worth from what they do or produce. In contrast to some who tout the value of rest because it gives people energy to do more, she writes, "We are not resting to be productive. We are resting simply because it is our divine right to do so. . . . The concept of filling up your own cup first, so you can have enough in it to pour to others feels off balance. It reeks of the capitalist language that is now a part of our daily mantras. Language like 'I will sleep when I am dead,' 'Rise and grind,' 'While they sleep, I grind,' 'If it doesn't make money, it doesn't make sense,' 'Wake up to hustle,' and many more."[34] Hersey's language echoes Heschel's affirmation that the Sabbath as a day of rest is "not for the purpose of recovering one's lost strength and becoming fit for the forthcoming labor. . . . Man is not a beast of burden, and the Sabbath is

30. Swoboda, *Subversive Sabbath*, 11.

31. Tricia Hersey (@thenapministry), September 21, 2022, https://tinyurl.com/y9d6u33p.

32. Napministry, "About," https://tinyurl.com/yc4zyv7r.

33. Tricia Hersey, *Rest Is Resistance: A Manifesto* (New York: Little, Brown, and Spark, 2022), 172.

34. Hersey, *Rest Is Resistance*, 62.

not for the purpose of enhancing the efficiency of his work."[35] Instead, Heschel proclaims that the Sabbath is a day for the sake of life.

Hersey also warns that her book does not offer a step-by-step rigid list of how to find rest[36] but rather offers a list of places to begin (note that there are ten places on the list), including encouraging people to "begin to heal the individual trauma you have experienced that makes it difficult for you to say no and maintain healthy boundaries" and "slowly accept you have been brainwashed. Your socialization in a capitalist culture makes this true. Begin to deprogram by accepting this truth," and "You are enough now. If you have to repeat this to yourself every day, do so. Begin to repair the way white supremacy and capitalism have wrecked your self-esteem and self-worth."[37]

Norbert Lohfink suggested that the specific wording in Deut 5:12–15 forms a chiasm, a literary structure that resembles the Greek letter X, as follows:

A Observe the sabbath day
  B the LORD your God has commanded you
    C The LORD your God
      D male and female slave
      D′ male and female slave
    C′ The LORD your God
  B′ the LORD your God has commanded you
A′ Keep[38] the sabbath day[39]

The terms "male and female slave," repeated twice, form the center of this chiasm. Levenson observes how this structure demonstrates that the commandment points to the "male and female slave" and thus reinforces the conclusion of the Sabbath commandment in Deuteronomy, that the people who are to keep a Sabbath must remember when they were slaves in Egypt.[40]

35. Heschel, *The Sabbath*, 14. Heschel contrasts this with the teaching of Aristotle, who asserted that relaxation should be done for the sake of activity for gaining strength for new efforts.

36. Heschel, *The Sabbath*, 125.

37. Hersey, *Rest Is Resistance*, 83–84.

38. The word here is "to do," *l'swt*, a different word than occurs at the beginning of the commandment, *šmr*.

39. Norbert Lohfink, "The Decalogue in Deuteronomy 5," in *Theology of the Pentateuch: Themes of the Priestly Narrative and Deuteronomy*, trans. Linda M. Maloney (Minneapolis: Fortress, 1994), 253.

40. Levenson, *Israel's Day of Light and Joy*, 87.

Alexandra Grund suggests that Deuteronomy makes the Sabbath into a sort of a weekly Passover festival, when the people remember their deliverance.[41]

Yet people continue to be obligated to work by those who do not respect the Sabbath. A Jewish legend teaches that Vashti, the queen deposed at the beginning of the book of Esther, was in the habit of forcing Jewish maids to spin and weave on the Sabbath; as an added cruelty, she would deprive them of their clothes. King Ahasuersus sent for Vashti on the seventh day of his feast (Esth 1:10–11), and the legend explains, "It was on the Sabbath, therefore, that her punishment overtook her, and for the same reason it was put into the king's heart to have her appear in public stripped of all clothing."[42] In June 2023, the Supreme Court ruled in favor of postal worker Gerald Groff who sued the US Postal Service when he was required to work Sundays delivering packages in rural Pennsylvania. Because Groff worked as a "rural carrier associate," his job included substituting for full-time workers, and it required flexibility and weekend work. Sundays had not been a day when mail was delivered until 2013 when Amazon struck a deal with the US Postal Service. Groff's supervisors made some accommodations but asserted that it was a significant burden to allow him to skip work on every Sunday, which was also in tension with a labor union agreement. Groff was disciplined for failing to report on Sundays, and he resigned in 2019. Groff explained, "Sunday's a day where we get together and almost taste heaven. We come together as believers. We celebrate who we are, together. We worship God. And so to be asked to deliver Amazon parcels and give all that up, it's just really kind of sad."[43] The Supreme Court ruling in Groff's favor clarified that increased costs to an employer when making religious accommodations must demonstrate "undue hardship" for the employer.[44] Again, some people aren't given a choice as to which day they must work; others may not have any choice to stop work for any day of the week.[45]

41. Levenson, *Israel's Day of Light and Joy*, 87.

42. Louis Ginzberg and David Stern, *Legends of the Jews*, trans. Henrietta Szold and Paul Radin (Philadelphia: Jewish Publication Society, 2003), 2:1135.

43. Adam Liptak, "Supreme Court Weighs Clash of Postal Worker's Sabbath and Sunday Deliveries," April 16, 2023, https://tinyurl.com/2k7sxa5n.

44. "Groff v. DeJoy," *Harvard Law Review* 137 (November 2023), https://tinyurl.com/2erkvjk9.

45. Emily Guendelsberger writes about her experience working jobs for an hourly wage, suggesting that the ideals of efficiency have come at the cost of humanity for many people. *On the Clock: What Low Wage Work Did to Me and How It Drives America Insane* (New York: Little, Brown and Company, 2019).

Sabbath in the Bible

Because the word "Sabbath" occurs more than a hundred times in the Hebrew Bible and some sixty-five times in the New Testament, this section cannot be exhaustive; instead, representative texts can demonstrate how "Sabbath" gets received in other biblical texts. The first time the noun occurs is in Exodus 16, when God provides manna for the Israelites in the wilderness, already mentioned above. Some Israelites fail to obey Moses's instruction to gather and save extra manna on the sixth day because the seventh day will be a day of Sabbath rest with no manna: they go out on the seventh day to gather it and find none (Exod 16:27). A Jewish legend connected the Israelite failure to properly observe that first Sabbath with the following chapter—Exodus 17—when the Amalekites attack in Rephidim (Exod 17:8). "They did not know, to be sure, what they had lost through their violation of the first Sabbath. Had Israel then observed the Sabbath, no nation would ever have been able to exercise any authority over them."[46]

After the Sabbath appears in the Ten Commandments in Exodus, further legislation extends the principle of resting one day a week, to resting one year every seven in a "sabbatical year" (Exod 23:10–11; cf. Lev 25:1–7). As Wirzba noted, mentioned above, this rest is for the land; Deuteronomy 15 also identifies that the seventh year is a time for canceling debts and setting free servants. Mark Biddle comments that Deuteronomy 15 "expands the notion of the Sabbath rest to include all manner of rest, liberation, and celebration."[47] The "sabbatical year" is itself extended even more, into a year of "jubilee." The people are instructed, "Count seven sabbath years—seven times seven years—so that the seven sabbath years amount to a period of forty-nine years. . . . Consecrate the fiftieth year and proclaim liberty throughout the land to all its inhabitants. It shall be a jubilee for you" (Lev 25:8–10). In this year of jubilee, each person is to return to their family property and clan, the land will rest, most property will be returned to its original owner (cf. Lev 25:30), and all debts are canceled. Jonathan Burnside refers to the year of jubilee as "Sabbath-squared," explaining that "it is a more intense form of Super-Sabbath than the sabbatical year because the jubilee does not only provide rest for land but also redemption."[48] John Calvin discusses the laws about jubilee under the heading

46. Ginzberg and Stern, *Legends of the Jews*, 1:572; cf. b. Shabbat 118b.

47. Mark E. Biddle, *Deuteronomy: Smyth & Helwys Bible Commentary* (Macon, GA: Smyth & Helwys, 2003), 250.

48. Jonathan P. Burnside, *God, Justice, and Society: Aspects of Law and Legality in the Bible* (Oxford: Oxford University Press, 2010), 201.

of "supplements to the fourth commandment" and describes the jubilee year as the "most illustrious Sabbath."[49]

Sabbath instructions also appear within the directions for creating the tabernacle in Exodus; they occur in Exodus 31 and 35, as bookends for the chapters about the golden calf. There are strict prohibitions against breaking the Sabbath in Exod 31:14–15, as well as in Exod 35:2; each of those verses proclaims that anyone who breaks the Sabbath by doing work will be put to death. Thus, the claim in Exod 31:16 is, "Therefore the children of Israel shall keep the sabbath, to observe the sabbath throughout their generations, for a perpetual covenant." In the early third-century midrashic collection from the school of Rabbi Yishmael, Rabbi Nathan argued that Exod 31:16 implies that if someone must break the Sabbath for the sake of saving the life of another person, it should be done, for then, that person will be able to observe many subsequent Sabbaths. That is, the person who died would not be able to perpetually keep the Sabbath (Mekhilta DeRabbi Yishmael, Tractate Shabbata 1:9). And the verse immediately following, Exod 31:17, explains that the Sabbath will be a sign between God and the children of Israel forever, "for in six days the LORD made the heaven and the earth, and on the seventh day he stopped, and was refreshed." That final verb only occurs in reference to the Sabbath in Exod 23:12 and 31:17 and in 2 Sam 16:14; it is the Niphal—passive—form of the Hebrew root *npš*, which in the noun form means "soul" or "life force." As above, most English translations translate this as "was refreshed," but it can also have the sense of catching one's breath or even having one's soul restored.[50]

The Israelites' failure to keep the Sabbath contributed to the destruction of Jerusalem and the Babylonian exile, according to Ezek 22:8 and 26. Though the entire chapter is about all "detestable practices" for which Jerusalem will be judged, Sabbath breaking is mentioned twice in the chapter as an example of the disobedience that led to the exile. A similar theme occurs in Nehemiah 13. When Nehemiah sees people in postexilic Judah and Jerusalem engaged in commerce, producing wine, selling and buying food, Nehemiah rebukes them, saying, "What is this wicked thing you are doing—desecrating the Sabbath day? Didn't your ancestors do the same things, so that our God brought all this calamity on us and on this city? Now you are stirring up more wrath against Israel by desecrating the Sabbath" (Neh 13:17–18). Nehemiah then orders the

49. John Calvin, *The Year of Jubilee*, vol. 2 of *Harmony of the Law* (Grand Rapids: Christian Classics Ethereal Library, 1999), 2:325, https://tinyurl.com/ycfmmrsj.

50. 2 Sam 16:14 explains that after the king and everyone with him arrived, exhausted, they were then "refreshed."

newly rebuilt gates of Jerusalem to be shut on the Sabbath day and stations guards to enforce that people will keep the Sabbath holy (Neh 13:19–22).

The New Testament authors' description of Jesus's actions on and teaching about the Sabbath is its own reception of the Sabbath commandment. Subsequently, those texts have generated much discussion about if and how Christians ought to practice the Sabbath. First, Jesus frequently heals on the Sabbath: the man with a withered hand (e.g., Matt 12:9–14; Mark 3:1–6; Luke 6:6–11), the crippled woman (Luke 13:10–17), the man with dropsy (Luke 14:1–6), the paralyzed man (John 5:3–18), and the blind man (John 9:1–17). When people question Jesus's actions, in most of these texts Jesus responds to his challengers by telling them it is lawful to do good and save life on the Sabbath. Second, when Jesus and his disciples are walking through fields on the Sabbath, the disciples pick grain and eat it (Matt 12:1–8; Mark 2:23–28; Luke 6:1–5). When Pharisees see and tell Jesus that eating on the Sabbath is not lawful, Jesus responds by appealing to the story from 1 Sam 21:1–6 when David and his men ate consecrated bread that was legally prohibited to them, only meant for the priests. In all three of the synoptic gospels, Jesus declares himself to be lord of the Sabbath (Matt 12:8; Mark 2:28; Luke 6:5); only in Mark 2:27 does Jesus proclaim, "The sabbath is made for humans, and not humans for the sabbath." Daniel Boyarin notes that Christian writers have frequently read that statement from Jesus "both as indicating total opposition to the keeping of Sabbath laws at all and as initiating a religion of love and not one of casuistry."[51] However, Boyarin points out how, while Jesus's views on the Sabbath were more expansive, many rabbis held closely related views. For example, in the Mekhilta Tractate Sabbath 1, Rabbis Ishmael, El'azar, and Akiva all affirm that the saving of a life supersedes the Sabbath. Rabbi Yose Hagelili says, "When it says 'But keep my Sabbaths,' the word 'but' makes a distinction: There are Sabbaths that you push aside and those that you keep [i.e., when human life is at stake, this supersedes the Sabbath]." Rabbi Shim'on, the son of Menasya, says, "Behold it says: Keep the Sabbath because it is holy to you; to you the Sabbath is delivered and not you to the Sabbath."[52] And as mentioned above, Rabbi Nathan affirmed that breaking one Sabbath to save someone means that

51. Daniel Boyarin, *The Jewish Gospels: The Story of the Jewish Christ* (New York: New Press, 2012), 63. Boyarin writes, "There is a tendency among certain Christian scholars to insist on an absolute contrast and hence conflict here between 'Judaism' (bad) and 'Christianity' (good). Exemplary of this tendency is Arland J. Hultgren. . . . Hultgren is precisely wrong; his sentence should read: 'The Sabbath is delivered to Israel as a gift, and therefore, it is permitted to heal Jews on the Sabbath'" (170n41).

52. Boyarin, *The Jewish Gospels*, 169.

the person will be able to keep many Sabbaths in the future. Without ignoring differences between Christian and Jewish practices of Sabbath, reception history also allows us to affirm the similarities in how the teachers understood the Sabbath.[53]

That Christians need not keep the Sabbath is one reception of Col 2:16, which concludes, "Therefore, do not let anyone condemn you in matters of food or drink or of observing festivals, new moons, or Sabbaths." For example, Michael Horton draws on Col 2:16–17 to suggest that because the list places the Sabbath "alongside the other rituals and celebrations of the ceremonial law," keeping the Sabbath day should be categorized as ceremonial law and not moral law, and the New Testament frees Christians from the practice of ceremonial law.[54] In contrast, John Chrysostom observes in his Homily 7 on Colossians that with regard to the festivals and Sabbath, "He [Paul] didn't say, 'Therefore don't observe them,' but 'let nobody judge you.'"[55]

The author of Hebrews discusses rest in Heb 4:1–11 after quoting Ps 95:8–11 when God declares that those who rebelled against God would not enter God's rest. The Greek word used is *katapausis* in verses 1, 3, 5, 10, 11, but then the author uses a word in Heb 4:9 that is unique in the NT, *sabbatismos*, sometimes translated as "Sabbath rest." The message—"So then, there remains a Sabbath rest for the people of God, for whoever has entered God's rest has also rested from his works as God did from his. Let us therefore strive to enter that rest" (Heb 4:9–11)—has been taken to refer to a future, eschatological rest as well as an encouragement to practice resting on the Sabbath day.[56] Timothy Keller referenced Hebrews 4 when explaining that keeping a Sabbath is more than resting one's body but also includes an inner rest of the soul. He writes, "We need rest from the anxiety and strain of our overwork, which is really an attempt to justify ourselves. . . . Avoiding overwork requires deep rest in Christ's finished work for your salvation (Heb 4:1–10)."[57]

53. Levenson observes that even when Christians acknowledge their indebtedness to a Jewish understanding of Sabbath, "echoes of an ancient and prominent strain of Christian anti-Judaism" may be present in their expositions, especially in casual and critical language about the legalism of the Pharisees, of which Jesus sets people free. Levenson, *Israel's Day of Light and Joy*, 168–70.

54. Michael S. Horton, *The Law of Perfect Freedom* (Chicago: Moody, 1993), 126–27.

55. Pauline Allen, *John Chrysostom, Homilies on Colossians* (Atlanta: SBL Press, 2021), 157.

56. Cf. Robert W. Wall, *Reading Hebrews: A Literary and Theological Commentary* (Macon, GA: Smyth & Helwys, 2024), 110–15.

57. Timothy Keller, "Wisdom and Sabbath Rest," July 13, 2021, https://tinyurl.com/22njwrkb.

Sabbath Personified

Jewish legends speak about the Sabbath as a queen or a bride; according to b. Šabb. 119a, "Rabbi Ḥanina would wrap himself in his garment and stand at nightfall on Shabbat eve, and say: Come and we will go out to greet Shabbat the queen. Rabbi Yannai put on his garment on Shabbat eve and said: Enter, O bride. Enter, O bride." Another rabbi taught, "One should put on beautiful clothes and rejoice as the Sabbath is coming in, like one who is going out to meet the king or one who is going out to meet a bride and groom" (Shulchan Arukh 262:3). Heschel explains that this language "is not a personification of the Sabbath but an exemplification of a divine attribute, an illustration of God's need for human love."[58]

But the Sabbath does take on a personified role in the midrash for Psalm 92; the superscription identifies this psalm as "for the Sabbath day." The midrash tells the story that Adam was created on the sixth day and sinned that very same day. When God was about to punish Adam, the Sabbath came to act as an advocate on Adam's behalf, saying to God, "No human being has ever been killed; why should it fall to my lot to be the first day on which a human is killed?" As a result of the Sabbath's plea, Adam was saved (Midrash Tehillim 92:2). The seventeenth-century commentary on the Torah Or HaChaim notes that when the Sabbath saved Adam's life, that also ensures existence for all humans. "It behooves us therefore to accord special honour to the Sabbath. The Sabbath proved to be our very life saver."[59]

Day of the Week

The Sabbath is referred to as the "seventh day" throughout the Bible. There is something special and significant about that seventh day in many texts, as thoroughly discussed by Levenson.[60] Apion, the Hellenized Egyptian grammarian from the first century, offers a strange explanation for the Sabbath: that on the seventh day after the Israelites left Egypt, they developed tumors in their groin, and so when they reached Judea they rested on that seventh day and called it *sabbaton* in reference to Egyptian terminology for a disease of the groin called "sabbo." Josephus refutes this—among other things—in his writing titled *Against Apion*;

58. Heschel, *The Sabbath*, 60.

59. Sefaria, citing "Or HaChaim on Exodus 20:8:3," Eliyahu Munk, Lambda, 1998, https://tinyurl.com/26r83u6d.

60. Levenson, *Israel's Day of Light and Joy*, 58–65.

Josephus attributes Apion's explanation to "either gross impudence or shocking ignorance; as there is a wide difference between *sabbaton* and sabbo."[61]

Josephus also claims that the custom of resting on the seventh day had spread throughout the eastern Roman empire, in all the cities of the Greeks, and barbarians, and all nations,[62] though Herold Weiss refers to this claim as "not only preposterous but contradicted by [Josephus's] own repeated defense of the Jewish observance of Sabbath rest vis-à-vis those who ridiculed it."[63] Still, historian Craig Harline suggests that a growing number of Roman pagans did observe a weekly rest day, initially on Saturn Day, or Saturday, the first day of the planetary week, which corresponded with the seventh day of the Jewish week, the Sabbath.[64] Harline also acknowledges that it is difficult to find consensus on the beginning of the Christian "Lord's Day" but that by at least the year 150 CE, most Christians observed the first day of the week by gathering to worship on that day to commemorate Jesus's resurrection.[65] As Calvin says, "The ancients did not substitute the Lord's Day . . . for the Sabbath without careful discrimination. The purpose and fulfillment of that true rest, represented by the ancient Sabbath, lies in the Lord's resurrection."[66] Sixteenth-century English clergyman Nicholas Bownde asserted that the shift of Sabbath to Sunday was made by Jesus and his apostles themselves and not later leaders in the church. Though the Jewish Sabbath had been observed on the seventh day to commemorate creation, Jesus chose Sunday as a replacement because Sunday marked the beginning of the new creation, inaugurated in the resurrection.[67]

61. Josephus, *Against Apion* 2.2, https://tinyurl.com/y6e6cs3m.

62. Josephus, *Against Apion* 2.40, https://tinyurl.com/y6e6cs3m.

63. Herold Weiss, "The Sabbath in the Writings of Josephus," *Journal for the Study of Judaism in the Persian, Hellenistic, and Roman Period* 29 (1998): 372.

64. Craig Harline, *Sunday: A History of the First Day from Babylonia to the Super Bowl* (New Haven: Yale University Press, 2011), 5.

65. Harline, *Sunday*, 9. Harline explains that there are three general competing interpretations: one is that the apostles established the Lord's Day as a weekly commemoration with Christ's resurrection on the first day of the week, but this day was not to be like the Sabbath; worship, and not rest, was emphasized. A second is that the apostles transferred the Sabbath in a new—and even perfected—form to the Lord's Day. The third is that the first day was chosen—either by the apostles or later leaders—for worship on the authority of the new Christian church, not because of a connection to the Sabbath commandment. Sabbath, which many early Christians still observed, was the same day that many pagan neighbors worshiped. *Sunday*, 7–8.

66. Calvin, *Institutes*, 399.

67. Nicholas Bownde, *The Doctrine of the Sabbath Plainely Layde Forth, and Soundly*

Sabbath—and the freedom to practice it with rigor and devotion—was especially important to the Puritans and a large part of what motivated them to leave Europe for the New World. As the introduction to this chapter indicates, the Puritans had stringent laws prohibiting regular work on the Sabbath, which was practiced on Sundays, plus any buying, selling, traveling, public entertainment, or sports.[68] These laws were particularly challenging for observant Jews who would not work or open their stores on Saturday, their Sabbath, and were also prevented by the blue laws from working on Sunday. In the 1950s, a group of Jewish merchants organized legally, arguing that the blue laws violated the First Amendment by supporting Sunday closing and favoring the holy day for Christians.[69] In 1961, the Supreme Court held that even though the blue laws were originally motivated by religion, they could be kept as long as states found secular reasons to justify them, such as setting aside a day in the week for rest and recreation.[70] While the blue laws were confirmed in theory, and present in nearly every state, they were increasingly ignored and limited in practice, superseded in America by the value of commerce.[71] And eventually, the emergence of the five-day workweek and its corresponding two-day weekend would allow for Sabbath keeping for both Jews and Christians.

I spent a year living in Egypt, working at an English-speaking, interdenominational Protestant church outside of Cairo. Because Friday is the holy day for Muslims, the church held worship services on Friday and "Friday School" instead of "Sunday School" for children and youth. A group in the church also persuaded the pastoral leaders to also add an evening service on

---

Proued by Testimonies Both of Holy Scripture, and also of olde and new ecclesiasticall writers, University of Michigan Library Digital Collections, 1:127–30, https://tinyurl.com/32keucr8.

68. Samuel A. Peters's *General History of Connecticut* (1781) includes several laws that were discredited or proved to be unreliable, such as "no woman shall kiss her child on the Sabbath day," or "The true-blue laws of Connecticut and New Haven and the false blue-laws invented by the Rev. Samuel Peters to which are added specimens of the laws and judicial proceedings of other colonies and some blue-laws of England in the reign of James I by J. Hammond Trumbull."

69. McGowan v. Maryland argued, "The Sunday observer may practice his faith and yet work six days a week, while the observer of the Jewish Sabbath, his competitor, may work only during five days, to the latter's obvious disadvantage. Orthodox Jewish shoppers whose jobs occupy a five-day week have no week-end shopping day, while Sunday-observing Christians do. Leisure to attend Sunday services, and relative quiet throughout their duration, is assured by law, but no equivalent treatment is accorded to Friday evening and Saturday services."

70. Library of Congress, "U.S. Reports: McGowan v. Maryland, 366 U.S. 420 (1960)," https://www.loc.gov/item/usrep366420/.

71. Harline, *Sunday*, 279–83.

Sunday, after the workday ended, because they were uncomfortable that there was not a worship service on Sunday. For some people, the day matters. Walter Harrelson suggests that a religiously plural society should allow one day in seven for worship and reflection for the major religions. The workweek would be four days, with "a day set aside for Jewish reflection and worship (the Jewish Sabbath), another for Christian worship and reflection (the Christian Sunday), and where necessary, another for Muslim worship and reflection (the Islamic Friday)."[72] As work patterns change, and remote work done during flexible hours becomes more common, practicing Sabbath rest and not working may also change.

Still, the day of the week continues to be debated in receptions about the Sabbath. During the eighteen years when Eugene Peterson was a Presbyterian pastor, Monday was his Sabbath, and he and his wife would go for walks in the forest around their Montana home. When he became a professor, he writes, "It became possible to keep a more conventional Sabbath. When I enter the church now, I no longer head for the pulpit, rather my wife and I take our places in a pew on Sunday mornings."[73] Swoboda and his family practice Sabbath each Wednesday. He explains, "My approach to our commitment is what I call the one-in-seven principle. That is, I don't believe the Sabbath must be observed on one specific day. . . . Rather we must find one day out of seven as a day of rest."[74] This "one-in-seven" principle certainly fits with biblical language about the Sabbath as the seventh day, and undoubtedly people who approach the Sabbath with more flexibility may be more able to keep a Sabbath given the genuinely complicated nature of human life and society today. But what may be gained in flexibility may be lost in community: certainly, one person or one family can choose to keep a Sabbath when it works for them, but that day may not be the same day others are similarly practicing the Sabbath. In reference to the switch from keeping a Monday Sabbath to a Sunday Sabbath, Peterson writes that while in some ways the practice is not very different, "there is one striking difference—community. We are now in the Sabbath company of children and men and women. . . . There is an element of festivity here that we never had walking alone on the forest trails."[75]

72. Walter Harrelson, *The Ten Commandments and Human Rights* (Philadelphia: Fortress, 1980), 90.

73. Eugene Peterson, "The Good for Nothing Sabbath," *Christianity Today*, April 4, 1994, https://tinyurl.com/2z8r2wp5.

74. Swoboda, *Subversive Sabbath*, 201.

75. Peterson, "The Good for Nothing Sabbath."

What Is Prohibited

The commandment prohibits "any work" (Exod 20:10; Deut 5:14). This gets detailed in a list of thirty-nine activities forbidden on the Sabbath, according to the Mishnah Shabbat 7:2: (1) sowing, (2) plowing, (3) harvesting, (4) binding sheaves, (5) threshing, (6) winnowing, (7) selecting, (8) grinding, (9) sifting, (10) kneading, (11) baking; (12) shearing wool, (13) bleaching it, (14) hackling it, (15) dyeing it, (16) spinning, (17) stretching the threads, (18) making two meshes, (19) weaving two threads, (20) dividing two threads, (21) tying, (22) untying, (23) sewing two stitches, (24) tearing in order to sew two stitches; (25) hunting a deer, (26) slaughtering it, (27) flaying it, (28) salting it, (29) curing its hide, (30) scraping it, (31) slicing it; (32) writing two letters, (33) erasing in order to write two letters; (34) building, (35) pulling down; (36) extinguishing, (37) kindling; (38) striking with a hammer; and (39) taking out from one domain to another. Some understand this list to represent primary types of labor, but Judith Hauptman argues that the list was created to explain that every sequential action in a process requires its own sin offering. That is, Hauptman believes that the redactor who added the list was not trying to be comprehensive but was focusing on large lists of "syntagmatically related labors" such as the first thirteen activities which would lead to producing a piece of cloth. Each activity in that list is a type of work that would need atonement.[76]

In reference to this list, Robert M. Johnston writes that reciting such Rabbinic Sabbath rules "might give the impression that the Sabbath was considered negative and burdensome, and for many it may have been so. But such an impression in general would be one-sided and distorted. The rabbis were concerned to make the Sabbath a delight (Isa 58:13), and it would seem that they largely succeeded."[77] Strict Christian Sabbatarians, on the other hand, might not have been very successful in making Sabbath a delight. Joy Davidman opines,

> It took the strict Puritans of England only ten years—from 1650 to 1660—so to disgust the people with legislated piety that they reacted into a license undreamed of before. Perhaps the willful license of our own Sun-

76. Judith Hauptman, "A New Interpretation of the 39 Forbidden Sabbath Labors," in *The Faces of Torah: Studies in the Texts and Contexts of Ancient Judaism in Honor of Steven Fraade*, ed. Christine Hayes, Michael Novick, and Michal Bar-Asher Siegal, Supplements to the Journal of Ancient Judaism 22 (Göttingen: Vandenhoeck and Ruprecht, 2017), 323–38.

77. Robert M. Johnston, "The Rabbinic Sabbath," in *The Sabbath in Scripture and History*, ed. Kenneth A. Strand (Washington, DC: Review and Herald, 1982), 83.

> days originated partly in a kind of bravado, a resentment of legislated controls and negative virtues. . . . Question a dozen modern infidels about their childhood, and half of them will trace their atheism to endless dull, bleak Sundays in a negatively "Christian" household which made a child's life seem hardly worth living. The ball games, the dances, the speeding automobiles, the crowded beaches of today's Sabbath—they are fugitive and inadequate pleasures, no doubt. Yet for many they may be an attempt, however fumbling, to restore to the Sabbath some of that holy gladness which it had before overzealous reformers turned the Fourth Commandment's "thou shalt" into a "thou shalt not." [78]

Two nineteenth-century authors—Samuel Langhorne Clemens (known as Mark Twain) and Charles Dickens—each write about the drudgery of Sabbath. Clemens's satirical essay "Letter II" is written from the perspective of Satan to his colleagues in heaven, Gabriel and Michael, trying to explain to them how absurd it is that humans expect heaven to be Sunday writ large, when on earth "these people cannot stand much church. . . . One day in seven; and even then they do not look forward to it with longing. And so—consider what their heaven provides for them: 'church' that lasts forever, and a Sabbath that has no end!"[79] Charles Dickens's writing was not fiction but a critique of a proposed Sabbath law in Great Britain in 1836, which would have outlawed all recreational and commercial activities on Sundays. Dickens writes, "Sunday comes, and brings with it a day of general gloom and austerity. The man who has been toiling hard all the week, has been looking toward the Sabbath, not as to a day of rest from labour, and healthy recreation, but as one of grievous tyranny and grinding oppression. The day which his Maker intended as a blessing, man has converted into a curse."[80]

The gloom of a strict Sunday Sabbath is also mentioned by author Laura Ingalls Wilder in *Little House in the Big Woods*: when Laura is forced to sit quietly, restricted in her activities, she shouts, "I hate Sunday!"[81] Journalist

78. Davidman, *Smoke on the Mountain*, 52–53. Davidman also references a—possibly apocryphal—story about a man in seventeenth-century Scotland who was hauled into court for smiling on the Sabbath day. She comments, "Considering the state of Scotland in his day, he should have been congratulated for managing to smile at all." *Smoke on the Mountain*, 56.

79. S. Bradley, R. Beatty, and E. Long, eds., *The American Tradition in Literature*, 3rd ed. (New York: Norton, 1967), 2:489.

80. Charles Dickens, "Sunday under Three Heads," https://tinyurl.com/ya4hwj5m. This was early writing for Dickens, under the pseudonym Timothy Sparks.

81. Laura Ingalls Wilder, *Little House in the Big Woods* (New York: HarperCollins, 1981), 86.

Chris Hedges describes Sundays in his New England boarding school in the late 1960s as "a day of deep depression."[82]

Specifically regarding depression on the Sabbath, the rabbis advise against praying all eighteen blessings of the Amidah prayer on the Sabbath, especially the prayer that refers to God as the one "who heals the ills of His people." The reasoning was, "if it should happen that a loved one was ill at home at the time of praying, the worshipper would be reminded of it while reciting the prayer . . . and would become depressed." Because the Sabbath was given to Israel "for sanctification, for joy and rest and not for sorrow," on the Sabbath day one must only recite the first and final three blessings and replace the blessings in the middle of the Amidah with the prayer of rest (Midrash Tanchuma, Vayera 1:5). Again, rabbinic teaching about the Sabbath, though sometimes maligned, emphasized the positive and beneficial aspects of the day even in what it asked people to give up. A similar idea, found currently, is that the Sabbath is a day when it is forbidden to worry. Hungarian pastor József Farkas says in addition to resting from the bondage of work on the Sabbath, it is a day when we can "relax the grip which our worries have upon us."[83]

Sabbath law in the Mishnah forbids carrying any weapons on the Sabbath; even if a person goes out into public unwittingly with a weapon, that person must then bring a sin offering (Mishnah Shabbat 6:4). According to Jub. 50:12, war is forbidden on the Sabbath, but the account in 1 Macc 2:29–41 suggests some ambivalence about not fighting on the Sabbath. The Jews who are the subjects of 1 Macc 2:32–38 believe they must not engage in war on the Sabbath, and they are killed. The leaders in 1 Macc 2:39–41 resolve to fight, on practical grounds; Levenson describes them as realizing the conviction that war is prohibited would spell "certain defeat."[84]

Scottish runner Eric Liddell is known for his insistence on observing the Sabbath in the 1924 Summer Olympics in Paris by not running in the heats for the hundred-meter dash—the race he was favored to win—because they were held on a Sunday. Instead, he competed in the four-hundred-meter race, which was held on a weekday. He won that race. In the 1981 movie *Chariots of Fire*, the character of Liddell says, "God made countries; God makes kings, and the rules by which they govern. And those rules say that the Sabbath is His. And I, for one, intend to keep it that way."

82. Chris Hedges, *Losing Moses on the Freeway: The Ten Commandments in America* (New York: Free Press, 2005), 73.

83. József Farkas, *Bench Marks*, trans. John R. Bodo (Richmond, VA: John Knox, 1969), 57–58.

84. Levenson, *Israel's Day of Light and Joy*, 67.

More recently, receptions of Sabbath practice emphasize refraining from using technology. "The Sabbath Manifesto" is a project developed by a small group of artists and media professionals who explain that, "while not particularly religious, [we] felt a collective need to fight back against our increasingly fast-paced way of living."[85] The project began in 2010 and includes a list of principles—ten, again—to help people practice a "weekly timeout" and a "National Day of Unplugging" for "communal digital detox."[86] The ten principles are (1) avoid technology, (2) connect with loved ones, (3) nurture your health, (4) get outside, (5) avoid commerce, (6) light candles, (7) drink wine, (8) eat bread, (9) find silence, and (10) give back. The website assures its readers that these principles are "completely open for your unique interpretation" and explain, "To some, 'avoid technology' means not sending text messages. To others, it means not using a stove or riding in an elevator. To some, 'be healthy' means running the next NYC marathon. For others, it means chewing each mouthful of food you eat real slow—18 chews a bite. You get the picture. Find the balance that works for you."[87] The "National Day of Unplugging" grew into a "Global Day of Unplugging," and organizers provide tips to help people take a break from technology, including selling a "resistor case kit": a case in which to store devices to help a person resist using them.[88]

American journalist Judith Shulevitz writes,

> Our schedules are not the only thing the Sabbath would disrupt if it could. It would also rip a whole in all the shimmering webs that give modern life its pleasing aura of weightlessness—the networks that zap digitized voices and money and data from server to iPhone to GPS. In a world of brightness and portability and instantaneous intimacy, the Sabbath foists on the consciousness the blackness of night, the heaviness of objects, the miles that keep us apart. . . . If we want to travel, it would make us walk, though not too far. If we long for social interaction, it would have us meet our fellow man and woman face-to face. If we wish to bend the world to our will, it would insist that we forgo the vast majority of the devices that extend our reach and multiply our efficacy.[89]

85. Sabbath Manifesto, "About," https://tinyurl.com/5ffaz6ve.

86. The National Day of Unplugging became the Global Day of Unplugging and is supported by the nonprofit member organization Unplug Collective, which was formed in 2020. Reboot, "National Day of Unplugging," https://tinyurl.com/4ezmtu5u; Global Day of Unplugging, "Our Team," https://tinyurl.com/sjfzd9nj.

87. Sabbath Manifesto, "About."

88. Global Day of Unplugging, "Resistor Case Kit," https://tinyurl.com/4axxy5k3.

89. Judith Shulevitz, *The Sabbath World: Glimpses of a Different Order of Time* (New York: Random House, 2010), 6.

In an interview with another American journalist, Ezra Klein, Shulevitz and Klein discuss what they call "the secularization of Sabbath," which often finds expression as these "digital Shabbats." As the example above from "The Sabbath Manifesto" admits, people need not be "particularly religious" to see the value in rhythms of unplugging from technology. Klein says he has mixed feelings and mixed experiences about the secularization of Sabbath, and Shulevitz responds, "I don't have a problem with people coming to this notion of the Sabbath in a secular way. I think that once you do it, though, you begin, in a way, to replicate what the religion meant to do. . . . If you become what I call a Sabbatarian, you're going to wind up finding your way to a community that makes it part of their life. And that's probably going to be a religious community."[90] Kelsey Osgood's 2002 article for *Wired* magazine is titled, "Why Your 'Digital Shabbat' Will Fail," and her reason boils down to the fact that while Sabbath is a good tool for spending time with family or preventing burnout, Orthodox Jews "do it for a very unfashionable, very simple, supremely awesome reason: because God told us to. . . . It's a behavioral manifestation of the covenant between God and the Jews, a way of imitating God's own cessation from creation in the Book of Genesis, a reminder of our calling to be holy and sanctified. God is a pretty central element in all these things, and it stands to reason that when you cut the core out of something, what's left will probably rot."[91]

The technology discussed above as forbidden on the Sabbath obviously did not exist when the Sabbath commandment first appeared. In 1950, the Committee on Jewish Law and Standards of the Conservative Movement published their legal opinion that the traditional prohibition of "riding" on the Sabbath day should no longer be observed, because the technology that allowed people to ride in cars was new. They explain, "The combustion of gasoline to produce power is a type of work that obviously could not have been prohibited before its invention. . . . [Therefore,] when attendance at services is made unreasonably difficult, without the use of the automobile, such use shall not be regarded as being in violation of the Sabbath."[92] It is important to note that final sentence, that the reason to clarify that using an automobile doesn't violate the Sabbath is to facilitate people's attendance at worship services especially when they live far enough away that to walk would be "unreasonably difficult." The committee's principle that the Sabbath commandment did not

90. "Transcript: Ezra Klein Interviews Judith Shulevitz," *New York Times*, January 3, 2023, https://tinyurl.com/3ycnh28d.

91. Kelsey Osgood, "Why Your 'Digital Shabbat' Will Fail," *Wired*, April 15, 2022, https://tinyurl.com/4czyzh3v.

92. Levenson, *Israel's Day of Light and Joy*, 210–11.

prohibit work—or technology—that had not yet been invented demonstrates how reception history can seek to distinguish between a text's original setting and how that text can be applied for people today.

What Is Permitted

In response to Nicholas Bownde's 1595 *Doctrine of the Sabbath* mentioned above—which took a strict position on the activities forbidden on the Sabbath—King James I of England and VI of Scotland published a *Book of Sports* in 1617, instructing that it should be read from pulpits. His son Charles I reissued the book in 1633 with added legal sanctions for anyone who refused to read it from the pulpit. The book promoted a number of fun activities for the Sabbath including archery and dancing.[93] According to the Talmud, "R. Shmuel the son of Nahmani said [that] R. Yonatan said: One may go to theatres and circuses to watch over public affairs on Shabbat; and a tanna of the school of Menashia taught: One may arrange for girls to be betrothed on Shabbat and about a boy to teach him the book and to teach him a trade" (Ket. 5a:3).

Theologian Marva Dawn writes that the Sabbath includes activities in four general categories: ceasing, resting, embracing, and feasting. The final category includes "feasting with music, feasting with food, feasting and festival"[94]— but even "ceasing the humdrum and meaningless" includes positive activities of celebration and delight.[95] Eugene Peterson appeals to the two different biblical versions of the Sabbath to explain that the two general Sabbath activities are praying and playing. "The Exodus reason directs us to the contemplation of God, which becomes prayer and worship. The Deuteronomy reason directs us to social leisure, which becomes play."[96] Pastor John Mark Comer identifies the two sole Sabbath activities as rest and worship.[97] Comer also created a digital workbook as a companion to his book, which gives suggestions for activities on the Sabbath that "spark joy, wonder, gratitude, and happiness, such as eating

93. Carl R. Trueman, "John Owen," in *The Decalogue through the Centuries: From the Hebrew Scriptures to Benedict XVI*, ed. Jeffrey P. Greenman and Timothy Larsen (Louisville: Westminster John Knox, 2012), 143.

94. Marva J. Dawn, *Keeping the Sabbath Wholly: Ceasing, Resting, Embracing, Feasting* (Grand Rapids: Eerdmans, 1989), 166–202.

95. Dawn, *Keeping the Sabbath Wholly*, 48–50.

96. Peterson, "The Good for Nothing Sabbath."

97. John Mark Comer, *The Ruthless Elimination of Hurry* (New York: Waterbrook, 2019), 161.

good food, walking in nature, spending time with family or friends, listening to music, playing games, making love to our spouse, or just having fun before God."[98] The creators of the Global Day of Unplugging have curated a list of over two hundred ideas about what to do, obviously, while unplugged.[99] These receptions are quick to emphasize that none of these activities are "required" and that they can be adapted and made personal, which continues to raise the question of how personal or communal Sabbath practice ought to be.

Benefits

Proper observance of the Sabbath, according to Isa 58:13, is "keeping from . . . doing as you please; honor it by not going your own way and not doing as you please or speaking idle words," advice that seems to fall into the category of things forbidden. It is striking that not doing as you please is repeated twice in this verse, which again may be in tension with those receptions that encourage a person to just do what works for them. But the subsequent promise in the passage is that "then you will find your joy in the LORD, and I will cause you to ride in triumph on the heights of the land and feast on the inheritance of your father Jacob" (58:14).

A legend in the Talmud is told about "Yosef who cherishes Shabbat." A gentile who lived in his neighborhood owned much property and was told by astrologers that "Yosef who cherishes Shabbat" would gain all of the gentile's property. The gentile sold all of his property, and with the money he bought a pearl, which he placed in his hat. But when he was crossing a river on a ferry, the wind blew his hat into the water, and a fish swallowed the pearl. That fish was caught close to sunset on Sabbath eve. The townspeople told the fishermen to bring the fish to "Yosef who cherishes Shabbat" because he regularly bought delicacies for the Sabbath. They brought the fish to him; he purchased it; and as he cut it open to prepare it he found the pearl, which he sold for great gain. The legend ends with the saying, "One who lends to Shabbat, Shabbat repays him" (b. Shabb 119a:5).

In addition to potential material benefits for keeping the Sabbath, the Talmud teaches that on the Sabbath day people are granted an extra, additional

98. John Mark Comer, "How to Un-hurry Workbook," https://tinyurl.com/yds8y589. Comer is careful to explain, "This is *not* a 'to do' list: there are no 'to do's' on Sabbath! No ought's or should's. This is just a list of activities many people find restful and restorative."

99. Global Day of Unplugging, "What to Do on Global Day of Unplugging . . . or Any Day of the Year!," https://tinyurl.com/spserkjx.

soul (Beitzah 16a:11–12). Sforno explains that this extra soul both "assists us in concentrating on the spiritual dimension of the day" but also helps humans to live up to the vision God had when creating humans in God's own image.[100] Matthew Sleeth's book on the Sabbath has the subtitle "A Prescription for a Healthier, Happier Life."[101] Sleeth is an MD, and though he writes about the Sabbath from a Christian perspective, as the subtitle indicates, he affirms that a weekly day of rest will increase someone's physical health through falling blood pressure and declining levels of stress hormones.[102]

Conclusion

There has been so much reception history on the Sabbath, and it will likely continue, especially as receptions debate when and how to keep it amidst an increasingly busy, technological Sabbath with competing tensions of the individual and community. Perhaps it is not surprising, though, that much has been said about the Sabbath, for R. Joshua the son of Hanina declared: The Holy One, blessed be He, said to Israel: "Keep the Sabbath, for it is equal to the entire law" (Midrash Tanchuma, Ki Tisa 33:6).

100. Sefaria, citing "Sforno on Exodus 31:17:1–2," Eliyahu Munk, HaChut Hameshulash, https://tinyurl.com/4aft5b2z.

101. Matthew Sleeth, *24/6: A Prescription for a Healthier, Happier Life* (Carol Stream, IL: Tyndale House, 2012).

102. Sleeth, *24/6*, 77.

5

"Honor Your Father and Mother"

Though the commandment to honor father and mother is longer than others because it includes a reason—"so that your days may be long in the land the LORD your God is giving you"— it, like the other commandments, is still brief and lacking details as to how this commandment should be lived out in the society. Walter Harrelson comments, "No penalties are stated. No threats appear. Just a laconic sentence sums up one of the most enriching and devastating aspects of the life of human beings upon the earth."[1] Harrelson's adjectives are striking, as relationships with parents can indeed be enriching or devastating—and sometimes both. Harrelson also declares that the relationship with parents is "an enormously complex relationship, perhaps the most complex of all human relationships not excluding that between husband and wife."[2] Marriages have their complexities, to be sure, but Harrelson's comment points to how the commandment about honoring parents is the only one that specifically addresses familial relationships. The commandment against adultery (Exod 20:14) or the commandment to not covet a neighbor's wife (Exod 20:17) may imply a relationship between a husband and wife, but their focus is more on broad social relationships, less on family.

In biblical narratives as well as in human life experience, honoring parents is complicated and often presented as relative to one's relationship with God. Jesus did say that unless people hate their father and mother (and wife, children, siblings, and even their own lives), they cannot be disciples (Luke 14:26). And yet, this commandment, to honor father and mother, is one that Jesus quotes explicitly (Mark 7:1–13 // Matt 15:1–9; Mark 10:17–22 // Matt 19:16–22 // Luke 18:18–25). So, as with other commandments, the reception history of this

1. Walter Harrelson, *The Ten Commandments and Human Rights* (Philadelphia: Fortress, 1980), 102.

2. Harrelson, *The Ten Commandments*, 94.

one helps to spell out what exactly it might mean to honor parents, and how this might be enacted in one's particular context and family life.

Placement within the "Tablets"

As mentioned in the introductory chapter to this book, many have debated where this commandment belongs: with the "first tablet" that consists of commandments about how to relate to God or in the "second tablet" that consists of commandments about how to relate to humans. Jewish midrashim frequently blur the distinctions by asserting that honoring parents is similar to honoring God. According to Mekhilta deR. Shimon b. Yoḥai, "Honoring one's father [and mother] is thus equated with honoring God." The Hellenistic Jewish Sibylline Oracles include the statement, "They honor only the Immortal who always rules, and then their parents"; and Pseudo-Phocylides urges, "Honor God foremost and afterward your parents."[3] One midrash explains that when people honor their parents, God says, "I consider it as if I had dwelled among men and they had honored Me," but if people do not honor their parents, God says: "It is good that I do not dwell among men, or they would have treated Me superciliously, too."[4] Another midrash says that parents are to be honored because people owe their existence to their parents; though God is the ultimate creator, "thy parents took part in thy creation."[5] Philo also noted how both parents and God are involved in creating a person and therefore described the commandment to honor parents as "on the borderline between the two sets of five." Philo's reason was that parents stand on the border between mortal and immortal existence: mortal because parents, like other humans and animals, have perishable bodies but immortal "because the act of generation assimilates [parents] to God, the generator of all."[6]

While Philo uses the language of "border" to describe the commandment about honoring parents, Patrick Miller uses the metaphor of a bridge to describe this commandment's location between commandments that deal with relationship to God and those that deal with relationship to neighbor. Miller notes

3. James L. Kugel, *The Bible as It Was* (Cambridge, MA: Belknap Press, 1997), 394.

4. Louis Ginzberg and David Stern, *Legends of the Jews*, trans. Henrietta Szold and Paul Radin (Philadelphia: Jewish Publication Society, 2003), 1:606.

5. Ginzberg and Stern, *Legends of the Jews*, 1:606.

6. Philo, *The Works of Philo: Complete and Unabridged*, trans. C. D. Yonge (Peabody, MA: Hendrickson, 2006), 527. Philo's language seems to draw a line between a mortal body and an immortal spirit or essence, a distinction that is not present in the Hebrew Bible.

that the phrase "the LORD your God" appears "from the Prologue through the Sabbath Commandment. After the Fifth Commandment this phrase—and any reference to God at all—disappears."[7] Connection to commandments about one's neighbor, Miller explains, is because all people have been in some sort of relationship with one's parents. "One may have no other kinship relations, but one always has a mother and father."[8] Miller also points out how, according to Ezek 22:6–8, negative treatment of father and mother is followed by bad treatment of other members of the community, especially the weaker or more vulnerable persons in the society: the immigrant, the orphan, and the widow.[9] Prov 30:11–14 has a similar progression, beginning by describing "those who curse their fathers and do not bless their mothers" (Prov 30:11) and ending with them devouring the poor and the needy (Prov 30:14).[10] In other words, a good, honoring relationship with one's parents can lead to faithfulness in keeping the other commandments about how to relate well with other people.

Martin Buber follows the convention of dividing the Ten Commandments into two main parts, the first "religious" and the second "ethical," but then identifies a "central section containing the commandment of the Sabbath and the commandment to honor parents."[11] These commandments—Sabbath and honoring parents—have two things in common. First is that they are both stated as positives instead of negatives, "you shall not." And second, as Buber puts it, "The two of them, and only these two among all of the Ten Commandments, deal with *time,* articulated time; the first with the closed succession of weeks in the year, the second with the open succession of generations in national duration. Time itself is introduced into the constitutional foundation of national life by being partly articulated in the lesser rhythm of the weeks, and partly realized in its given articulation through the greater rhythm of the generations. . . . Both of them together ensure the continuity of national time; the never-to-be-interrupted consecution of consecration, the never-to-be-broken consecution of tradition."[12]

7. Patrick D. Miller, *The Ten Commandments* (Louisville: Westminster John Knox, 2009), 172.

8. Miller, *The Ten Commandments*, 169.

9. Miller, *The Ten Commandments*, 173.

10. David Hazony writes that Prov 30:11–14 describes a logical progression from dishonoring parents to being generally bad people. *The Ten Commandments: How Our Most Ancient Moral Text Can Renew Modern Life* (New York: Scribner, 2010), 133.

11. Martin Buber, *Moses: The Revelation and the Covenant* (New York: Harper and Row, 1958), 132.

12. Buber, *Moses*, 132.

In other words, for Buber, the commandments for Sabbath and honoring parents both support the continuity of national time in Israel, as that time gets marked by weekly Sabbaths and the generations that continue whenever a child is born to parents.

Theologians Stanley Hauerwas and William Willimon also draw a connection between the Sabbath command and the command to honor parents. They explain, "Even as the third commandment tells us that we must live in time as a gift, rather than as an arena of our achievements and assertions, so the fourth commandment commands us to live as those who know their very being is a gift. Our lives are not self-derived."[13] Buber's connection between the commandments centers around the idea of time, but Hauerwas and Willimon see the similarity in how the commandments emphasize receiving a gift rather than earning or striving. Remembering that we were born to parents without "doing something" to earn that life—it is a gift—can resemble a Sabbath practice when we stop working to prove ourselves.

Josephus advocated that five commandments would be assigned to each Table, though John Calvin took umbrage with this based on a reading of Matt 19:19, where Jesus says, "Honor your father and mother; also, you shall love your neighbor as yourself." This verse is part of Jesus's list of commandments in response to the question from the rich young man as to what he must do to have eternal life. Calvin allows that Josephus made the division of five and five "no doubt according to the common agreement of his age" but then declares, "This is contrary to reason in that it confuses religion and charity; furthermore, it is refuted by authority of the Lord, who according to Matthew puts the commandment to honor one's parents in the canon of the Second Table."[14] Perhaps Calvin's language also follows the common agreement of his age but might need some explication now: by "religion," Calvin is referencing only those commandments that relate to God, which Calvin numbers as one through four; "charity" refers to those commandments—five through ten—that explain how humans relate to each other. Then, because Matt 19:19 lists the commandment to honor parents in the same verse as love of neighbor, Calvin reads the command to honor parents in "the Second Table."

Earlier in the Christian tradition, Augustine advocated for dividing the commandments into a group of three and a group of seven, so that the com-

13. Stanley M. Hauerwas and William H. Willimon, *The Truth about God: The Ten Commandments in Christian Life* (Nashville: Abingdon, 1999), 69.

14. John Calvin, *Institutes of the Christian Religion*, ed. John T. McNeill, trans. and indexed by Ford Lewis Battles (Philadelphia: Westminster, 1960), 379.

mandment about parents would be the first commandment on the "second tablet." Augustine did so on the basis of Eph 6:2, which calls this commandment to honor parents "the first commandment with a promise"; apparently, Augustine understood the first clause as meaning that the commandment to honor parents was the first commandment on the second tablet, paying less attention to the latter part of the claim in Eph 6:2 that it was the first commandment "with a promise."[15]

John Ames, the first-person narrator of Marilynne Robinson's novel *Gilead*, acknowledges that there are different defensible ways to view the commandments but muses about the possibility that "honoring your mother might be the last in the sequence relating to right worship rather than the first in the series relating to right conduct."[16] This is because, as Ames explains, "Right worship is right perception . . . and here the Scripture commands right perception of people you have a real and deep knowledge of."[17] Ames observes that there is a pattern in the Ten Commandments of setting things apart in order to perceive their holiness: first God, then God's name, then the Sabbath, and then father and mother: "Every human being is worthy of honor, but the conscious discipline of honor is learned from this setting apart of the mother and father, who usually labor and are heavy-laden, and may be cranky or stingy or ignorant or overbearing. Believe me, I know this can be a hard Commandment to keep. But I believe also that the rewards of obedience [to the commandment] are great, because at the root of real honor is always the sense of the sacredness of the person who is its object."[18]

This section of *Gilead* concludes with Ames declaring that based on his reasoning, he has persuaded himself that "the Fifth Commandment belongs on the first tablet"[19] and honoring parents means to perceive them correctly, as sacred and worthy of honor.

What Does It Mean to Honor?

The Hebrew word in the commandment adds more dimensions to what honoring might mean: it is *kbd*, which can also be translated as "glory," as well as

15. Augustine, "Sermon 33: On What Is Written in the Psalm: *O God, I Will Sing You a New Song*," in *The Works of Saint Augustine*, vol. 3.2, *Sermons*, ed. John E. Rotelle, trans. Edmund Hill (Brooklyn, NY: New City Press, 1990), 156.

16. Marilynne Robinson, *Gilead* (New York: Picador, 2004), 135.

17. Robinson, *Gilead*, 135.

18. Robinson, *Gilead*, 139.

19. Robinson, *Gilead*, 139.

"heavy/weighty."[20] The semantic overlap of these words and ideas suggests that to "honor" a person means to treat them as if they have weight or substance. Aviya Kushner translates the commandment as saying, "Treat your father and mother with heft. . . . The idea is to treat your parents with heavy consideration, to make sure they have a serious place in your life."[21] The opposite would be to treat them as if they are insubstantial, or "lightly"; that latter word corresponds to the Hebrew word *qll*, which also means "curse." In fact, Exod 21:17 and Lev 20:9 explicitly forbid a person from cursing father and mother,[22] such that the positive commandment to "honor" (*kbd*) parents in the Ten Commandments (Exod 20:12; Deut 5:16) has its counterpart in these negative commandments to not "curse" (*qll*). As Ibn Ezra comments, "The commandment *Honor thy father and thy mother* means that we should not do the opposite; that is, we should not curse or make light of our parents."[23] Additionally, Exod 21:15 forbids a person from "striking" (*nkh*) a parent, suggesting that physical violence against a parent is another way to dishonor them. This idea—of children abstaining from force against their parents—gets mirrored in broader ancient southwest Asian society: a Middle Babylonian document references a man who was imprisoned for beating his mother.[24]

Rather than the word "honor" to describe treatment of parents, Lev 19:3 commands a person to "fear" or "respect" (*yr'*) father and mother (Lev 19:3). Instructions in the intertestamental book of Sirach combine "honor" and "respect," albeit with the Greek terms (Sir 3:3–4) *timan* and *doxazōn*, not the Greek word *phobos*.

Another reception of what it may mean to honor can be found in the story in Deut 21:18–21 of a rebellious son who will not "hear/obey" (*šm'*) the voice

20. The word appears multiple times in the ark narrative of 1 Sam 4–6, where it seems to be deliberately employed to suggest those different meanings: when the Philistines capture Israel's ark, Eli's dying daughter-in-law names her child "Ichabod," which translates into "Where is (the) glory?" (1 Sam 4:21). But God's hand is "heavy" on the Philistines until they return the ark back to Israel. C. S. Lewis is trading on both meanings of the word *kbd* in his piece titled *The Weight of Glory*.

21. Aviya Kushner, *The Grammar of God: A Journey into the Words and Worlds of the Bible* (New York: Spiegel & Grau, 2015), 134.

22. Prov 20:20 and 30:11 also utilize language about cursing father and mother, though instead of an explicit command forbidding it, the verses describe the negative consequences of such actions. For example, Prov 20:20 asserts, "If someone curses their father or mother, their lamp will be put out in pitch darkness."

23. Sefaria, citing "Ibn Ezra on Exodus 20:12," H. Norman Strickman and Arthur M. Silver, Menorah, 1988–2004, https://tinyurl.com/25b9j6s37.

24. Karel van der Toorn, *Sin and Sanction in Israel and Mesopotamia: A Comparative Study* (Assen: Van Gorcum, 1985), 14.

of his parents and is therefore killed. There is a parallel to this in the Code of Hammurabi, but it only commands cutting off of a hand as punishment. According to the Talmud, Rabbi Shimon said that such a rebellious son never existed, and the Torah only told this story for educational purposes, but Rabbi Yonatan disagreed, saying, "I was once in a place where a stubborn and rebellious son was condemned to death, and I even sat on his grave after he was executed" (Sanh. 71a.15). The writer of the letter to the Ephesians introduces the commandment to honor parents with the paraenesis, "Children, obey your parents in the Lord, for this is right" (Eph 6:1) and then quotes "Honor your father and mother" (Eph 6:2). Even though the words "honor" and "obey" are different, certain receptions suggest that obedience to parents may be part of how honor gets applied.

In the *Illustrated Bible*, with scenes chosen by Melanchthon and illustrated by Cranach's woodcuts, this commandment is depicted with an image of the drunken and naked Noah; his son Ham is pointing to his nudity. Melanchthon referenced this story in his commentary on the commandment as an example of how the commandment to honor parents includes being patient with physical infirmities in both parents and rulers. He wrote, "When Noah lay uncovered, his son Ham wantonly mocked him, and today young people often mock infirmities in true rulers."[25] Understanding Noah's drunkenness as "an infirmity" notwithstanding, more on the overlap between honoring parents and honoring those in authority will be discussed below.

British Puritan Thomas Watson explained that people show honor to parents, first, by a "reverential esteem of their persons"[26] and, second, by "careful obedience," which includes listening to them, complying with their commands, and relieving their wants. As an example of taking care of parents' wants, Watson wrote about "young storks, who, by an instinct of nature, bring meat to the old ones when, by reason of age, they are not able to fly."[27] Philo also referenced storks in his discussion of this commandment, writing that "the old birds remain in their nests because they are unable to fly, but their children . . . traverse the whole of earth and sea, and from all quarters provide their parents with what is necessary for them."[28] The provision of food—and clothing, and drink—was stipulated in Babylonian records of adoption, which

25. Philipp Melanchthon, *Melanchthon on Christian Doctrine: Loci communes 1555*, trans. and ed. Clyde L. Manschreck (Grand Rapids: Baker, 1965), 105.

26. Thomas Watson, *Body of Divinity: Contained in Sermons upon the Assembly's Catechism* (Grand Rapids: Baker, 1979), 315.

27. Watson, *Body of Divinity*, 317.

28. Philo, *Works*, 528.

commanded the adoptee to "revere and honor" (Akkadian *palāḫu* and *kubbutu*) the adopted parents, by providing for their material needs.[29]

Harrelson took pains to note that the commandment does not say "love your mother and father,"[30] although Joy Davidman wrote how in the Western world in the twentieth century,

> we no longer *need* our families—we are therefore free to love them with complete unselfishness. Now at last we might do for love what our ancestors did for self-interest; now at last it is possible to honor our parents genuinely, because they no longer have the power to kill us if we don't. The old sort of honor was sometimes an ugly sham—the son who respects Father only out of fear of punishment is not much of a son, just as the Christian who worships God only out of fear of hell is precious little of a Christian.[31]

Davidman urged, "Let us, then, practice and pray for love, and the honor will take care of itself."[32]

Unlike Davidman, Calvin did not include the idea of "love" for parents but writes that the sum of the commandment is "that we should look up to those whom God has placed over us, and should treat them with honor, obedience, and gratefulness. It follows from this that we are forbidden to detract from their dignity either by contempt, by stubbornness, or by ungratefulness."[33] Calvin, however, qualifies his statement by appealing to Eph 6:1, that we are "bidden to obey our parents only 'in the Lord.'"[34] He explains, "If they spur us to transgress the law, we have a perfect right to regard them not as parents, but as strangers who are trying to lead us away from obedience to our true Father. . . . It is unworthy and absurd for their eminence so as to prevail as to pull down the loftiness of God. On the contrary, their eminence depends upon God's loftiness and ought to lead us to it."[35] In Pedro de Córdoba's *Doctrina christiana* of 1544, a catechism produced for Spanish colonies in the modern-day Dominican Republic, he states that if parents ordered their children to

29. Van der Toorn, *Sin and Sanction*, 14.

30. Harrelson, *The Ten Commandments*, 102.

31. Joy Davidman, *Smoke on the Mountain: An Interpretation of the Ten Commandments* (Philadelphia: Westminster Press, 1954), 67–68.

32. Davidman, *Smoke on the Mountain*, 70.

33. Calvin, *Institutes*, 401.

34. Calvin, *Institutes*, 403.

35. Calvin, *Institutes*, 404.

return to idolatry, the children must not obey, "as well as if they ordered you to lie or to steal, or to do harm to others, or not go to the sermons, or to make some sacrifice or to worship idols."[36] God's authority and instruction superseded that of a parent, especially if the two were in conflict.

More contemporary receptions of the commandment to honor parents similarly acknowledge that honoring does not mean unqualified or simplistic acceptance of everything they do and say. Many receptions deal with the problem of cruel, harmful, or abusive parents. Journalist Chris Hedges writes,

> The commandment to honor your parents is a commandment to honor yourself, honor the life force that created you, the good and the bad mingled within us, but not to honor abuse. Those who were abused, who wince at the name of father or mother, cannot be asked to honor the memory of the abuse or the abuser. But at the same time, however painful, we have to see in parents, even bad parents, reflections of ourselves, if only to guard against and keep at bay the demons within us. We cannot wish our parents away. They will always be a major, overpowering force in our life. We cannot undo abuse, but we can find a way to honor life, even their lives, by turning that abuse into compassion not only for ourselves, which is necessary for healing, but more important for all who suffer. Those who use personal pain to mitigate the pain of others, who take the experience of sorrow and suffering and use it to lead a life of compassion, honor their parents, even as they rise above them. They honor life, which is what their parents gave them. They honor what is holy and good. They take out of tragedy a regenerative power. They fulfill the commandment.[37]

March Moyle writes about how to honor parents who are "profoundly dishonorable or, at best, show well-meaning but imperfect love,"[38] suggesting that a mature form of honoring would look like acknowledging parents' failings and limitations. Eugenia Ann Gamble writes that people honor the life given to them by their parents by working to be free from the negative things that may have been present in the family or throughout the generations. Gamble

36. Luis Resines, "American Catechisms of the Sixteenth Century," in *The Decalogue and Its Cultural Influence*, ed. Dominik Markl (Sheffield: Sheffield Phoenix, 2013), 248.

37. Chris Hedges, *Losing Moses on the Freeway: The Ten Commandments in America* (New York: Free Press, 2005), 90–91.

38. Marsh Moyle, *Rumors of a Better Country: Searching for Trust and Community in a Time of Moral Outrage* (London: Inter-Varsity Press, 2023), 141.

gives examples such as alcoholic parents or parents whose interactions with children were especially critical, rigid, or angry, asserting, "It is . . . profoundly honoring of our parents when we stop the pain with us and choose to nurture the life in ourselves that they could not."[39]

Hungarian pastor József Farkas places the commandment to honor parents in conversation with the description in Gen 2:24 of a man leaving his father and mother to cling to his wife. Farkas explains, "God's thought is that when a man and woman found a new family, they leave their parents on the one hand, but on the other hand they look back upon them and honor them. God, then, intends parents to leave their parents *and* to honor them. And the whole truth of the commandment is summed up in this dialectic."[40] In addition to the dialectic, Farkas also locates the meaning of the commandment as between two extremes: "self-centered rebellion against parents and blind obedience to them."[41] Those who cannot separate themselves from their parents and live their own lives are not fulfilling the commandment, but neither is a person who has "kicked over everything, turning his back on his parents in a grand show of radicalism."[42] Honoring parents, he explains, means that people need to shape their own lives and at the same time respectfully contemplate the strivings, failures, mistakes, and quest of former generations. Farkas's explanation is a good illustration of how receptions move beyond the historical context of the text and into the world of the person interpreting the text. While Farkas does seek for a balance between extremes, his encouragement that people shape their own lives as they seek to honor their parents makes good sense in individualistic Western societies and may fit less neatly into other times and places.

Adult Children as the Addressee

Many receptions of this commandment stress that the proper addressee is adult children, not young children, though this is not specified in the laconic commandment.[43] Because Farkas connects the commandment to honor par-

39. Eugenia Ann Gamble, *Words of Love: A Healing Journey with the Ten Commandments* (Louisville: Westminster John Knox, 2022), 96.

40. József Farkas, *Bench Marks*, trans. John R. Bodo (Richmond, VA: John Knox, 1969), 63.

41. Farkas, *Bench Marks*, 66.

42. Farkas, *Bench Marks*, 68.

43. Miller cautions that, although care for older parents as a basic intent of this commandment may be inferred, it "is not laid out elsewhere in the legal statutes of the Torah

ents with the verse about marriage, it follows that the children to whom the commandment is addressed are of marriageable age. Farkas makes that clear as he writes that God "is not telling children that they should honor adults. Rather he is telling *adults* that they should honor their *elders*."[44] Charlie Trimm argues, "A close reading of the Decalogue encourages the interpretation that the command to honor parents was specifically for adults."[45] Scholar Georg Beer explains that the commandment to honor parents means, "The aged parents, those over sixty years, whose capacity for work and whose valuation has diminished (Lev 27:7), are not to be treated harshly by the Israelite; he is not to begrudge them the bread of charity, or force them to leave the house or take the way of voluntary death, or even to kill them himself."[46] Prov 23:22 tells a child, "do not despise your mother when she is old," and Sir 3:12–14 also specifically mentions an elderly parent, urging the child to "help your father in his old age . . . even if his mind fails, be patient with him; because you have all your faculties do not despise him."

In contrast with receptions that emphasize that this commandment was addressed to (only) older children, theologian Karl Barth included a discussion of how the commandment would need to be followed by a young or a small child.[47] Harrelson suggests that Barth misunderstood this commandment, especially the idea of the "length of days."[48] Harrelson draws on Exod 21:15, the verse that forbids "striking" a parent, and Deut 21:18–21, about the rebellious son who will not obey his parents, and reasons that those presuppose a young adult who will no longer listen to elderly parents, writing, "That suggests that the parents are aged or frail and have become a nuisance to the active adults who would very much like to be relieved of further responsibility for such aged ones."[49] Harrelson asserts that the commandment to honor parents was not primarily intended to support parents' discipline of unruly children but "had

---

or even in the Old Testament generally as the meaning or intent of the commandment, which is why one should resist seeing in this important responsibility the sole meaning of the commandment." *The Ten Commandments*, 181. Of course, a project in reception history would warn against any interpretation that claims to be "the sole meaning" of a text.

44. Farkas, *Bench Marks*, 63.

45. Charlie Trimm, "Honor Your Parents: A Command for Adults," *JETS* 60 (2017): 248.

46. Beer, *Exodus*, 102.

47. Barth, *Church Dogmatics*, III.4, 253.

48. Harrelson, "Karl Barth on the Decalogue," *Sciences Religieuses* 6/3 (1976–77): 237. Harrelson writes, "Barth's most unsatisfactory exegesis appears in connection with the commandment to show honor to one's parents."

49. Harrelson, *The Ten Commandments*, 94.

in view, rather, the care of the aged, the treatment of old parents with dignity and thoughtfulness by their adult children."[50]

Harrelson's application of the commandment for today includes reference to practices of care for the elderly; he writes,

> it would be wrong and wicked for us quickly to suggest that some of the present used alternatives for caring for aged parents are instances of "cursing" father and mother, for example, placing them in nursing homes, visiting them infrequently. No, the import of a commandment to care for aged parents and not to treat them with contempt finds applicability today in much more subtle ways. Who can really be sure whether it is a kindness or a curse to keep the elderly in one's home when they are not able to cope with the normal demands of life in such a home and must appear more and more to the other members of the household as unfit, incapable of managing life?[51]

Like Miller, who used Ezek 22:6–8 to connect the commandment to honor parents with care for the widow and orphan, Harrelson also notes how care for elderly who are unable to care for themselves is a mark of one's ability to care for others in society who are more needy: the poor, the orphan, the widow. Harrelson writes, "For it is how one deals with the helpless . . . and with such helpless ones against whom one has a lifetime of grievances for wrongs done or imagined, that provides the test of one's moral and human commitments."[52] Indeed, it may be easier to give care to those with whom we have less history and less deep relationships—to an unknown widow or orphan, or even to a recent immigrant to our country—than to a parent who has or may have done us wrong in our lives.

Both Father and Mother

Both parents are identified in the commandment, which is striking in the androcentric world of the Old Testament. Both Lev 27:7—referenced by Beer above—and Lev 27:3–4 value a woman less than a man: a male between the ages of twenty and sixty is valued at fifty shekels, and only at fifteen shekels

50. Harrelson, *The Ten Commandments*, 98.
51. Harrelson, *The Ten Commandments*, 98.
52. Harrelson, *The Ten Commandments*, 98.

when he is over sixty, but a female between twenty and sixty is valued at thirty shekels and only at ten shekels after she is sixty. (Though journalist Gay Talese's book *Honor Thy Father* identifies only one of the parents, the subject of the book is the Mafia; the titular "father" is the patriarch or "don" of an organized crime family.) A Jewish midrash explains that a person receives from each of his parents five parts of his body, which is why both mother and father are included in the commandment: bones, veins, nails, brain, and the white of the eye come from the father, while skin, flesh, blood, hair, and the pupil of the eye come from the mother. God gives each person breath, soul, light of countenance, sight, hearing, speech, touch, sense, insight, and understanding.[53]

The book of Proverbs—still in this androcentric world—tells the proverbial child to heed instruction and teaching from both father and mother (Prov 1:8; 6:20), and the oracle in Prov 31:1–9 is from King Lemuel's mother. In the Midrash Rabbah of Numbers, "Lemuel" is identified as Solomon,[54] which would make Bathsheba the mother of "Lemuel" and therefore as his mother responsible for teaching him wisdom. Rabbinic commentators suggest that the "instruction" or, in Hebrew, "torah" of your mother in Prov 1:8 is the "oral tradition" of torah, which complements the written torah and helps guide children on the proper path.[55] In the deuterocanonical book of Tobit, the title character tells his son, "My son, when I die, give me a proper burial. Honor your mother and do not abandon her all the days of her life. . . . Remember her, my son, because she faced many dangers for you while you were in her womb" (Tob 4:3–4). In comparison, Sir 7:27 instructs one to "honor your father and do not forget the birth pangs of your mother." So, while Tobit tells his son specifically to honor his mother after Tobit dies and the text from Sirach instructs honoring a father, both texts acknowledge a mother's potential dangers and pain in childbirth.

Though both parents are to be honored, according to the Ten Commandments, and "respected," according to Lev 19:3, the father is listed before the

53. Ginzberg and Stern, *Legends of the Jews*, 1:606.

54. "R. Ishmael said: on the selfsame night that Solomon completed the work of the Holy Temple he married Bathiah, the daughter of Pharaoh, and there was great jubilation on account of the Temple, and jubilation on account of Pharaoh's daughter, and the jubilation on account of Pharaoh's daughter exceeded that of the Temple; as the proverb says, 'Everybody flatters the king.' The reason why he was called Lemuel is because he cast off the yoke of the kingdom of heaven from his shoulders; as if to say, *Lammah lo el.*" *Midrash Rabbah Numbers*, trans. Judah Slotki (London: Soncino, 1983), 352. The Hebrew consonants form the letters of Lemuel's name; a literal translation of the phrase would be "why to him God," which is interpreted to mean, "why should there be to him—Solomon—what is divine?"

55. Sefaria, citing "Midrash Mishlei 1:7," Sefaria community translation, https://tinyurl.com/4b2v49w4.

mother in Exod 20:12 and Deut 5:16, but the mother is listed before the father in the passage in Leviticus. The Talmud offered the following reason compiled in Rif Kiddushin 12 b.7: a child will tend to honor a mother more than a father, because a mother speaks and "cajoles" with kind words, so the Ten Commandments put "father" before mother so we will not diminish the honor due him. A child will tend to respect a father more than a mother because fathers are the one to teach Torah, so Lev 19:3 puts "mother" before father when commanding respect, so we will not diminish the awe due to her.[56]

Seventeenth-century Puritan James Durham writes that if it was asked why the mother was added to the commandment, the answer is "because although the mother be not so qualified for the rule and government of the Children, yet she is no less entitled to their acknowledgment and this parental honour by the labour, toil, and tenderness of their birth and education. . . . She is added to show that it is not only the most eminent Superiour or Neighbour to whom honour is due, but even those who have more weakness, and especially the Mother."[57]

These receptions give varying reasons why a mother should be honored as well as a father; another reason is that Jesus modeled such honor to his own mother. Patrick Miller describes Jesus's words in John 19:26–27 as "an act of obedience to the commandment to honor father and mother. . . . The respectful son has now provided for the care of the mother."[58]

Honoring Parents and Confucianism

In 2022 in Hong Kong, the commandment to honor parents was appealed to when a primary school introduced a "filial piety" curriculum related to Chinese tradition. In the initiation ceremony for the curriculum, children cut their parents' nails and knelt to serve them tea, among other activities. Reporter Karen Wong explains that many in Hong Kong criticized what they saw as a way to compel children to blindly follow or unconditionally obey authority—a concern in Hong Kong since it was returned to China in 1997.[59] The

56. Cf. Rachel S. Mikva, *Broken Tablets: Restoring the Ten Commandments and Ourselves* (Woodstock, VT: Jewish Lights, 1999), 62.

57. James Durham, *The Law Unsealed, or, a practical exposition of the Ten Commandments. With a resolution of several momentous questions and cases of conscience*, Early English Books Online, https://tinyurl.com/phfsuw6v, 192.

58. Miller, *The Ten Commandments*, 218.

59. Karen Wong, "'Honoring' Your Father and Mother Isn't Always Biblical," *Christianity Today*, February 15, 2023, https://tinyurl.com/nardyza3.

school's principal defended the curriculum by referencing the commandment to "honor your father and mother," as well as Buddhist Master Hsing Yun's teaching about filial piety.[60] Wong examines the difference between Christian instruction to honor parents and traditional Confucian teaching about filial piety, arguing that the two are not the same: a parent's authority over their children is something God-given, and any human authority is ultimately accountable to God. Drawing on texts from Ephesians and Colossians, Wong concludes, "Neither practicing blind obedience nor demanding the same from others in our lives is godly."[61]

Theologian Daniel D. Lee places the commandment to honor parents in conversation with the commandment to have no other gods, reading them with a Confucian hermeneutic. Lee describes the tension between God and parents as the ultimate locus of authority in a Confucian framework, noting that even when one puts God first and parents second, certain Confucian values persist, often in the lived legacy of imperial neo-Confucianism. Lee is concerned for the theological implications of such practices, especially for one's relationship with and understanding of God. For example, Lee explains that when one's parent is seen as the embodiment of law, authority, and discipline within one's family, a relationship with that parent becomes legalistic. Lee writes, "This kind of filial piety would be a far cry from the covenantal relationship that God has with God's people with . . . wrestling and often lament."[62] Another example is when a parent's care and sacrifice demand that children respond with filial piety, such as when an "immigrant parent who has come to America, maybe working in excruciating conditions for their children . . . demands that their children respond in obedience, sacrifice, and outstanding academic achievement."[63] Lee points out that such links mean that "the love of parents is not necessarily free, it is part of a social contract. . . . All this becomes projected to God the parent."[64] Though writing in an Asian American context, Lee makes

60. Huang Xuzhi, "Fújiàn fùxiǎo xiàodào lǐ zāo wǎngmín pī yú xiào xiàozhǎng zhuànwén fǎnbó: Xià guì fèng chá shì zūnjìng fùmǔ" ("The filial piety etiquette of Fujian Affiliated Primary School was criticized by netizens for being foolish and filial. The principal wrote an article to refute: Kneeling down to serve tea is to respect your parents"), *Hong Kong 01*, September 5, 2022, https://tinyurl.com/4d9tdphs.

61. Wong, "'Honoring' Your Father and Mother Isn't Always Biblical."

62. Daniel D. Lee, "The First and Fifth Commandments: Confucian Family–Centricity in Asian American Hermeneutics," presentation at the Institute for Biblical Research, Asian-American Biblical Interpretation Research Group, San Antonio, TX, November 17, 2023, 7.

63. Lee, "The First and Fifth Commandments," 7–8.

64. Lee, "The First and Fifth Commandments," 8.

clear that he does "not believe that scripture offers ethnical casuistry" but points us toward concrete and actual encounters with God and that each person must attend to such divine encounters as they seek to express honoring parents.

Reciprocity

Lee is careful to caution against parental sacrifice being deployed as debt that children are then forced to repay. Certainly, the command to honor parents does focus on the child, but many receptions of this commandment suggest a level of reciprocity between children and parents. For example, in both Ephesians 6 and Colossians 3, parents are given clear instructions about treatment of children; after admonishing children to "obey your parents in the Lord" (Eph 6:1) and quoting the commandment to honor parents (Eph 6:2–3), the subsequent verse commands parents, "Do not provoke your children to anger, but bring them up in the discipline and instruction of the Lord" (Eph 6:4). Though Colossians 3 does not quote the commandment to honor parents, it otherwise has a similar message for both children and parents: "Children, obey your parents in everything, for this is your acceptable duty in the Lord. Fathers, do not provoke your children, or they may lose heart" (Col 3:20–21). The book of Malachi ends with a description of what will happen when Elijah returns before the day of the LORD: Elijah "will turn the hearts of parents to their children and the hearts of children to their parents, so that I will not come and strike the land with a curse" (Mal 4:5). Even if this is something supernatural—that is, that Elijah through God's power is the one turning their hearts rather than parents and children choosing to turn toward each other—there is still a level of reciprocity described between the generations.

Van der Toorn writes that, in ancient southwest Asian texts, a child's filial care of parents had the "counterpart" of a parent's love for their child. "Usually, however, this is not prescribed but considered a spontaneous affection. Thus, when Akkadian 'prophecies' want to convey the grimness of an impending famine, they will say that 'people will sell their children . . . mother will bar the door to daughter.'" In the same vein the *Epic of Erra* depicts how during a devastation "the son will not concern himself about the father, nor the father about the son; amid laughter the mother will plot her daughter's evil."[65] Care for parents by children and vice versa is so natural to ideals of flourishing in a society that its absence can only be imagined as an ominous sign.

65. Van der Toorn, *Sin and Sanction*, 14–15.

Thomas Watson's language, above, that honoring a parent meant "relieving parent's wants" reminded me of a friend who told me that in her family her father's wants and even whims were frequently elevated above the children's needs; when her father wanted to spend extra time at the museum, that's what they did, though the children needed to go get lunch. A level of reciprocity for wants and needs for both children and parents seems to be another ideal to strive for in family life. American Jewish writer and activist Leonard Fein connected reciprocity with "contingency," explaining that his own parents taught him to deprecate ascribed status in people, and it was better to give one's parents honor because and when they deserved it.[66] Again, there seems to be a balance in application of this commandment; parents are not given carte blanche for their actions toward their children and are not unconditionally entitled to demand that the children show them honor. But to make the honor entirely contingent on whether the parents deserve honor may push things too far in the other direction.

American country singer Collin Raye's 1998 song "The Eleventh Commandment" deals with the issue of child abuse. After singing about examples of parents harming their children, the lyrics first ask, "Did God overlook it, what ought have been written, The eleventh commandment: honor thy children?" After listing the commandments to not kill, steal, or take the Lord's name in vain, the song ends with the declarative, "Thou shalt not cause thy children pain / God does not overlook it what ought have been written / The eleventh commandment: honor thy children."

The First Commandment with a Promise

In Eph 6:2, the author describes the commandment to honor parents as "the first commandment with a promise," even though the commandment to not make idols in Exod 20:6 includes the clause that God will show steadfast love to those who love God and keep the commandments. As mentioned in the first sentence in this chapter, the promise in this commandment in Exod 20:12 and Deut 5:16 is that "your days will be long in the land the LORD your God is giving you." Other references to long days occur in Deut 6:2; 32:45–47, where a person is admonished to observe general "laws and commandments" to

66. Leonard Fein, "I Was Young, and I Have Also Grown Older," in *Broken Tablets: Restoring the Ten Commandments and Ourselves*, ed. Rachel S. Mikva (Woodstock, VT: Jewish Lights, 1999), 66.

lengthen their days. God gives a specific promise to Solomon in 1 Kgs 3:14 to lengthen his days if Solomon will walk in God's ways and keep God's statutes and commandments. The promise gets expanded in Deuteronomy's version of the commandment; not only will one's days be long, but "it may go well with you in the land" (Deut 5:16); J. J. Stamm describes this as a strengthening and enriching of the pledge for long life.[67]

Other receptions of this commandment express the benefit in different ways. Sirach 3:5 promises that those who honor their father will have joy in their children, and their prayer will be heard by God. Aquinas declares that five "desirable things" are promised to those who honor their parents: (1) grace in the present life and glory in the life to come, (2) life, (3) grateful and pleasing children, (4) a good name, and (5) wealth.[68]

Luther states as the fruit and reward of this commandment that the one who keeps it will not only live many years but will also "have everything that should go with long life, such as health, wife and offspring, peace, good government, etc. without which this life can neither be happily enjoyed nor continue for long."[69] Then after describing the benefits of honoring parents, Luther details the pitfalls of disobedience, saying, "So if you do not want to obey father and mother nor let yourself be properly brought up by them, then go ahead and obey the hangman, and if not the hangman than the reaper Death. God, in short, insists that you obey Him, love Him, and serve Him, in which case He will richly reward you with every kind of good thing; but if you anger Him, He will send both death and the hangman after you."[70] Obviously, Luther's language here conflates honoring parents with obedience to them and also conflates such obedience of parents with obedience to God.

Hauerwas and Willimon declare, "If you are uneasy about this commandment's promise of blessing and reward for those who are obedient, get over it. It is either the good news or the bad news of the Decalogue that our actions have

67. Johann Jacob Stamm, with M. E. Andrew, *The Ten Commandments in Recent Research* (London: SCM, 1967), 14. "Both the sanctification of the sabbath and the honouring of parents are strengthened in Deuteronomy by the sentence: 'as Yahweh your God commanded you.' . . . [God] has enriched the pledge of long life in the promised land with the words: 'and that it may go well with you.'"

68. Aquinas, *The Commandments of God: Conferences on the Two Precepts of Charity and the Ten Commandments*, trans. Laurence Shapcote, OP, with an introduction by Thomas Gilby, OP (London: Burns, Oates & Washbourne, 1937), 52–54.

69. Martin Luther, *Luther's Large Catechism with Study Questions*, ed. F. Samuel Janzow (St. Louis: Concordia, 1978), 34.

70. Luther, *Large Catechism*, 34.

consequences. . . . God takes note of obedience and is willing to stoop even to reward."[71] If the language of God being "willing to stoop" to give rewards seems less certain, they also give an example of a woman who gives sacrificial care to her mother during the mother's final days and assert that even when the world will not reward the woman, "God rewards."[72] They conclude that honoring parents ought to be done in worship of God rather than in expectation of reward, but, for most people, God will graciously give long and happy lives to those who obey.[73]

Who Else Is to Be Honored?

Van der Toorn explains how in ancient southwest Asia, the first encounter with hierarchy was in the family, so submissiveness to parents could be considered paradigmatic of all other relationships of authority and obedience.[74] As an example, King Esarhaddon described moral evils in Babylon before he established his rule by relating children's disrespect of parents to a slave's disobedience: "The son cursed his father in the street, the slave [did not obey] his master, [the slave girl] did not heed [the command] of her mistress."[75] Using the strong simile that children will "serve" (Greek *douleusei*) their parents as "masters" (Greek *despotais*), Sir 3:7 explicitly connects the honor and respect due parents with that of slaves/servants to their owners/masters/despots.

There is a long Christian tradition of receiving this commandment to honor parents as extending broadly to a whole range of Christian social relationships between superiors and inferiors: teachers and hearers, ministers and congregants, benefactors and patrons. For example, seventeenth-century Puritan Durham wrote that father and mother "are here to be largely and synecdochically understood" as all superiors "in church or common-wealth" such as both "supreme and subaltern" magistrates, ministers, teachers, or overseers, "in a word, any sort of eminence [that puts] one in that role of Fathers largely taken, though they not be properly such."[76] Watson writes "Father is of different kinds: the political, the ancient, the spiritual, the domestic, and

71. Hauerwas and Willimon, *The Truth about God*, 77.
72. Hauerwas and Willimon, *The Truth about God*, 77.
73. Hauerwas and Willimon, *The Truth about God*, 78.
74. Van der Toorn, *Sin and Sanction*, 13.
75. Van der Toorn, *Sin and Sanction*, 14.
76. Durham, *The Law Unsealed*, 191–92.

the natural."[77] Calvin assumes that leaders—"those whom God has placed over us"—have been put in their positions through God's will, writing, "It makes no difference whether our superiors are worthy or unworthy of this honor, for whatever they are they have attained their position through God's providence—a proof that the Lawgiver himself would have us hold them in honor."[78] Again, any reception is influenced by its setting and context. Those who were part of the Magisterial Reformation like Luther and Calvin were supported by secular authorities such as princes or magistrates, and they experienced positive things in their submission to political authority. Those in the Radical Reformation—and so many others in history—who were persecuted and punished by governmental authorities would find it harder to swallow this reception of the commandment.

Marilynne Robinson's first-person narrator of *Gilead*, John Ames, declares, "The old commentators usually say 'your father and mother' means anyone in authority over you, but that is the way people thought for a long time and a lot of harm came from it."[79] As an example, John Winthrop, the leading figure in founding the Massachusetts Bay Colony, and its first governor, organized the colony along loosely theocratic lines: voting citizenship was only for white men in good standing with the colony's official church. When a faction within the colony pushed for more democratic representation and some restriction from what they perceived as arbitrary rulings from magistrates—such as an incident involving possession of a runaway pig—Winthrop condemned democracy as "the meanest and worst of all forms of government" and specifically as a violation of the commandment to honor father and mother. Though the Puritans were themselves dissident Anglicans, Winthrop understood government as that which united church and state, but government would not tolerate dissent.

Additionally, though it was the norm after the Protestant Reformation to apply the commandment to honor parents to a range of hierarchical relationships, other and different receptions of this commandment still occurred. For example, in Thomas Solme's treatise printed in Antwerp in 1540, he wrote that the commandment "is a particulere commaundement for the carnall father & sone, and by nomens can suffere an allegory or popysche morall"; as the last

77. Watson, *Body of Divinity*, 311. For an overview of these perspectives, cf. John P. Burgess, "Reformed Explication of the Ten Commandments," in *The Ten Commandments: The Reciprocity of Faithfulness*, ed. William P. Brown, Library of Theological Ethics (Louisville: Westminster John Knox, 2004), 78–99.

78. Calvin, *Institutes*, 402.

79. Robinson, *Gilead*, 135.

example indicates, Solme was particularly critical of the category of "spiritual father" when it was applied to the papacy.[80] Overall, however, interpreters expanded the number of individuals in named offices and categories to whom this commandment was deemed to apply.

Historian Jonathan Willis asserts that during the Reformation in England, authors "enlarged the scope of the commandment in ways which had the effect of significantly diluting the very principle of authority they sought to describe."[81] For example, in 1606 John Brinsley explained that this commandment was instituted by God "for preserving the honour and dignitie which he hath bestowed upon everyone," with special duties owed "towards equalls" and "ourselves."[82] In William Whatley's *Pithie, Short, and Methodicall opening of the Ten Commandements* from 1622, he asserted that the commandment applied both to self and to others, requiring people to take notice of their place and duties, as well as relating with virtue and kindness to others.[83] Willis writes, "In other words, the injunction to honour mother and father was taken by some . . . to create a binding code of conduct which applied to every conceivable human relationship, even with oneself."[84]

Thomas Mann wrote that the commandment to honor father and mother had a wider meaning than anyone suspected at first, that it should be extended to anyone old enough to be your parents, to anyone who had "a gray head." But Mann also connected the commandment to honor parents with the subsequent commandment to not murder, writing, "The only consolation was that since your neighbor was not permitted to kill you, you had a reasonable prospect of becoming yourself old and gray, so that the others would have to arise before you."[85] Polish director Krystof Kieślowski's "Four," in his series *Dekalog*, tells the story of a young adult who must negotiate her relationship with her father after learning that he, in fact, was not her biological father.

Bruno Frank's short novel, "Honor Thy Father and Mother," published in 1944 as part of the collection subtitled *Ten Short Novels of Hitler's War*

80. Jonathan Willis, *The Reformation of the Decalogue: Religious Identity and the Ten Commandments in England, c. 1485–1625* (Cambridge: Cambridge University Press, 2017), 91.

81. Willis, *The Reformation of the Decalogue*, 93.

82. Willis, *The Reformation of the Decalogue*, 93.

83. William Whatley, *A pithie, short, and methodicall opening of the Ten commandements.* London: Printed by John Haviland for Thomas Pauier and Leonard Greene, 1622, Early English Books Online, https://tinyurl.com/yc58ervc, 97–102.

84. Willis, *The Reformation of the Decalogue*, 94.

85. Thomas Mann, "Thou Shalt Have No Other Gods Before Me," trans. George R. Marek, in *The Ten Commandments: Ten Short Novels of Hitler's War against the Moral Code*, ed. Armin. L. Robinson (New York: Simon & Schuster, 1944), 47.

against the Moral Code, tells the fictional story of a family whose father is promoted within the Nazi party. At one point in the story, the daughter gets in a fierce argument with her father, and then waits for him to argue back. But, as Frank writes,

> the Standartenführer did not raise his voice to remind his daughter of the dictates of the fifth commandment. Nothing was so emphatically, so furiously, denied by the new state, nothing was so violently stamped out of the heart of German youth as filial devotion. "Honour thy father and thy mother"—to the ears of German boys and girls the words had a feeble-minded, idiotic, in fact, a treasonable quality. Today's commandment was: "Honor thy Führer and thy state, and sacrifice to them thy parents. Spy upon them, for they are suspect, watch them, threaten them. Report them—that is not only permitted; it is thy duty. Deliver them unto bondage, to the lash of the gaoler, or unto the hangman. Thou canst not, if it serves thy party and thy state, commit an injustice to thy father and thy mother."[86]

The double negative in that last sentence communicates that someone can commit an injustice to one's father and mother, the opposite of the positive commandment to honor one's parents. In the story, the father himself is informed on by his son, a leader in Hitler's youth, and is killed. Though this rather bleak tale may be an extreme reception of how the commandment to honor parents gets broken, the quote above indicates how loyalty to family could compete with loyalty to government and other authorities.

Conclusion

Again, relationships between children and parents are complicated in life as well as in the Bible. David Hazony references how Abraham abandoned his father's home and religion (Gen 11:31–12:4) and how Absalom challenged David's rule (2 Samuel 15–18), concluding, "Looking at the Bible alone, the Fifth Commandment remains something of a mystery."[87] In addition to the complicated stories and relationships—Rachel taking the household idols of

86. Bruno Frank, "Honor Thy Father and Thy Mother," in *The Ten Commandments: Ten Short Novels of Hitler's War against the Moral Code*, ed. Armin L. Robinson (New York: Simon & Schuster, 1944), 202.

87. Hazony, *The Ten Commandments*, 115.

her father Laban, Jacob tricking Isaac into giving him the blessing—the relationship between Ruth and Naomi demonstrates a level of covenantal love and loyalty, which is notable especially because this mother and daughter are related through marriage, not through biology. It may be helpful to point to these extreme biblical cases as exemplary both of what not to do, or what to do, in honoring parents. But it may also be helpful to consider what it looks like to honor parents in mundane situations of everyday life. Though complicated and challenging, there is, after all, the promise of a reward.

6

"Don't Kill"

On the back of Neal Shusterman's 2016 young adult novel *Scythe* in large font are the words "Thou Shalt Kill." This is the first of the Ten Commandments for the "Scythedom," a group in the novel tasked with keeping the population in check in a world and time when advances in technology have given effective immortality to humans.[1] In this fictional setting, death is reversible; a person who dies because of illness or accidents will get revived, so the population would grow beyond the capacity of the earth to support it without the professional reapers (Scythes) who randomly kill (or "glean"). When a Scythe kills someone, it is permanent. I was reminded of the premise of this novel when I read a student's opinion that the commandment to not kill is the most important one, because killing is a permanent act. First-century Jewish philosopher Philo also emphasized that killing is especially unjust because the act is irreversible.[2]

Obviously, the biblical commandment states the exact opposite from Shusterman with its declaration, "you shall not kill" (Exod 20:13 and Deut 5:17). This is the first of the very brief commandments, with only two Hebrew words,

1. The full list of Scythedom commandments is as follows: "1) Thou shalt kill; 2) Thou shalt kill with no bias, bigotry, or malice aforethought; 3) Thou shalt grant an annum of immunity to the beloved of those who accept your coming, and to anyone else you deem worthy; 4) Thou shalt kill the beloved of those who resist; 5) Thou shalt serve humanity for the full span of thy days, and thy family shall have immunity as recompense for as long as you live; 6) Thou shalt lead an exemplary life in word and deed, and keep a journal of each and every day; 7) Thou shalt kill no scythe beyond thyself; 8) Thou shalt claim no earthly possessions, save thy robes, ring, and journal; 9) Thou shalt have neither spouse nor spawn; 10) Thou shalt be beholden to no laws beyond these." Neal Shusterman, *Scythe* (New York: Simon & Schuster, 2016), 67.

2. Philo considers every attack of a human being against another human being as unjust; but the irreversibility of death heightens the injustice in killing. J. Cornelius De Vos, "Murder as Sacrilege: Philo of Alexandria on the Prohibition of Killing," in *"You Shall Not Kill": The Prohibition of Killing in Ancient Religions and Cultures*, ed. J. Cornelius de Vos, Hermut Löhr, and Juliane Ta Van (Göttingen: Vandenhoeck and Ruprecht, 2018), 149.

but though it may seem like a simple and even absolute prohibition against (all) killing, many questions have been generated throughout reception history. Does the commandment forbid any and every type of killing? What about when killing is commanded by a government, such as in wars or capital punishment? Does God sanction killing? Is this commandment limited to forbidding the act of taking a person's life, or could it include other less literal ways we engage in dealing death, such as killing someone's reputation or even killing hopes and dreams? Of course, reception history will also offer a variety of answers to these questions, but most—even Shusterman—agree that the sanctity of life is of ultimate importance.

Murder or Kill

So much conversation about this commandment revolves around how to translate the verb *rāṣaḥ*: "murder" or "kill"? The word only appears forty-six times in the Hebrew Bible, in contrast with other analogous words for causing death: *hārag* ("to kill")[3] occurs 165 times and *hēmît* ("to put to death") (the Hiphil of *mût*) 201 times.[4] The latter two are used in contexts that describe killing a personal or political enemy, including killing in battle; killing one punishable according to the law; and even death as God's judgment. In contrast, *rāṣaḥ* is used to describe killing only a personal enemy, not a political or national one. So, while there is some overlap between terms for killing, *rāṣaḥ* only once—in Num 35:30—refers to killing someone who is guilty of breaking the law, and it is never used to describe killing in the context of war.[5]

The word *rāṣaḥ* is rarely used in biblical law: it only appears in the Ten Commandments in Exodus, not at all in Leviticus, and in Numbers and Deuteronomy it occurs in reference to the cities of refuge, places to which a "murderer" can flee (e.g., Num 35:6, 11, 12; Deut 4:42; 19:3, 4; these cities and instructions about them are also mentioned in Joshua 20). In addition to describing the cities of refuge, Numbers 35 and Deuteronomy 19 also clarify what type of

3. This is the word used in Eccl 3:3, which proclaims, "there is a time to kill," so technically, the commandment "you shall not kill" does not contradict the statement in Eccl 3:3.

4. At least ten Hebrew words get translated as "kill": in addition to the three mentioned above, *zābaḥ*, *ḥālāl*, *ṭābaḥ*, *nākâ*, *qāṭal*, and *šāḥaṭ* are all translated in some verse as "kill."

5. Johann Jacob Stamm, *The Ten Commandments in Recent Research* (London: SCM, 1967), 98–99. As discussed later in the chapter, many other receptions come to similar conclusions: that the commandment allows for killing in war and state-sanctioned killing as punishment for crimes.

killing would be punished by death—when one strikes someone with a weapon of stone or wood that could cause death—that is, "murder" (*rāṣaḥ*), and the one who caused death with the weapon will be killed. But if a person causes death by pushing someone suddenly without enmity (Num 35:22), or unintentionally drops a stone on a person (Num 35:23), or is in the forest to chop wood and swings his axe and the axe head flies off and kills another (Deut 19:5), then even though that person is a "murderer" (*roṣeaḥ*; Deut 19:6), he can flee to the city of refuge and be safe therein. Jonathan Burnside comments, "The laws of asylum illustrate how biblical law tries to strike a balance between harm and culpability. Asylum is available in the case of the 'spur of the moment' but not the premeditated killing. However, in biblical law, even an accidental killing can be treated as seriously as murder. Biblical law takes seriously the value of human life—both the value of the victim's life and the need to protect the life of the offender, in certain circumstances."[6]

If we limit our understanding of this commandment to simply the verb itself as it gets used within the legal material of the Hebrew Bible, it seems to be prohibiting a specific and certain kind of killing of another person. Johann Stamm suggests, "The life of the Israelite was protected in this way from illegal impermissible violence. The commandment thus has its place in a community in which capital punishment exists and war is permitted or even sometimes commanded."[7] But, of course, the rub in reception history is that it is not limited only to the context of the legal material or even the context of the Hebrew Bible. We read this commandment as it looks backward to discussions about death in Genesis and forward into Jesus's association of killing with anger (Matt 5:21–22). We also read this commandment in our historical time, knowing that "an itemized total sum of deaths in wars and conflicts during the 20th century of those killed or allowed to die by human decision is approximately 231 million,"[8] a number that cannot capture the calculus of suffering, grief, and loss of those whose loved ones died, a number that does not include those killed in the twenty-first century through mass shootings, terrorist attacks, and numerous "invasions" (if not outright "wars").

The word *rāṣaḥ* appears in very few narratives: in the passive form, it describes the Levite's concubine as "the woman who was murdered" (Judg 20:4). Her death—a culmination of the horrific events in Judges 19—is a clear

6. Jonathan P. Burnside, *God, Justice, and Society: Aspects of Law and Legality in the Bible* (Oxford: Oxford University Press, 2010), 283.

7. Stamm, *The Ten Commandments in Recent Research*, 99.

8. Milton Leitenberg, "Deaths in Wars and Conflicts in the 20th Century," Cornell University Peace Studies Program Occasional Paper #29, 3rd ed. (2006), 9.

violation of the commandment. And God says that King Ahab "murdered" Naboth for his vineyard in 1 Kgs 21:19;[9] that chapter contains the story of multiple commandments being broken, including the commandment to not bear false witness and the commandment to not covet, as will be discussed later in this book.

When the Septuagint translates the commandment in Exodus and Numbers, it uses the Greek word *phoneuō*, which more often gets translated as "kill" than "murder" but has the connotation of violence and brutality. When commenting on the commandment, Philo uses the word *androphonein*, specifying that this is about killing a human, but also uses the words *phonos* and *kteinein* ("to kill"). J. Cornelius De Vos writes that Philo does not make a distinction between killing and murder "in a modern legal way in which murder is restricted to a series of well-defined very severe forms of killing," for Philo uses all three Greek words synonymously.[10] Josephus, like Philo, also uses the word *phonos*. Silvia Castelli explains that in Greek law, *phonos* "is generally divided at least into the two categories of *phonos akousios*, 'unintentional murder,' and *hekousios* 'intentional murder,'" but Josephus does not specify if the commandment only concerns intentional murder.[11] Castelli also writes that Josephus "is merely interested in the general principle, postponing any specific case to the Mosaic constitution."[12] In many ways, that sentence is a perfect description of how reception history on the Ten Commandments notes the general principle in each commandment in Exodus and Deuteronomy, and only later observes specific cases in biblical law, narrative, and subsequent commentary.

Wilma Bailey discusses the history of English translations of the commandment, noting how earlier translations use "kill" and later ones "murder," though she also notes that Roman Catholic Bibles consistently translate *rāṣaḥ* as "kill." Bailey argues that "kill" is a better translation for the commandment because it is more general and inclusive than "murder"; she suggests that many people are complicit in killing when, for example, they vote for certain leaders or policies.[13] Similarly, Joy Davidman writes that to translate

9. The prophet Elisha's description of the king of Israel in 2 Kgs 6:32 as the "son of a murderer" could be referencing Ahab as the murderer.

10. De Vos, "Murder as Sacrilege," 144.

11. Silvia Castelli, "Murder and Murder Prohibition in Josephus," in *"You Shall Not Kill": The Prohibition of Killing in Ancient Religions and Cultures*, ed. J. Cornelius de Vos, Hermut Löhr, and Juliane Ta Van (Göttingen: Vandenhoeck and Ruprecht, 2018), 163.

12. Castelli, "Murder and Murder Prohibition in Josephus," 163.

13. Wilma Ann Bailey, *"You Shall Not Kill" or "You Shall Not Murder"? The Assault on a Biblical Text* (Collegeville, MN: Liturgical Press, 2005), 81.

the commandment as "you shall not murder" is "too obvious, too limited a prohibition, perhaps, for our own time, with its increased awareness of the sanctity of human life—and its morbid fear of death."[14] Later in the same chapter, Davidman writes that people commit "murders by willful negligence or omission—hit-run drivers, say, or company directors who save money on safeguards and send miners to agonizing death. . . . Anyone who studies our poisonous drugs, our denatured food, our deathtrap automobiles and houses, our lung-rotting cities, must conclude that we accept a good deal of murder as inevitable simply because it is done to make or save money."[15] So, while Davidman seems to advocate for the use of the word "kill" rather than "murder" because the latter might be limited to acts of intentional killing, her language in her examples expands the understanding of "murder" to make it more broad. I see the value in translating *rāṣaḥ* as "murder" because it is more specific and limited than all the other Hebrew words translated as "kill," and so "murder" is how I would translate the word in the commandment. Yet I also agree with those who resist translating the word as "murder" because it is legally limited to an act committed with malice or premeditation and so admit that the word "kill" better reflects certain receptions of the commandment. Therefore I will tend to quote the commandment as "thou shalt not murder," even though I will also discuss situations that are more properly or legally understood as "kill."

Why Not?

Many receptions of the commandment appeal to Gen 9:6 as an explanation of why murder is prohibited; the verse declares, "The one who sheds the blood of a human, by a human his blood will be shed, for God made humans in God's image." For example, Rabbi Akiva says, "Whoever spills blood, behold, that person causes the image [of God] to be diminished, as it is said, 'One who sheds a man's blood, by a man his blood shall be shed, [for God made man in His image]'" (Tosefta Yebamot 8:5). Abarbanel did not specifically reference Gen 9:6 but alluded to it when teaching that the commandments parallel each other, saying, "Five on one tablet and five on the other. It is written, 'I am the Lord your God,' and opposite it, 'You shall not murder'—since spilling blood is tan-

14. Joy Davidman, *Smoke on the Mountain: An Interpretation of the Ten Commandments* (Philadelphia: Westminster, 1954), 73.

15. Davidman, *Smoke on the Mountain*, 78.

tamount to diminishing the likeness [of God]."[16] Seventeenth-century English Puritan Thomas Watson's comment is representative of many; he writes, "Life is the most precious thing; and God has set this commandment as a fence about it, to preserve it. He made a statute which has never to this day been repealed. 'Whose sheddeth man's blood, by man shall his blood be shed' (Gen 9:6)."[17]

Only Humans

Biblical scholar Karlheinz Rabast offers a more expansive translation of Exod 20:13: in German, it is "Du sollst nicht einen Menschen an seiner Seele töten." A wooden translation would be, "you shall not kill a person of his soul/life."[18] Another translation would be, "You shall not kill a person in their person." Rabast seems to have taken some license in this, his personal translation of the commandment; he does not say as much, but perhaps he alludes to Lev 24:17, which states that any person who kills the soul/life (*npš*) of a human (*ʾdm*) will surely die. Both Rabast's language about a "person" and the specification in Lev 24:17 of a "human" seem to suggest another reception of the commandment: that it does not apply to animals, only humans.

The prohibition on killing as restricted to humans is exemplified in Aquinas's explanation that "in the natural order plants are intended for the nourishment of animals; some animals for the nourishment of others; and all for the nourishment of man. . . . The sense [of the commandment] is then *Thou shalt not kill men*."[19] Seventeenth-century Scottish minister John Durham wrote that

16. Sefaria, citing "Abarbanel on Torah, Exodus 20:13," Sefaria Community Translation, https://tinyurl.com/25ukbepn.

17. Thomas Watson, *Body of Divinity: Contained in Sermons upon the Assembly's Catechism* (Grand Rapids: Baker, 1979), 307. Lancelot Andrewes uses similar reasoning as he explains, "Thou must not deface the image of God which thy neighbor beareth." *A Pattern of Catechistical Doctrine*, 219. Matthew Henry writes, "The sixth commandment concerns our own and our neighbour's life (v. 13): '*Thou shalt not kill;* thou shalt not do any thing hurtful or injurious to the health, ease, and life, of thy own body, or any other person's unjustly.' This is one of the laws of nature, and was strongly enforced by the precepts given to Noah and his sons, Gen. 9:5, 6."

18. Karlheinz Rabast, *Das Apodiktische Recht im Deuteronomium und im Heiligkeitsgesetz* (Berlin-Hermsdorf: Heimatdienstverlag, 1949), 35. In commenting on this translation, Stamm suggests that Rabast has added the Hebrew word *npš* to the commandment. *The Ten Commandments in Recent Research*, 20. Any distinction between a person's "soul" and "physical body" would not be implied by the Hebrew word; the point is to emphasize the death.

19. Thomas Aquinas, *The Commandments of God: Conferences on the Two Precepts of*

the commandment "cannot be considered as relating to beasts, as if they were not to be killed, because God gave man all the beasts for his use to feed on them (Gen 9:3)."[20] Yet Durham clarifies that a person may "offend" by "breaking out into anger and passion at brutes, as when a horse rideth not well, a Dog runneth not well, a hawk flyeth not well, etc." or by "striking a beast" with unreasonableness, cruelty, or bitterness, as Balaam did when he hit his donkey.[21] Even in these readings that imply human exceptionalism, there are ethical limits with regard to treatment of animals, which might suggest limits in killing animals.

It may not be surprising that more ancient receptions do limit this commandment to humans; scholarly receptions today tend to be silent on the issue, though the Light of the Spirit Monastery (Atma Jyoti Ashram) located in New Mexico teaches that the killing of animals is prohibited by the commandment, explaining, "'You shall not take life' is the command. An integral part of life is *consciousness*, so we can never take conscious life—that is, any form of life above plant life (and we should respect the lives of plants as well)."[22] Again, how the commandment is translated would affect its reception: if it refers to all "killing," it could include killing of animals for food. Many omnivores would be loath to say that they are engaging in "murder" by eating meat, though Morrissey, animal protector and vegetarian lead singer of the British band the Smiths, emphasized the moral complexity to eating animals in the band's 1985 song "Meat Is Murder."

War

Philo, though fundamentally opposed to killing, rarely discusses the wars in the Bible and often skips or allegorizes them. His stance on killing in warfare is somewhat ambivalent. J. Cornelius DeVos explains, "The Pentateuch forces [Philo] to be ambivalent. It states that God created humans in his own image, and reports on the use of death penalty and killings from religious

---

Charity and the Ten Commandments, trans. Laurence Shapcote, OP, with an introduction by Thomas Gilby, OP (London: Burns, Oates & Washbourne LTD, 1937), 57.

20. James Durham, *The Law Unsealed, or, a practical exposition of the Ten Commandments. With a resolution of several momentous questions and cases of conscience*, Early English Books Online, https://tinyurl.com/phfsuw6v, 109.

21. Durham, *The Law Unsealed*, 109.

22. Light of the Spirit Monastery, "Thou Shalt Not Kill," *Original Christianity*, https://tinyurl.com/2tenhk2y.

zeal."[23] Philo was neither the first nor the last in reception history to observe tensions between these things: first, that humans are created in God's image and therefore to kill another human is to deface God's image; and second, killing is sanctioned as a punishment, and God's faithful people fight and kill in many wars.

In addition to reviewing English translations and their use of "murder" or "kill," Bailey also reviews denominational statements on war and peace. She finds that, in general, before the 1940s, when denominations quote from Exod 20:13, they use the term "kill" and argue that Christians may not participate in war. But after the 1940s, because of the influence of the World Wars, they use the term "murder." For example, in April of 1917, the Assemblies of God adopted a resolution that cites "you shall not kill" and states, "We cannot conscientiously participate in war and armed resistance which involves the actual destruction of human life since this is contrary to our view of the clear teachings of the inspired Word of God, which is the sole basis of our faith." The California Evangelistic Association states in their "Article XVII: Relation to War" from 1939, "Whereas, our Bible teaches us 'Thou shalt not kill,' therefore be it resolved that in the time of war, we shall be glad to be of service to our government in any way consistent with non-combative service."[24] Similar language is found from Holiness leader John Alexander Dowie during the Boer War in 1900. Referencing the commandment, he argues, "We feel that all War is wrong, and that without exceptions. It is sinful for Christian men to fight and destroy life. We read that the command of God is: 'thou shalt not kill.' No human or demoniacal sophistry can every justify murder in any form especially for the members of the Christian Catholic Church who stand on each side, whom we have earnestly exhorted not to fight. We are willing that our people should go, if need be, on the firing line to remove the wounded and dying, and to minister to them."[25]

The managing editor of the periodical *The Foursquare Crusader*, Pastor C. W. Philleo, titled his 1938 article "Should a Christian Take Up Arms in Time of War?" He writes, "The question is perhaps, a little late. It already has been answered—IN THE BIBLE. Until the Ten Commandments are repealed the

23. J. Cornelius De Vos, "Murder as Sacrilege: Philo of Alexandria on the Prohibition of Killing," in *"You Shall Not Kill": The Prohibition of Killing in Ancient Religions and Cultures*, ed. J. Cornelius de Vos, Hermut Löhr, and Juliane Ta Van (Göttingen: Vandenhoeck and Ruprecht, 2018), 157.

24. Jay Beaman and Brian K. Pipkin, eds., *Pentecostal and Holiness Statements on War and Peace* (Eugene, OR: Pickwick, 2013), 149.

25. Beaman and Pipkin, *Pentecostal and Holiness Statements*, 26–27.

Christian has no alternative but to stay aloof from war and its consequent destruction of human life."[26]

However, in 1968, the Assemblies of God—which in 1917 quoted from Exod 20:13 in their resolution against involvement in war—describes Exod 20:13 as follows: "The Hebrew word used here in the ancient manuscripts is descriptive of an act of willful and personal vengeance. While the outcome may be similar to the killings of war, the motive and driving force are quite different. The language of Exodus 20:13 does not suggest that we are to disallow participation in war, even if that participation involves killing."[27] The double negative in their statement demonstrates that in 1968 the Assemblies of God received this commandment as suggesting that participation in war is allowed. Similarly, in a 1975 *Christianity Today* article titled "Can a Christian Go to War?," George W. Knight argues that the commandment is limited to murder and therefore would not apply to killing in war.

Christian shifts in their receptions about the commandment's application to war had already occurred in the fourth century. Anders-Christian Jacobsen observes that the church fathers interpreted the commandment as a total prohibition against killing other humans but were mostly silent about a Christian's participation in warfare. He points out that such silence is to be expected in the pre-Constantinian era when Christians are a minority without political power and responsibility. Jacobsen writes, "As soon as Christians begin to take part in the political power, the theologians start rethinking the prohibition about taking part in wars and as a consequence of that also the total prohibition against killing human beings."[28] Augustine's "Just War" theory, for example, came after Constantine.

Journalist Chris Hedges was a war correspondent for several decades, covering conflicts in Central America, Europe, and the Middle East. Hedges interviews a Vietnam veteran, who tells him, "I violated the commandment, 'Thou Shalt Not Kill.' Nothing will be gained by intellectualizing this. I killed

26. Beaman and Pipkin, *Pentecostal and Holiness Statements*, 174. A number of these statements from Pentecostal and Holiness traditions also state that Christians should not hold government in contempt, but must not engage in warfare because of Exod 20:13.

27. Murray Dempster, "Pacifism in Pentecostalism: The Case of the Assemblies of God," in *The Fragmentation of the Church and Its Unity in Peacekeeping*, ed. Jeffrey Gros and John D. Rempel (Grand Rapids: Eerdmans, 2001), 138.

28. Anders-Christian Jacobsen, "The Prohibition of Killing in the Ethics of the Church Fathers," in *"You Shall Not Kill": The Prohibition of Killing in Ancient Religions and Cultures*, ed. J. Cornelius de Vos, Hermut Löhr, and Juliane Ta Van (Göttingen: Vandenhoeck and Ruprecht, 2018), 265.

other people. I took lives. It was exactly that."[29] Hedges writes, "There is a difference between killing someone who is trying to kill you and killing someone who does not have the power to harm you. The first is killing. The second is murder. But murder, in insurgencies like Vietnam and Iraq, often becomes more common than killing."[30] Hedges is quite sympathetic to veteran soldiers and "the terrible wounds, visible and invisible"[31] they sustain during war. His position against war is clear, and he criticizes religious institutions "whose texts are unequivocal about murder" but have "failed to address in times of war the sinful state of war."[32]

Capital Punishment

The question of the death penalty in the Bible is complicated by the fact that the same word is used in the commandment to prohibit killing and to instruct killing, as in Numbers 35 and Deuteronomy 19. Most scholars acknowledge that the commandment does not rule out death as a punishment for crimes. Many other verses in the Old Testament—including other legal texts—are drawn upon as evidence that death sentences occurred in ancient Israelite culture. Johannes Schocks distinguishes between receptions that allow for biblical laws about capital punishment because of the social and cultural contexts of the world of the text and those that legitimize the death penalty through theological justifications. In other words, if capital punishment is part and parcel of the social domain of the world of the text it can be explained more easily, but death penalties prescribed by God are "highly problematic for interpretation."[33]

29. Chris Hedges, *Losing Moses on the Freeway: The Ten Commandments in America* (New York: Free Press, 2005), 104–5.

30. Hedges, *Losing Moses on the Freeway*, 108–9.

31. Hedges, *Losing Moses on the Freeway*, 107.

32. Hedges, *Losing Moses on the Freeway*, 109.

33. Johannes Schnocks, "When God Commands Killing: Reflections on Execution and Human Sacrifice in the Old Testament," in *"You Shall Not Kill": The Prohibition of Killing in Ancient Cultures and Religions*, ed. J. Cornelius de Vos, Helmut Löhr, and Juliane Ta Van (Göttingen: Vandenhoeck & Ruprecht, 2018), 124. He writes, "The results for the Book of the Covenant and the Deuteronomic law point toward the social domain, even though these bodies of law are fundamentally divinely legitimized. In Priestly texts in Leviticus and Numbers, in contrast, arguments can be found in which death sentences for murderers could be prescribed in the context of cultic ideas of purity, i.e. within theological concepts." These Priestly texts, for Schnocks, are the difficult ones.

Of course, because the world of the text does include theological permission for killing, making very clear distinctions may be easier said than done.

Martin Luther, in his *Large Catechism*, asserts that neither God nor the government is included in the commandment; thus, it only applies to individual humans.[34] The implication is that if God kills, it would not break the commandment, nor would a government break the commandment by punishing someone with death. As mentioned in the previous chapter, Luther, as part of the Magisterial Reformation, was both supported by and supportive of the state. British Puritan Lancelot Andrewes has a similar interpretation, reasoning that because the commandment is addressed to private individuals, the government can put people to death, especially "if any one part be so corrupt that that it endangereth the whole."[35]

More recent receptions, however, do use the commandment to argue that capital punishment would be included in the type of killing prohibited. For example, Polish filmmaker Krzysztof Kieślowski's film *Dekalog: Five* depicts a brutal murder and the subsequent punishment for the murderer through a legal execution. The lawyer for the perpetrator argues for the immorality of the death penalty but is forced to witness the execution of his guilty client. The final scene in the film shows the lawyer sitting in his car, repeating in anguish, "I abhor it, I abhor it."

In an op-ed for the *New York Times* in 2019, written shortly after an execution in Tennessee, journalist Margaret Renkl identifies her own reason for wanting to end the death penalty: "As a Christian, I keep coming back to exhortations like, 'Thou shalt not kill' and 'He that is without sin among you, let him first cast a stone,' and 'Blessed are the merciful, for they will be shown mercy.'" The title of Renkl's piece is, "What Part of 'Thou Shalt Not Kill' Don't We Understand?"[36] In ways similar to Renkl, Christian activist and pacifist Shane Claiborne tends to draw more on Jesus's teaching and Jesus's own experience as an "executed savior"[37] than the commandment in his writings against

34. Martin Luther, *Luther's Large Catechism with Study* Questions, ed. F. Samuel Janzow (St. Louis: Concordia, 1978), 41.

35. Lancelot Andrewes, *A Pattern of Catechistical Doctrine and Other Minor Works* (Oxford: John Henry Parker, 1846; New York: AMS, 1967), 221. Andrewes is also careful to explain that a magistrate must be kept within his limits, and any death penalty needs a lawful trial, with the verdict that he is "a guilty man and justly punishable." *A Pattern of Catechistical Doctrine*, 222.

36. Margaret Renkl, "What Part of 'Thou Shalt Not Kill' Don't We Understand?," *New York Times*, August 19, 2019, https://tinyurl.com/4b26hhpp.

37. Shane Claiborne, *Rethinking Life: Embracing the Sacredness of Every Person* (Grand Rapids: Zondervan, 2023), 66.

the death penalty. But Claiborne quotes Tertullian as an example of an early Christian who "categorically denounced the death penalty," when Tertullian said, "The Creator puts his prohibition on every sort of man-killing by that one summary precept, 'Thou shalt not kill.'"[38]

Gun Violence

Claiborne also supports greater gun control laws in the United States but only briefly mentions the commandment to not kill in his 2019 *Beating Guns: Hope for People Who Are Weary of Violence* when quoting Maryland pastor David Anderson, who says about Americans, "We are better at protecting the Amendments than the Commandments." Claiborne adds, "one of [the commandments] is 'Thou shalt not kill.'"[39] As the title of Claiborne's book would suggest, he draws more on Isa 2:4 and Mic 4:3, as well as Jesus's words in the Sermon on the Mount, for biblical references to argue against death from guns.[40] But Brian A. Haggerty, in his book on the Ten Commandments from the 1970s, presciently highlighted the problem with guns and lack of gun control laws in the United States as a violation of this commandment.[41] Haggerty rewords this commandment to say, "You shall not threaten the lives of others by your aggressive or irresponsible behavior."[42] Opposite Haggerty, in an article in *Time* magazine from 1998, evangelical gun owners explain that the commandment prohibits "murder" and not "killing," again drawing the line between the words; these gun owners argue that their "guns are for self defense."[43] Of course, guns did not exist in ancient Israel, but the biblical law that held people responsible for death from instruments of iron or wood that could kill, may prove an analogy for reading the commandment as speaking to prohibitions of guns.

38. Claiborne, *Rethinking Life*, 77.

39. Shane Claiborne and Michael Martin, *Beating Guns: Hope for People Who Are Weary of Violence* (Grand Rapids: Brazos, 2019), 145.

40. Claiborne's book is written with Michael Martin, a Mennonite and amateur blacksmith. To promote the book, Claiborne and Martin held vigils in places across the country where mass shootings or other gun violence had occurred; the vigils included collecting guns, melting them down in a mobile forge, and inviting survivors of the violence to help beat the metal into hoes and spades as an enactment of Isa 2:4.

41. Brian A. Haggerty, *Out of the House of Slavery: On the Meaning of the Ten Commandments* (New York: Paulist, 1978), 84–89.

42. Haggerty, *Out of the House of Slavery*, 136.

43. Zed Nelson, "Up in Arms," *Time*, July 6, 1998, 36.

Suicide, Euthanasia, Abortion

Because so many other biblical texts permit killing through war or capital punishment, Aquinas interprets the commandment as "not forbidding killing altogether. . . . The sense is then: *Thou shalt not kill on thine own authority*."[44] In other words, like Luther and Andrewes, Aquinas believes a government could have the authority to kill but an individual human would not. Yet, for Aquinas, this reasoning led him to assert that suicide was forbidden, with some fascinating exceptions: "If then it is unlawful to kill a man save by God's authority, neither is it lawful to kill oneself, except either by God's authority or at the instigation of the Holy Ghost, as in the case of Samson."[45]

Andrewes specifically identifies suicide as prohibited by the commandment, explaining that life is a gift from God and God has authority over a person's life and death. Andrewes also writes about how suicide harms a community: "No man is his own, but is a part of the society of commonwealth wherein he liveth, and so cannot injure or kill himself but he brings detriment and damage to the whole company."[46]

A number of receptions identify Saul's act of suicide in 1 Sam 31:4 as breaking the commandment. In a booklet on euthanasia published by the Christian Medical Fellowship, an organization of Christian doctors and nurses in London, Peter Saunders also highlights how an Amalekite tells David that he had killed Saul after Saul asked him to do so because he was so badly wounded (2 Sam 1:9–10), an instance of euthanasia in the Bible.[47] Saunders titles his writing "Thou Shalt Not Kill: The Christian Case against Compassionate Killing" and draws on biblical, theological, philosophical, ethical, and legal material to argue that euthanasia is wrong for Christians, though his title emphasizes the commandment against killing.[48]

Few ancient receptions identify abortion in relationship to the commandment; when the Didache discusses the practice of child exposure, it mentions,

44. Aquinas, *The Commandments of God*, 58.

45. Aquinas, *The Commandments of God*, 58–59.

46. Andrewes, *A Pattern of Catechistical Doctrine*, 219.

47. This story is complicated by the fact that the Amalekite's story contradicts the narrator's version of events in 1 Sam 31, when Saul asked his armor-bearer to kill him because he was so badly wounded (1 Sam 31:3–4). When the armor-bearer refused, Saul fell on his own sword, after which the armor-bearer also fell on his sword and died (1 Sam 31:5). And, because Amalekites are Israel's prototypical enemies, the default position in the Bible is that killing them is positive.

48. Peter Saunders, "Thou Shalt Not Kill: The Christian Case against Compassionate Killing," *The Euthanasia Booklet* (Christian Medical Fellowship), https://tinyurl.com/38b47rpz.

"do not murder a child by abortion or kill a new-born infant" (Didache 2:1–2). But contemporary receptions that connect abortion to Exod 20:13 tend to be univocal in saying that the commandment forbids abortion. Of the nineteen pages in the chapter on the commandment "do not kill" in her book on the Ten Commandments, cofounder of the L'Abri Christian community Edith Schaeffer spends ten pages discussing abortion as a specific way people break the commandment.[49] The Assemblies of God quotes Exod 20:13 in their statement about the "sanctity of life" that includes abortion, suicide, and euthanasia.

Stanley Hauerwas and William Willimon write that the commandment calls for the type of peaceful community in which "such violent acts as abortion, suicide, and euthanasia" would not take place. They proclaim, "We ought to live with and love one another in such a way that none of us are ever so alone that suicide seems a possibility. We ought to so honor and care for our elders that euthanasia seems irrelevant. We ought to never have sex (as we shall see in the next commandment) in a manner that a life conceived through that sex should tempt us to end life. Descriptions like suicide, abortion, euthanasia, words not in the Bible, are descriptions meant to help extend our understanding of how God would have us reverence life."[50]

Many receptions also make a move from the negative commandment, "you shall not kill" to the positive affirmation of revering life, as will be discussed below.

In the New Testament: Jesus and Anger

Jesus references the commandment "don't murder" when he includes it in lists of the commandments, as in Matt 15:19 (and its parallel in Mark 7:21) and Matt 19:18 (and its parallels in Mark 10:19 and Luke 18:20). But Jesus's specific reception of the commandment is found in his teaching about it in the Sermon on the Mount, when Jesus says, "You have heard it said to those of ancient times,

49. Edith Schaeffer, *Lifelines: The Ten Commandments for Today* (Westchester, IL: Crossway, 1982), 121–31.

50. Stanley M. Hauerwas and William H. Willimon, *The Truth about God: The Ten Commandments in Christian Life* (Nashville: Abingdon, 1999), 88. David Hazony also declares that abortion and euthanasia relate to "the intention of the sixth commandment," especially as the commandment is developed through the centuries; he acknowledges that contemporary debates about abortion and euthanasia assume levels of medical specificity and social issues that were not shared by those in ancient Israel. Hazony, *The Ten Commandments: How Our Most Ancient Moral Text Can Renew Modern Life* (New York: Scribner, 2010), 115.

'you shall not murder' and 'whoever murders will be liable to judgment.' But I say to you that if you are angry with a brother or sister, you will be liable to judgment, and if you insult a brother or sister, you will be liable to the council, and if you say, 'you fool,' you will be liable to the hell of fire" (Matt 5:21–22). Thus, Jesus extends the prohibition of murder to include anger and speaking insults against others. Jesus's teaching gets echoed in 1 John 3:15, which identifies anyone who hates a brother or sister as a murderer.

In Aquinas's treatment of the commandment, he spends much more time writing about anger than killing, including listing five ways a person should beware: (1) of being quickly provoked, (2) of nursing anger, (3) lest anger leads us to hatred, (4) lest we give vent to our anger in words, and (5) lest anger provoke us to deeds.[51] Aquinas comments of Jesus, "Like a good physician who removes not only the external symptoms, but also the very root of the malady, lest there be a relapse he would have us avoid the very beginnings of sins, and therefore anger as the beginning of murder."[52]

Andrewes—among others—is careful to say that Jesus does not prohibit anger in general, for, after all, Jesus expressed anger. Instead, he claims that what Jesus says the commandment is about is sinful anger, which he defines as "when it is without a cause or not kept within due bounds and measure."[53] Jesus's reception of this commandment seems to move inwardly, from the deed of murder to a motive for it, and to also emphasize the relationship to the community through the use of family language of brother and sister. Linguist Anna Wierzbicka describes Jesus's teaching in the Sermon on the Mount as follows:

> Whereas it purported to do no more than fully articulate God's will behind the commandment "You shall not murder," the demand it made on listeners must have seemed, then as now, exceedingly difficult to fulfill, perhaps even more so since one was not expected to turn oneself emotionally into a stone and forgo strong emotions altogether. But Jesus did not urge people to exert superhuman efforts and to aim at superhuman ethical achievements. Rather, he invited them to live with God (in the kingdom of God), assuring them at the same time that "things which are impossible with people are possible with God." (Luke 18:27)[54]

51. Aquinas, *The Commandments of God*, 61–64.
52. Aquinas, *The Commandments of God*, 65.
53. Andrewes, *A Pattern of Catechistical Doctrine*, 214–15.
54. Anna Wierzbicka, *What Did Jesus Mean? Explaining the Sermon on the Mount and*

Beyond the Literal Act

Jesus's teaching is not the only reception that advocates for understanding this commandment as going beyond the literal, physical act of murder. A teaching from the Talmud declares, "Anyone who humiliates another in public, it is as though he were spilling blood." In response to this saying, Rav. Naḥman bar Yitzḥak answers that after a humiliated person blushes, the red color leaves his face and he becomes pale, which is tantamount to spilling his blood (Bava Metzia 58b:12). Rabbeinu Yonah Gerondi affirms this teaching, explaining, "The dust of murder is whitening [someone else's] face (embarrassing someone). Since his face turns white and the ruddy appearance leaves [it], it is similar to [the draining of blood] caused by murder" (Sha'arei Teshuvah 3:139). So, to humiliate or embarrass someone is akin to breaking the commandment against murder.

Referencing this teaching, Rachel Mikva notes that while gossip or criticism cannot be considered murder in a real sense, they do cause pain and wounds. She adds,

> Other kinds of assaults against people are also seen as murderous. Some, like rape, obviously destroy aspects of life that cannot be recovered. Some require a greater stretch of our imagination. If you cause people to lose their livelihood, the Talmud says it is as if you murder them. If you pretend to be a scholar and hand down halachic decisions without having attained the proper level of wisdom, or if you have the knowledge and experience yet refrain from teaching—you strike down many students. Even a host who fails to provide travelers with sufficient provisions and an escort to ensure their safety is described as a shedder of blood. While the punishment for these transgressions is not like the punishment for murder—in fact many have no punishment at all—the teachings make abundantly clear our obligation to protect and enrich the lives of others in all circumstances.[55]

Abarbanel writes that the commandment also includes that one must not refrain from charity to the poor. He explains, "For one who withholds charity

---

the Parables in Simple and Universal Human Concepts (Oxford: Oxford University Press, 2001), 70–71.

55. Rachel S. Mikva, *Broken Tablets: Restoring the Ten Commandments and Ourselves* (Woodstock, VT: Jewish Lights, 1999), 75.

is killing the souls of the poor and the destitute. And also included in this negative commandment is the release of Hebrew slaves on the seventh year. . . . For if he detains them more than is the law, it is like killing and negating them from the world."[56]

Puritan James Durham drew on Jesus's teaching in the Sermon on the Mount to affirm that the commandment is broken by words, specifying that those who speak "imprecations, cursings, wrathful wishes, disdainful and passionate speeches" will be called to account. Durham also writes that the commandment is broken "in gestures, such as high looks, fierce looks, gnashing with the teeth . . . foaming with the mouth, and such like"; in deeds including "extortion, exaction, usury, litigious wrangling, violent compulsion, raising and racking of Land or House-rents beyond the just value"; and by "withholding what might be useful and refreshful, as by neglecting the sick and distressed, want of hospitality, specially to the poor."[57] In addition to abstaining from committing any of the things in his long list, Durham says, "We must also make conscience to practice all contrary duties."[58] Eugenia Ann Gamble gives examples of a broad understanding of the word and commandment, writing, "If we crush a person's spirit, that is murder. If we cause someone to lose their job, that is murder. If we use blame as a weapon and an excuse, that is murder. If we constantly criticize and rarely applaud, that is murder. If we think the work of attaining our own goals necessitates taking others down, that is murder."[59]

Most receptions focus on another person when they describe these nonliteral ways of killing, but some even apply the commandment to oneself. For example, seventeenth-century English Puritan William Whatley wrote that obedience to the commandment would include care for one's own physical state and "our bodily condition in this present life" as regards "good and needful things" like food, apparel, rest and sleep, and exercise.[60] Farkas tells the story of a man who gave up painting because he felt he had no time for it, though he had enjoyed the activity as well as how it allowed him to contemplate beauty in the world and writes that "whoever ties off the spiritual blood circulation is actually committing suicide . . . for it is himself he puts to slow

56. Sefaria, citing "Abarbanel on Torah, Exodus 20:13:1," Sefaria Community Translation, https://tinyurl.com/mr86kxpf.

57. Durham, *The Law Unsealed*, 213.

58. Durham, *The Law Unsealed*, 213.

59. Eugenia Anne Gamble, *Words of Love: A Healing Journey with the Ten Commandments* (Louisville: Westminster John Knox, 2022), 118.

60. Whatley, *A Pithie, short and methodicall opening of the Ten Commandments*, 143–44.

torture and death. Thus when we are told, 'You shall not kill,' this includes not only killing others but also killing ourselves!"[61] Farkas's example is not about literal death; he clarifies that death can also include "tying off a gift or a part of life" and the death of joy for the person who does that.[62]

Popular Culture

David Hazony suggests that this commandment is challenging for people today who have been desensitized to killing, writing, "Our music and movies and literature condone violence to a radical degree. We embrace romantic political ideologies, thrilled by their simple answers and optimism, without caring about all the historical precedents that show how often they lead to the widespread killing of innocents. We entertain ourselves with flirtations and fantasies of violence, killing, and barbarism, watch *The Sopranos* and boxing and hang posters of Che Guevara on the wall."[63]

Marsh Moyle suggests that such desensitization to violence—which, he says, is problematic for keeping the commandment—is evident in casual language used to describe interactions, such as "he stabbed me in the back" or "she got thrown under the bus."[64] At some point, any person receiving the commandment would need to decide how far to take the nonliteral aspect of what it forbids: Would "not killing" include not participating in violent video games? Or watching crime shows? Or reading murder mysteries? Interestingly, ancient southwestern Asian empires, which regularly boasted of actions we would consider war crimes, nonetheless disapproved of murder. Karel Van der Toorn points out how in Mesopotamia a murderer is "polluted with blood," and an Old Assyrian letter suggests that the royal throne is blemished when the king commits bloodshed. He writes, "The recurrent topos of the triumphant king who washes his weapons in the waters of the Mediterranean Sea after a victorious campaign, attested to in Mesopotamia's literary tradition from the second half of the third millennium onward, can therefore be regarded as a reference to a rite of purification. The gods themselves had to bathe after they had slaughtered one of their fellows."[65]

61. Farkas, *Bench Marks*, 77.

62. Farkas, *Bench Marks*, 76.

63. Hazony, *The Ten Commandments*, 143–44.

64. Marsh Moyle, *Rumors of a Better Country: Searching for Trust and Community in a Time of Moral Outrage* (London: Inter-Varsity Press, 2023), 157.

65. Karel van der Toorn, *Sin and Sanction in Israel and Mesopotamia: A Comparative Study* (Assen: Van Gorcum, 1985), 15–16.

Thomas Mann's short novel from 1944, "The First Commandment," includes Moses commenting on the other commandments, including murder. Moses tells the people they must say "Amen" to God's prohibitions against murder, and Mann then writes,

> And they said Amen, still hoping that with the ban on murder killing alone was meant. For few of them had the desire to kill, and those who did had it only occasionally. But it turned out that Jahwe gave that word as wide a meaning as he had given the word adultery and that he meant by it all sorts of things, so that "murder" and "killing" began with almost any transgression of the code. Almost every wound which one man inflicted upon another, whether through deceit or through fraud (and almost all of the people hankered a little after deceit and fraud), Jahwe considered bloodshed.[66]

In the same collection of novels, Jules Romain depicts a character who is discussing situations in which a person may be ordered to break the commandment, "thou shalt not kill." The character says, "If you can *in all sincerity* translate the order thus: 'We are required to break the commandment which forbids us to take life. But it is clear that in bowing to necessity we deplore this with our whole hearts, and our essential aim, even in doing this continues to be promoting upon this earth the triumph of the commandment *Thou shalt not kill.*' If, on the contrary, you cannot so translate the order without laughing or shrugging your shoulders, then you are acting in a bad cause."[67]

Two separate movies were released in 2008, both titled *The Fifth Commandment*: one, produced in Mexico, is about a serial killer,[68] and the other, produced in the United States, is about an assassin.[69] A BBC 2023 miniseries titled *The Sixth Commandment*—again, the numbering of the commandments is not standardized—is about the murders of two people in 2015 and 2017 in a small village in England.

In the 2021 murder mystery *The Last Commandment*, a serial killer com-

66. Thomas Mann, "Thou Shalt Have No Other Gods Before Me," trans. George R. Marek, in *The Ten Commandments: Ten Short Novels of Hitler's War against the Moral Code*, ed. Armin L. Robinson (New York: Simon & Schuster, 1944), 46–47.

67. Jules Romain, "Thou Shalt Not Kill," in *The Ten Commandments: Ten Short Novels of Hitler's War against the Moral Code*, ed. Armin L. Robinson (New York: Simon & Schuster, 1944), 230–31.

68. *The Fifth Commandment*, directed by Rafael Lara (Cyclus Producciones, 2008), https://tinyurl.com/2dc79hs5.

69. *The Fifth Commandment*, directed by Jesse V. Johnson (Freestyle Releasings, 2008), https://tinyurl.com/pvvmanxx.

mits murders of people he believes have violated each commandment. When he is caught and confronted, the detective says, "But each time you took a life, you were violating one of the Commandments, the sixth. 'Thou shalt not kill.' How do you explain that?" The killer quotes from Ezek 18:21–22 and tells the detective, "All previous transgressions will be forgiven because of the righteousness a man has done once he has turned from a life of sin." The detective then asks, "One sin pardons another? . . . According to the word of the Lord?" The killer answers, "Most definitely."[70] This dialogue not only demonstrates the irony of a serial killer who murders people for violating the Ten Commandments, one of which prohibits murder, but also—albeit in a heightened way—illustrates how certain receptions of biblical texts are used to justify terrible behavior or actions.

Positive: Value Life

The positive way of stating "do not murder" would be "value life." Hazony muses, "Maybe our problem is that we don't value life enough"[71] and then encourages people to ask for "the most basic moral instinct . . . the instinct to cherish the lives of others."[72] Calvin writes that the commandment "contains . . . the requirement that we give our neighbor's life all the help we can. . . . God forbids us to hurt or harm a brother unjustly, because he wills that the brother's life be dear and precious to us. So at the same time he requires those duties of love which can apply to its preservation."[73] Harrelson proposes guidelines to help people follow the commandment: that life is a gift to be treasured, that an individual life is treasured best when it is shared in association with the lives of others, that actions that enhance rather than damage life in community are preferred.[74] Bailey, who preferred translating the commandment as "kill" because she believed it was more accurate and inclusive, writes, "We are all complicit in wars and other policies that end human life prematurely, but happily we are also all complicit in actions that enhance and protect life. Those of us who do have a say can work to increase the latter and decrease the former."[75] In other words, following the commandment is about working to

70. Scott Shepherd, *The Last Commandment* (New York: Mysterious Press, 2021), 255–57.
71. Hazony, *The Ten Commandments*, 145.
72. Hazony, *The Ten Commandments*, 146.
73. Calvin, *Institutes*, 375–76.
74. Harrelson, *The Ten Commandments*, 122.
75. Bailey, *"You Shall Not Kill" or "You Shall Not Murder?,"* 83.

increase actions and policies that enhance and protect life. Claiborne similarly encourages advocacy for life on a comprehensive level, explaining that "a consistent ethic of life . . . requires pursuing whatever allows people to flourish and fighting everything that crushes life."[76] Claiborne writes that he wants to be "pro-life for the whole of life" with "the conviction that all of life—from womb to tomb—matters."[77]

Conclusion

In 2022, the Center for Literacy Education at the University of Notre Dame awarded Shusterman's *Scythe* novel the Alexandria Award. This award is for young adult books that "advance Gospel values and tenets of Catholic Social Teaching while portraying adolescents who espouse St. Catherine of Alexandria's brave and tenacious character."[78] While being interviewed about winning the award, Shusterman explained that a driving issue in his book was the sanctity of life, and the main characters, though tasked with the order to kill, were ultimately seeking to preserve the dignity of life in their world.[79] Again, the "Scythe" commandment, "Thou Shalt Kill" is the opposite of the biblical commandment, but the novel as a reception of the commandment paradoxically upholds some of the same values as in other receptions, which encourage a love of and care for life.

76. Claiborne, *Rethinking Life*, 5.

77. Claiborne, *Rethinking Life*, 5.

78. Center for Literacy Education, "The Alexandria Book Award," https://tinyurl.com/5n6m8e38.

79. Vimeo, "The Alexandria Award—Interview with 2022 winner Neal Schusterman," December 1, 2022, https://tinyurl.com/2s4yb8bz.

7

"Don't Commit Adultery"

In London in 1631, publishers Robert Barker and Martin Lucas printed a version of the King James Bible that came to be known as the "Wicked Bible," because it omitted the word "not" from Exod 20:14, and the verse read, "Thou shalt commit adultery." This Bible was also known as the "Sinner's Bible" or the "Adulterous Bible." While there is some debate as to whether this was simply an embarrassing error or deliberate act of sabotage from a rival printer,[1] the official response—the publishers were called into court, fined, and deprived of their printing license[2]—makes clear that endorsing adultery would be categorically wrong. Yet as regards the commandment itself, contemporary commentators observe that its meaning is not entirely clear. For example, Shalom Albeck wrote, "From the simple law, 'You shall not commit adultery' it is impossible to know what is sexually prohibited and what is permitted."[3] Similarly, Walter Harrelson noted, "This commandment is extremely terse and short, leaving aside many of the matters in the sexual realm that must have confronted the judges and lawgivers every day."[4] Harrelson also declared that because the commandment gave no definitions and drew no distinctions, "It is the kind of statement that clearly will in times to come, encourage an appli-

1. According to a worker at Bonhams auction house, the misprint was "possibly perpetrated by [printer Robert] Barker's rival Bonham Norton, to politically embarrass Barker." Allison Flood, "Extremely Rare Wicked Bible Goes on Sale," *Guardian*, October 21, 2015, https://tinyurl.com/4vmstkfd.

2. Most copies of this Bible were destroyed, but around a dozen still exist, including one at the British Library in London, and another in the collection of rare books at the New York Public Library. Peter Campbell, "The Codex Sinaiticus," *London Review of Books*, July 23, 2009, https://tinyurl.com/39xpkdhp.

3. Shalom Albeck, "The Ten Commandments and the Essence of Religious Faith," trans. Chaim Pearl, in *The Ten Commandments in History and Tradition*, ed. Ben-Zion Segal, English version ed. Gershon Levi (Jerusalem: Magnes, 1990), 281.

4. Walter Harrelson, *The Ten Commandments and Human Rights* (Philadelphia: Fortress, 1980), 128.

cation broader than it probably had in view."[5] Certainly that latter comment describes reception history of the commandments writ large, in that they are applied in more specific and broad ways as time goes on.

Adultery: Terms and Definitions

The Hebrew word *n'p* gets translated in virtually every English translation as "adultery";[6] and as with the other Ten Commandments, the verbs occur in the second masculine singular form. In Lev 20:20, though, the word occurs in both masculine and feminine nominal forms, such that a man can be an adulterer and a woman can be an adulteress; the verse also explains that both the man and the woman should be killed. Proverbs 30:20 critiques the way of the "adulterous woman"; in this verse, the word occurs as an adjective to modify the noun "woman." Although both men and women could be adulterous, biblical adultery was understood legally as consensual sexual intercourse between a married woman and a man who was not her husband; it did not matter if the man was himself married or unmarried. As British professor of Biblical Law at the Law School at the University of Bristol Jonathan Burnside explains,

> Adultery is seen in androcentric terms as an infringement by a third party of the husband's marital rights over his wife. It is *not* adultery if a married man has intercourse with an unbetrothed woman. This is because there is no husband whose marital interests are threatened. Nowadays this strikes us as unfair asymmetry between men and women: in one case, the sexual relationship is classed as "adultery" whereas in the other, it is merely "an affair." However, this may reflect the view that in biblical society, men are the protectors of women. It may also be because married men needed to be sure of the paternity of their offspring who will, after all, inherit the family property.[7]

5. Harrelson, *The Ten Commandments*, 124.

6. The exceptions are in the Contemporary English Version, which translates the verse as "be faithful in marriage," and the Tyndale Bible of 1526 and the Coverdale Bible of 1535, which have "Thou shalt not breake wedlocke."

7. Jonathan P. Burnside, *God, Justice, and Society: Aspects of Law and Legality in the Bible* (Oxford: Oxford University Press, 2010), 367. Burnside, drawing on Ken Stone's *Sex, Honor, and Power in the Deuteronomistic History* (Sheffield: Sheffield Academic Press, 1996), makes the point that sexual wrongdoing in biblical texts can be interrogated according to

While the medieval rabbi Rashi agreed that adultery happens only with another man's wife, the late medieval rabbi Ibn Ezra challenged that view, writing, "The matter is not so. . . . The word *ni'uf* (adultery) is the equivalent of *zenutth* (whoredom)."[8] Other receptions of the idea of adultery similarly broadened the concept. For example, twenty-first-century scholar J. Duncan M. Derrett argued that the Hebrew word *n'p*, which appears in Exod 20:14, is associated with fornication or sexual activity in general. He wrote, "Thus the seventh commandment is understood to forbid any kind of sexual intercourse between unmarried people who will not or cannot marry."[9] Thirteenth-century Franciscan Bonaventure explained that adultery could happen in different sexual acts, and though it would be called different things, it was still breaking the commandment. Bonaventure explained: "Someone can sin against the chastity of marriage, and this is called adultery. Or someone can sin . . . with an unmarried person and it is called fornication, or with a tramp and prostitute and it is called harlotry. Now if someone sins against privileged chastity, that is virginity, it can be done in one of two ways. Either it is done with an additional condition, which is defloration and is called debauchery; or it is done with a woman consecrated to God and then it is called sacrilege, namely, when someone violates a woman consecrated to God."[10]

Bonaventure also included in his examples what he referred to as a "sin against nature," which in the medieval era usually referred to homosexuality but could also include bestiality.[11] All of these sexual acts were, for Bonaventure, examples of adultery. Calvin wrote that the summary of the commandment was that "we should not become defiled with any filth or lustful intemperance of the flesh."[12] A reception that at least focused the meaning, if not narrowed it, came from the school of Rabbi Yishmael, which taught, "When it is stated in the Ten Commandments: 'You shall not commit adultery' (Exodus 20:13[14]), this means that there shall not be adultery among you, whether you masturbate by hand or whether with one's foot" (Niddah 13b:4).

---

what they tell us not about relationships between men and women but about relationships between men. Burnside, *God, Justice, and Society*, 375.

8. Sefaria, citing "Ibn Ezra on Exodus 20:13," H. Norman Strickman and Arthur M. Silver, Menorah, 1988–2004, https://tinyurl.com/3vtkvy9u.

9. J. Duncan M. Derrett, *Law in the New Testament* (London: Darton, Longman and Todd, 1970), 371.

10. Bonaventure, *St. Bonaventure's Collations on the Ten Commandments*, trans. Paul J. Spaeth (New York: Franciscan Institute, 1995), 89.

11. Bonaventure, *Collations on the Ten Commandments*, 89.

12. John Calvin, *Institutes of the Christian Religion*, ed. John T. McNeill, trans. and indexed by Ford Lewis Battles (Philadelphia: Westminster, 1960), 405.

In composer Joseph Haydn's canon *The Ten Commandments* from 1810, he did not use the typical German word for adultery, *Ehebruch*, but rather used the broader German word *Unkeuschheit*, which more literally translates as "unchastity." Seventeenth-century Puritan James Durham writes that the commandment forbids not only adultery but everything that could lead to it, including "idleness, gluttony, drunkenness, impudence, gaudiness and unchasteness in apparel or nakedness, dancing, singing of bawdy songs, and loose company or fellowship."[13] Today, the term "infidelity" sometimes gets used synonymously with "adultery," though others use "infidelity" as a blanket term to refer to any sort of marital or relational unfaithfulness that could include "adultery," with "adultery" specifically referring to a sexual encounter; "infidelity" could include emotional affairs.[14] Another example of a reception of the commandment that broadened the understanding of adultery is that of Hungarian pastor József Farkas, who writes, "Whenever sexual energy is being used in a joyful, releasing, redemptive way, there it is being used well. Wherever sexual energy is being used in an animalistic way for mutual violence and torture, there is adultery—even if there is a marriage certificate on hand."[15]

Reception history also has equated the commandment against adultery with the commandment against coveting. In his book on the Ten Commandments, for example, Emmet Fox does not have a separate chapter on the two commandments, explaining that "they are different aspects of the same thing."[16] Karol Wojtyła, the given and pen name of Pope John Paul II, wrote that being faithful in marriage is expressly addressed in the commandment against adultery, which forbids the external action, and in the commandment against coveting, which forbids the internal action.[17] Journalist Gay Talese's book *Thy Neighbor's Wife* does not explicitly reference either the commandment against adultery or the commandment against coveting, where the phrase "your neighbor's wife" occurs. Rather, the book is about changing sexual mores in the United States in the 1970s, with specific attention to the "free love" movement in marriages, discussed further below. This is the same author who wrote another book with a

13. James Durham, *The Law Unsealed, or, a practical exposition of the Ten Commandments. With a resolution of several momentous questions and cases of*, Early English Books Online, https://tinyurl.com/phfsuw6v, 215.

14. For example, cf. Morse Investigation Services, https://tinyurl.com/4az8kph3.

15. József Farkas, *Bench Marks*, trans. John R. Bodo (Richmond, VA: John Knox, 1969), 87.

16. Emmet Fox, *The Ten Commandments: The Master Key to Life* (New York: Harper and Row, 1953), 113.

17. Karol Wojtyła (Pope John Paul II), *Love and Responsibility*, trans. H. T. Willetts (San Francisco: Ignatius Press, 1993), 147–48.

title borrowed from the commandments: *Honor Thy Father*, which is not about the commandment, but about the mob, and was discussed in chapter 6.

What precisely defined adultery continued to be debated socially and legally. Voltaire's entry on "Adultery" in his *Philosophical Dictionary* (ca. 1764) tells about a senior magistrate in a French town who left his persistently unfaithful wife but was not permitted by the Roman Catholic Church of the eighteenth century to divorce her. According to Voltaire, though the magistrate "needs a woman," unfortunately any sexual relationship would make him an "adulterer."[18] Until the divorce law reforms in Britain in the late 1960s, "adultery" was one of the only grounds for divorce, but scholar Michael Freeman notes how a petitioner in *Barnacle v. Barnacle* in 1948 thought that adultery involved illicit connection between two unmarried persons with the consequent production of a child. Others thought it was not adultery "during the daytime" and yet another averred that it was not adultery if the woman was "over 50."[19] Adultery is still considered a crime in almost twenty US states: it is a felony in Oklahoma, Michigan, and Wisconsin and a misdemeanor in states including New York. As of the spring of 2024, a bill to repeal the crime of adultery in New York State had passed both the senate and the assembly.

Louise DeSalvo, an American author and scholar, who wrote a memoir about her husband's affair, describes adultery as "very, very adolescent. It's when a grown person tries to feel the way they did when they were in love in high school."[20] DeSalvo also explains, "Adultery is about saying, through our actions, that, regardless of who I am, of what vows I have taken, of what responsibilities I have (and especially *because* of the responsibilities I have), I have the right to do whatsoever I choose so long as I don't harm anyone. (That adultery inevitably harms another seems never to be taken into consideration.)"[21]

The first line in DeSalvo's obituary from 2018 notes that she died in her home, "with her husband . . . of 55 years by her side."[22] Adultery—when one

18. Voltaire, "Adultery," *Philosophical Dictionary*, trans. H. I. Woolf (New York: Knopf, 1924), https://tinyurl.com/2ke2z6xw. Voltaire was not only defining "adultery" but criticizing what he saw as the hypocrisy in the Roman Catholic Church in this eighteenth-century French town. He specifically referenced Jesus's teaching in Matt 19:9 to say that because the woman had been unfaithful—which seemed to fit Jesus's exception clause of "sexual immorality"—the magistrate should have been granted a divorce by the church.

19. M. D. A. Freeman, "The Law and Sexual Deviation," in *Sexual Deviation*, ed. Ismond Rosen (Oxford: Oxford University Press, 1979), 393.

20. Louise DeSalvo, *Adultery* (Boston: Beacon Press, 1999), 114.

21. DeSalvo, *Adultery*, 107.

22. Jaimie Julia Winters, "Obituary: Louise A. DeSalvo," *Montclair Local*, October 31, 2018, https://tinyurl.com/27czkf4t.

married partner has sex with someone else, without the knowledge of their partner—does not mean the marriage will or must end.

Adultery in the Old Testament

The Sotah Ritual in Numbers 5

Though the word for "adultery" (*n'p*) does not appear in Num 5:11–31, the Sotah ritual (from the Hebrew word *sṭh*, meaning "to go aside") described in those verses explains what would happen when a husband suspected his wife of infidelity.[23] A priest at the tabernacle would perform a series of ritual acts, including making a "meal offering of jealousy" consisting of ground barley without oil or frankincense (Num 5:15). The woman was required to swear by oath that she only had sexual relations with her husband, and the priest wrote the words down on a scroll and then rubbed off the writing into water mixed with dirt from the floor of the tabernacle. Her guilt or innocence was determined after she drank the mixture, called the "waters of bitterness." If guilty, the water would cause her "thigh to fall and her belly to distend" (Num 5:27), phrases that are likely euphemisms for harm to sexual organs, indicating the infertility that would result from her drinking the water. But if she was innocent, the water would do her no harm. Because a "trial by ordeal" was atypical in biblical law, Jacob Milgrom suggested that the Sotah ritual was adopted to save women from public death, the typical punishment for an adulteress or an adulterer (cf. Lev 20:10).[24] The laws in the Talmud tractate with the title "Sotah," however, are less about a divine trial of a woman suspected of infidelity and more about a woman against whom there is evidence of her immoral behavior. Ishay Rosen-Zvi writes, "The extreme character of the ritual and its essential inequality have led to different ways of coping with it, ranging from apologetics to severe criticism."[25]

23. In addition to the word "gone aside" (*sṭh*), Num 5:11–31 also describes how the woman "transgressed" (*m'l*) against her husband, another man had sex with her, and they kept it secret from her husband.

24. Jacob Milgrom, *The JPS Torah Commentary: Numbers* (Philadelphia: Jewish Publication Society, 2003), 354.

25. The Sotah ritual has its own fascinating reception history. Daniel Boyarin referred to it as "a particularly obnoxious rite in which a woman is shamed, stripped bare, dirtied, and cursed in public, and all because her husband has suspected—merely suspected—her of adultery" in "Women's Bodies and the Rise of the Rabbis: The Case of Sotah," in *Jews and*

King David's Adultery with Bathsheba

Just as the Hebrew word for adultery (*n'p*) doesn't occur in the Sotah ritual in Numbers, it is also absent in the narratives of 2 Samuel 11–12. In fact, when Nathan the prophet confronts David, he accuses David of "taking" Uriah's wife (2 Sam 12:9). This language demonstrates how, in the biblical legal world where a wife was understood as the property of her husband, an act of adultery was akin to theft. Neither does the Hebrew word for adultery occur in the superscription to Psalm 51, despite the English NIV translation: "When the prophet Nathan came to him after David had committed adultery with Bathsheba." Most other English translations are more literal, reflecting the Hebrew word in the superscription that says David "went to her."[26] Yet there is a link in reception history between David's action with Bathsheba and the commandment against adultery. For example, in a Reformation-era Bible illustrated by Lucas Cranach's woodcuts, the reformer Philipp Melanchthon chose 2 Samuel 11—when David sees Bathsheba, takes her, and lies with her—as the narrative to illustrate the commandment "you shall not commit adultery." In a fourth-century homily on penitence, John Chrysostom preached about how God says in the law not to commit adultery, but David the adulterer was redeemed.[27] Seventeenth-century bishop Lancelot Andrewes explains that the vices of gluttony and idleness can

---

Gender: The Challenge to Hierarchy, Studies in Contemporary Jewry 16, ed. Jonathan Frankel (Oxford: Oxford University Press, 2000), 89. Feminists have critiqued the ritual; Alice Bach's "Good to the Last Drop" is exemplary of the critiques and concerns. Bach, "Good to the Last Drop: Viewing the Sotah (Numbers 5.11–31) as the Glass Half Empty and Wondering How to View It Half Full," in *Women in the Hebrew Bible: A Reader*, ed. Alice Bach (New York: Routledge, 1999), 503–22. But Boyarin also points out the counterview within the tractate itself, which declares that if a father teaches his daughter Torah, that would give a merit to her that would mitigate the possible ill effects of the ritual if she were ever to be subjected to it. The phrase is, "A man is obligated to teach his daughter Torah, so that if she drinks [the bitter water], she will know—for merit mitigates." Moreover, interpretations within the Palestinian and Babylonian versions of the tractate differ. The Palestinian reading is that the merit of having studied Torah will mitigate the punishment in the Sotah ritual, so a father ought to teach a daughter Torah. But the Babylonian Talmud seems to advise a father to only teach his daughter that merit mitigates, not the whole of the Torah. Cf. Boyarin, 94–97.

26. The NET Bible translation, however, has "after David's affair."

27. Chrysostom also noted how the law proclaimed that prostitution was forbidden, but through Joshua, God also proclaimed that Rahab the prostitute should live. Chrysostom described both Rahab the prostitute and David the adulterer as "pearls mixed up in the mire," but not in this case before swine; rather, he linked the two redeemed sexual sinners to an image of a precious heavenly pearl. Gus George Christo, *St. John Chrysostom on Repentance and Almsgiving* (Washington, DC: Catholic University Press, 1998), 98–99.

lead someone to adultery and referenced 2 Sam 11:2 as his example of idleness. Andrewes suggests that David's idleness—rising from his bed late in the day, which is when he saw Bathsheba—led to David's adultery with her.[28]

A few Talmud tractates offer the idea that David did not commit adultery with Bathsheba because Bathsheba was not married to Uriah; b. Šabb. 56a explains that everyone who went to war during David's reign wrote a letter of divorce for their wives before going to battle. This theme is repeated in b. Ketub. 9b and in b. Meṭ. 58b, which refers to Bathsheba as a "doubtful married woman"; that is, it is doubtful that she was married at the time to Uriah. And yet, the Talmud is clear that David did wrong: several rabbis taught that Bathsheba was created by God to be David's wife, "but he partook of her unripe, before the appointed time. David would have ultimately married her in a permitted manner after the death of Uriah" (b. Sanh. 107a 9). The same section of the Talmud teaches that David had been warned by God that God would test David in regard to a married woman, with whom sexual relations were forbidden.

> Rav Yehuda says: Once David heard the nature of his ordeal, he sought to prevent himself from experiencing lust. He transformed his nighttime bed into his daytime bed, i.e., he engaged in intercourse with his wives during the day, in an attempt to quell his lust. But a *halakha*, i.e., a Torah statement, escaped him: There is a small limb in man that he employs in sexual intercourse. If he starves the limb, and does not overindulge, it is satiated; but if he satiates the limb and overindulges in sexual intercourse, it is starving, and desires more. Therefore, his plan had the opposite effect. (b. Sanh. 107a:3–4)

The tractate continues with a story of how the sages would interrupt their study and ask David about the penalty for adultery. David answered, "His death is by strangulation, and he has a share in the World-to-Come. But one who humiliates another before the multitudes has no share in the World-to-Come" (B. Sanh. 107a 11). Thus, according to David, publicly embarrassing another was a worse transgression than David's sin of having sex with a married woman.

Reception history illustrates how the word "adultery" need not occur in the biblical text for the idea of adultery to be attached to the story of David and Bathsheba. Again, the biblical legal definition of adultery requires the woman to be married to another—even though David had seven identified wives at this

28. Andrewes, *A Pattern of Catechistical Doctrine*, 239.

point in the narrative, if Bathsheba had been unattached, it would not have been considered adultery—and also understands the sexual act to be consensual. The very brief clause in 2 Sam 11:4, which reads "and she came to him," has been magnified in reception history by those who assert that Bathsheba was a willing participant in the sexual act;[29] it was not until 2010 that a biblical scholar called David's act "rape."[30] In part, this can be explained by the fact that the Hebrew verb that describes rape (of Dinah in Genesis 34, the Levite's concubine in Judges 19, and Tamar in 2 Samuel 13) is not present in 2 Sam 11:4, which says David "lay with" Bathsheba after he "sent" messengers and "took" her. But with new conversations about consent and power differentials today, especially after the #metoo movement, the ancient technical and legal distinction between adultery and rape may seem like splitting hairs. As scholar David T. Lamb wrote in 2015, "Based on the huge power differential between the king and his subject, it's more accurate to call this power rape rather than adultery. Bathsheba couldn't say no. She didn't even have a choice."[31] And in an interview from 2019, Lamb explained, "By not calling it 'rape,' but 'adultery,' we are ignoring perhaps one of the clearest examples of sexual abuse in the Bible."[32]

Adultery and Idolatry

The word for adultery (*n'p*) appears only a handful of times in the legal books but is more frequent in the prophetic books of Jeremiah, Ezekiel, and Hosea.

29. For example, A. F. Kirkpatrick writes, "Bath-sheba can not be acquitted from blame, for it does not appear that she offered any resistance." *The Second Book of Samuel* (Cambridge: Cambridge University Press, 1880), 326. Carl Friedrich Keil and F. Delitzsch explain, "In the expression, 'he took her and she came to him' [2 Sam 11:4], there is no intimation whatever that David brought Bathsheba into his palace through craft or violence, but rather that she came at his request without any hesitation, and offered no resistance to his desires. Consequently Bathsheba is not to be regarded as free of blame." *Biblical Commentary on the Books of Samuel*, trans. James Martin (Edinburgh: T&T Clark, 1868), 383.

30. Suzanne Scholz, *Sacred Witness: Rape in the Hebrew Bible* (Minneapolis: Fortress, 2010), 100. In 2015, Anne Létourneau, "Bathing Beauty: Concealment of Bathsheba's Rape and Counter-Power in 2 Sam 11:1–5," presented at Society of Biblical Literature meeting, Atlanta, GA, November 21, 2015; and David T. Lamb, *Prostitutes and Polygamists: A Look at Love, Old Testament Style* (Grand Rapids: Zondervan, 2015), 134.

31. David T. Lamb, "David Was a Rapist, Abraham a Sex Trafficker," *Christianity Today*, October 22, 2015, https://tinyurl.com/2xxpd3ha.

32. Adelle M. Banks and Emily McFarlan Miller, "Speaking of Abuse: Baptist News Service, Bible Scholars Grapple with Language," *Religion News Service*, October 10, 2019, https://tinyurl.com/ya85jmbe.

Adultery is listed among sins committed by the people (e.g., Jer 29:23; Hos 4:2), but more typically, these prophets use adultery as a metaphor for idolatry. Ezekiel 23:37 makes the connection succinctly, explaining, "they have committed adultery with their idols." The metaphor is extended in Hosea when the prophet is commanded to marry the prostitute Gomer; then in Hos 3:1, Hosea is commanded to love (another) woman: "Love a woman . . . who is committing adultery, just as the LORD loves the children of Israel, and they look to other gods." Unlike Hosea's metaphor with Gomer, and Ibn Ezra who equates adultery with prostitution, Ezek 16:31–32 clarifies that God's people have not been like a prostitute; instead, they are like a wife committing adultery against her husband. Eleventh-century rabbi Rashbam connected idolatry and adultery in reference to the Israelites' punishment in Exod 32:20 when Moses ground the golden calf into powder, mixed it with water, and forced the Israelites to drink it. Rashbam commented that Moses "examined their truthfulness by making them drink this mixture, just as a Sotah suspected of infidelity has to drink water [mixed with ground dust; Num 5:11–31]."[33] For those who divide the Ten Commandments into two tablets of five each, idolatry and adultery are parallel; each one is in the second position on its tablet.[34]

The idea of idolatry as "spiritual adultery" is not limited to the prophets or to commentary on the golden calf. At the end of the fifth century, Pope Gelasius of Rome wrote a treatise against a Roman magistrate who had recommended that people in Rome continue to observe the ancient Roman rite of Lupercalia, the festival commemorating Rome's legendary founding when Romulus and Remus were nursed by a wolf.[35] A local priest had been found guilty of adultery, and his action had led to a charge of hypocrisy against the Roman church—and therefore against Gelasius himself. Gelasius, however, responded by declaring that by supporting Lupercalia, the magistrate and other members in the senate were committing spiritual adultery. Biblical scholar Jennifer Knust and theologian Tommy Wasserman describe Gelasius as saying, "A local priest may have committed adultery in the flesh, but the Roman aristocrats who accuse him reveal that they are worse sinners: guilty of fornicating with idols, they nevertheless dare to throw stones."[36]

33. Sefaria, citing *Rashbam on Exodus*, https://tinyurl.com/9ausp63s.

34. Rachel S. Mikva, *Broken Tablets: Restoring the Ten Commandments and Ourselves* (Woodstock, VT: Jewish Lights, 1999), 88.

35. Details about exactly how Lupercalia was celebrated are sparse.

36. Jennifer Knust and Tommy Wasserman, "Telling Stories in Church: The Early Medieval Liturgy and the Reception of the *Pericope Adulterae*," in *To Cast the First Stone: The Transmission of a Gospel Story* (Princeton: Princeton University Press, 2008), https://doi.org/10.23943/princeton/9780691169880.003.0009.

CHAPTER 7

Adultery in the New Testament

In the Sermon on the Mount, Jesus reinterprets the commandment against adultery by saying that anyone who looks at a woman lustfully has already committed adultery with her in his heart (Matt 5:28). Church fathers followed Jesus's teaching here, such as Justin Martyr who writes that Jesus "condemns not only the man who commits the act of adultery, but the man who desires to commit adultery, since not only our actions but our thoughts are manifest to God."[37] Sociologist Annette Lawson muses, "In our own times, perhaps Jimmy Carter's chances in the United States presidential elections in 1980 might have been improved had he not admitted that he had sinned, lusting in his heart after other women."[38] Though not misquoted, Carter was certainly misunderstood; in his 2015 memoir, he wrote that he was simply trying to explain the Sermon on the Mount.[39]

Jesus also connected divorce to adultery, proclaiming, "Anyone who divorces his wife, except for sexual immorality, makes her the victim of adultery and anyone who marries a divorced woman commits adultery" (Matt 5:32 and 19:9; cf. Mark 10:11–12; Luke 16:18). William Heth and Gordon Wenham describe Jesus's statement here as a novelty: that, through divorce, a man could commit adultery against his own wife.[40] Contemporary theologians Jeannine K. Brown and Kyle Roberts express a common perspective when they explain how Jesus seems to be interpreting Deut 24:1, which allowed men to divorce their wives; they write, "In this context of relatively 'easy divorce,' Jesus shores up the

37. *Early Christian Fathers*, ed. Cyril Richardson (Philadelphia: Westminster, 1953), 1:230.

38. Annette Lawson, *Adultery: An Analysis of Love and Betrayal* (New York: Basic Books, 1988), 38. Lawson's comment references an interview published by *Playboy* magazine in 1976 with then-governor Carter, with the full quote being, "I try not to commit a deliberate sin. I recognize that I'm going to do it anyhow, because I'm human and I'm tempted. And Christ set some almost impossible standards for us. Christ said, 'I tell you that anyone who looks on a woman with lust has in his heart already committed adultery.' I've looked on a lot of women with lust. I've committed adultery in my heart many times. This is something that God recognizes I will do—and I have done it—and God forgives me for it." *Playboy*, November 1976, https://tinyurl.com/bdw7zc48.

39. Carter writes, "My own campaign suffered, perhaps even more, from an ill-advised inverview I granted to *Playboy* magazine, in which I was explaining Jesus' Sermon on the Mount and stated that, like other men, I had 'lusted' for women. I could not think of an effective way to further explain my blunder and decided just to live with it. Within a few days, I dropped almost 15 percentage points in public opinion polls." *A Full Life: Reflections at Ninety* (New York: Simon & Schuster, 2015), 117.

40. William A. Heth and Gordon J. Wenham, *Jesus and Divorce: The Problem with the Evangelical Consensus* (Nashville: Nelson, 1985), 48.

stability and integrity of lifelong monogamy, thereby protecting women from the whims of a dissatisfied husband."[41] Apparently, even a dissatisfied husband would think twice about accusing a wife of adultery. Augustine underscored Jesus's teaching, saying that even when it was legal for men to divorce wives who were barren, whoever did so was guilty of "adultery by the law of the gospel, though not by this world's rule."[42] New Testament scholar Amy-Jill Levine describes Jesus's teaching about adultery and divorce as "building a fence" against adultery and divorce, a rabbinic expression from the Mishnaic tractate *Pirke Avot*, which encouraged limiting actions such that a person would not get close to breaking a law. So, by forbidding remarriage, Jesus built a fence around divorce; by forbidding lust, Jesus built a fence around adultery.[43]

The Woman Caught in Adultery in John's Gospel

In addition to Jesus's teaching about adultery, the narrative tells of Jesus's encounter with and response to the woman caught in the act of adultery (John 8:1–11). This story has a complicated manuscript history; even today, many Bibles include notes that the narrative was not included in the earliest manuscripts of the Gospel of John.[44] Augustine proposed an explanation for its omission, arguing that the reason the story is not found in every copy of John is that "men of slight faith" were afraid that their wives might commit adultery after hearing about the woman and deleted it.[45] Certainly, adultery scenes were common in ancient literature: New Testament scholar Jennifer Knust describes them as pervasive and discusses three particular stories that she describes as enjoying "an indisputably wide currency": the tale of Lucretia, the Roman wife of Collatinus; the deuterocanonical story of Susanna; and a mime script called the "Jealous Mistress."[46] Knust notes how each of these adultery scenes, though

41. Jeannine K. Brown and Kyle Roberts, *Matthew* (Grand Rapids: Eerdmans, 2018), 60.

42. Augustine, "On Marriage and Concupiscence," in *The Works of Augustine*, trans. Marcus Dods (Edinburgh: T&T Clark, 1885), 109.

43. Amy-Jill Levine, *Sermon on the Mount: A Beginner's Guide to the Kingdom of Heaven* (Nashville: Abingdon, 2020), 30–37.

44. The scholarly consensus is that this story is not of Johannine authorship: rather, it is a piece of oral tradition that became incorporated into different gospel manuscripts in different textual locations and at different times in history. For further details, see Jennifer Knust and Tommy Wasserman, *To Cast the First Stone: The Transmission of a Gospel Story* (Princeton: Princeton University Press, 2018).

45. Knust and Wasserman, *To Cast the First Stone*, 98.

46. Knust, "Can an Adulteress Save Jesus? The *Pericope Adulterae*, Feminist Interpreta-

different in details, "begins with a case of adultery against a young wife (who may have been set up rather than guilty) and each is resolved by a narrative reinstatement of male dominance and female passivity," and wonders if the scene between Jesus and the woman is a similar type.[47] Jesus does tell the woman to "sin no more" but also encourages her to leave, declaring, "neither do I condemn you" (John 8:11).

In William Blake's poetic reception of the woman caught in the act of adultery, "The Everlasting Gospel," in his larger work, *The Marriage of Heaven and Hell*, he identifies the woman with Mary Magdalene and writes:

> The morning blushd fiery red:
> Mary was found in Adulterous bed:
> Earth groand beneath & Heaven above
> Trembled at discovery of Love
> Jesus was sitting in Moses Chair
> They brought the trembling woman There
> Moses commands she be stond to Death.
> What was the sound of Jesus breath
> He laid his hand on Moses Law
> The Ancient Heavens in Silent Awe
> Writ with Curses from Pole to Pole
> All away began to roll . . .
> And she heard the breath of God
> As she heard by Edens flood
> Good & Evil are no more
> Sinai's trumpets cease to roar (Exod. 19:16)
> Cease finger of God to write (Exod 31:18)
> The Heavens are not clean in thy Sight
> Thou art Good & thou Alone
> Nor may the sinner cast one stone.[48]

tion, and the Limits of Narrative Agency," in *The Bible and Feminism: Remapping the Field*, ed. Yvonne Sherwood (Oxford: Oxford University Press, 2017), 425. Cf. Saundra Schwartz, "From Bedroom to Courtroom: The Adultery Type-Scene and the Acts of Andrew," in *Mapping Gender in Ancient Religious Discourse*, ed. Todd Penner and Caroline Vander Stichele, Biblical Interpretation Series 84 (Leiden: Brill, 2007), 267–311.

47. Knust, "Can an Adulteress Save Jesus?," 429.

48. Blake, "The Everlasting Gospel," in *The Complete Poetry and Prose of William Blake*, ed. David V. Erdman (New York: Doubleday, 1988), 521.

Clearly, Blake is drawing a line between Moses as a representative of the law, which commands death by stoning, and Jesus, who while "sitting in Moses' chair" rolls away the curses and may even stop God's finger from writing down the law, as was described in Exod 31:18.

David Bamidele Oluwole considers the Yoruba traditional penal system for adultery in light of John 8:1–11. Olowole writes, "This is believed to have the capacity to address the overemphasis on sexual sin as if it is the only abominable thing that can ever happen, and the untold castigation of those caught in same by the church, which seems to be engrossed in the traditionally prescribed penalties even at a time when the grace to save is available in and through Christ."[49] Oluwole's comment focuses on how the church can extend mercy or forgiveness—grace—toward those who have done wrong, especially when seeking to follow Jesus's example and model. But grace ought not to be made cheap, as Dietrich Bonhoeffer famously noted, and a spouse who chooses to forgive their adulterous spouse may also experience the costliness of such forgiveness.

Punishments

Responses to adultery in the Bible, and throughout history, span the spectrum from the death penalty, on the one hand, to mercy and forgiveness, on the other hand. When the Ten Commandments are understood as apodictic, absolute laws, the death penalty is implied for those who break them, as discussed in the introduction, but no specific punishment is stated in the words of either Exod 20:14 or Deut 5:18. As mentioned above, it is Lev 20:20 (and Deut 22:22) that declares that both the adulterer and adulteress should die, though as Burnside notes, there is not a clear distinction in Hebrew between a mandatory "he shall die" and a permissive "he may die." Burnside writes, "Consequently, in Deuteronomy 22:22, it is up to the husband whether he wants to prosecute the offenders or not. Likewise, the penalty is a matter for the husband's discretion."[50] According to Prov 6:34–35, a monetary payment is possible, though the gist of those verses is to warn a would-be adulterer that the husband may refuse to accept such a settlement.

49. David Bamidele Oluwole, "Sexual Sin, Punishment and Saving Grace: A Study of the Yoruba Penal Practices in the Light of John 8:1–11," *Ogbomoso Journal of Theology* 22 (2017): 101–2.

50. Burnside, *God, Justice, and Society*, 368.

Fourth-century theologian Basil of Caesarea writes about how an adulterer would be excluded from the sacraments for fifteen years: "He must weep for four years [outside the door of the church during the service], then he must listen for five years [in the vestibule], be prostrated [among the catechumens] for four years and then stand upright [among the full congregation] for two years without receiving communion."[51]

In sixteenth-century Protestant Europe, clerical authors argued that because adultery was a breach of God's law, it deserved the level of punishment as did other crimes such as murder. For example, British Bible translator George Joye wrote a treatise in 1549 titled *A contrayre (to a certayne manis) consultacion: that adulterers ought to be punished with deathe*. The titular "certain man" was martyrologist John Foxe who had published a treatise in Latin in the previous year arguing for merciful treatment of adulterers. Joye's argument is signaled by his title: contrary to Foxe, Joye argued that the seriousness of adultery meant that adulterers deserved the death penalty.[52] After all, the law in Lev 20:10 did say that the man and the woman would be killed, and Deut 22:22—though not containing the word "adultery"—likewise explained that if a man was found having sex with the wife of another man, they would both be put to death. In the seventeenth-century British Interregnum, the Puritan government issued an "Act for suppressing the detestable sins of Incest, Adultery, and Fornication" on May 10, 1650, which also made adultery punishable by death; fornication was punished by three months in prison. Historian Keith Thomas explains that convictions of adulterers were very infrequent, the harshest sentences in this act were rarely imposed, and the act lapsed ten years later and was not renewed.[53] Thomas writes, "To modern commentators, for whom sexual morality is a private matter, the very aims of the adultery act appear alien and tyrannical," and notes that many at the time also thought that the death penalty for adultery was "too hard and too cruel."[54] Still, even if the people at the time were loath

51. Saint Basil, Canon 58, in *The Letters*, Loeb Classical Library 243, 3:248–49. By contrast, the Cappodocian church only insisted on seven years of withholding communion from an adulterer: one year spent weeping, two listening, three being prostrate, and then one standing in the congregation without receiving communion (Canon 77).

52. Jonathan Willis, *The Reformation of the Decalogue: Religious Identity and the Ten Commandments in England, c. 1485–1625* (Cambridge: Cambridge University Press, 2017), 269.

53. Keith Thomas, "The Puritans and Adultery: The Act of 1650 Reconsidered," in *Puritans and Revolutionaries: Essays in Seventeenth Century History Presented to Christopher Hill*, ed. Donald Pennington and Keith Thomas (Oxford: Clarendon Press, 1978), 258. Thomas also observes that the adultery act of 1650 "followed Old Testament precedent in defining adultery as adultery of the married *woman*. Intercourse by a married man with a single woman was only fornication" (261).

54. Thomas, "The Puritans and Adultery," 280.

to enforce the death penalty, at that time and place the reception history of adultery made it into a capital criminal offense.

In Nathaniel Hawthorne's nineteenth-century novel *The Scarlet Letter*, the unwed and pregnant Hester Prynne is sentenced to wear an embroidered scarlet "A" for adultery. One woman in the crowd, whom Hawthorne describes as among those who "appeared to take a peculiar interest in whatever penal infliction might be expected to ensue," comments, "What do we talk of marks and brands, whether on the bodice of her gown or the flesh of her forehead? . . . This woman has brought shame upon us all, and ought to die; is there not law for it? Truly there is, both in the Scripture and the statute-book."[55] Hawthorne describes this speaker as "the ugliest as well as the most pitiless of these self-constituted judges" of Hester Prynne.[56] If she had no pity, she was nonetheless correct about the "statute book." *The Scarlet Letter* is set in the Massachusetts Bay Colony during 1642–49, and in 1631 the Colony's Court of Assistants passed a law making adultery a capital offense. In that same year, for the first and only time, two death sentences were issued for Mary Lathan of Marshfield, MA, described by historian Mary Beth Norton as "a young wife unhappily married to a much older man,"[57] and James Britton of Weymouth. Both Lathan and Britton expressed remorse and repentance before they were killed, and subsequent punishments were limited to whipping or banishments instead of death. In 1641, adultery charges were brought against another couple, but eleven people in the colony—eight of whom were men of high status—helped the couple escape from custody. When the couple was recaptured, the Bay Colony's Court of Assistants ordered only a symbolic hanging, with the couple sitting on the gallows for an hour with ropes around their necks, and then banished the woman but not the man.[58] Again, while there was a range of punishments for adultery historically, the trajectory does seem to move toward more leniency over time, especially as Western social contexts emphasized individual freedom.

Adultery's Place in the Commandments

Some receptions note a seeming causal connection between the order of the commandments, with Exodus 20 and Deuteronomy 5 listing murder, adul-

55. Nathaniel Hawthorne, *The Scarlet Letter* (Minneapolis: Lerner, 2014), 50.

56. Hawthorne, *The Scarlet Letter*, 50.

57. Mary Beth Norton, *Founding Mothers and Fathers: Gendered Power and the Forming of American Society* (New York: A. A. Knopf, 1996), 342.

58. Norton, *Founding Mothers and Fathers*, 342.

tery, then theft.[59] Peter S. Knobel comments, "The Torah seems to be saying that if we improperly cross the boundary of intimacy, it destroys something more significant than property rights, something almost as sacred as human life itself—but not quite."[60] Aquinas suggests that the reason the commandment against adultery follows the one against murder is that husband and wife are as one body: "The prohibition of murder is followed by the prohibition of adultery, and with reason, since husband and wife are as one body."[61] This order—murder, adultery, theft—also occurs in Mark 10:19 (and its parallel in Matt 19:18–19) when Jesus lists the commandments in response to a questioner who asks Jesus what he must do to inherit eternal life. However, in Luke's version of the account, Jesus lists adultery *before* murder, which is also the order of the commandments in the Septuagint Vaticanus manuscript, in the Nash Papyrus (which likely follows the Septuagint Vaticanus), Philo and Pseudo-Philo, and in Rom 13:9.[62] In Eduard Nielsen's discussion of the variations in order of adultery and murder in the commandments, he asserts, "That the prohibition of killing should come before that of adultery appears to us as obvious as it is difficult to explain why some witnesses to the text should give these two commandments in the opposite order."[63] Philo's reception of the order of commandments, however, takes the opposite approach from Nielsen. Philo explains that adultery is the first commandment on the "second table" of the law, prohibiting offenses against one's neighbor, because it is the greatest violation against one's neighbor:

> For in the first place, it has for its source the love of pleasure, which enervates the bodies of those who indulge in it, and relaxes the tone of the soul, and destroys the essences of it, consuming every thing that it touches, like unquenchable fire, and leaving nothing which affects human

59. This order also occurs in the Samaritan Pentateuch, the Syriac Peshitta, and several Septuagint manuscripts.

60. Peter S. Knobel, "Sacred Boundaries," in *Broken Tablets: Restoring the Ten Commandments and Ourselves*, ed. Rachel S. Mikva (Woodstock, VT: Jewish Lights, 1999), 91.

61. Thomas Aquinas, *The Commandments of God: Conferences on the Two Precepts of Charity and the Ten Commandments*, trans. Laurence Shapcote, OP, with an introduction by Thomas Gilby, OP (London: Burns, Oates & Washbourne, 1937), 66.

62. Hos 4:2 places adultery last, after cursing, lying, murder, and stealing.

63. Eduard Nielsen, *The Ten Commandments in New Perspective: A Traditio-historical Approach*, trans. David J. Bourke (London: SCM, 1968), 42. However, Nielsen seems to subscribe to the text-critical principle of preferring the more difficult reading, as he then writes, "On grounds of intrinsic content we prefer the order attested by the witnesses that flip them)." *The Ten Commandments in New Perspective*, 42.

> life uninjured, inasmuch as it not only persuades the adulterer to commit iniquity, but also teaches him to join others in wickedness, making an association in things in which there ought to be no such participation. For when this violent passion seizes on a man it is impossible for the appetites to arrive at the accomplishment of their object by one person alone, but it is indispensable that two should share in the action. . . . Since then, illicit cohabitation produces such great calamities, adultery is very naturally a detestable thing hated by God, and has been set down as the first of all transgressions.[64]

Issues: Marriage

While Martin Luther acknowledged that this commandment is broadly directed against "all manner of impurity" (and urged people not to engage in said impurity), he affirmed that the commandment against adultery "is aimed directly at the state of matrimony." Correspondingly, the bulk of Luther's teaching about this commandment in his *Large Catechism* is about marriage. Luther wrote that God gloriously "honors and extols this estate, inasmuch as by His commandment He both sanctions and guards it." Luther explains that the commandment to honor father and mother already demonstrates that God sanctioned marriage, but here, God "hedged it about and protected it." In Luther's teaching, God "created man and woman separately (as is evident), not for lewdness, but that they should live together, be fruitful, beget children, and nourish and train them to the honor of God." Luther also reveals his own context and perspective as a former monk when he critiques the "popish rabble, priests, monks, and nuns, [who] resist God's order and commandment, inasmuch as they despise and forbid matrimony, and presume and vow to maintain perpetual chastity."[65] Calvin takes a similar stance in being skeptical about people who try to remain celibate as he discusses the commandment against adultery. He writes that God ordained marriage "as a necessary remedy to keep us from plunging into unbridled lust."[66] Because for Calvin, the commandment forbids any type of lustful sexual behavior, those who "cannot

64. Philo, *The Works of Philo: Complete and Unabridged*, trans. C. D. Yonge (Peabody, MA: Hendrickson, 2006), 529.

65. Martin Luther, *Luther's Large Catechism with Study Questions*, ed. F. Samuel Janzow (St. Louis: Concordia, 1978), 44–46.

66. Calvin, *Institutes*, 405.

prevail in the struggle should turn to matrimony to help them preserve chastity," and a person should "abstain from marriage only so long as he is fit to observe celibacy. If his power to tame lust fails him, let him recognize that the Lord has now imposed the necessity of marriage upon him."[67]

Adultery is referred to as the "great sin" in the ancient western Asian legal codes of Egypt and Ugarit,[68] but the gods are not involved in prohibiting adultery in those cultures. Nahum Sarna writes, "In Israel by contrast, the marriage bond has a sacral dimension and the prohibition of adultery is divinely ordained."[69] Evangelical biblical scholar Carmen Imes agrees; she explains the commandment against adultery as saying, "Each neighbor has a right to marriage free from competition. . . . Sexual intimacy is reserved for marriage because marriage is a reflection of the covenant with Yahweh. In both, two enter into an exclusive commitment: 'I am yours; you are mine.' For marriage to work as God designed, both parties must give themselves wholly to each other and to no one else."[70]

Lawson, who researched adultery over decades through an extensive project, observed how in the twentieth century the "Myth of Romantic Marriage" contributed to people's choice to have an affair. In this myth, your spouse is your soulmate, and romantic love is not only the basis for marriage but such love for your spouse—and only for your spouse—will last as long as you both live. Lawson writes that within the Myth of Romantic Marriage, "It is the quality of the relationship that must carry the weight of marriage; this is valued, not the solidity of the institution itself."[71] In her memoir, DeSalvo wrote, "Knowing that my marriage nearly ended once has made me value it more because I value it less and I value myself more. . . . His adultery signaled a challenge to our marriage; it didn't mean its end (unless he or I or we chose to end it)."[72]

In his discussion of the commandment against adultery, David Hazony referred to the "problem of marriage," explaining that many people view marriage

67. Calvin, *Institutes*, 406–7.

68. Cf. Jacob J. Rabinowitz, "The 'Great Sin' in Ancient Egyptian Marriage Contracts," *JNES* 18 (1959): 73; and W. L. Moran, "The Scandal of the 'Great Sin' at Ugarit," *JNES* 18 (1959): 280–81.

69. Nahum Sarna, *The JPS Torah Commentary: Exodus* (Philadelphia: Jewish Publication Society, 2003), 114.

70. Carmen Joy Imes, *Bearing God's Name: Why Sinai Still Matters* (Downers Grove, IL: IVP Academic, 2019), 55.

71. Lawson, *Adultery*, 24. Lawson also writes about how the "Myth of Me" which has as its goal the peak of self-actualization, may be subsumed in the Myth of Romantic Marriage, but may also compete with it and may even offer a justification for breaching the boundaries of marriage when one believes the self is best found in adulterous relationships. *Adultery*, 26.

72. De Salvo, *Adultery*, 128.

as a cure to existential loneliness, rather than a framework for the project of partnership and love. He explains that marriage at its best can create conditions for love to prosper, but that requires an investment and taking inventory to deepen what is good and correct what is bad.[73] Joy Davidman wrote, "The adultery forbidden in the Seventh Commandment originally meant any infringement of the man's rights—and, possibly, nothing more. Jesus took this old negative prohibition of adultery and turned it into the positive affirmation of marriage."[74]

Different understandings of marriage throughout the centuries will, understandably, lead to different understandings of adultery. Psychotherapist Esther Perel writes, "When marriage was an economic arrangement, infidelity threatened our economic security; today marriage is a romantic arrangement and infidelity threatens our emotional security."[75] Interestingly, there is no Hebrew word for "marry": a man would "take" (*lqḥ*) a woman as his wife.[76] Also, multiple wives were common in most marriages in the Old Testament. When marriage was about the integrity of the family and the community—as in the biblical world—adultery would harm the community. Cultures and times that value individual freedom in marriage will see adultery more as a threat to the integrity of the couple.

Betrayal

The English word "adultery" is related to the Latin *adulterare*, which has connotations of diluting, poisoning, polluting, or debasing.[77] One participant in a study on adultery conducted in Great Britain in the 1980s said about her husband's previous adultery, "I still feel now that it spoilt our relationship. It spoilt it, just spoilt it."[78] Marsh Moyle describes a scandal in the Austrian wine industry in the 1980s when, after some poor harvests, unscrupulous winemakers added chemicals similar to antifreeze to enhance the taste of the

73. David Hazony, *The Ten Commandments: How Our Most Ancient Moral Text Can Renew Modern Life* (New York: Scribner, 2010), 186.

74. Joy Davidman, *Smoke on the Mountain: An Interpretation of the Ten Commandments* (Philadelphia: Westminster, 1954), 87.

75. Esther Perel, *The State of Affairs: Rethinking Infidelity* (New York: HarperCollins, 2017), 51.

76. Neither are there distinct words for "husband" or "wife" in Hebrew, just the word "man" (*'yš*) and "woman" (*'šh*).

77. *Oxford English Dictionary*, 2nd ed. (1989), under "adultery."

78. Lawson, *Adultery*, 36.

wine. He writes, "The adulterated wine tasted better but . . . when drunk in large enough quantities could seriously damage your health. When the scandal broke, people were shocked and then outraged. The vintners had violated the promise of purity. Trust, won over centuries had been betrayed. . . . Most people experience adultery as a painful betrayal."[79]

Seventeenth-century English Puritan John Downame wrote that the adulterous husband becomes to his wife "a most grievous tormentor, filling her heart with grief and jealousy and her face with shame when she seeth herself rejected and set at naught."[80] DeSalvo describes the French author Colette's book *My Apprenticeships* as follows: "It talks, frankly, about how unhealthy and unwholesome living in an adulterous household can be. . . . [Colette] speaks of how her husband Willy's adulteries literally made her sick. Of how his spending money on other women meant that she went without a warm coat in the winter. Of how she felt like a prisoner within her marriage. Of how she lost her soul."[81] DeSalvo admitted regarding her own husband's infidelity, "This 'tough broad' tone I take is, of course, a cover for how hurt I then was, for how betrayed I felt."[82] An entry on "infidelity" on the American Association for Marriage and Family Therapy website explains that after the initial disclosure of an affair, it can be common for both spouses to experience depression, and the "injured party" may have reactions that resemble symptoms of post-traumatic stress disorder. "Common reactions to the loss of innocence and shattered assumptions include obsessively pondering details of the affair; continuously watching for further signs of betrayal; and physiological hyperarousal, flashbacks and intrusive images. The most severely traumatized are those who had the greatest trust and were the most unsuspecting. The involved partner may fear that they will be punished forever for the betrayal while they grieve for the lost dreams associated with the affair."[83]

79. Marsh Moyle, *Rumors of a Better Country: Searching for Trust and Community in a Time of Moral Outrage* (London: Inter-Varsity Press, 2023), 173.

80. John Downame, *Foure treatises tending to disswade all Christians from foure no lesse hainous then common sinnes; namely, the abuses of swearing, drunkennesse, whoredome, and briberie*, Early English Books Online, https://tinyurl.com/4s923uua, 180–81.

81. DeSalvo, *Adultery*, 94–95.

82. DeSalvo, *Adultery*, 111.

83. American Association for Marriage and Family Therapy (AAMFT), "Infidelity," https://tinyurl.com/muz2dm4f. Multiple other sources exist online and elsewhere, such as a website titled "Affair Recovery" (https://www.affairrecovery.com), "Affair Healing" (https://www.affairhealing.com/), and "Emotional Affair Journey" (https://www.emotionalaffair.org/), which is not surprising, given that according to the AAMFT, some national surveys indicate that 15 percent of women and 25 percent of men have sex outside their long-term

Former Methodist missionary Al Vom Steeg tells the story about a couple in his congregation who salvaged their marriage after one spouse committed adultery, with time and much intentional work. Vom Steeg used the term "moral dry rot" to describe adultery, proclaiming that it "is eating away at the foundation of marriages, is destroying families, and will eventually, if left unchecked, destroy our society."[84] The commandment against adultery, he explains, is "more than just a concept of legalism. It is meant to be a safeguard for us."[85] Of course, Vom Steeg's story illustrates that adultery need not end a marriage, and the entry on "infidelity" on the AAMFT website includes the "good news" that "the majority of relationships not only survive infidelity, but marriage and family therapists have observed that many marriages can become stronger and more intimate after couples therapy." Even though—as noted above—DeSalvo's marriage did not ultimately end, its endurance does not negate her feelings of betrayal at the time.

There seems to be a difference between adultery, where one spouse does not know about the other's extramarital sexual relationship, and what is termed "consensual/ethical non-monogamy"; the "ethical" aspect of this is that the people in the relationship are informed about any non-monogamous encounter. Lawson explains that for those engaged in such sexual relationships, "Their commandment reads not, 'Thou shalt not commit adultery,' but 'Thou shalt tell thy spouse of any other sexual relationship thou hast.'"[86]

Sex and Sexuality

In fact, Talese's book, *Thy Neighbor's Wife*, mentioned above, is an exploration of sexuality in America, with a notable discussion of what was known as the "free-love" subculture. In preparation for writing the book, Talese resided for months at the clothing-optional resort "Sandstone Retreat" founded by John and Barbara

---

relationship, and when including emotional and sexual intimacies without intercourse, the rates increase by 20 percentage points, to 35 percent of women and 45 percent of men.

84. Al Vom Steeg, *Freedom to Live: A Guide to a Free and Abundant Life as Revealed through the Ten Commandments* (Des Moines, IA: Meredith, 1984), 80.

85. Vom Steeg, *Freedom to Live*, 86.

86. Lawson writes, "This [new] commandment involves a heavy burden—changing as it does ideas about love, possession, and jealousy—and those who adhere to it do not believe any less strongly in their chosen ideal than the more conventionally religious, but they do remove the inherent conflict in, for example, being a devout Christian and also adulterous." *Adultery*, 89.

Williamson in Los Angeles, California, in 1969. Talese explained that in the late 1960s and early 1970s, "group sex and consensual adultery were kind of a new thing. . . . The big mission of John and Barbara Williamson was to try to make people feel that extramarital sex didn't reflect a bad marriage—that you could have a central relationship and satellite relationships and not harm your partner."[87] Yet, while Talese's book was a best seller, he later discussed how participating in open sexual relationships as he wrote the book almost ended his own marriage.[88]

Certainly a detailed discussion about open marriages is beyond the scope of this book, but reception of this commandment includes considering how such relationships relate to the commandment. Harrelson argued that open marriages might even be helpful for marriages today, writing,

> It might be possible to say that this commandment, perhaps more than any other in the list, must be set aside today, as persons have learned a new joy and fulfillment in life through the adoption of much freer relations between human beings sexually. Many a person today—indeed, many a Christian theologian today—will wish to urge upon the Christian community that it never again get trapped into espousing a notion of what is permitted sexually that does terrible damage to individuals and to families and to the larger human community. . . . As in the case of killing, it cannot be claimed that this commandment should become an absolutistic and unbreakable norm, issuing in a commitment never to have sexual relations with anyone other than the marriage partner. But unlike the sixth commandment, this seventh commandment does allow for scrupulous adherence without necessary harm at all.[89]

Instead of advocating for setting the commandment aside, the Hungarian pastor Farkas explained that the commandment in the contemporary world ought to be interpreted as having three implications: first, do not harm or ruin the love life of another; second, do not worship sex; and third, do not be afraid of sex. Farkas explained that sex is "a divine help in the process of becoming human. . . . Sex exists that there may be joy in this earthly life."[90]

Aquinas had a similar, if somewhat less positive interpretation of how

87. Alex Mar, "What Happened to 'The Most Liberated Woman in America'?," *Atlas Obscura*, June 7, 2016, https://tinyurl.com/ms3uv8d9.

88. Mar, "What Happened to 'The Most Liberated Woman in America'?"

89. Harrelson, *The Ten Commandments*, 129–30.

90. Farkas, *Bench Marks*, 86.

the commandment against adultery related to sex in marriage, writing, "*Thou shalt not commit adultery* forbids not only adultery, but all carnal corruption except that which is part of matrimony. And yet there are some who say that marital intercourse is not devoid of sin, but this is heretical, for the Apostle says (Heb 13:4) *Let marriage be honourable in all and the bed undefiled.* In fact sometimes not only is it void of sin but even meritorious for eternal life, in those who are in a state of grace."[91]

Positive Formulations of the Commandment

Calvin writes that the negative commandment "do not commit adultery" corresponded to "the affirmative commandment that we chastely and continently regulate all parts of our life."[92] Harrelson wrote that the commandment might be restated "to support partners in committing themselves to one another sexually in such a way as actually to reflect the commitment they are making to each other as a whole."[93] He claimed that the chief implications of this commandment for human sexual activity are that the sexual relationship should be mutually beneficial and pleasurable, as well as life-giving, to both participants.[94] Durham, who expanded the prohibition against adultery to include a number of activities that might lead to it, also expounds upon the virtues "which are required in this Command, and are very useful for a holy life," including chastity, modesty, temperance, and lawful marriage.[95] And Farkas writes that the commandment "is designed not so much to prohibit the love life as to protect the family."[96]

Conclusion

A midrash explains how one who commits adultery breaks all ten of the commandments. Remembering that the first Jewish commandment is "I am the

91. Aquinas, *The Ten Commandments*, 69–70. Daniel Boyarin's *Carnal Israel: Reading Sex in Talmudic Culture* (Berkeley: University of California Press, 1995) demonstrates how rabbinic Judaism was substantially different from Greek-speaking Judaism in how it represented and spoke about the body and sexuality.

92. Calvin, *Institutes*, 405.

93. Harrelson, *The Ten Commandments*, 131.

94. Harrelson, *The Ten Commandments*, 131.

95. Durham, *The Law Unsealed*, 215.

96. Farkas, *Bench Marks*, 81.

LORD your God," the adulterer and adulteress deny that there is a God who exists who can see and know what they have done in private. They break the second commandment, which includes the description of God as a "jealous God," because they engage in activity that makes the husband of the woman jealous. They break the commandment about not taking God's name in vain because they swear in vain that they have not committed adultery. The rabbis give very specific examples of how they break the commandments about keeping the Sabbath or honoring parents, by telling stories of how the wife of a priest commits adultery and has a son whose father is not from the priestly tribe; when the child grows up and serves as a priest on the Sabbath, he is profaning the Sabbath. Or, when a child does not know the identity of his biological father—because he is a product of adultery—he honors his mother's husband because he believes he is his father, but when he walks through the market, the child hits the adulterer because he thinks he is not his father. The adulterer breaks the commandment against murder because if he is caught, he will be killed. The rabbis note that, obviously, the commandment against adultery is broken because he is committing adultery, but they explain that the adulterer breaks the commandment against stealing because he steals his neighbor's wife. The adulteress breaks the commandment about not bearing false witness when she tells her husband that she is pregnant from him, though she conceived the child after adultery. And the commandment against coveting is broken because the husband will give all his possessions to a son who is not his own. The rabbis concluded, "It turns out that the adulterer covets whatever belongs to his friend" (Midrash Tanhuma, Nasso 2:1). At first reading, the examples in this midrash may appear to be too specific, as if only an adulterous wife of a priest would have an illegitimate son who would profane the Sabbath. Yet, reception of any given text often is, and probably should be, very specific for it to apply to the lives of the people who seek to follow its instructions.

Also as noted above, because understandings of adultery are so connected with understandings of marriage, changing norms and values about marriage—including same-sex marriages and polyamorous marriages—will continue to yield different receptions of the commandment. While no reception history can ever be truly exhaustive, it is particularly true that all permutations surrounding marriage and adultery couldn't be dealt with in this chapter. Additionally, experiences of adultery are vast and varied. Perel describes her experience as a psychotherapist for couples dealing with infidelity, explaining, "The stories I heard ran the gamut. Marriages fell apart, the affair an irreparable breach. . . . Marriages limped along, at times locking horns and other times locked in silence. Marriages came out stronger, the crisis of infidelity serving as a springboard to greater intimacy, commitment, and sexuality. And sometimes new marriages emerged, with the former affair partners becoming the new spouses."[97] Perel observes that because marital relational ethics in the West for many people are no longer dictated by religious authority, definitions of infidelity reside with people, which leads to more freedom and also more uncertainty. Perel therefore counsels, "Couples must draw up their own terms."[98] Such sage advice seems to be at a vast distance from ancient Israel where a marriage was negotiated by the society. Yet Perel often laments the over-privatization that can happen in a marriage in the West, especially when a person expects their (only) spouse to provide everything that a village once did; she encourages people to involve their community to help keep marital relationships strong and faithful.[99] So, even as receptions change through time and societies, connections still remain.

97. Perel, *The State of Affairs: Rethinking Infidelity* (New York: HarperCollins, 2017), 281.

98. Perel, *The State of Affairs*, 22.

99. Perel talks about this frequently, e.g., "Letters from Esther #1—Connection," https://tinyurl.com/38vf6dew.

8

"Don't Steal"

Relatively frequently when I teach that the commandment proclaims "you shall not steal" (Exod 20:15; Deut 5:19), someone in a class will ask, "What about Jean Valjean?" The character from Victor Hugo's powerful nineteenth-century novel *Les Misérables* stole bread for his starving sister and her family and was imprisoned for five years, with another fourteen years added onto his sentence for his numerous attempts at escape. Yes, he was a thief, but for a good reason, and the consequences seem excessive. The benevolent bishop provides a more inspiring example of generosity and mercy; after Valjean has stolen his silverware and has been hauled back by the police, the bishop declares that he had given it to Valjean as a gift and presses the expensive silver candlesticks on him as well. With this gift of silver, the bishop explains, he has bought Valjean's soul for God. On the one hand, Valjean is a good example of an extreme reception of the commandment, when stealing—anything and for any reason—leads to disproportionate, merciless punishments. Additionally, that Valjean is brought up as an example demonstrates how there are reasons to justify breaking each and any of the Ten Commandments, for surely it is not wrong to steal bread for someone who is starving. According to Prov 6:30–31, "People do not despise a thief if he steals to satisfy his hunger when he is starving. Yet if he is caught, he must pay sevenfold, though it costs him all the wealth of his house." This inner-biblical reception of the commandment—and its similarity to the situation of starving peasants in late eighteenth-century France—demonstrates how, yes, one can understand why a person does steal. And yet there are also consequences if that person is caught. Reception history illustrates the extreme and frankly harmful receptions of a commandment, as well as the more benign receptions that seek to justify behavior that seem in contrast with the meaning of the word or its application in the community.

The Act of Stealing

The commandment is simple and brief—another that is only two words in Hebrew—and relatively straightforward, especially in comparison with other southwest Asian laws about theft.[1] The word *gnb* ("steal") only occurs forty times in the Hebrew Bible, with the related nouns "thief" and "stolen object" occurring another nineteen times. This word differs from *lqḥ* ("take") or *gzl* ("rob, seize"): those two words frequently have a connotation of violence or force, but David L. Baker suggests that likely the word used in the commandment "was intended to express the whole semantic range covered by the English words, 'steal,' 'rob,' 'seize,' and 'take by force.'"[2] That is, the word *gnb*, used in Exod 20:15 and Deut 5:19, can reference any number of types of theft: it is a general word. Bonaventure's definitions of different types of theft give an illustrative contrast, as he explains,

> If it is done by pure deceit and in secret, then it is called stealing. If it is done by violence, either the violence is done in the open and is called plundering, or it is hidden and is called a robbery. If the taking of things belonging to another is done by fraud, this can involve an agreement in one of three ways. It can be done with an agreement that is either fraudulent, sinful, or sacrilegious. The first way happens in business and can be done in one of three ways: in weight, or in number, or in measure. . . . If it is done by a sinful agreement it is called usury, in which that is sold is public, namely time. If it is done by a sacrilegious agreement, in which things belonging to God are sold, it is called simony.[3]

Analogous to how the Ten Commandments are so brief that they can be received in a number of ways, this commandment is brief and general enough that it could include plunder, usury, or any of the above. The commandment does not define every possible type of theft;[4] instead, it forbids (all) theft as an action that disrupts the community life of the people of God.

1. David L. Baker explains, "The simplicity of the eighth commandment is unparalleled in all other ancient Near Eastern laws on theft." *The Decalogue: Living as the People of God* (Downers Grove, IL: InterVarsity Press, 2017), 125.

2. Baker, *The Decalogue*, 125.

3. Bonaventure, *St. Bonaventure's Collations on the Ten Commandments*, trans. Paul J. Spaeth (New York: Franciscan Institute, 1995), 91.

4. Baker, *The Decalogue*, 126.

CHAPTER 8

Stealing of People

Frequently, the commandment to not steal was understood as prohibiting stealing a person, as in slavery or kidnapping. Exodus 21:16 warns, "The one who steals a human, and sells him, or if he is found in his hand, will surely die." Certain English versions translate the verb as "kidnap" (NASB, NIV, NRSV), but the word is the same as in the commandment, *gnb*. Deuteronomy 24:7 calls one who "steals any of his fellow Israelites" a "thief," also using the word from the commandment.

Rashi's commentary on this commandment includes his process of reasoning, in a quote worth including in its entirety. He writes,

> Scripture here is speaking about a case of one who steals human beings, whilst the command (Leviticus 19:11) "Ye shall not steal" speaks about a case of one who steals money (another person's property in general). Or perhaps this is not so, but this speaks about the case of one who steals money and the other about the case of one who steals human beings! You must, however, admit that the rule applies: a statement must be explained from its context. How is it in regard to, "Thou shalt not murder" and "Thou shalt not commit adultery"? Each speaks of a matter for which one becomes liable to death by sentence of the court; similarly, "Thou shalt not steal" must speak of a matter for which one becomes liable to death by sentence of the court, and this is not so in the case of theft of money but only in that of kidnapping (Sanhedrin 86a).[5]

In other words, because the commandments against murder, adultery, and theft are all in the same verse in the Hebrew Bible, Rashi understands that committing each act is punishable by death. Yet, because stealing someone's property is not a capital offense—for example, according to Exod 22:1, one who steals an ox or sheep and kills or sells it must pay back five cattle for the ox and four sheep for the sheep—but stealing another human is punishable by death, the commandment refers to the stealing of another human being.[6]

5. Sefaria, citing "Rashi on Exodus 20:13," M. Rosenbaum and A. M. Silbermann, London, 1929–34, https://tinyurl.com/skh7ur3v. With the commandments against murder, adultery, and theft all in the same verse in the Hebrew Bible, Rashi reasons that it is because they are all liable to the death penalty. He further reasons that stealing someone's property is not punishable by death, but stealing a human is, so suggests that the commandment focuses more on stealing a person.

6. In Karlheinz Rabast's translation of Exod 20:15, he added the nouns to have it say, "you shall not steal a man or a woman." Johann Jacob Stamm, with M. E. Andrew, *The Ten Commandments in Recent Research* (London: SCM, 1967), 20.

This reception was important for, and frequent among, abolitionists. The Westminster Larger Catechism of 1647 answered question 142 by identifying the sins forbidden "in the eighth commandment" as "theft, robbery, man-stealing, and receiving anything that is stolen." In 1815, George Bourne, an English-born Presbyterian pastor living in Virginia, was expelled from ministry by his local presbytery after Bourne took a public stance at the General Assembly meeting in Philadelphia in 1815. Jeremy Schipper explains, "Since the catechism considers 'manstealing' a violation of the eighth commandment, [George] Bourne reasoned, Presbyterians should not condone slavery. Bourne's argument did not win the [General] Assembly over, and when he returned home to Virginia, he was defrocked. But Bourne was not deterred. The following year he published a fulsome condemnation of slavery titled *The Book and Slavery Irreconcilable.* This landmark book wove together a wide array of biblical texts and commentaries by earlier theological authorities to show that slavery is a sin."[7] The transatlantic slave trade, because it stole human beings, is considered a violation of the commandment. Nineteenth-century abolitionist Frederick Douglass criticizes those white American Christians who "hug to their communion a man-stealer" but "would be shocked at the proposition of fellowshipping with a sheep-stealer."[8]

These earlier receptions, that the commandment explicitly prohibits the stealing of another human, are echoed in Albrecht Alt's 1953 article, though Alt's argument would not have been helpful for the abolitionists because Alt emphasizes that the human who was protected from theft was the free Israelite male, not a slave. Alt explores the similarities and differences between the commandments against coveting and stealing, suggesting that to covet and to steal are essentially the same transgression at different stages, so what distinguishes the two is the objects, not the action. Noting that the commandment against coveting protects the free Israelite male's household—including his slaves—but not the man himself, Alt argues that the commandment against coveting prohibits the desire for and the taking of a man's property, and the commandment against stealing prohibits taking of the man.[9] Cheryl B. Anderson's discussion of Alt's argument illustrates, again, a feature of reception history as a methodology: Anderson reads the commandment against stealing

7. Jeremy Schipper, *Denmark Vesey's Bible: The Thwarted Revolt That Put Slavery and Scripture on Trial* (Princeton: Princeton University Press, 2022), 25–26.

8. Frederick Douglass, "Slaveholding Religion and the Christianity of Christ," in *African American Religious History: A Documentary Witness*, ed. Milton C. Sernett, 2nd ed. (Durham, NC: Duke University Press, 1999), 106.

9. Albrecht Alt, "Das Verbot des Diebstahls im Dekalog," in *Kleine Schriften zur Geschichte des Volkes Israel, I* (Munich: Beck, 1953), 333–40.

in the light of Martin Luther King Jr.'s vision of the beloved community and is concerned that when the protected person "was defined originally as only an Israelite and only a male," that is "a restriction contrary to King's more inclusive vision." But Anderson continues, "However, what is significant about the commandment, if it also prohibits the stealing of a person, is the way it can be applied more inclusively in our contemporary setting."[10] Indeed, as Anderson notes, an "original definition" does not preclude—in reception history—different applications of the text. Even if Alt's argument has academic merit, it does not prevent Joy Davidman, in her discussion on the commandment, from identifying slaveholding as undoubtedly "the ultimate form of theft."[11]

Like Alt, Christian ethicist Lewis Smedes makes a distinction between the types of things stolen, explaining, "Kidnapping is a sin against what is stolen more than against who is stolen from. You reduce a person to a brute thing; you shrink him to something you can steal like a machine and sell for profit."[12] Unlike Alt, Smedes's reception includes the possibility that the person stolen was the slave or property of another and was stolen for a dehumanizing purpose. Brian Haggerty agrees that the commandment can apply to a human being and suggests that the commandment is broken any time one human takes away—steals—the freedom or dignity of another. In fact, Hagerty suggests the commandment should be reworded as "you shall not deprive other people of their freedom."[13] This reception comes from the theological principle that one member of the community should not exercise control over another; rather, all should be free and equal, because only God is sovereign over people. Haggerty explains, "In sum, we serve the purpose of the commandment not to steal when we respect the freedom and equality of other members of society and remove from our lives whatever threatens to deprive them of their freedom or to deny them equal dignity."[14]

10. Cheryl B. Anderson, "The Eighth Commandment: A Way to King's 'Beloved Community'?," in *The Ten Commandments: The Reciprocity of Faithfulness*, ed. William P. Brown, Library of Theological Ethics (Louisville: Westminster John Knox, 2004), 285–86.

11. Joy Davidman, *Smoke on the Mountain: An Interpretation of the Ten Commandments* (Philadelphia: Westminster, 1954), 100.

12. Lewis Smedes, *Mere Morality: What God Expects from Ordinary People* (Grand Rapids: Eerdmans, 1983), 184.

13. Brian A. Haggerty, *Out of the House of Slavery: On the Meaning of the Ten Commandments* (New York: Paulist, 1978), 136.

14. Haggerty, *Out of the House of Slavery*, 109.

Indirect Theft

Haggerty's statement about stealing someone's freedom or dignity points to another dimension of this commandment: that theft can be of something immaterial and can take place indirectly. A human heart and its corresponding loyalty and devotion can be stolen, according to the story of Absalom's attempt to usurp the throne of his father David in 2 Sam 15–18; 2 Sam 15:6 tells that "Absalom stole the hearts of the people of Israel" using the same word as in the commandment. The Talmud connects Absalom's theft with his death, explaining,

> And because he [Absalom] stole three times, committing three thefts of people's hearts: The heart of his father, as he tricked him by saying that he was going to sacrifice offerings; the heart of the court, as he tricked them into following him; and the heart of the Jewish people, as it is stated: "So Absalom stole the hearts of the men of Israel" (II Samuel 15:6), therefore three spears were embedded into his heart, as it is stated: "Then said Joab: I may not tarry like this with you. And he took three spears in his hand, and thrust them through the heart of Absalom, while he was yet alive" (II Samuel 18:14). (Sotah 9b:7)

Richard N. Levy gives examples of other nonphysical things, explaining, "The prohibition against stealing extends even to non-material thefts, which we hardly think of as stealing at all—to keep other people waiting, thus stealing their time; to forget to credit the author of an idea of a felicitous expression, thus stealing their creativity."[15]

In relationship to stealing something in an indirect manner, Baker writes, "In today's world too, this commandment is not only for burglars and pickpockets—it if were, most of us could claim we have kept it without fail. Rather, it prohibits all kinds of improper gain, whether by marketing inferior-quality goods, charging excessive prices, being involved in financial corruption, filing dishonest tax returns, profiting from others' ignorance, giving and receiving bribes, pilfering at work, traveling on trains or buses without a ticket, ignoring copyright laws, or buying and selling unfairly traded goods."[16] Baker points out that the laws in Deuteronomy about honest weights and measures

15. Richard N. Levy, "A Bit of a Thief," in *Broken Tablets: Restoring the Ten Commandments and Ourselves*, ed. Rachel S. Mikva (Woodstock, VT: Jewish Lights, 1999), 103.

16. Baker, *The Decalogue*, 128.

(Deut 25:13–16) encourage fair trade, whereby one person does not take advantage of another. He admits that it would be naïve to assume that the motives of all fair-trade promoters today are altruistic[17] but that purchasing things produced fairly can be especially important for local workers.

Davidman writes that it is easy to identify theft when it is overtly physical, such as when we see someone stealing a car or breaking into a bank. "But swindling, on the other hand! But rigging contracts, bribing officials, finding loopholes in the tax laws, playing tricks with foreign exchange, lying about the goods we sell and selling trash! How cleverly all these forms of dishonesty can masquerade themselves as legitimate business methods."[18] The Heidelberg Catechism uses similar language, explaining, "In God's sight theft also includes cheating and swindling our neighbor by schemes made to appear legitimate, such as: inaccurate measurements of weight, size, or volume; fraudulent merchandising; counterfeit money; excessive interest, or any other means forbidden by God." Calvin writes that thefts occur in many ways, including "in a more concealed craftiness, when a man's goods are snatched from him by seemingly legal means. Still another lies in flatteries, when one is cheated of his goods under the pretense of a gift."[19] Luther put it in broad terms, explaining stealing as "nothing other than acquiring someone else's property by unjust means. . . . This includes taking advantage of our neighbor to his loss in any sort of dealing."[20]

In 1600, Robert Allen included an extensive list of ways that one might break the commandment by unjustly "getting other men's goods out of their hands":[21] in relation to buying, one might pretend something is worth less than its true value or might pay with counterfeit money. Concerning selling, the examples include overpricing, selling average or substandard goods as though they were of the best quality, using false weights and measures, selling lands or titles with false or forged evidence, and passing off sickly animals as healthy. Landlords specifically break the commandment by raising rents, taking away common land, or allowing nearby properties to remain desolate in order to live more privately. Allen warns those renting land or houses against exhibiting

17. Baker, *The Decalogue*, 130.

18. Davidman, *Smoke on the Mountain*, 97–98.

19. John Calvin, *Institutes of the Christian Religion*, ed. John T. McNeill, trans. and indexed by Ford Lewis Battles (Philadelphia: Westminster, 1960), 409.

20. Luther, *The Large Catechism*, 47–48.

21. Robert Allen, *A treasurie of catechisme, or Christian instruction. The first part, which is concerning the morall law or ten Commandements of Almightie God: with certaine questions and aunswers preparatory to the same*, Early English Books Online 2, https://tinyurl.com/4jvsv8jw, 209.

greed in outbidding one another. Borrowers may break the commandment by not paying back their debts, not paying enough, or paying too slowly. Lenders must not refuse to lend without some pawn if a neighbor is in need and you sustain no loss or hindrance through lending. Allen encourages those who pay wages to not keep money that is due to workers and not to defer payment overlong. Those working must keep the commandment by not being negligent nor presuming above their level of skill. Those in partnership must not fail in work or in oversight. Allen ends the list by advising all readers to not try to gain material advantage through trickery in games such as loading dice or packing cards.[22] Notwithstanding the sheer volume of Allen's examples, many of them are not what one would consider direct theft.

Contemporary pastor Al Vom Steeg identifies a person not tithing as another way to break the commandment. He explains, "When the Church lacks money to accomplish its Godly purposes, it is not because God does not supply it, but because the people of God have chosen not to give it and are stealing from God."[23] God already owns everything, Vom Steeg explains, and to give back to God is a reminder to us of that fact. He writes, "The tithe is to help us keep our possessions from possessing us. . . . The tithe is a biblical injunction for my sake."[24] In other words, by *not* giving God—and the church—a tithe, a person indirectly breaks the commandment, "you shall not steal."

Stealing and Poverty

As the example of the peasant Jean Valjean from the beginning of the chapter demonstrates, poverty and injustice are important dimensions in the reception of this commandment. Some suggest that the prohibition against theft is primarily in the interest of the wealthy. For example, David J. A. Clines argues that the commandment protects the rich who have possessions they want to hold on to.[25] Allen Verhey writes, "Let's be honest. The eighth commandment has always been the favorite commandment of the propertied class. The rich cherish both the authorization it seems to afford to their possessions and the

22. Allen, *A treasurie of catechisme*, 209–12.

23. Al Vom Steeg, *Freedom to Live: A Guide to a Free and Abundant Life as Revealed through the Ten Commandments* (Des Moines, IA: Meredith, 1984), 101.

24. Vom Steeg, *Freedom to Live*, 100.

25. David J. A. Clines, "The Ten Commandments: Reading from Left to Right," in *Interested Parties: The Ideology of Writers and Readers of the Hebrew Bible*, ed. David J. A. Clines (Sheffield: Sheffield Phoenix, 2009), 42.

protection it evidently provides against any who would take them away—including (and especially) the poor. The economically powerful have frequently read the commandment in self-serving ways, defending their tightfisted grip on their own prosperity and security as a faithful performance of the law of God."[26] In fact, in Calvin's treatment of the commandment, he includes his assumption that what every person has—and correspondingly, what every poor person does not have—is distributed by God and God's dispensation.[27]

By contrast, J. Gordon McConville explains that the commandment "you shall not steal" is particularly important for protecting the poor; those who have such limited property that what they have is necessary for survival.[28] Similarly, Robert Gnuse asserts that modern scholars "recognize the command to be an attempt to protect persons, especially the poor," explaining, "We have for too long used this command as the safeguard for the institution of private property against the human needs of the poor and dispossessed."[29] Walter Harrelson suggests that, instead of emphasizing private ownership and possession, a better application of the commandment today would be for people to commit "to sharing the goods of the earth more widely and more fairly."[30] Harrelson sees the society of ancient Israel as one where property is never as important as, or even more important than, the life of other humans and asserts, "Therein lies the continuing import of this commandment for today."[31]

Another biblical proverb about theft and poverty—in addition to the verses in Prov 6:30–31 mentioned at the beginning of the chapter—connects poverty, stealing, and taking God's name in vain. In the sayings of Agur, he asks God, "Remove far from me falsehood and lying, give me neither poverty nor riches; feed me with the food that I need, lest I be full and deny you and say, 'Who is the LORD?' or I be poor and steal and profane the name of my God" (Prov 30:8–9). Notably, both wealth and poverty would lead to misuse of God's name, but being poor is what leads to stealing; the word in Prov 30:8 is the

26. Allen Verhey, "Calvin and the 'Stewardship of Love,'" in *The Ten Commandments for Jews, Christians, and Others*, ed. Roger E. Van Harn (Grand Rapids: Eerdmans, 2007), 157.

27. Calvin, *Institutes*, 409.

28. J. Gordon McConville, *Deuteronomy*, Apollos Old Testament Commentary 5, ed. David W. Baker and Gordon J. Wenham (Downers Grove, IL: IVP Academic; Nottingham: Apollos, 2002), 130.

29. Robert Karl Gnuse, *You Shall Not Steal: Community and Property in the Biblical Tradition* (Eugene, OR: Wipf & Stock, 1985), 9.

30. Walter Harrelson, *The Ten Commandments and Human Rights* (Philadelphia: Fortress, 1980), 7.

31. Harrelson, *The Ten Commandments*, 138.

same as in the commandment. The prolific hymn writer Isaac Watts has a song titled "The Ten Commandments" with one line for each commandment. The commandments against adultery and theft are reworded to rhyme as "Abstain from words and deeds unclean; nor steal, though thou art poor and mean."[32] Watts adds no other description to any of the other commandments, so the addition of a situation in which a person is "poor and mean" is noteworthy, as if to say that stealing is forbidden no matter what.

Many of the Puritan receptions of the commandment specify that in addition to prohibiting stealing, it encourages generosity to those who are in need. Lancelot Andrewes, for example, explains that obeying this commandment in relationship to other people means "liberality to them that want. We must let our fountains run abroad, something must be given to the poor."[33] Seventeenth-century Scottish Puritan James Durham writes about giving alms as a way to keep the commandment and specifies that there are three degrees of need among the poor: (1) common need, to which others should give out of their abundance;[34] (2) "pinching" need, that may require some effort from the giver, such as when a person has two coats, they must give one; and (3) extreme need when a person "cannot subsist," and which asks of the giver "to sell all and divide it," though Durham clarifies that such giving "is not always called for."[35] Levy asserts, "Stealing is a serious crime in Jewish tradition. So is the sin of encouraging stealing by refusing to share the bounty God has temporarily entrusted to us."[36]

Theft Today

In 1991, the American animated television series *The Simpsons* aired an episode titled "Homer vs. Lisa and the 8th Commandment." Homer—the patriarch of the family—pays for an illegal cable hookup from a dishonest cable man, and

32. Isaac Watts, *Divine and Moral Songs for the Use of Children* (London: John Van Voorst, 1848), 68.

33. Lancelot Andrewes, *A Pattern of Catechistical Doctrine and Other Minor Works* (Oxford: John Henry Parker, 1846; New York: AMS, 1967), 260.

34. Calvin similarly encourages, "Let us share the necessity of those whom we see pressed by the difficulty of affairs, assisting them in their need with our abundance." *Institutes*, 410.

35. James Durham, *The Law Unsealed, or, a practical exposition of the Ten Commandments. With a resolution of several momentous questions and cases of conscience*, Early English Books Online, https://tinyurl.com/phfsuw6v, 252.

36. Levy, "A Bit of a Thief," 108.

the family enjoys watching all the new channels. The oldest daughter, Lisa, however, is suspicious about the cable hookup, and after a Sunday school lesson in church about the Ten Commandments, when the teacher gets to "you shall not steal," she envisions her house fading away, replaced by the fires of hell where the devil has joined her family on the couch to watch cable with them. Satan invites her to join them, saying there is no cost: "except your soul!" A few days later the cable installer lets himself into the Simpson house, offering to sell Homer stolen stereo equipment, assuming that because Homer was open to pirated cable, he would be open to other stolen goods. Homer refuses but then becomes worried about how easily the cable installer had gained entry into his house, so he installs bars on his windows and places a sign saying "No Thieves" on his lawn. He tells his wife, "There are thieves everywhere, and I'm not talking about the small forgiveable stuff." Taking the advice of their pastor, Lisa protests by no longer watching television with the family. Her father is eventually persuaded to cut the cable but only after he has hosted his friends to watch a cable TV boxing match.

This reception of the commandment illustrates several contemporary issues surrounding stealing. Writer Jeff Martin explains that when creating this episode the staff decided to use "a very strict construction of the eighth commandment," even though cable theft is "essentially a victimless crime, the kind of thing that many, many good people do."[37] Certainly, the episode shows the possibility of a (too?) strict punishment, similar to Valjean's years in prison for stealing a loaf of bread: Would people go to hell for purchasing an illegal cable hookup? Is this sort of theft that bad? Homer's language of "small forgivable stuff" and Martin's description that this is "the kind of thing that many, many good people do" indicate once again a level of justification. Nor is a casual acceptance of types of theft something new; centuries ago Luther wrote, "Now, stealing is a widespread, common vice, but so little notice is taken of it that it has gotten very much out of hand. If all who are thieves but do not want to admit it were strung up on the gallows, the world would soon be emptied and there would not be enough gallows and hangmen."[38] Luther, also, does not shy away from discussing harsh punishment.

Another issue raised in *The Simpsons* episode is the nature of theft in a world where many goods are provided by corporations, not individuals. The

37. Mark I. Pinsky, *The Gospel according to the Simpsons, Bigger and Possibly Even Better! Edition* (Louisville: Westminster John Knox, 2007), 106.

38. Luther, *Large Catechism*, 47.

term "victimless crime" was popularized in 1965 by sociologist Edwin Schur;[39] the idea is that it describes a crime without an identifiable victim. Certainly, the theft of a cable hookup is quite different from stealing a specific personal item that belongs to a specific person. Would the victims be the amorphous entity of the cable company or the employees of the company? If the latter, would it be the owners, the shareholders, the workers? Is any stealing from a large retail corporation "a victimless crime"? Is it different for a small business than for a large corporation? According to the International Centre for Retail Research, the cost of retail theft in 2018–19 was $35 billion in the United States and almost $25 billion in Europe.[40] In 2022, it was estimated by the Global Retail Theft Barometer that US retailers would lose $1.8 million in stolen merchandise in just the four weeks leading up to Christmas.[41] Stores have attempted to combat retail theft of commonly stolen items such as toothpaste or laundry detergent by locking those items up so that a shopper would need to ask to purchase them; such efforts also deter shoppers from making in-store purchases, with sales of those items dropping 15–25 percent.[42] The retail theft examples above still have to do with people stealing physical items, but another complicating issue today is what it means to steal something digital or electronic. When unlimited copies are available for download, or multiple people can watch the same entertainment through their cable cords, is stealing less problematic?

The Simpsons often references other cultural products; the opening scene of the episode "Homer vs. Lisa and the 8th Commandment" parodies the 1956 Cecil B. DeMille film *The Ten Commandments*. This raises other issues related to theft today regarding copyrights, trademarks, and intellectual property, including creative artistic works. When is a piece of music "sampling" another one, and when has it stolen a melody from elsewhere? When is a scene parodying or borrowing from another one, and when has it stolen from it? When is a paper drawing on other scholars' insights, and when has it tipped over into plagiarism? Technological advances, including more advanced AI,

39. Edwin Schur, *Crimes without Victims: Deviant Behavior and Public Policy; Abortion, Homosexuality, Drug Addictions* (Englewood Cliffs, NJ: Prentice Hall, 1965).

40. Centre for Retail Research, "Crime Comparisons: Retail Crime in the U.S., UK and Europe 2019," https://tinyurl.com/559x6hef.

41. Amy L. Knapp, "The Season of Taking: Shoplifting Jumps, Exposing Depth of Problem," *The Independent*, December 21, 2022, https://tinyurl.com/y7tkw8x9.

42. Kelly Tyko, "Shoplifting Deterrents Drive Down Sales," *Axios*, February 20, 2023, https://tinyurl.com/vmfckxy3.

certainly complicate the nature of theft, but perhaps that is why there is something refreshing about the simplicity of the statement "you shall not steal."

Broader Implications

Baker suggests that the commandment "may also be taken as a challenge to reflect on larger economic structures. Such structures within and between nations can make robbery an institution and ensure the rich stay rich while others are permanently poor." Baker includes issues like inflation and debt as examples of those larger economic structures.[43] The Heidelberg Catechism explains that the commandment additionally "forbids all greed." Such a broad application would certainly touch on many issues around money, wealth, and possessions.

Andrewes specifically discusses the question of wanting and acquiring possessions as it relates to the commandment. He explains that "you shall not steal" forbids "the lust of the eyes"[44] but permits what he calls "lawful desire." For example, he writes, one might desire to have more when his household grows and he needs more; one might also desire to have more to be able to give to the church, to pay tribute to the king or taxes for the commonwealth, or to give to "the poor saints" and to whoever is in need. But, according to Andrewes, going into "desire out of measure" will first "come in the end to a murmuring and envying of others in better estate than ourselves; secondly to an unquiet overcare and taking thought what we shall eat and what we shall do (Matt 6:31, Luke 12:17); and thirdly, to breed a nest of horse leeches, which are worms, that have *linguam bisulcam*, 'a cloven' or 'a forked tongue,' and cry, 'bring, bring'; *unde habeas nihil refert, sed oportet habere*, 'no matter whence you get it, have it you must'; and this is that which we may call *suppurationem concupiscentiae*, 'an inward rankling of concupiscence.'"[45] In other words, a person who keeps this commandment may desire and even acquire possessions, but too much wanting could lead to a state where internal pests with insatiable desires are constantly asking for more. Similarly, centuries later, Hungarian pastor József Farkas clarifies what it means to want without transgressing the commandment, explaining,

43. Baker, *The Decalogue*, 120.
44. Andrewes, *A Pattern of Catechistical Doctrine*, 247.
45. Andrewes, *A Pattern of Catechistical Doctrine*, 252.

> Many believers would answer, in God's name, that God would command us to be content with what we have—to be modest, undemanding, resigned; if therefore, you feel that there is something more you want in your life, call this feeling sin, uproot it from your heart, and then you will not steal. This sounds good, and I'm not saying that it does not contain some truth. However, I do not believe that this is essentially God's thought. I would express God's thought in this way: "Man, you are right in your desire for a richer life. I myself would have you live an abundant life. You are right if you want more. But you are not supposed to take this 'more' from others. You are supposed to *create it yourself*."[46]

Several Puritan commentators add that this commandment forbids two extremes: "niggardliness" and "prodigality." Andrewes defines "niggardliness" as "too much sparing" by which "a man may commit theft toward himself."[47] "Prodigality," on the other hand, is "too much wasting." It also is stealing from oneself in that when one wastes superfluously, Andrewes explains, one will eventually want and need things.[48] Allen similarly expresses that people may have an unjust relationship with their own possessions, "either by a niggardly and fast keeping of them, or contrariwise, by an overlavish and prodigal misspending of them."[49] Durham refers to such practices as "inordinateness," encouraging that people avoid the extremes and seek to keep within just boundaries in relationship with their possessions.[50] Harrelson reflects on what he calls "the incredible wastefulness of much of Western life," which he sees as evident in people who replace furnishings of their homes and even the homes themselves "to such extent and with such frequency that we are virtually without personal possessions that count for anything."[51] Harrelson contrasts that with people whose possessions are either treasured or essential for their life, saying, "For persons of average means, however, loss of property

46. József Farkas, *Bench Marks*, trans. John R. Bodo (Richmond, VA: John Knox, 1969).
47. Andrewes, *A Pattern of Catechistical Doctrine*, 258.
48. Andrewes, *A Pattern of Catechistical Doctrine*, 259.
49. Robert Allen, *A treasurie of catechisme, or Christian instruction. The first part, which is concerning the morall law or ten Commandements of Almightie God: with certaine questions and aunswers preparatory to the same*, Early English Books Online 2, https://tinyurl.com/4jvsv8jw, 213.
50. Durham, *The Law Unsealed*, 238.
51. Walter Harrelson, *The Ten Commandments and Human Rights* (Philadelphia: Fortress, 1980), 140.

was not a matter of life and death. And yet the commandment not to steal stands right along with those prohibiting murder and adultery. It does so because persons do depend for a wholesome life upon the materials with which that life is surrounded."[52]

Positive Implications

Allen summarizes much of the above discussion about a healthy relationship with one's possessions when saying that "preservatives against theft and all kinds of unrighteousness include well using and well bestowing of the same outward goods of this world."[53] Allen and Andrewes both also advocate contentment: for Allen, keeping the commandment requires "a full and settled contentment of mind," followed by other virtues of seeking after God's kingdom, having faith in God's providence, love of righteousness, love of neighbor "with joy in his prosperity as it if were our own," diligence in one's own labor, praying to God to bless that labor, and fearing God's punishment of all of our unrighteous actions.[54]

Calvin teaches that a positive expression of the commandment is to faithfully help all people by our counsel and to aid them in keeping what is theirs; he urges, "Let this be our constant aim."[55] A teaching in the Talmud explains that if someone stole a wooden beam and built it into his building, he should tear down the entire building and return the beam to its owner (Taanit 16a:13).

Luther's definition of stealing as "taking advantage of our neighbor," discussed above, may be nuanced slightly with a story told by Gregory Boyle who works in Los Angeles with the rehabilitation of gang members. During an interview with Anderson Cooper, Cooper told Boyle, "The police say you're naïve. That gang members take advantage of you." Boyle writes, "I always have the same answer at the ready, 'How can someone take my advantage when I'm giving it?'"[56] In other words, not only is Boyle preventing theft by generously giving to those with whom he is in a relationship, he may also be obeying the commandment by not taking from them.

52. Harrelson, *The Ten Commandments*, 141.

53. Allen, *A treasurie of catechism*, 217.

54. Allen, *A treasurie of catechism*, 217–18.

55. Calvin, *Institutes*, 409–10.

56. Gregory Boyle, *Barking to the Choir: The Power of Radical Kinship* (New York: Simon & Schuster, 2017), 86.

Conclusion

In relationship to stealing, Aquinas says, "No sin is so dangerous as this. Of other sins a man quickly repents, for instance of murder when his anger ceases, or of fornication, when his lust has subsided, and so on: whereas although a man sometimes repents of stealing, he does not easily atone for it; especially in view of his obligation not only to restore what he took, but also to indemnify the owner for the loss incurred, which is besides his obligation to repent of his sin."[57] As mentioned in the introductory chapter, each commandment has someone proclaiming that it is "the most" significant or important, so Aquinas's opinion on this commandment is shared by others regarding other commandments. If there is a significance to the order in which commandments are listed in Jer 7:9, "steal" does precede "murder and adultery." But we may want to add some qualification to Aquinas's assertion; surely other sins may be as dangerous, or perhaps it is that the danger is worse depending on what is stolen, from whom, and how. Philo's comment on theft may be more easy to agree with; he explains that stealing anything is problematic because even if it is the smallest trifle, it may become habitual.[58]

Though I am the one who collected the various examples of stealing for this chapter, I nonetheless still marvel at their range: stealing a human being for slavery is quite different from stealing a loaf of bread for a starving family member, which is different still from stealing a streaming service for a televised sporting event. Yet the brevity of the commandment is what enables all the various examples in reception history. Certainly, while the examples are not the same, they all demonstrate legitimate areas in which to understand and apply the commandment in our own lives.

57. Thomas Aquinas, *The Commandments of God: Conferences on the Two Precepts of Charity and the Ten Commandments*, trans. Laurence Shapcote, OP, with an introduction by Thomas Gilby, OP (London: Burns, Oates & Washbourne, 1937), 75.

58. Philo, *The Works of Philo: Complete and Unabridged*, trans. C. D. Yonge (Peabody, MA: Hendrickson: 2006), 530.

9

"Don't Bear False Witness"

Early twentieth-century American Egyptologist James Henry Breasted reflects,

> I remember that when I fibbed I found consolation in the fact that there was no commandment, "Thou shalt not lie," and that the Decalogue forbade lying only as a "false witness" giving testimony before the courts where it might damage one's neighbor. In later years when I was much older, I began to be troubled by the fact that a code of morals which did not forbid lying seemed imperfect; but it was a long time before I raised this interesting question: How has my own realization of this imperfection arisen? Where did I myself get the moral yardstick by which I discovered this shortcoming in the Decalogue?[1]

Some of Breasted's fascinating ideas cannot be unpacked here, including that there is a "shortcoming" in the Decalogue and that he received a moral yardstick outside of revealed and taught biblical law. By his own admission, he was considering only the Ten Commandments, and it is true that the commandment in Exod 20:16 and Deut 5:20 does not specifically state "you shall not lie." However, his "consolation" was incorrect, because Lev 19:11 does admonish, "Do not lie, do not deceive one another," and 19:16 says, "Do not go about spreading slander among your people." Additionally, Breasted's quote points to how many receptions of this commandment do simplify and abbreviate it as "don't lie," when it is one of the longer ones in the so-called second tablet. While the commandments to not murder, commit adultery, or steal consist of only two Hebrew words, this commandment is five words in Hebrew (*l' t'nh br'k 'd šqr*), which I translate as "you shall not testify against your neighbor as a lying witness."

1. James Henry Breasted, *The Dawn of Conscience* (New York: Charles Scribner's Sons, 1933), xi.

A commitment to truth is certainly part of this commandment but to reduce the commandment to simply "don't lie" is, well, reductionistic in two ways. First, it misses out on the legal dimension of this commandment. Second, and significantly, the words in Exod 20:16 and Deut 5:20 include the term "your neighbor." So, instead of an absolute and abstract commandment to never in any circumstance tell a lie, this commandment highlights the importance of telling truth about your neighbor, particularly in legal situations but always in a context of generosity, trust, and relationship.

Testifying and Witnessing: Legal Setting

The Hebrew language "testify" and "witness" suggests a legal setting; Martin Luther writes that the "first and most obvious sense of this commandment relates to public courts of justice."[2] When this commandment is echoed in the book of the covenant, a legal setting is clear: "You shall not spread a false report. You shall not join hands with the wicked to act as a malicious witness. You shall not follow a majority in wrongdoing; when you bear witness in a lawsuit, you shall not side with the majority so as to pervert justice, nor shall you be partial to the poor in a lawsuit" (Exod 23:1–3). In ancient Israel, the location for legal deliberations includes the "assembly," as in the story of Naboth's vineyard, when two *bny-bly'l* (literally "sons of Belial" or "scoundrels") falsely accuse Naboth of cursing God and the king (1 Kgs 21:9–13), which leads to Naboth's death by stoning. The two "wicked" elders—who are also judges—in the book of Susanna falsely testify in the assembly that Susanna had sent her maids away so that she could have sex with a young man (Sus 1:36–41).[3] "A lying witness who testifies falsely" (Prov 6:19) is included in the list of seven things that the LORD hates. And Amos 5:10 describes the level of corruption in Israel as a hatred for the one who speaks truth and "reproves in the gate"—the gate being the location for public courts.

2. Martin Luther, *Luther's Large Catechism with Study Questions*, ed. F. Samuel Janzow (St. Louis: Concordia, 1978), 53.

3. The assembly is also the location where the Levite is called to explain "this wickedness" against his concubine. Arguably, his "witness" is false, or at least not entirely true, as he omits the detail that he had shoved her out of the house to the mob, who raped her. He also testifies that the mob wanted to kill him, whereas in Lev 19 they "only" want to rape him; and as Phyllis Trible has convincingly demonstrated, it is not clear if she had died before he cut her up into pieces, as he also testifies. *Texts of Terror: Literary-Feminist Readings of Biblical Narratives* (Minneapolis: Fortress, 2022), 79. (The LXX does say that she had died in ch. 19, before his testimony in ch. 20.)

In the account of Jesus's trial in Matthew's gospel, the chief priests and Sanhedrin look for "false evidence" against Jesus, and many "false witnesses" come forward, including two who testify that Jesus said he could destroy the temple and rebuild it in three days (Matt 26:59–61). And in the book of Acts, Stephen is stoned after members of the so-called Synagogue of the Freedmen produce false witnesses against him (Acts 6:9–14). These stories illustrate how, despite the clarity of the commandment, people continue to testify falsely in the Bible.

Legal codes attempt to dissuade false testimony by asking witnesses to swear oaths; the contemporary oath to "tell the truth" in a court setting traces back to ancient southwestern Asian Law codes.[4] Such oaths assume that punishment would occur at least in the next life, if not in this one, but several legal codes include detailed and imaginative punishments for committing perjury.[5] Perhaps pessimism—or realism—about the persistence of false witnesses is why Deut 19:15–20 explains that one witness is not enough to convict anyone accused of a crime, and if the witness proves to be false, the witness will suffer the punishment intended for the accused.[6] Num 35:30 mandates that no one will be put to death because of the testimony of a single witness. Then again, as the cases against Naboth, Susanna, and Jesus illustrate, it is not hard to find two false witnesses.

Indeed, false witnesses in legal settings are prevalent and persistent throughout history. Richard H. Underwood suggests that they started with Cain, who, though he did not have much a trial by contemporary standards, responded to God's question about Abel's location with a lie that an American lawyer today might characterize as "the original 'exculpatory no.'"[7] From

4. Richard H. Underwood, "False Witness: A Lawyer's History of the Law of Perjury," *Arizona Journal of International and Comparative Law* 10 (1993): 219–22. Underwood observes, for example, how the Egyptian Instructions of Amen-Em Opet state that a person must not "bear witness with false words" and how the Code of Hammurabi states, "If a man make a false accusation against a man, putting a ban upon him, and cannot prove it, then the accuser shall be put to death."

5. For example, the Hindu *Laws of Manu*, ca. 200 BCE, include the statement, "Naked and shorn, tormented with hunger and thirst, and deprived of sight, shall the man who gives false evidence go with a potsherd to beg food at the door of his enemy." Underwood, "False Witness," 226.

6. Aviya Kushner speculates that this law in Deuteronomy is why Rashi doesn't discuss this commandment in his comments about the commandments in the Hebrew version of Exod 20:13, which are all related to each other. *The Grammar of God: A Journey into the Words and Worlds of the Bible* (New York: Spiegel & Grau, 2015), 130.

7. Underwood, "False Witness," 215. The "exculpatory no" in criminal law draws from the Fifth Amendment right against self-incrimination and says that a person cannot be

biblical examples onward, there are too many false witnesses to exhaustively recount, but famous examples include the soldier John Scofield, who, after being involved in an altercation in 1803 with the artist and poet William Blake, falsely accused Blake of sedition against the king. Blake was eventually acquitted, but spent a year in jail.[8] US Senator Burton K. Wheeler was falsely indicted while fighting corruption in Warren G. Harding's presidential administration during the 1920s; his story loosely inspired the fictional Mr. Jefferson Smith in the Frank Capra movie *Mr. Smith Goes to Washington*. Several books that share the title "False Witness" discuss historical examples, two of which relate to communism in America. In Harvey Matusow's memoir *False Witness*, he was the one who falsely accused hundreds of people as Communists or Communist sympathizers in the early 1950s, while Melvin Miller Rader was himself accused of being a Communist in 1948 by the Washington State Legislature's Committee on Un-American Activities in 1948.[9] As the subtitle indicates, Patricia Lambert's 1999 *False Witness: The Real Story of Jim Garrison's Investigation and Oliver Stone's Film JFK* focuses on New Orleans District Attorney Jim Garrison and his investigation of John F. Kennedy's murder. The Equal Justice Initiative in the United States challenges wrongful convictions in the courts; according to a 2016 report, half of those could be traced to witnesses who lied in courts or made false accusations.[10] False witnesses even outside the courtroom can lead to terrible consequences, as was made salient in the horrific murder of Emmett Till in 1955, who was falsely accused by Carolyn Bryant of making verbal and physical advances against her. Bryant testified as much in court, but five decades later she admitted that she had lied on the stand of the trial against his murderers about Till; her false accusations before his death led directly to his brutal death.[11] The title of Journalist Dorothy Rabinowitz's

---

punished for lying about their guilt when questioned by an investigator. The US Supreme Court, however, in 1998 decided that this rule does not apply in US federal law. Brogan v. United States, 522 U.S. 398 (1998), https://tinyurl.com/yc3xmash.

8. Kenneth R. Johnston, "Blake's *America*, the Prophecy That Failed: William Blake (1757–1827)," in *Unusual Suspects: Pitt's Reign of Alarm and the Lost Generation of the 1790s* (Oxford: Oxford University Press, 2013), 307–22.

9. Rader was a paid FBI informer who named hundreds of people as Communists or Communist sympathizers in the early 1950s; after the publication of his book in 1955, he was imprisoned for perjury.

10. The National Registry of Exonerations, "Basic Patterns," November 2016, https://tinyurl.com/55t2wfrj. Similar statistics can be found on the website for the Innocence Project (https://innocenceproject.org/), with false witnesses being particularly high against people of color.

11. In an interview with Timothy Tyson in Raleigh, NC, on September 8, 2008, Carolyn

2004 book is suggestive, if perhaps slightly hyperbolic: *No Crueler Tyrannies: Accusation, False Witness, and Other Terrors of Our Times.*

If tyranny is the experience of the one against whom the witness gives false testimony, Puritan Lancelot Andrewes describes the false witness using analogies of a weapon wielded against other parties in a lawsuit. Andrewes compares the false witness to a hammer to the judge, hitting the judge on the head so that the judge does not know how to determine the case, and a sword to the person who hires the false witness: a sword that fights for the cause of the one who hired him "but withal a sword to kill his soul, because he is his instrument against the truth."[12]

False witnesses may not always be malicious. As interrogation expert James L. Trainum explains, some make honest mistakes of memory, especially because memory is so malleable; data suggests that the more a person is questioned, the more likely it is that a memory could be contaminated by the investigator. Others may be under the influence of suggestion from investigators who use leading questions to contaminate or even manipulate the testimony. Sometimes witnesses know they are lying but persist in their story because of the consequences they may suffer if they tell the truth.[13] The difference between a witness who intentionally lies and one who tells a falsehood—for whatever reason—may be encapsulated in the difference between the adjectives given for the witness in the commandment in Exodus and Deuteronomy. In Exod 20:16, the commandment forbids acting as a "lying (*šeqer*) witness"; and in Deut 5:20, it is a "false (*šāwʾ*) witness." The distinctions will be discussed in more detail below.

Bryant Donham told him that her testimony was not true, saying, "Nothing that boy did could ever justify what happened to him." Tyson, *The Blood of Emmett Till* (New York: Simon & Schuster, 2017), 6–7. Tyson writes about the many possibilities for blame, concluding, "We blame them to avoid seeing that the lynching of Emmett Till was caused by the nature and history of America itself and by a social system that has changed over the decades, but not as much as we pretend." *The Blood of Emmett Till*, 208.

12. Lancelot Andrewes, *A Pattern of Catechistical Doctrine and Other Minor Works* (Oxford: John Henry Parker, 1846; New York: AMS, 1967), 270–71. The simile Andrewes uses for the one against whom the person is witnessing falsely is an arrow. As Andrewes discusses the many various parties who might also commit "false witness" in a legal situation, he includes the accuser who may be a false witness by his untrue accusation, the defendant by his untrue defense, the judge by the wrong determination, the notary or registrar by entering the sentence amiss, and the advocate by informing amiss.

13. James L. Trainum, *How the Police Generate False Confessions: An Inside Look at the Interrogation Room* (Lanham, MD: Rowman & Littlefield, 2016), 175.

False Witness beyond the Courtroom

Testimony in a legal setting is very specific, and even limited, which is likely why the scope of application of this commandment broadens out as a general prohibition against lying. An early reception of this may be in the statement in Lev 19:11 and 16, already mentioned above: the Hebrew word for "slander" in Lev 19:16 (*rkyl*) never occurs in legal settings but refers generally to a person who tells false tales. While Prov 6:19, also mentioned above, specifically refers to a "false witness," earlier in the list of the things God hates is the more broad "lying tongue" (Prov 6:17). A number of illustrated versions of the Ten Commandments accompany this commandment with images of the lying spies in Numbers 13 or Jacob increasing his flocks over and against Laban's by his clever, albeit deceitful, animal husbandry (Genesis 30).[14] And while Matt 15:19 includes "false witness" as something evil that comes out of the heart, the list there also includes the more general term "slander."[15]

Several receptions acknowledge that the courtroom was the initial focus of the commandment but that it was not limited to that setting. For example, twentieth-century commentator Johann Stamm asserts that, because the courtroom was the primary location for this commandment, extending the commandment to the sphere of lying "must take place only secondarily. But here it may be done with a good conscience, and not only because false witness itself is an extreme particular case of lying, but also for the reason that the Old Testament, when it designates the false witness frequently as lying witness, has seen the essence of the false witness in the lie itself."[16] Luther similarly agrees that the commandment focuses at first on legal testimony but then broadens its application to prohibit "lying and malevolent talk outside of the courtroom" and then, even beyond, to "all sins of the tongue against one's neighbor. . . . Included is especially the repulsive, shameful vice of scandalmongering or slander, to which the devil spurs us on."[17]

14. Ilja Veldman, "The Old Testament as a Moral Code: Old Testament Stories as Exempla of the Ten Commandments," *Simiolus: Netherlands Quarterly for the History of Art* 23 (1995): 218, 220, 232.

15. As discussed in the first chapter of the book, this reference seems to be a partial list of the Ten Commandments, including murder, adultery, sexual immorality, theft, and therefore it is interesting that false witness and slander are both mentioned. (As discussed in chapter 7, Matt 15 also seems to extend "adultery" to include "sexual immorality.")

16. Johann Jacob Stamm, with M. E. Andrew, *The Ten Commandments in Recent Research* (London: SCM, 1967), 109–10.

17. Luther, *Large Catechism*, 54.

The study catechism approved by the 1998 General Assembly of the Presbyterian Church (USA) includes a question that explains that the commandment also forbids racism and other forms of negative stereotyping. Question 115 is answered in the catechism as follows: "In forbidding false witness against my neighbor, God forbids me to be prejudiced against people who belong to any vulnerable, different or disfavored social group. Jews, women, homosexuals, racial and ethnic minorities, and national enemies are among those who have suffered terribly from being subjected to the slurs of social prejudice." Miroslav Volf and Linn Tonstad suggest that such prejudices are not deliberately bearing false witness because often we slip into judgment without even considering if it is based on sufficient knowledge or justified grounds, but to avoid persisting in false witness we have the responsibility to acquire knowledge necessary to make correct judgments.[18]

With some sarcasm, John Calvin writes, "And yet it is wonderful with what thoughtless unconcern we sin in this respect time and again! Those who do not markedly suffer from this disease are rare indeed. We delight in a certain poisoned sweetness experienced in ferreting out and in disclosing the evils of others. And let us not think it an adequate excuse if in many instances we are not lying." Calvin also gives very specific examples, saying that the commandment "even extends to forbidding us to affect a fawning politeness barbed with bitter taunts under the guise of joking. Some do this who crave praise for their witticisms, to others' shame and grief, because they sometimes grievously wound their brothers with this sort of impudence."[19]

Calvin uses the term "evilspeaking," which is similar to the Hebrew phrase *lashon hara'* ("evil tongue"); it is roundly critiqued in rabbinic teaching. Maimonides explains, "The Sages said: there are three transgressions for which a person is punished in this world and has no share in the world to come—idolatry, illicit sex, and bloodshed—and evil speech is as bad as all three combined. They also said: whoever speaks with an evil tongue is as if he denied God. . . . Evil speech kills three people—the one who says it, the one who accepts it, and the one about whom it is said" (Hilchot Deot 7:3). The Talmud has Rabbi Yoḥanan saying (in the name of Rabbi Yosei ben Zimra) that God spoke to the tongue, saying, "All the other limbs of a person are upright, but you are lying horizontally. All the other limbs of a person are external, but

18. Miraslov Volf with Linn Tonstad, "Bearing True Witness," in *The Ten Commandments for Jews, Christians, and Others*, ed. Roger E. Van Harn (Grand Rapids: Eerdmans, 2007), 184.

19. John Calvin, *Institutes of the Christian Religion*, ed. John T. McNeill, trans. and indexed by Ford Lewis Battles (Philadelphia: Westminster, 1960), 1:412.

you are internal. And moreover, I have surrounded you with two walls, one of bone, i.e., the teeth, and one of flesh, the lips. What shall be given to you and what more shall be done for you, to prevent you from speaking in a deceitful manner, tongue?"[20] Additionally, Rav Ḥisda said that Mar Ukva said, "With regard to anyone who speaks malicious speech, the Holy One, Blessed be He says about him: He and I cannot dwell together in the world" (Arahkin 15b:5–6). Evil speech may be distinct from "bearing false witness," but the seriousness of it demonstrates how significant speech is that causes harm.

Aquinas describes the commandment as God forbidding anyone to injure a neighbor by word.[21] This led Volf and Tonstad to explain that the commandment is an answer to the question, "How are we to speak about each other so as not to injure each other?"[22] Aquinas gives several examples of how one could break this commandment "in ordinary conversation," including by repeating what one has heard from someone else, engaging in "detraction" and "those who listen to detractors," and by "murmurers."[23] Like Aquinas, Andrewes also identified those who listen as well as those who speak as those who break the commandment. Andrewes castigated people who tell lies but also those who have "that which we call *pruritus aurium*, 'itching ears'; if there were no willing hearers of lies, there would not be so many tellers . . . we must not only not slander our neighbor, but not receive an evil and false report against him."[24]

How to Speak

As Andrewes identifies what the commandment forbids—slander, hearing lies—he also identifies that it encourages us to rebuke and admonish our neighbors.[25] Andrewes's language echoes Lev 19:17: "Rebuke your neighbor frankly so you will not share in their guilt." Calvin also identifies what is negative and positive in this commandment, as he wrote that the commandment

20. In the letter of James, the potential harm and power of a tongue are discussed through similes of bits for horses, rudders for ships, and a fire (Jas 3:2–6).

21. Thomas Aquinas, *God's Greatest Gifts: Commentaries on the Commandments and the Sacraments* (Manchester, NH: Sophia Institute Press, 1992), 65.

22. Volf with Tonstad, "Bearing True Witness," 179.

23. Thomas Aquinas, *The Commandments of God: Conferences on the Two Precepts of Charity and the Ten Commandments*, trans. Laurence Shapcote, OP, with an introduction by Thomas Gilby, OP (London: Burns, Oates & Washbourne, 1937), 78–79.

24. Andrewes, *A pattern of catechistical doctrine*, 269.

25. Andrewes, *A pattern of catechistical doctrine*, 277.

not only prohibits a person from maligning anyone with slander or injuring anyone with falsehood or evil speech, but it also implies that "we should faithfully help everyone as much as we can in affirming the truth, in order to protect the integrity of his name and possessions."[26] Luther's summary of the commandment is similar: "No one shall harm his neighbor with his tongue, be he friend or foe. We are not to say anything bad about him whether the statement is true or false. The only exception is whatever must be said as a matter of official duty or for the purpose of helping the wrongdoer to change. We are to use the tongue only to speak the best we can about everyone, covering his sins and weaknesses by presenting them in the best light possible and by veiling them behind his more honorable and attractive qualities."[27]

In other words, Luther advocates speaking the best about your neighbor. The Heidelberg Catechism teaches that the commandment means "I should love the truth, speak it candidly, and openly acknowledge it. And I should do what I can to guard and advance my neighbor's good name." The catechism from the Presbyterian Church (USA) adds that God requires me "to speak well of my neighbor when I can, and to view the faults of my neighbor with tolerance when I cannot."

Beyond speaking well of neighbors, Volf and Tonstad explain that the commandment urges people to speak well of themselves: this commandment discourages false modesty. "Just as we are forbidden to make ourselves out to be better than we are, we are also discouraged from undercutting ourselves in dealing with others, even as we do seek to foster their well being and promote their interests in a way equal to or greater than our own. . . . To speak about ourselves as though we were of little value—say, when we have failed to reach goals we have set for ourselves or when we have wronged others—is to speak falsely about God's beloved creatures."[28]

False or Lying

As mentioned above, the adjective for the witness differs in Exodus and Deuteronomy. In Exod 20:16, the commandment forbids acting as a "lying [*šeqer*] witness"; and in Deut 5:20, it is a "false [*šāwʾ*] witness." The book of the covenant offers yet another adjective: "a malicious/violent [*ḥms*] witness"

26. Calvin, *Institutes*, 411.

27. Luther, *Large Catechism*, 58.

28. Volf with Tonstad, "Bearing True Witness," 189.

(Exod 23:1). Stamm suggests, "[Deuteronomy's] striving for more precision is probably the reason why the 'lying witness' of Exodus has been replaced in Deut. 5 by 'false witness', since one who was called a 'false witness' could not claim, as one who was called a 'lying witness' perhaps could, that he had not actually told a lie."[29] The term *šeqer* seems to suggest a knowledge of the truth and an outright lie; *šāw'* can mean "deceit," which is synonymous with lying but also is translated as "false, vain, empty."

As discussed in chapter 3, the word *šāw'* appears in the commandment about God's name, which can have the connotation of false bearing of God's name. Various receptions link the commandment about God's name with the commandment about bearing witness against a neighbor. According to David Hazony, thirteenth-century Franciscan theologian Ramón Lull went so far as to physically relocate the ninth commandment after the third, so convinced he was that they are essentially saying the same thing.[30] In contrast, Andrewes and Calvin made a distinction between these commandments: Andrewes clarified that the falsehood condemned in the earlier commandment touches God's glory, but in this commandment it hurts one's fellow humans.[31] Calvin apparently would not include the commandment about false witness in a legal setting, claiming, "Perjuries, in so far as they profane and violate God's name, are sufficiently dealt with in the Third Commandment. Hence this commandment is lawfully observed when our tongue, in declaring the truth, serves both the good repute and the advantage of our neighbors."[32]

Philosophical definitions of honesty and lying make the distinction on the basis of whether or not the self knows the truth. If one knows something to be untrue and says it anyway, that is a lie. If one erroneously believes something to be true and says the thing, it is false but not a lie. So, for example, I could say, "She was in the library," and it could be false, but if I believe she was there, it is not a lie. If I know she was at the park and I still say, "She was in the library," that is a lie. Philosopher and ethicist Sissela Bok defines a lie as "an intentionally deceptive message in the form of a statement,"[33] explaining that the moral question of whether a person is lying or not does not get settled by merely the truth or falsity of what that person says. Instead, the moral

29. Stamm, *The Ten Commandments in Recent Research*, 15.

30. David Hazony, *The Ten Commandments: How Our Most Ancient Moral Text Can Renew Modern Life* (New York: Scribner, 2010), 211.

31. Andrewes, *A pattern of Catechistical doctrine*, 270.

32. Calvin, *Institutes*, 411.

33. Sissela Bok, *Lying: Moral Choice in Public and Private Life*, 2nd ed. (New York: Vintage Books, 1999), 15.

question of a lie gets settled on the basis of whether or not the person intends their statement to mislead.[34]

Several terms further illustrate complications surrounding truth and lies. American philosopher Harry Frankfurt's 2005 book *On Bullshit* defines the word as speech intended to persuade without any concern for the truth. He specifically identifies this as a concern for people in public life, such as politicians, who are pressured to give answers about things they don't know.[35] "Gaslighting" is a term that derives from a 1944 film but grew in popularity starting in the mid-2010s and refers to a person who lies to another systematically, eventually accusing the other of untruth if they question the narrative. Psychologist and bioethicist Will Gaylin coined the term "truth-dumping" to convey the harm that can be wreaked by brutal, needless, or uncaring truth-telling.[36] "Virtue-signaling" is another relatively recent term: someone who might say something specific to suggest a level of virtue or care but who might not follow that up with related action.[37]

The Talmud instructs, "One should not promise to give a child something and then not give it to him, because as a result the child will learn to lie" (b. Sukkah 46b). One can imagine a parent giving such a promise not as an intentionally deceptive statement, as Bok identifies a lie, but perhaps just forgetting. Then again, parents sometimes tell their children untruths to pacify. Journalist A. J. Jacobs writes about trying to follow commandments as literally as possible, so he truthfully tells his toddler son that they don't have any bagels and does not pretend that a different baked good is a bagel. This honest admission results in Jacobs's son's tantrum (and his wife's extreme exasperation).[38] Jacobs admits he could have justified breaking this commandment for the sake

34. Bok, *Lying*, 6.

35. This was originally published as an essay in 1986. Frankfurt distinguishes "bullshit" from lying because a lie presumes knowledge of the truth. People who engage in "bullshit" do not care whether what they say describes reality correctly. Instead, they merely pick out things to say, or make things up, to suit their purposes. Frankfurt writes that it is "unavoidable when circumstances require someone to talk without knowing what they are talking about . . . when a person's obligations or opportunities to speak about some topic are more excessive than knowledge of the facts that are relevant to that topic." Because it does not reject the authority of the truth as a liar does but rather pays no attention to the truth, Frankfurt asserts, it "is a greater enemy of the truth than lies are."

36. Bok, *Lying*, xxi–xxiii.

37. B. D. McClay, "Virtue Signaling," *Hedghog Review* (summer 2018), https://tinyurl.com/4e3y6phd.

38. A. J. Jacobs, *The Year of Living Biblically: One Man's Humble Quest to Follow the Bible as Literally as Possible* (New York: Simon & Schuster, 2007), 55–56.

of peace in the household with his child and his wife. Then again, while he recognizes the short-term disadvantages of a toddler tantrum, he justifies his honesty given the long-term consequences of a child who has learned to lie.

Walter Brueggemann identifies euphemisms as a "public pattern of false witness against neighbor," referencing a 1995 lecture by linguist and political activist Noam Chomsky. Brueggemann sees euphemisms as particularly prevalent in the areas of finance, such as when unemployment is called "downsizing," and in the military industry, when weapons capable of massive destruction are given peaceable names.[39] For example, from 1985 to 2005, the United States produced and deployed a missile originally known as the MX for "Missile, Experimental, but eventually called the "LGM-118 Peacekeeper."

Always and Never?

In several teaching tools for children, the commandment also gets restated either as "never tell a lie" or "always tell the truth." Certainly truth telling is important, and lying can be harmful. In 2020, the John Templeton Foundation funded "The Honesty Project," which is studying topics such as behavioral and motivational requirements for honesty, the consequences of honesty and dishonesty in relationships and groups, and the conditions—if any—under which dishonesty is justified.[40]

Some believe dishonesty is never justified: Augustine, for example, thought that all lies are sins.[41] Aquinas agreed but made a distinction between types of lies—officious lies meant to help, jocose lies told in jest, and mischievous or malicious lies—and suggested that the only lies that were mortal sins were those told so that a person would seem wise and a malicious lie told to harm a neighbor.[42] Philosopher Immanuel Kant saw no need to distinguish between types of lies because he argued that it was never permissible to lie: Kant was an absolutist, which means that for Kant, the duty to tell the truth was "an unconditional duty which holds in all circumstances."[43] Kant's famous example—for

39. Walter Brueggemann, "Truth-Telling as Subversive Obedience," in *The Ten Commandments: The Reciprocity of Faithfulness*, ed. William P. Brown, Library of Theological Ethics (Louisville: Westminster John Knox, 2004), 295.

40. The Honesty Project, https://tinyurl.com/2r3vvrm.

41. E.g., Augustine, *The Enchiridion on Faith, Hope, and Love* (Washington, DC: Regnery, 1996), 29.

42. Aquinas, *The Commandments of God*, 30.

43. Immanuel Kant, *The Doctrine of Virtue* (New York: Harper & Row, 1964), 92–96.

which he often is scorned[44]—is of a murderer who asks someone the location of his intended victim. Kant argues that to tell a lie to the murderer, even if it were to save the life of the victim, was not permissible. A lie would always be harmful to society because "it vitiates the source of law" and also harms the liar by destroying his dignity.

As often is the case, the biblical narrative is more morally complicated, telling stories of people who lie without any statement of condemnation against their falsehood. The wife-sister stories in Genesis 12, 20, and 26, for example, have Abraham and Isaac lying about the nature of their relationships with Sarah and Rebekah, respectively.[45] These three stories are not identical,[46] and the variants are significant, but Abraham is arguably rewarded by Pharaoh with wealth and possessions for his lie. Jacob and Rebekah deceive Isaac so that Jacob can receive the blessing that was meant for Esau (Genesis 27).[47] In the book of Judges, deceit leads to the killing of oppressors: Ehud assassinates King Eglon of Moab (Judg 3:15–23); and Jael kills Sisera after inviting him into her tent under the pretense of safety (Judg 4:18–21). Rahab tells the messengers from the king of Jericho that the Israelite spies have left, when in fact she had taken them up to her roof and hidden them there (Josh 2:6). And Michal lies to Saul's men by saying that David is sick in bed, when she had helped David to flee; she also lies to her father, telling him that David had threatened her life if she wouldn't help him escape (1 Sam 19:11–17). Several of these are women, and there has been a lot of scholarship on how they are utilizing what they can in their situations. The tendency is to refer to them not as "liars" but as "tricksters."[48]

The example of Shiphrah and Puah itself has a fascinating reception history: the two midwives tell Pharaoh that the reason why they do not carry out

44. Helga Varden, "Kant and Lying to the Murderer at the Door . . . One More Time: Kant's Legal Philosophy and Lies to Murderers and Nazis," *Journal of Social Philosophy* 41 (December 2010): 403.

45. Some point out that for Abraham, this was not a full lie but only partial, because Sarah was his half-sister, according to Abraham himself in Gen 20:12. Genesis 11:31 suggests something different, although the discrepancies between the two verses do get attributed to different source material.

46. For example, God reveals the truth to Abimelech, whereas Pharaoh only knows the truth after he is punished.

47. While there is no clear condemnation for Jacob in the narrative of Gen 27, there are consequences for his deception, including Esau's hatred and Jacob then fleeing to Haran.

48. Cf. Melissa A. Jackson, "Trickster Matriarchs: Lot's Daughters, Rebekah, Leah, Rachel, Tamar," in *Comedy and Feminist Interpretation of the Hebrew Bible: A Subversive Collaboration* (Oxford: Oxford University Press, 2012), 41–66; and Susan Niditch, *A Prelude to Biblical Folklore: Underdogs and Tricksters* (Urbana: University of Illinois Press, 2000).

his command to kill the Hebrew baby boys is that the Israelite women are so strong and vigorous that they give birth before the midwives can reach them in time. Are their words a lie? Should they have told Pharaoh the truth, that they refused to follow his command because it was morally repugnant? Augustine references them in his treatise on lying and concludes that although they were rewarded with their own families (Exod 1:20–21), it was because of their benevolence to Israel, not their deceit. Again, for Augustine, lying is not justified. Gregory the Great argued that lying is reprehensible, and Shiphrah and Puah were rewarded on earth because they will not be rewarded in heaven. Calvin wrote that their lies were reprehensible to God, but since no action is free of sin, God rewarded their good works, though the works themselves were impure. A marginal note in the Geneva Bible says that the midwives' disobedience was lawful, but their deception was evil. And Luther wrote that Shiphrah and Puah were a model for life under the pressures of persecution; their lies are justified because they meant to aid rather than injure.[49]

If an absolutist moral stance on lying is complicated because biblical characters tell lies, how much more so would it be if God tells a lie? In the Mormon Book of Abraham, the patriarch does not come up with the "lie" about his wife being his sister; rather, God tells Abraham to tell Sarah to identify herself to Pharaoh as Abraham's sister (the Book of Abraham 2:22–25). That event does not occur in Genesis. But in reference to the visit from the three men in Gen 18, Rashi claimed that God told a (white) lie for the sake of peace to Abraham in Gen 18:13: when Sarah heard that she would have a son in her old age, she laughed and said in Gen 18:12, "After I am grown old, will I have pleasure, for my lord [Abraham] is old?" When God confronts Abraham, however, God reports to Abraham that she had said, "How can I bear a child when I am old?" (Gen 18:13), neglecting to include that Sarah had said that Abraham was old. According to Rabbi Ishmael's school, it was taught, "Great is the cause of peace, seeing that for its sake even the Holy One modified a statement" (Bava Metzia 87a:11). Rashi commented that for the sake of peace between a husband and a wife, lying is acceptable.[50] Others disagreed with Rashi, arguing that this was not an outright lie, rather an omission, for God does not lie. The twelfth- to thirteenth-century commentary Daat Zkenim on Gen 18:13 includes an alternate opinion, that the angel did not alter her words, he only did not report all of her words, thereby preventing any hard feelings on the part of Abraham. The

49. Brevard Childs, *The Book of Exodus: A Critical, Theological Commentary* (Philadelphia: Westminster, 1974), 23–24.

50. Sefaria, citing "Rashi on Genesis 18:13:2," https://tinyurl.com/3mpu69pu.

commentary explains, "It is totally absurd to argue that anything appearing to us as a lie could have been uttered by G-d or His agent, an angel," though "any ordinary person, other than a Divine creature, is permitted to tell white lies in order to preserve בית שלום [*byt šlwm*], family harmony."[51]

Justified Lies

In other words, the rabbis taught that a lie would be permitted in limited situations, such as when it would bring peace or family harmony. Some rabbis understood what Joseph's brothers said in Gen 50:16–17 in a similar light. Rabbi Ile'a said in the name of Rabbi Elazar, "It is permitted for a person to depart from the truth in a matter that will bring peace, as it is stated: 'Your father commanded before he died, saying: So you shall say to Joseph: Please pardon your brothers' crime, etc.' (Genesis 50:16–17). Jacob never issued this command, but his sons falsely attributed this statement to him in order to preserve peace between them and Joseph (Yebamot 65b:7)."

According to the Talmud tractate Babia Metzia 23b:11 and 24a:1, there are three incredibly specific matters in which one may "amend their statements and deviate from the truth": (1) if asked directly if he has studied a particular tractate, a scholar may say no out of a sense of modesty and humility; (2) if asked if he slept in a particular bed, he may say no to avoid shame if there is "unseemly residue" found on a bed; and (3) one can falsely say that a host was not gracious in order to prevent more people from taking advantage of that host's hospitality.

The Schools of Shammai and Hillel debate over how honest one must be when speaking about a bride: Shammai, referencing Exod 23:7, says that a bride should be described honestly, but the School of Hillel says one must always describe a bride as "beautiful and graceful," even if that was not objectively true. The reasoning was that because one must refrain from causing another anguish, once a groom had married his bride, anyone else should praise her beauty (Ketubot 17a).[52] A different example of a similar situation in which

51. Sefaria, citing "Da'at Zekenim on Genesis 18:13:1," Eliyahu Munk, https://tinyurl.com/rbkebnwb.

52. Laura Gellar's explanation of this differs from the one given in the Talmud, that it would not be right to cause anguish to a groom who married an unattractive bride. Gellar writes, "Perhaps telling an unattractive bride she is beautiful isn't really lying; it is simply making an ambiguous statement. While she might not be physically beautiful, the bride is (most likely, anyway) a beautiful person inside!" "Competing Values," in *Broken Tablets:*

telling the truth would upset someone was given through the example of a rabbi who mistakenly thought other rabbis had come to meet him. One rabbi told him honestly that they did not, but because this fact/truth upset the first rabbi, it was concluded that because it upset him, it was not necessary to be entirely truthful. Also, because he misled himself, they didn't intentionally mislead him (Chullin 94b). All these lies that are justified in the Talmud seem to fit under Bok's definition of a white lie as "a falsehood not meant to injure anyone, and of little moral import."[53] Such lies are also the opposite of what Calvin referred to as "evilspeaking," which comes "from evil intent and wanton desire to defame."[54] Joy Davidman, after acknowledging that one might have various benign reasons for telling a white lie, nevertheless concludes, "All the same, it is possible that most of our white lies are told, not for charity, but for laziness and for cowardice—to save the work of thinking up a real answer, or to avoid a trivial social discomfort."[55]

Aquinas gives other various reasons why people would tell a lie, including "for the benefit of another, in order, for instance, that they may escape death, or danger, or loss."[56] It is one thing to tell a falsehood to do no wrong, that is, to not cause another anguish or embarrassment as in the examples above, and maybe more powerful to tell a lie for someone's good or benefit. Krzysztof Kieślowski's film *Dekalog: Eight* tells the story in 1943 Warsaw of a six-year-old Jewish girl who is brought to a Catholic couple who have promised to be her godparents to protect her from the Nazis. But at the last minute, the woman says they cannot lie about a fake baptism because it would be bearing false witness, effectively sentencing the child to death. The child survives the Holocaust and meets up with the woman—now an ethics professor—decades later. Both have been haunted by what happened: the child traumatized because the couple did not rescue her and the woman by guilt for her decision. As they process the past, the woman reveals the real reason behind their refusal: she and her husband were involved in the Polish resistance, and were told—falsely—that the man who brought the child was a Nazi collaborator; they feared they would be caught if they accepted the girl. Kieślowski's episode was based on the true story of the journalist Hanna Krall, whose family was killed in the Holocaust and

Restoring the Ten Commandments and Ourselves, ed. Rachel S. Mikva (Woodstock, VT: Jewish Lights, 1999), 118.

53. Bok, *Lying*, 58.

54. Calvin, *Institutes*, 412.

55. Joy Davidman, *Smoke on the Mountain: An Interpretation of the Ten Commandments* (Philadelphia: Westminster, 1954), 110.

56. Aquinas, *The Commandments of God*, 82.

whose own survival depended on being hidden by Polish citizens.[57] Thousands of children survived because they were hidden by others who were willing to lie to the Gestapo, as was recorded by Anne Frank and Corrie Ten Boom.[58] The conclusion is that it is more ethical to lie—or not be honest—about the existence of Jewish people in a home, than to tell the truth about their presence. This raises the question made explicit in the language of the commandment: who is our neighbor? For people living in occupied Poland, it would seem that the neighbor is the Jewish refugee, not the occupying SS officer.

Neighborhood and Community

It is in this commandment that the word "neighbor" appears for the first time in the Ten Commandments. Though we can certainly assume the idea of a neighbor earlier—that is, we ought not murder our neighbor or steal from our neighbor—here it gets specified. And that raises the question about the identity of our neighbor. When Jesus was asked, pointedly, in the gospels, "who is my neighbor?" (Luke 10:29), Jesus answered by telling the parable of the Good Samaritan. A neighbor is one who has mercy on the one in need (Luke 10:36–37); unlike the priest or the Levite, the Samaritan was the one who cared emotionally, physically, and financially for the man who had been attacked.[59] Neighborliness, therefore, includes awareness of the one who is in need; the one who has been hurt; the one who is poor, marginalized, or meek; the one who needs protection. In Kant's example, the potential victim of the murderer is the neighbor, not the murderer. For Shiphrah and Puah, the pregnant women and their children are the neighbors, not Pharaoh. Again, the words of the commandment are not only "don't lie" but include the identity of the one whom we must not bear false witness against, the neighbor. The commandment makes explicit that we must not lie about, or lie in a matter that would harm, our neighbor.

57. Monika Adamczyk-Garbowska, "Hanna Krall," *The Shalvi/Hyman Encyclopedia of Jewish Women*, June 23, 2021, https://tinyurl.com/bddkc9aj.

58. A grim variation on the more positive stories of families who take in or protect children during the Nazi regime is Hendrik Willem Van Loon's short novel, "Thou Shalt Not Bear False Witness against Thy Neighbor," in *Ten Commandments: Ten Short Novels of Hitler's War against the Moral Code* (New York: Simon & Schuster, 1944), in which a Dutch family takes in a young German child who is a war orphan. The child frequently lies to the family about relatively minor things such as eating sugar when it had been forbidden by the strict parents and is punished by those parents. Much later, the child who is now grown, tells a falsehood about the patriarch of the house, which results in the man's execution.

59. The Samaritan had pity, bandaged the man's wounds, and paid for his continual recovery (Luke 10:33–35).

When brutal honesty would harm a Jewish person under Nazi occupation, or an Israelite baby in Pharaoh's Egypt, or a potential murder victim, to tell a lie to save that neighbor would be keeping this commandment.

The Hebrew word for neighbor can also be translated as friend or companion, as it is in a Jewish legend, which explains the consequences of bearing false witness. "The ninth commandment reads: 'O My people Israel, bear not false witness against your companions, for in punishment for this the clouds will scatter, so that there may be no rain, and famine will ensue owing to drought.' God is particularly severe with a false witness because falsehood is the one quality that God did not create, but is something that men themselves produced."[60]

Luther and Calvin extend this commandment beyond the neighbor to "anyone"; as discussed above, Luther describes the summary of this commandment as not doing any injury with one's words to a neighbor, "be he friend or foe," but we are to "speak the best we can about everyone."[61] Calvin's summary of the commandment was similar: "Let us not malign *anyone* with slanders or false charges. . . . To this prohibition the command is linked that we should faithfully help *everyone* as much as we can in affirming the truth."[62] What if the truthfulness for one—the SS Officer at the door, for example—would harm the other? It is significant that Luther acknowledges that we might not always feel friendly toward a neighbor, that a neighbor could be a foe. If there are competing gains in telling the truth, that would need to be negotiated. Moreover, the categories of intent and impact apply to this commandment. One may speak truthfully, intending to faithfully help as Calvin encourages, but the impact of the person's words could do injury, as Luther warns against. To negotiate such a situation, and do repair, would require a level of trust, indeed, a relational generosity, with the person taking seriously the impact of the words and the other taking seriously the intent.

As with so many of these commandments, this abstract idea does not come with a formula that can be applied in any situation. It takes hard work to make it concrete and live it out in practice, especially when one's understanding of one's neighbor and even one's community becomes more complicated. Hazony points out, "While our community was once chosen for us—where we lived, our religious affiliations, our trade—today we share so many different things with so many different people, and it is so much easier than ever before to connect with them, it becomes unclear what is or is not a community for us.

60. Louis Ginzberg and David Stern, *Legends of the Jews*, trans. Henrietta Szold and Paul Radin (Philadelphia: Jewish Publication Society, 2003), 1:607.

61. Luther, *Large Catechism*, 58.

62. Calvin, *Institutes*, 411.

Living in a major city, do we create community with the other tenants of our apartment building? Our fellow sweat-soakers at the gym? Fellow Pentecostals or Jimi Hendrix lovers around the world?"[63] Hazony's questions seem to start with people who are physically close, but he extends this to people "around the world." Moreover, Hazony suggests that one can bear false witness against a public figure who is not personally known, writing, "Turn on any cable news channel or visit any public-affairs website, and you are likely to find an effervescent flow of evil tongues. I am not speaking of disagreement and the clash of values and ideas, or of the careful look that is taken at a public figure's record—all these are not just legitimate but essential to any democratic society. I am speaking of these with which motives are impugned, lifestyles derogated, name-calling condoned, individuals and groups demonized."[64] Hazony concludes that the false witness "attacks not only his victim but his entire community. He is, in fact, the paradigmatic destroyer of communal life."[65]

Commitment to Truth

Regarding this commandment, Aquinas commented, "Lying is the destruction of social life because men live together in society which would be impossible if they told not the truth to each other."[66] Zech 8:16–17 includes both positive and negative commandments from God, saying, "These are the things you are to do: Speak the truth to each other, and render true and sound judgment in your courts; do not plot evil against each other, and do not love to swear falsely." And the letter to the Ephesians tells each of them to "put off falsehood and speak truthfully to your neighbor, for we are all members of one body" (Eph 4:25). So, commitment to speaking truth is a way to keep this commandment.

To lie—to and about others—will cause harm. And to tell only the partial or brutal truth to and about others also causes harm. But it does not only harm the neighbor; it also harms the one who speaks in such ways. Ronald Rolheiser identifies lying with the oft speculated about blasphemy against the Holy Spirit (cf. Matt 12:31), saying that lying begins to distort and warp the heart of the liar.

> If you lie to yourself long enough, eventually you will lose sight of the truth and believe the lie and become unable any longer to tell the dif-

63. Hazony, *The Ten Commandments*, 226.
64. Hazony, *The Ten Commandments*, 215.
65. Hazony, *The Ten Commandments*, 212.
66. Aquinas, *The Commandments of God*, 80.

ference between truth and lies. What becomes unforgiveable about that is not that God does not want to forgive, but that you no longer want to be forgiven. God easily forgives all of your weaknesses and will always forgive anyone who wants to be forgiven, but you can so warp your own conscience that you see God's truth and forgiveness itself as a lie, as Satan, and you see your own lie as truth and forgiveness. That is the only sin that truly puts us outside of God's mercy, not because God refuses to extend mercy further, but because you can look mercy in the eye and call it a lie.[67]

Arnold Jacob Wolf extends the commandment beyond speech to how one lives one's life, writing, "I am troubled not so much by verbal lies as by a life that is fundamentally inauthentic. . . . I can only hope to become more truthful, not only in what I say but in who I am. As witness, we are all (partially) false."[68]

Conclusion

Several TV shows and movies present characters who are unable to lie: in an episode from *The Twilight Zone* in 1961, "The Whole Truth," an unscrupulous used-car salesman is no longer able to tell lies after purchasing a vintage Ford Model A from an elderly gentleman. The main character in the 1997 comedy *Liar Liar* is a lawyer who can only speak the truth for an entire day. A character in the 2019 film *Knives Out* suffers from a condition that causes her to vomit whenever she tells a lie, or in the words of the detective character, she has "a regurgitative reaction to mistruthing." The latter's character's honesty is a major plot point for the movie, but the others—a lawyer, a used-car salesman—are the type of character often stereotyped as dishonest. Being compelled to be truthful is one thing, but choosing to speak—and even live—in honest ways, in commitment to others, and with a rootedness in a community, is a way everyone can apply the commandment to not bear false witness against a neighbor in their own lives.

67. Rolheiser, *The Holy Longing*, 227.

68. Arnold Jacob Wolf, "Ten More Words," in *Broken Tablets: Restoring the Ten Commandments and Ourselves*, ed. Rachel Mikva (Woodstock, VT: Jewish Lights, 1999), 135.

10

"Don't Covet"

David Hazony writes, "At first blush, there is something petty about the Tenth Commandment. One of the world's greatest moral works, which opens with the overwhelming declaration of *I am the Lord your God* and over nine earth-shaking pronouncements presenting a whole vision of God, man, and society, now comes to a close with a trifle about our stuff. *His ox or his ass*—do we really need a list of mundane longings for other people's belongings?"[1] Of course, Hazony doesn't stop there. He then describes the commandment using the simile of "a summit of a soaring mountain": it may seem small to those standing on the peak but towers over other mountains. He explains that while the tenth commandment reflects back on the previous nine, it adds a new dimension, "a sin of the spirit so egregious as to warrant closing on this note, so deeply hidden as to have to wait until the end."[2] Yes, the commandment against coveting does include a list of specific objects, but the list is not trifling, nor should it be understood as limited to only those things, as it concludes with the sweeping inclusion of "*anything* that belongs to your neighbor" (Exod 20:17; Deut 5:21).

Reception history of the commandment to not covet centers around two main questions. First, what is being prohibited: all desire, or a certain type of desire? In other words, what does it mean to "covet"? Second, how can this commandment be observed and enforced? As Hazony notes, this sin can be deeply hidden. Unlike commandments that get broken by someone's action—a murder is committed, an object is stolen, a false testimony is spoken—this commandment mostly exists in the heart and mind of the person who may be coveting, without anyone else seeing or knowing. Certainly, the commandment, "you shall not covet" is neither petty nor mundane, and many join Hazony in viewing it as a fitting conclusion to the entire Ten Commandments.

1. David Hazony, *The Ten Commandments: How Our Most Ancient Moral Text Can Renew Modern Life* (New York: Scribner, 2010), 233.

2. Hazony, *The Ten Commandments*, 233.

Definitions

The first question, of what it means to "covet," is complicated by the two different Hebrew words in Exodus and Deuteronomy. In Exod 20:17, the verb is *ḥmd*, which gets translated in virtually every English version as "covet," but elsewhere in the Hebrew Bible it is translated as "desire" and is used in contexts where it has neutral or even positive connotations.[3] For example, the suffering servant is described as having "nothing in his appearance that we should desire him" (Isa 53:2), and the beloved one "desires" to sit in "the shade" of the apple tree that is her lover in Song 2:3. Sometimes the Hebrew root word is used as an adjective to describe something desirable, pleasant, or handsome: the beloved is wholly "desirable (*mḥmdym*)" in Song 5:16, and the trees God creates in the garden for food are "pleasing (*nḥmd*) to the eye" (Gen 2:9). But then, Eve sees that the fruit of the tree of the knowledge of good and evil is "desired . . . to make one wise" (Gen 3:6). Even if Eve's desire was good—and the jury is out on that—the consequences of her eating the fruit might support a translation that the fruit was "coveted . . . to make one wise."

The word *ḥmd* also appears as a description of the clothing of Esau in Gen 27:15. Many English translations simply refer to these as "the best" or "favorite" clothes of Esau, but scholar Rachel Adelman traces the Jewish legend that tells that these clothes were worn by Nimrod, the mighty hunter (Gen 10:8–9); in fact, it was the clothing that gave him prowess with the animals. Rabbi Yehudah explained that when Nimrod put on the clothing, "all beasts, animals, and birds . . . came and prostrated themselves before him" (*Pirke DeRabbi Eliezer* 24.4). As the legend continues, Rabbi Meir made the connection between Nimrod and Esau, who also is described in Gen 25:27 as a skilled hunter, saying, "Esau, the brother of Jacob, saw the coats of Nimrod, and in his heart he coveted them, and he slew him, and took them for himself. How (do we know) that they were desirable in his sight? Because it is said, 'And Rebecca took the coveted clothing of Esau [בגדי עשו . . . החמודות], her elder son'" (Gen. 27:15; *Pirke DeRabbi Eliezer* 24.12). Rachel Adelman explains, "The cloak engenders covetousness, חמדנות, in the eyes of the beholder. In this case, Esau covets the clothing and murders Nimrod, in order to possess it, hence the term 'the best (lit. coveted) clothes of her older son Esau'" (Gen. 27:15).[4]

3. Patrick D. Miller notes how it is similar to English, in that desire can be either "proper or improper." *The Ten Commandments* (Louisville: Westminster John Knox, 2009), 390.

4. Rachel Adelman, "Primeval Coats," TheTorah.com, 2015, https://tinyurl.com/438f2zwe. According to the legend, God made this amazing clothing from the skin of the serpent who tempted Adam and Eve in the garden; it was held in the ark and then given to Noah by Nimrod.

In Exod 34:24, God promises that no one will covet (*ḥmd*) a person's land when that person makes pilgrimages to Jerusalem. Sixteenth-century Jewish interpreter Sforno referenced the verse when explaining that the commandment means "the object you covet should be considered by you as so utterly unattainable that you will not even begin to hatch schemes of how to acquire it."[5] Sforno's explanation introduces the idea that coveting often leads to actions of acquisition, and other texts affirm such a progression. For example, Deut 7:25 warns against coveting the silver and gold on the images of the gods of the other nations, and taking that silver and gold, because it will ensnare the one who does so. Achan confesses in Josh 7:21 that he coveted things he saw in the plunder from Ai, and took them. Micah 2:2 similarly describes how those who plot evil "covet fields and seize them, and houses, and take them."

Deuteronomy 5:21 uses the same verb as in Exod 20:17 (*ḥmd*) to prohibit "coveting" a neighbor's wife but then uses a different word (*'wh*) to warn against "desiring" a neighbor's house, field, or servants. Patrick D. Miller writes that this latter verb connotes desire and longing and often involves one's bodily appetite, as when people desire food (cf. Deut 12:15, 20, 21) or have a great thirst (cf. 2 Sam 23:15). This verb also has negative and positive connotations. In Numbers 11, and the references to the story in Ps 78:30 and 106:14, the Israelites "desire" or "crave" meat instead of manna; these references thus suggest a desire born out of discontent rather than mere physical hunger. The same verb appears in Prov 13:4, which contrasts the "desire" of the lazy one who has nothing with the diligent one who is satisfied. The lazy one's desire also gets referenced in Prov 21:25–26, "The desire of the lazy one kills him, for his hands refuse to work; all the day he desires with desire,[6] but the righteous give and do not spare." The verb (*'wh*) appears in Jer 2:24 to describe the wild donkey sniffing the wind in her "desire." Several translations make clear that this metaphorical donkey's desire is sexual, using words like "heat," as in an animal in heat, ready to mate. Along those lines, Stanley Hauerwas and William Willimon explain that the Hebrew word used "also entails 'lust'"[7]; Johann Stamm suggests that "lust after" is a possible translation.[8]

5. Sefaria, citing "Sforno on Exodus 20:14:1," Eliyahu Munk, HaChut Hameshulash, Lambda, https://tinyurl.com/42ra5p6k.

6. The Hebrew grammar here uses two forms of the same root word for emphasis, so something like "covet covetously" would also be appropriate; many English translations use "covet greedily" (KJV, ASV, ERV, JPS) to communicate that sort of emphasis.

7. Stanley M. Hauerwas and William H. Willimon, *The Truth about God: The Ten Commandments in Christian Life* (Nashville: Abingdon, 1999), 129.

8. Johann Jacob Stamm with M. E. Andrew, *The Ten Commandments in Recent Research* (London: SCM, 1967), 14.

But in Deut 14:26, the Israelites are permitted, even encouraged, to spend money on whatever they "desire," so the same word that had negative connotations in other texts is positive here. Biblical scholar James K. Bruckner explains that in this context, "'whatever you desire' means 'whatever you desire that [God has] given for the purpose of desiring.'"[9] In 1 Kgs 11:37, the prophet Ahijah promises Jeroboam that he will be king of Israel and will rule over "all his heart 'desires'"; here, too, the desire has a permissive sense, even when the following verse includes the caveat that God will be with Jeroboam if Jeroboam chooses to follow and obey God.

The meaning of the verb also shifts, depending on the subject. For example, the Psalms describe a wicked person's "desire" (e.g., Ps 10:3; 112:10; 140:8; cf. Prov 21:10), which contrasts with the "desire" of a meek person, as in Ps 10:17, or "the desire of a righteous person" in Prov 11:23, which "ends only in good." The prophet Amos laments, "Woe for you who 'desire' the day of the LORD" (Amos 5:18), but the desire itself is not necessarily negative nor is the object of that desire—the day of the LORD—something bad; rather, as throughout the book of Amos, the misguided arrogance of the people who think the day of the LORD will be positive for them is what Amos warns against. The verb also occurs in several texts where it is unequivocally positive, as in Isa 26:8–9, which describes people "desiring" God's name, renown, and even "desiring God." According to Ps 132:13–14, God "desired" Zion for God's dwelling.

Types of Desire

To summarize, use of the verb *'wh* in the Hebrew Bible suggests that it depends on who is doing the desiring: a wicked person's "desire" will be negative, but a righteous, meek person—or, of course God—will "desire" in good and right ways. Additionally, the object of the desire also colors the meaning of the word. When someone desires God, or goodness, or something that they are permitted to have, something given to them, then the desire is good. The same is true for the word *ḥmd*: its connotation depends on the context. Puritan Lancelot Andrewes wrote that it was good to desire the spirit against the flesh; and natural desires like a desire for food when hungry and a desire for rest when weary

9. James K. Bruckner, "On the One Hand . . . On the Other Hand: The Twofold Meaning of the Law against Covetousness," in *To Hear and Obey: Essays in Honor of Fredrick Carlson Holmgren*, ed. Bradley J. Bergfalk and Paul E. Koptak (Chicago: Covenant, 1997), 100.

were also positive.[10] But desire is negative when someone desires something negative; and especially—to return to the commandment—when something belongs to a neighbor. Though this commandment often is abbreviated into the prohibition "you shall not covet," the full versions in both Exodus and Deuteronomy specify that the objects are "your neighbor's." In fact, the word "neighbor" gets repeated three times in Hebrew in Exod 20:17 and Deut 5:21, and each object also has the possessive "his" attached in Hebrew: his wife, his house, his ox and donkey, etc. Andrewes describes these things as "baits to allure us . . . and hooks to draw us into sinning."[11]

Reinhard Hütter's explanation is representative of many receptions. He writes,

> To be clear: Desire as such is not the problem; it is not "bad." Indeed we are created as creatures with desires; to be human is to be desiring. All of our desires, however, are created to come to a rest in their one ultimate good, communion with God. Augustine's famous sentence from the *Confessions*—"You have made us and drawn us to yourself, and our heart is unquiet until it rests in you"—expresses how our desires find rest and fulfillment only in God. If other created things are elevated to the position of the ultimate good in ceaseless exchange, coveting is the unavoidable result, since none of these created things will ultimately bring our desiring to a rest. Without desire we would cease to be human; without God as desire's ultimate end, we become inhumane.[12]

Aquinas similarly drew on Augustine's description of the heart's desire and asserted that desire is something innately human.[13] Walter Harrelson wrote that to obey this commandment, it was necessary to distinguish covetousness "from a deep hunger for life that is wholesome, full and good."[14]

10. Lancelot Andrewes, *A Pattern of Catechistical Doctrine and Other Minor Works* (Oxford: John Henry Parker, 1846; New York: AMS, 1967), 283.

11. Andrewes, *A Pattern of Catechistical Doctrine*, 285–86.

12. Reinhard Hütter, "The Twofold Center of Lutheran Ethics: Christian Freedom and God's Commandments," in *The Promise of Lutheran Ethics*, ed. Karen L. Bloomquist and John R. Stumme (Minneapolis: Fortress, 1998), 47.

13. Thomas Aquinas, *The Commandments of God: Conferences on the Two Precepts of Charity and the Ten Commandments*, trans. Laurence Shapcote, OP, with an introduction by Thomas Gilby, OP (London: Burns, Oates & Washbourne, 1937), 83–84.

14. Walter Harrelson, *The Ten Commandments and Human Rights* (Philadelphia: Fortress, 1980), 153–54.

Many contemporary receptions of this commandment add adjectives to clarify what is prohibited by this commandment. For example, Philo interpreted the commandment as prohibiting passionate desire, which meant for him "excessive," "immoderate" or "tyrannical desire."[15] Miller writes that "coveting" can be understood as "inordinate" or "ungoverned" desire, desire "let loose and uncontrolled," or "unrestrained."[16] Marsh Moyle similarly defined covetousness as "a desire that is out of control."[17] Hauerwas and Willimon define coveting as "disordered desire,"[18] and Eugenia Ann Gamble uses the term "predatory desire,"[19] explaining, "Covetousness makes others expendable to our desires."[20]

Emotions, Actions, or Both?

Medieval French interpreter Chizkuni asserts in his commentary on Deut 5:18 that the expression "to covet" from the Hebrew root *'wh* is only used "when it describes the desire of one's heart, not when one plans to act upon that desire."[21] Chizkuni contrasts this sort of "coveting" with that found at the beginning of the verse, which uses the Hebrew root *ḥmd*. Chizkuni explains the difference using the example of a person who becomes aware that his neighbor is experiencing pressure that makes the neighbor consider selling land or a house. When the person, "instead of financially supporting his neighbor, exploits his reduced circumstances and decides in his mind to buy it from him, he has violated this commandment [*wl' tt'wh*, from the verb *'wh*)]. When he expressed

15. Philo, *The Works of Philo: Complete and Unabridged*, trans. C. D. Yonge (Peabody, MA: Hendrickson, 2006), 530. Hanz Svebakken observes how Philo's assumptions about desire are philosophically similar to middle Platonic ideals, where desire is a nonrational emotion. One who indulges in passionate desire not only violates the Tenth Commandment but also risks what Philo sees as a ruinous outcome, allowing desire to usurp reason. In *Philo of Alexandria's Exposition on the Tenth Commandment* (Atlanta: Society of Biblical Literature, 2012), 185.

16. Miller, *The Ten Commandments*, 396–401.

17. Marsh Moyle, *Rumors of a Better Country: Searching for Trust and Community in a Time of Moral Outrage* (London: Inter-Varsity Press, 2023), 213.

18. Hauerwas and Willimon, *The Truth about God*, 129, 136.

19. Eugenia Ann Gamble, *Words of Love: A Healing Journey with the Ten Commandments* (Louisville: Westminster John Knox, 2022), 185.

20. Gamble, *Words of Love*, 188.

21. Sefaria, citing Chizkuni, "Deuteronomy 5:18:1," trans. Eliyahu Munk, https://tinyurl.com/2jpr2mvm.

his intention by mouth, he has violated the commandment of לא תחמד, as written at the beginning of verse 18."[22]

Maimonides had a similar reception, writing that if you see something desirable in the possession of someone else, and you can't stop thinking about and craving it, you have violated the commandment against desire. "But if your desire for the object is so strong that you take measures to acquire it, and you don't stop importuning the owner and exerting pressure on him to sell it to you or to exchange it for something of greater value . . . and you achieve your purpose, you have also violated, 'You shall not covet.'"[23]

Maimonides's caveat about how someone could still be coveting even if trading beyond the value of the item echoes a principle in the Talmud, that payment for the coveted item does not negate the coveting. One breaks the commandment when they take an item from another by force or deceit, even when they pay for the item (b. Metzia 5b:19). Hungarian pastor József Farkas wrote, "The full meaning of the word *chamad* is: if you covet something, do not begin to exert yourself, to try by fair means or foul, to acquire it."[24]

Medieval Spanish interpreter Ibn Ezra asserted that because Moses in Deuteronomy "employs *ve-lo titavveh* (neither shalt thou covet) (v. 18) in place of *lo tachmod* (thou shalt not covet) (Ex. 20:14)," that is "proof" that the root *ḥmd* "has two meanings in Hebrew. One is to rob, to extort, to take someone's property by force and compulsion. . . . The second meaning is to desire in the heart without acting."[25] That is to say, Ibn Ezra seems to presume that the two verbs in the Deuteronomy commandment must offer a distinction in meaning, but since Ibn Ezra also presumes that the commandment in both Exodus and Deuteronomy must mean the same thing, therefore the single word *ḥmd* must embrace two meanings.

Similar debates about coveting as more of an emotion or an action reoccurred in Western scholarship of the twentieth century. J. Hermann, in 1927, argued that *ḥmd* did not only denote an emotion but also included the action that stemmed from it. Albrecht Alt followed Hermann in 1949, as did J. Stamm. But William Moran disagreed; in 1967, he published a piece in which he pointed out that Prov 6:25 utilized the verb *ḥmd* without any corresponding action, thus arguing that it references an internal desire without necessarily

22. Sefaria, citing Chizkuni, "Deuteronomy 5:18:1."

23. Maimonides, *Book of the Commandments*, trans. C. B. Chavel (London-New York 1967), 250.

24. József Farkas, *Bench Marks*, trans. John R. Bodo (Richmond, VA: John Knox, 1969), 106.

25. Sefaria, citing "Ibn Ezra on Deuteronomy 5:18:1," H. Norman Strickman and Arthur M. Silver, Menorah, 1988–2004, https://tinyurl.com/3kye2zbw.

including action that would lead to acquiring the desired object. Moran also argued that many Semitic verbs that suggest desire are related to subsequent action, but those don't influence the denotation proper of that verb.[26] Brevard Childs weighed in with the opinion that "covet" (*ḥmd*) included both the emotion and actions. Assuming that the commandments in Exodus preceded those in Deuteronomy, Childs writes, "The original command was directed to that desire which included . . . those intrigues which led to acquiring the coveted object. The Deuteronomic substitution of the verb *hit'aweh* did not mark a qualitative difference of approach which had the effect of internalizing a previously action oriented commandment. . . . Rather, the Deuteronomic recension simply made more explicit the subjective side of the prohibition which was already contained in the original command."[27]

LXX uses the Greek word *epithumeō* to translate both Hebrew words for "covet"; this word is defined by *The Greek-English Lexicon of the Septuagint* as "to set one's heart upon, to long for, to desire." Leonard Greenspoon writes, "The Greek verb *epithumeō* is different from the English verb 'covet' since it can be used for positive as well as negative desires. . . . For this reason, readers interpreting the Greek Bible (as opposed to the Hebrew version) were likely to miss the specific connection between ḥ-m-d and 'taking.'"[28] Other receptions of this commandment, while not delving into distinctions in Hebrew and Greek terms, also seem to suggest that coveting is more a state of mind or will than an action. For example, the late medieval *Dives and Pauper* asserts that in the previous commandments, God forbids all "wicked werkes," but in this last commandment God forbids all "wicked wylles."[29] John Calvin preached, "For if we only read 'You shall not be a thief, You shall not be a murderer, You shall not be an adulterer,' then we would each think that we are innocent. But when we come to this commandment: 'You shall not covet,' then that provides God with a sharper lancet for not only sounding the bottom of our heart, but

26. Brevard Childs, *The Book of Exodus: A Critical, Theological Commentary* (Philadelphia: Westminster, 1974), 425–26.

27. Childs, *The Book of Exodus*, 427. The English word "covet" is used to describe a move in the video game Pokémon, in which a user steals an item from another player. The description of the move is that the user "endearingly approaches" and then steals the item held by the other. While nothing necessarily connects this with the commandment, that it is a "move" suggests that coveting is ultimately an action. Pokémon Database, "Move:Covet," https://tinyurl.com/45rjnahe.

28. Leonard Greenspoon, "Do Not Covet: Is It a Feeling or an Action?," TheTorah.com, 2018, https://tinyurl.com/y7sjzy7c.

29. Jonathan Willis, *The Reformation of the Decalogue: Religious Identity and the Ten Commandments in England, c. 1485–1625* (Cambridge: Cambridge University Press, 2017), 143.

all our thoughts and imaginations."[30] Calvin's move is similar to those who distinguish between actions of theft, murder, or lying, which are prohibited in earlier commandments, and the inward state of coveting prohibited in this commandment.

Examples of Coveting

Many receptions also see covetousness in biblical stories that lack either Hebrew word for "covet." The *Illustrated Bible* from the Reformation, with scenes chosen by Melanchthon and illustrated by Cranach's woodcuts, use two stories from Genesis for this commandment: Jacob's animal husbandry with Laban's flocks (Genesis 30) and Potiphar's wife wanting to have sex with Joseph (Genesis 39). Hazony proclaims that coveting "is the sin of insecurity" and uses the story of Cain in Genesis 4 and the spies in Numbers 13 to demonstrate such insecurity.[31] Many receptions reference the story of Ahab wanting Naboth's vineyard (1 Kings 21) and David wanting Bathsheba (2 Samuel 11). Miller comments, "When one encounters instances of coveting in the Old Testament, they are largely *acts of royalty and the wealthy*" (emphasis his).[32]

A number of receptions also then understand coveting as "greed."[33] Bruckner suggests that in Mark's version of the story of the rich young ruler with whom Jesus references the commandments, the word "defraud," which appears only in Mark 10:19, is a stand-in for the commandment against coveting, for the rich take what they covet from others by defrauding them.[34] Journalist Chris Hedges specifically criticizes self-help author and speaker Anthony J. Robbins for fueling other people's desire for wealth, describing Robbins's teaching techniques as encouraging people to covet wealth and power.[35] Gamble names Jeff Bezos and Mark Zuckerburg, CEOs of Amazon and Facebook, respectively, as cautionary examples of those who are unable to say they have enough, based on their profits during the COVID-19 pandemic.[36] Hauerwas and Willimon write, "The commandment against covetousness may be one

30. Calvin, *Sermons*, 233.

31. Hazony, *The Ten Commandments*, 234.

32. Miller, *The Ten Commandments*, 396.

33. Chris Hedges, *Losing Moses on the Freeway: The Ten Commandments in America* (New York: Free Press, 2005), 157–68.

34. Bruckner, "On the One Hand," 112.

35. Hedges, *Losing Moses on the Freeway*, 157.

36. Gamble, *Words of Love*, 189. Gamble does admit that their products were helpful to

of the most accusatory for those of us who live in a society of seemingly unquenchable acquisitiveness, where greed appears to be a necessary component to keep the economy running smoothly. The Constitution tells us that America exists to give people what we want, without judging the comparative worth of our wants. To not want is almost un-American."[37]

Theologian Bernd Wannenwetch, whose argument that covetousness reflects the core of idolatry for many today was mentioned in chapter three of this book, also proclaims, "Covetousness is the dominant celebratory of the capitalist religion."[38] He traced developments in advertising, noting how in the years following World War II, most companies focused on the utility values of their products, for example, advertising that a vacuum worked well. But then, once every household had a vacuum, the advertising would shift to emphasize the value of immaterial benefits that promised to accompany the product, such as happiness or prestige. Eventually, the product itself received little to no focus, and instead, the deeper desires for those immaterial benefits would be advertised. Wannenwetch gives examples of ads for BMW cars. In the 1950s, the advertisements had close-up images of the vehicle. In the 1970s, the close-up was of a driver, who was then approached by an attractive person. More recently, the car was incidental to the advertisement, shown only at the end. Because the commandment prohibits coveting specific objects that belong to a neighbor, Wannenwetch asks, "Has the recent shift towards self-referential desire perhaps rendered this commandment anachronistic? Since the object of my desire is my desire not my neighbour's, is the commandment no longer capable of . . . convicting me of sin?"[39]

Regarding advertising and acquisition as almost inevitable in the United States, several clergy in the greater Los Angeles area weighed in on the question, "Can We Raise Children Not to Covet?" in an op-ed from December 2011 in the *LA Times* newspaper. Many acknowledged that during the Christmas season, it would be difficult to hinder children wanting things. Steven Gibson from the South Pasadena Atheist Meetup wrote, "Children often grow up to reflect the society they are raised in. This society is filled with covetousness, greed and unnecessary desires." Some opined that it would be helpful to have

connect people and provide services during the pandemic; she also perhaps blurs the lines between a company and the one in charge of the company.

37. Hauerwas and Willimon, *The Truth about God*, 135.

38. Bernd Wannenwetch, "The Desire of Desire: Commandment and Idolatry in Late Capitalist Societies," in *Idolatry: False Worship in the Bible, Early Judaism and Christianity*, ed. Stephen C. Barton (New York: Continuum, 2007), 313.

39. Wannenwetch, "The Desire of Desire," 321.

legislation that would ban or limit advertising for children, though others wrote that it was the responsibility of parents, not the government to guide and teach children. The Rev. Amy Pringle encouraged parents, "Teach your children to avoid commercialism by, you know, avoiding commercialism." The Rev. Bryan Griem wrote, "Adults have to lead by example. If we're living like we believe the one who dies with the most toys wins, what chance do kids have? By the way, this conversation is based upon the Tenth Commandment. Apart from God's directive, why should anyone think covetousness is wrong?"[40]

Making a distinction between "covetousness" and "jealousy," Gamble suggests that while jealousy is often deeply problematic, it can act as a motivator, but "Covetousness is always a thief and a liar. It has no positive application."[41] Moyle compares covetousness with envy, and while he acknowledges that the reference to "biting and devouring one another" in Gal 5:15 is not literal, he writes, "The ultimate act of coveting is cannibalism! Historically, cannibals did not eat other humans for calories but to acquire the life force in their victim; this is the heart of envy."[42] Moyle also wrote, "We hide covetousness in social convention, behind pleasant smiles over the garden wall, in the barbed observations at the academic dinner table, or in supposedly objective peer reviews."[43]

Lists of Objects That Are Coveted

Erhard Gerstenberger observed that the commandment against coveting divides a person's things into three categories: real estate, people under him—including a wife, though more will be said about the spouse below—and animals.[44] Deuteronomy's version of the commandment adds the word "field" to the "real estate"; David Baker notes how this creates a list of three pairs—house or field, male or female slave, ox or donkey—with a concluding phrase, for a total of seven items.[45] Baker argues that, because the Hebrew word *byt* means

40. "In Theory: Can We Raise Children Not to Covet?," *Glendale News-Press*, December 10, 2011, https://tinyurl.com/22sypxx3.

41. Gamble, *Words of Love*, 188–89.

42. Moyle, *Rumors of a Better Country*, 215.

43. Moyle, *Rumors of a Better Country*, 216.

44. Erhard S. Gerstenberger, *Leviticus*, OTL Commentary Series (Louisville: Westminster John Knox, 1996), 441.

45. David L. Baker, *The Decalogue: Living as the People of God* (Downers Grove, IL: InterVarsity, 2017), 146. Baker also notes how "house and field" are paired in Gen 39:5; 2 Kgs 8:3, 5; Isa 5:8; and Mic 2:2.

both "house" and "household," it has the second meaning in Exodus and the first in Deuteronomy; in Exodus, he suggests, "it really means 'house*hold*' and includes all of a man's possessions that are economically significant . . . specified in decreasing order of importance."[46] The wife's economic importance is because she brought capital to the marriage through her dowry.

In Chizkuni's commentary on Deut 5:18, he follows the order from Exodus, explaining that there "Moses arranged the order of the examples quoted in the tenth commandment, according to how people develop desires as they grow older. First they desire a better house, one that they could not afford previously. Next, they desire a woman who they feel has more to offer them than the one they had married when relatively young and inexperienced. Next they also desire such assets as make life more comfortable, even if they have to acquire them by making someone who owns them part with theirs."[47] But in contrast to Chizkuni, who observed significance in the order of the objects, Puritan James Durham suggests that because the commandment listed several, it was not really about the objects themselves but about a new way of acting in reference to that object. Durham explains that this commandment to not covet condemns directly a sin that hadn't been condemned previously, "so that it also seems to be added to the other as a full and more clear explication of that spiritual obedience that is required in the rest."[48]

French philosopher René Girard writes:

> In reading the Tenth Commandment one has the impression of being present at the intellectual process of its elaboration. To prevent people from fighting, the lawgiver seeks at first to forbid all the objects about which they ceaselessly fight, and he decides to make a list of these. However, he quickly perceives that the objects are too numerous: he cannot enumerate all of them. So he interrupts himself in the process, gives up focusing on the objects that keep changing anyway, and he turns to what never changes. Or rather, he turns to that one who is always present, the neighbor. One always desires *whatever belongs to that one*, the neighbor.[49]

46. Baker, *The Decalogue*, 146.

47. Sefaria, citing *The Contemporary Torah*, ed. David E. S. Stein et al. (Philadelphia: Jewish Publication Society, 2006), https://tinyurl.com/mrv3s2wy.

48. James Durham, *The Law Unsealed, or, a practical exposition of the Ten Commandments. With a resolution of several momentous questions and cases of conscience*, Early English Books Online, https://tinyurl.com/phfsuw6v, 269.

49. René Girard, *I See Satan Fall Like Lightning*, trans. James G. Williams (Maryknoll, NY: Orbis Books, 2001), 9.

Wannenwetch explains, "We may concede that the commandment summons any new generation to update the list that comprises the potential objects of coveting according to its own time and circumstances."[50] When I teach the Ten Commandments, I invite students to brainstorm an "updated list" of things we might covet from another person. The list inevitably includes material objects—a person's car, a person's iPhone (these are college students)—but they also identify less material things, such as a person's confidence, or sense of humor, or ability to write well. Though the objects change, the desire for what belongs to another persists.

The Wife as Distinct

As noted above, Deuteronomy and Exodus use different verbs and have a different order. Exodus lists "house" then "wife." Both Exod 20:17 and Deut 5:21 have two prohibitions, such that Exod 20:17 reads, "You shall not covet your neighbor's house, neither shall you covet your neighbor's wife, etc." Deuteronomy's version of the commandment lists wife first and uses two separate verbs, such that Deut 5:21 reads, "You shall not covet your neighbor's wife, neither shall you desire your neighbor's house, his field. . . ." Anthony Phillips suggests that the Deuteronomic editors thought women had a higher status, which resulted in the change in order from Exodus to Deuteronomy,[51] but William L. Moran demonstrates how the end of the commandment reflects traditional types of a list of possessions elsewhere in ancient southwest Asia, such as at Ugarit, so Deuteronomy's version can be as old as Exodus.[52] Miller writes that, even though it is difficult to read the status of women into Deuteronomy's sequence of objects, because the Deuteronomic version of the Ten Commandments separates the wife from the other property categories, it therefore focuses attention on her and her protection.[53] Bernard Levinson

50. Wannenwetch, "The Desire of Desire," 321.

51. Anthony Phillips, "The Decalogue: Ancient Israel's Criminal Law," in *Essays on Biblical Law*, JSOT Supp 344 (Sheffield: Sheffield Academic Press, 2002), 8.

52. William L. Moran, "The Conclusion of the Decalogue (Ex 20,17 = Dt 5,21)," *CBQ* 29 (October 1967): 548–52.

53. Miller, *The Ten Commandments*, 395. But Miller also acknowledges, in that historical context, that the wife is part of the personal and economic integrity of a household, when he suggests that the laws about Levirate marriage in Deut 25:5–6 are an exception to the basic prohibition of the commandment to not covet a neighbor's wife. He writes that in this instance, it is not only acceptable, but the brother is obligated to take the sister-in-law.

writes, "By removing her altogether from the list of other chattels, [the editors] establish that the law does not regard the woman as merely one commodity among others comprising a house."[54]

Though reception history cannot definitively explain the reason for the difference in the two versions of the Ten Commandments, it clearly demonstrates that the version in Deuteronomy led later readers to separate Exod 20:17 and Deut 5:21 into two distinct commandments. Augustine was the first to do so, followed by Roman Catholics; and Luther continued to subscribe to that enumeration. Protestants treated Exod 20:17 and Deut 5:21 as a single commandment that could be summarized by the last clause in the verse, "you shall not covet anything of your neighbor's." An effect of separating out coveting into two commandments is that the ninth commandment, "you shall not covet your neighbor's wife," would correspond to the previous commandment, "you shall not commit adultery," and the tenth commandment, "you shall not covet your neighbor's house . . ." would correspond to the previous commandment, "you shall not steal." Someone who obeys the commandment to not covet a neighbor's wife would not commit adultery; someone who obeys the commandment to not covet a neighbor's belongings would not steal. Indeed, Calvin—while following the numbering that combined everything into a single commandment to not covet—is typical of many when he acknowledges that this commandment may seem superfluous given that previous commandments forbade adultery and stealing; he justified this commandment based on the distinctions between intent and action.[55]

Historian Jonathan Willis argues that the Reformed combination of two commandments for coveting into one served to emphasize Reformed theology around original sin and justification by faith. For example, sixteenth-century English bishop John Hooper writes,

> In this precept is declared specially our infirmity and weakness, that we are all miserable sinners. . . . In this commandment is not only forbid the effect of ill, but also the affect and desire towards ill: not only the affect,

Miller, *The Ten Commandments*, 403. This idea raises the question if one can "covet" and "take" something once the neighbor is dead and gone.

54. Bernard Levinson, "Deuteronomy: Introduction and Annotations," in *The Jewish Study Bible*, ed. Adele Berlin and Marc Zvi Brettler (New York: Oxford University Press, 2004), 378.

55. John Calvin, *Institutes of the Christian Religion*, ed. John T. McNeill, trans. and indexed by Ford Lewis Battles (Philadelphia: Westminster, 1960), 413. In 2 Sam 12:9 when the prophet Nathan accuses David of his sins, Nathan uses the language "you took [Uriah's] wife" and not "you committed adultery" with her.

> lust, concupiscence, proneness, inclination, desire, and appetite towards ill; but also when man is most destitute of sin and most full of virtue . . . yet is his works so imperfect that if it were not for the free, liberal, and merciful imputation of justice in Christ Jesu, man were damned. . . . He that considereth this precept well, shall the better perceive the greatness of God's infinite mercy, and understand the article and doctrine of free justification by faith.[56]

Scott Shepherd's mystery novel *The Last Commandment* is about a serial killer who murders victims who have each broken one of the Ten Commandments. The book reveals at the end that the killer is the brother of Detective Austin Grant of Scotland Yard, and what set him off was that Grant had married a woman with whom his brother had previously been involved. In the book's climactic confrontational scene, Grant tells his murderous brother, "If anyone is guilty of the last commandment, it's you, brother. You're the one who coveted his neighbor's wife. Not me."[57] A few chapters before the end, the brother had expressed that a person who covets commits "the worst transgression of all."[58]

Connections with Other Commandments

As mentioned above, many receptions connect the commandment to not covet a neighbor's wife with the commandment forbidding adultery and the commandment to not covet a neighbor's possessions with the commandment forbidding stealing. Gamble relates this commandment to each of the previous ones, describing how breaking it could lead to violation of all nine others. Referring to a commandment as a "Word," she writes:

> Covetousness can lead us to believe that something other than God can salve our wounds, free us, manage our emotions, and become our little gods (Words One and Two). It can lead us to misuse God's name, "O Lord, let me win the lottery!" (Word Three). It can rule us to the point

56. John Hooper, *Early Writings Comprising the Declaration of Christ and His Office, Answer to Bishop Gardner, Ten Commandments, Sermons on Jonas, Funeral Sermon*, ed. Samuel Carr for the Parker Society (Cambridge: Cambridge University Press, 1843), 410–11.

57. Scott Shepherd, *The Last Commandment* (New York: Mysterious Press, 2021), 349.

58. Shepherd, *The Last Commandment*, 335.

> that we never stop and rest, to see God's provision or work for God's justice (Word Four). It can blind us to seeing what and who really brings us life (Word Five). It can lead us, metaphorically or even literally, to kill anyone who gets in the way of our getting what we want (Word Six). It can lead us to cheapen our relationships (Word Seven). It can lead us to steal (Word Eight). And it can lead us to lie about it (Word Nine).[59]

Harrelson explains that he suspected that commandments against idols and to keep the Sabbath would produce in Israel "a very common envy of those who could have plastic images of the deity and who could avoid the commitment to Sabbath observance. In this way the community was already being prepared to covet the ways of the neighboring peoples."[60] Abraham Joshua Heschel also related the commandment to keep the Sabbath with the commandment to not covet, by explaining that the final commandment forbids coveting anything that belongs to one's neighbor because God has given the Sabbath. "It is as if the command: *Do not covet things of space*, were correlated with the unspoken word: *Do covet things of time*."[61]

Heschel also related the commandment to not covet with the first (Jewish) commandment by seeing that both were about liberty. Heschel wrote,

> Nothing is as hard to suppress as the will to be a slave to one's own pettiness. Gallantly, ceaselessly, quietly, man must fight for inner liberty. Inner liberty depends upon being exempt from domination of things as well as from domination of people. There are many who have acquired a high degree of political and social liberty, but only very few are not enslaved to things. This is our constant problem—how to live with people and remain free, how to live with things and remain independent. In a moment of eternity, while the taste of redemption was still fresh to the former slaves, the people of Israel were given the Ten Words, the Ten Commandments. In its beginning and end, the Decalogue deals with the liberty of man. The first Word—I am the Lord thy God, who brought thee out of the Land of Egypt, out of the house of bondage—reminds him that his outer liberty was given to him by God, and the tenth Word—Thou shalt not covet!—reminds him that he himself must achieve his inner liberty.[62]

59. Gamble, *Words of Love*, 185.
60. Harrelson, *The Ten Commandments*, 150.
61. Abraham Joshua Heschel, *The Sabbath* (New York: Farrer, Straus and Giroux, 2005), 90.
62. Heschel, *The Sabbath*, 89–90.

Antidotes

The quote from Heschel, that it is up to each person to "achieve inner liberty," suggests that enforcing the commandment to not covet is something personal and individual. This may be especially true when coveting remains in the realm of one's intention and does not move into action. Theologian Kevin DeYoung includes four ways someone could know that they "might be coveting": if they hurt others in order to get more for themselves; if they are preoccupied with making and accumulating more; if they are unwilling to give up what they already have; and if they are frequently grumbling about their house, spouse, quality or quantity of possessions, and the general state of their life.[63] As an antidote to these, DeYoung references 1 Tim 6:6, "Godliness with contentment is great gain."[64]

Many receptions suggest that contentment is an antidote to coveting. Rabbi Lord Jonathan Sacks of Great Britain restated the commandment as: be content with your own blessings.[65] Puritan James Durham wrote that a person should have "a full contentation with the lot that God had carved out to you, without the least ordinate motion or inclination to the contrary, which may . . . be inconsistent with love to [neighbor], or with contentment and a right composure of spirit in yourselves."[66] The Westminster Catechism explains, "The Tenth commandment forbids all discontentment with our own estate"; put positively, it encourages contentment.

Ibn Ezra's teaching on the commandment begins with the statement, "Many people are amazed at this commandment. They ask, how is it possible for a person not to covet in his heart all beautiful things that appear desirable to him?" Ibn Ezra's answer comes in a parable about a peasant—of sound mind—who sees a beautiful princess and won't entertain any covetous thoughts about sleeping with her because he knows it is impossible. The peasant will not think "like the insane who desire to sprout wings and fly to the sky, for it is impossible to do so."[67] Ibn Ezra also appeals to the idea of being content, even happy, with the lot God has apportioned, explaining,

63. Kevin DeYoung, *The 10 Commandments: What They Mean, Why They Matter, and Why We Should Obey Them* (Wheaton, IL: Crossway, 2018), 162–64.

64. DeYoung, *The 10 Commandments*, 164.

65. "Was Jacob Right to Take Esau's Blessing?," *Covenant & Conversation* (blog), *Jonathan Sacks: The Rabbi Sacks Legacy*, https://tinyurl.com/3sbp9xft.

66. Durham, *The Law Unsealed*, 269.

67. Sefaria, citing "Ibn Ezra on Exodus 20:14:1," H. Norman Strickman and Arthur M. Silver, Menorah, 1988–2004, https://tinyurl.com/5n6b5x65.

> So must every intelligent person know that a person does not acquire a beautiful woman or money because of his intelligence or wisdom, but only in accordance with what God has apportioned to him. He will therefore be happy with his lot and will not allow his heart to covet and desire anything which is not his. For he knows that that which God did not want to give him, he cannot acquire by his own strength, thoughts, or schemes. He will therefore trust in his creator, that is, that his creator will sustain him and do what is right in His sight.[68]

Liturgist Douglas McKelvey's prayer titled "A Liturgy for Those Who Covet the Latest Technology" includes the refrain "Content my soul in you, O Christ, who alone are sufficient to my longings" and includes the specific petition,

> Let me be content, O Lord, with what I truly need to accomplish the necessary tasks before me. Nay, let me be content with nothing but thee. . . .
> using technologies to further good ends,
> while never seeking them as ends in themselves.[69]

The language of need is another important aspect of understanding coveting; Rabbi Corey Helfand wrote in an online column in 2018, "The act of coveting becomes a way of avoiding dealing with our own insecurities by distracting ourselves with what others have, rather than what we ourselves might need."[70] Helfand drew on David Hazony's explanation of this commandment that coveting is "the product of insecurity"; Hazony proclaims that insecurity—which may be expressed in various ways from a lack of belief in oneself, to avoiding hard questions, to channeling fears into hatred toward others—"is the antithesis of redemption."[71] Hedges also writes that coveting comes from "deep, burning insecurity . . . our feelings of unworthiness."[72] Antidotes to coveting, then, would include knowing what we genuinely need, distinguishing between a mere desire and a need, and, according to these receptions, having a sense of security and self-worth would be positive hindrances to coveting.

68. Sefaria, citing "Ibn Ezra on Exodus 20:14:1."

69. Douglas McKelvey, "A Liturgy for Those Who Covet the Latest Technology," in *Every Moment Holy* (Nashville: Rabbit Room, 2017), 160–61.

70. "What Do You Covet and What Does It Say About You?," *The Jewish News*, July 27, 2018, https://tinyurl.com/sm2sujtv.

71. Hazony, *The Ten Commandments*, 250.

72. Hedges, *Losing Moses on the Freeway*, 158.

Generosity, gratitude, and humility provide further antidotes to coveting. Proverbs 21:26 uses antithetical parallelism to contrast the lazy person who covets with the righteous person who "gives and does not refrain." Giving—generously—counters covetousness. And Gamble does not use the word contentment but asserts that "gratitude" for one's own life, possessions, and state of being will prevent coveting what belongs to someone else.[73] Moyle argues that humility is the root, and out of humility will grow contentment, gratitude, and worship. He writes, "If the first instruction of the Decalogue calls for humility before the ever-present and active Creator to whom we must answer, the tenth calls us to humility towards everyone else."[74]

Luther includes explanations of both what is forbidden and what is encouraged as he defines the "ordinary meaning" of the commandment against coveting in his Catechism. Luther writes, "We are here forbidden to wish our neighbor's harm, to contribute to it, or to give occasion for it. If he has property, we are to be glad about it, allow him to enjoy it, and promote and protect everything that may be of service and profit to him, as we would wish him do for us."[75] Luther's advice here is very practical: be happy about what your neighbor possesses, be that something material or some quality in their personality. What's more, help them enjoy that themselves, promote and protect it for them. Luther's reception also seems to link the commandment against coveting with the so-called golden rule, that we love our neighbors by treating them as we would wish to be treated.

Love of Neighbor

Thus, yet again, the pattern of love of God and love of neighbor is evident in the Ten Commandments, with the final words in the final commandment being "your neighbor." Alexander Rofé examines four other laws in Deuteronomy—19:14; 23:25[24], 26[25]; and 24:10—which seem to be minor infringements against property. Yet, Rofé observes that the general rule on behalf of a neighbor's property in the commandment is made specific and concrete with these other laws about the neighbor's field, vineyard, standing grain, and the pledge that is within the house. Rofé also notes how each of these verses uses the phrase "your neighbor," and 23:23 uses it twice.[76]

73. Gamble, *Words of Love*, 200–201.

74. Moyle, *Rumors of a Better Country*, 221.

75. Luther, *Large Catechism*, 62.

76. Alexander Rofé, "The Tenth Commandment in the Light of Four Deuteronomic

If the four laws in Deuteronomy concretize how to love a neighbor by caring for their property in very specific ways, other receptions of the commandment broaden it out in their explanation and application. Aquinas proclaims that coveting "kills love of our neighbor—since according to Augustine, the more a man loves, the less he covets and the more he covets the less he loves."[77] Miller asserts, "No single commandment embodies the love of neighbor more than the commandment against coveting, for it is the prohibition that from the start inhibits whatever inclinations we may have to do in our neighbor's life, property, marriage, honor, and all that is our neighbor's."[78] Moyle proclaims succinctly, "Covetousness is an inversion of love."[79]

Calvin expresses that the purpose of this commandment against coveting is that, "Since God wills that our whole soul be possessed with a disposition to love, we must banish from our hearts all desire contrary to love. To sum up, then: no thought should steal upon us to move our hearts to a harmful covetousness that tends to our neighbor's loss. To this corresponds the opposite precept: whatever we conceive, deliberate, will, or attempt is to be linked to our neighbor's good and advantage."[80]

Conclusion

Luther comments, "This last commandment therefore is given not for rogues in the eyes of the world, but just for the most pious, who wish to be praised and be called honest and upright people, since they have not offended against the former commandments."[81] Certainly, we could critique Luther's rhetoric, as if the rogues in the world wouldn't also benefit from attention to their attitude as well as their actions.[82] And Luther seems to intend this negatively, as a criticism that no one is able to keep the Ten Commandments; he explains that though God wants people to have a pure heart, "like all the other commandments, this commandment, too, constantly accuses us and shows us what our

---

Laws," trans. Arnold Schwartz, in *The Ten Commandments in History and Tradition*, ed. Ben-Zion Segal, English version ed. Gershon Levi (Jerusalem: Magnes, 1990), 54–56.

77. Aquinas, *The Commandments of God*, 85.

78. Miller, *The Ten Commandments*, 412–13.

79. Moyle, *Rumors of a Better Country*, 214.

80. Calvin, *Institutes*, 413.

81. Luther, *Large Catechism*, 60.

82. And certainly, Luther's anti-Judaism is in full force when he identifies "the Jews" especially, and negatively, as those who believe themselves pious.

righteousness really amounts to in the eyes of God."[83] But in the same way that negative "you shall not" commandments imply something positive, it would seem that we could receive Luther's word in a more positive manner: that being pious is not only about outward appearances but inward attitude and the heart and that to love a neighbor may begin and end with attitudes of love for that neighbor and appreciation for what they have. Indeed, as this commandment reminds us of how thoroughly the Ten Commandments ask us to relate well to our neighbor, with late sixteenth-century commentor Robert Allen, we might say this commandment "is a most worthie conclusion of all the rest."[84]

83. Luther, *Large Catechism*, 62.

84. Robert Allen, *A treasurie of catechisme, or Christian instruction. The first part, which is concerning the morall law or ten Commandements of Almightie God: with certaine questions and aunswers preparatory to the same*, Early English Books Online 2, https://tinyurl.com/4jvsv8jw, 267.

CONCLUSION

This reception history of the Ten Commandments has not sought to be exhaustive but hopefully has been representative enough to demonstrate that there is never a single one right way to interpret and apply a commandment. Instead, particularly because of the nature of the—brief—Ten Commandments, it is always a both/and. We can keep the commandment not to bear God's name in vain by how we live out our lives as representatives of God and by avoiding speech about God that is false, blasphemous, or trivializing. We can honor our parents by listening to them patiently, by repeatedly helping them with new technology, and also by maintaining boundaries with them. These applications of the Ten Commandment are not, and need not be, mutually exclusive. Moreover, in different situations and times, a commandment may need to be applied differently. The abstract principles and virtues of loving God can be made concrete in a specific practice of keeping Sabbath; loving neighbor can be made concrete when it is my literal next-door neighbor whose property I help protect by picking up a package delivered when she is out of town so it will not be stolen.

Martin Luther's language about the Ten Commandments tends toward the superlative. He describes them as "the greatest treasure given to us by God,"[1] writing,

> They are the true fountain and channel from which all that is to qualify as good works must spring and flow. Apart from the Ten Commandments no deed or conduct can be good or pleasing to God, however great or valuable it may be in the eyes of the world. . . . It will be a very long time before humans introduce a doctrine or a social order that matches up to the Ten Commandments, the demands of which are so high that no one

1. Martin Luther, *Luther's Large Catechism with Study Questions*, ed. F. Samuel Janzow (St. Louis: Concordia, 1978), 67.

> can fulfill them by mere human strength. . . . Focus on them, really test yourself, apply all the strength and ability you have, and you then will really find so much to work at that you will not look for nor pay attention to any other works or types of holiness.[2]

Luther is not alone in describing the Ten Commandments in such glowing terms; subtitles to books about the Ten Commandments similarly advertise their helpful/useful qualities. For example, Emmet Fox's 1953 book on the Ten Commandments is subtitled "The Master Key to Life."[3] David Hazony's subtitle is "How Our Most Ancient Moral Text Can Renew Modern Life."[4] Edith Schaeffer titles her book on the Ten Commandments *Lifelines*,[5] and Al Vom Steeg's book is titled *Freedom to Live: A Guide to a Free and Abundant Life as Revealed through the Ten Commandments*.[6] So many of these titles promise that knowing the Ten Commandments and practicing them in life will yield freedom, renewal, and even life itself.

While each commandment has its own focus, there are common themes that run through several commandments, such as trusting in God, knowing and remembering who God is; practicing honesty in speech and acts directed to both God and to other people; minimizing work, production, and accumulation, especially when those things threaten to define life; valuing life; and helping others in the community thrive in their own relationships and lives.

Even as each commandment can and should be made concrete in the life of an individual, Cheryl B. Anderson identifies a concern, writing, "Problems arise, however, when the Decalogue is applied in such a way that its requirements address how an individual treats his or her own group while the deeper societal ills affecting a different group are ignored."[7] Reception history does encourage attention to the context—historically and socially—in which the reception occurs, but this does not give carte blanche to anyone to ignore the

2. Luther, *Large Catechism*, 63–64.

3. Emmet Fox, *The Ten Commandments: The Master Key to Life* (New York: Harper and Row, 1953).

4. David Hazony, *The Ten Commandments: How Our Most Ancient Moral Text Can Renew Modern Life* (New York: Scribner, 2010).

5. Edith Schaeffer, *Lifelines: The Ten Commandments for Today* (Westchester, IL: Crossway, 1982).

6. Al Vom Steeg, *Freedom to Live: A Guide to a Free and Abundant Life as Revealed through the Ten Commandments* (Des Moines, IA: Meredith, 1984).

7. Cheryl B. Anderson, "The Eighth Commandment: A Way to King's 'Beloved Community'?," in *The Ten Commandments: The Reciprocity of Faithfulness*, ed. William P. Brown, Library of Theological Ethics (Louisville: Westminster John Knox, 2004), 281.

historical and social—or literary and theological—setting of the text. The Ten Commandments come from a society that is communal and connected, concerned with the flourishing and the well-being of the whole. These concerns are also rooted in faith in the God who gave the commandments, the same God who set God's people free from dehumanizing slavery to love God and one another.

Obviously, the various receptions of the Ten Commandments throughout the ages are not the same. Some are trivial and perhaps even humorous. Others are tragic and serious. Again, the aim has been to demonstrate representative ways of interpreting and applying each commandment and the implications for those receptions. Luther writes, "I should think that we would have our hands full trying to keep these commandments and to practice gentleness, patience, and love toward enemies, chastity, kindness, and so on, together with everything else connected with these virtues. . . . Focus on them, really test yourself, apply all the strength and ability you have, and you then will really find so much to work at that you will not look for nor pay attention to any other works or types of holiness."[8] Such language might also be slightly hyperbolic, but I agree with Luther that a focus on the Ten Commandments can be an invitation to apply their virtuous patterns in our own lives.

8. Luther, *Large Catechism*, 63–64.

ACKNOWLEDGMENTS

Arnold Jacob Wolf wrote, "It is much harder to write about crucial, famous texts than about more obscure and apparently less persuasive ones. What, after all, is left to be said about the Ten Words that has not been said a thousand times?"[1] I couldn't agree more: my academic writing has focused on minor characters such as Balaam, Bathsheba, and the two Tamars, and it was relatively easy to write about seemingly trivial characters in fairly obscure biblical narratives. It is hard to write about the Ten Commandments. Also, Wolf is not wrong that much has already been said about the "Ten Words." Entire books have been written on the single commandment about Sabbath; Abraham Heschel, Walter Brueggemann, Tricia Hersey, and Jon Levenson—to name only a few!—have explained and clarified what Sabbath means and why and how it can be kept. But obviously, instead of taking Wolf's words as permission to stop this project, I see his question as a challenge to justify writing this book. It is not that I believe that I have something utterly new to say, but rather, Eerdmans has given me a new opportunity to gather (some of) what has been written about the Ten Commandments into a single volume. I have long admired the design of the Talmud, where editors codified various rabbinic teaching into one place. Certainly, this book will not be authoritative in any way similar to the Talmud, but perhaps it will be helpful to readers to have various, even competing, perspectives on each of the Ten Commandments in one place.

I have wanted to avoid too much prescription or legalism in this book. When I told a friend that, she responded, "Well, you are writing a book on the law." Still, I hope that the various receptions discussed throughout the book give freedom and permission to every person who receives and applies the commandments in their own lives. I also sincerely hope that this book may be useful, in the sense that all Scripture is described as useful in 2 Tim 3:16–17.

1. Arnold Jacob Wolf, "Ten More Words," in *Broken Tablets: Restoring the Ten Commandments and Ourselves* (Woodstock, VT: Jewish Lights, 1999), 133.

I have to thank all the friends and colleagues who supported and encouraged me while I was writing. First, Amy K. Erickson and G. Brooke Lester, thank you for your patient and careful reading of my drafts and your many suggestions for improvement. You two know how much I value you; it always bears repeating. Jennifer McKinney and Karen Snedker have helped me maintain the discipline of writing even during the academic year and through some tumultuous times. Here's another "outcome" from our "support group"! Thanks to many other colleagues at Seattle Pacific University for conversations, suggestions, and answers to my seemingly random questions, including Matthew Benton, Esther Cen, Jeff Keuss, Brian Lugiyoyo, Leland Saunders, Chakrita Saulina, Ashley Skinner-Creek, Rick Steele, and Rob Wall. Special thanks to librarian Steve Perisho for tracking down all manner of sources and references for me and for taking the picture of our library's Torah scroll. My children Madeleine and Max encouraged me frequently, especially in the final months of writing, and my husband Matthew's support was essential: thank you, family.

I am very grateful to Andrew Knapp for the initial invitation to write this book for Eerdmans as well as his patient encouragement during the time it took me to complete it. Editors Kimberley Benedict and Laurel Draper at Eerdmans and copyeditor Trent Hancock corrected typos and made sure that my references were accurate, and I appreciate all their attention and care. Thanks also to Rebekah Eklund, whose lovely reception history of the Beatitudes was the inspiration for this one.

As an undergraduate student at Seattle Pacific University, I took more classes with Bob Drovdahl than any other professor. When I began teaching at my alma mater, Bob embraced me as a full colleague, not just a former student. Bob and I have been learning guitar together, taught by various instructors, for a good long time. After one of those guitar lessons, I told him I was trying to figure out how to describe my approach to the commandments, wanting to encourage interpretive flexibility without it sounding utterly relative. Bob's framework, that the commandments are abstract and only become concrete when they get applied in biblical stories and the lives of the people who seek to obey them, became a helpful shift in focus for me as is evident in the first chapter of this book. For this reason, and with gratitude for all the ways Bob has invested in my life over the years, I dedicate this book to him.

SELECTED BIBLIOGRAPHY

Adelman, Rachel. "Primeval Coats." TheTorah.com. 2015. https://tinyurl.com/438f2zwe.

Albeck, Shalom. "The Ten Commandments and the Essence of Religious Faith." Translated by Chaim Pearl. Pages 261–89 in *The Ten Commandments in History and Tradition*. Edited by Ben-Zion Segal. English version edited by Gershon Levi. Jerusalem: Magnes, 1990.

Albright, William Foxwell. *From the Stone Age to Christianity: Monotheism and the Historical Process*. 2nd ed. Baltimore: Johns Hopkins University Press, 1957.

Alexander, T. Desmond. *Exodus*. Downers Grove, IL: IVP Academic, 2017.

Allen, Pauline. *John Chrysostom, Homilies on Colossians*. Atlanta: SBL Press, 2021.

Allen, Robert. *A treasurie of catechisme, or Christian instruction. The first part, which is concerning the morall law or ten Commandements of Almightie God: with certaine questions and aunswers preparatory to the same*. Early English Books Online 2. https://tinyurl.com/4jvsv8jw.

Allison, Dale C. "The History of the Interpretation of Matthew: Lessons Learned." *In die Skriflig/In Luce Verbi* 49 (2015): https://tinyurl.com/2ptp4hex.

Alt, Albrecht. "Das Verbot des Diebstahls im Dekalog." Pages 333–40 in *Kleine Schriften zur Geschichte des Volkes Israel, I*. Munich: Beck, 1953.

———. "The Origins of Israelite Law." Pages 101–71 in *Essays on Old Testament History and Religion*. Translated by R. A. Wilson. Garden City, NY: Doubleday, 1967.

Amissah, Patrick Kofi. *The Prophetic Voice of Amos on Contemporary Social Justice*. Biblical Interpretation Series 215. Leiden: Brill, 2023.

Anderson, Cheryl B. "The Eighth Commandment: A Way to King's 'Beloved Community'?" Pages 276–89 in *The Ten Commandments: The Reciprocity of Faithfulness*. Edited by William P. Brown. Library of Theological Ethics. Louisville: Westminster John Knox, 2004.

Andrewes, Lancelot. *A Pattern of Catechistical Doctrine and Other Minor Works*. Oxford: John Henry Parker, 1846; New York: AMS, 1967.

Aquinas, Thomas. *The Commandments of God: Conferences on the Two Precepts of Charity and the Ten Commandments*. Translated by Laurence Shapcote, OP, with an introduction by Thomas Gilby, OP. London: Burns, Oates & Washbourne, 1937.

———. *God's Greatest Gifts: Commentaries on the Commandments and the Sacraments*. Manchester, NH: Sophia Institute Press, 1992.

Augustine. *The Enchiridion on Faith, Hope, and Love*. Washington, DC: Regnery, 1996.

———. "On Marriage and Concupiscence." In *The Works of Augustine*. Translated by Marcus Dods. Edinburgh: T&T Clark, 1885.

———. "Sermon 33." In *The Works of Saint Augustine*. Vol 3.2, *Sermons*. Edited by John E. Rotelle. Translated by Edmund Hill. Brooklyn, NY: New City Press, 1990.

Bach, Alice. "Good to the Last Drop: Viewing the Sotah (Numbers 5.11–31) as the Glass Half Empty and Wondering How to View It Half Full." Pages 503–22 in *Women in the Hebrew Bible: A Reader*. Edited by Alice Bach. New York: Routledge, 1999.

Bailey, Wilma Ann. *"You Shall Not Kill" or "You Shall Not Murder"? The Assault on a Biblical Text*. Collegeville, MN: Liturgical Press, 2005.

Baker, David L. *The Decalogue: Living as the People of God*. Downers Grove, IL: InterVarsity Press, 2017.

Baranov, Vladimir A. "Origen and the Iconoclastic Controversy." Pages 1043–52 in *Origen and the Alexandrian Tradition: Papers of the 8th International Origen Congress, Pisa, 27–31 August 2001*. Edited by L. Perrone. Leuven: Leuven University Press, 2003.

Barclay, John M. G. "Snarling Sweetly: Josephus on Images and Idolatry." Pages 365–85 in *Idolatry: False Worship in the Bible, Early Judaism, and Christianity*. Edited by Stephen C. Barton. London: T&T Clark, 2007.

Barth, Karl. *Church Dogmatics*. Vol. III, part 4. Edited by G. W. Bromiley and T. F. Torrance. Edinburgh: T&T Clark, 1961.

Basil. *The Letters*. Translated by Roy J. Deferrari. Loeb Classical Library 243. Cambridge, MA: Harvard University Press, 1986.

Baugh, Lloyd. "The Reception of the Decalogue in Film: Krzysztof Kieślowski's *Decalogue*." Pages 343–53 in *The Decalogue and Its Cultural Influence*. Edited by Dominik Markl. Sheffield: Sheffield Phoenix, 2013.

Beal, Timothy K. *Roadside Religion: In Search of the Sacred, the Strange, and the Substance of Faith*. Boston: Beacon Press, 2006.

Beaman, Jay, and Brian K. Pipkin, eds. *Pentecostal and Holiness Statements on War and Peace*. Eugene, OR: Pickwick, 2013.

Beard, Mary. *How Do We Look: The Body, the Divine, and the Question of Civilisation*. New York: Liveright, 2018.

Beduschi, Luciane. "Joseph Haydn's *Die heiligen zehn Gebote als Canons* and Sigismund Neukomm's *Das Gesetz des alten Bundes, oder die Gesetzgebung auf Sinai*: Exemplification of Changes in Musical Settings of the Ten Commandments during the Eighteenth and Nineteenth Centuries." Pages 296–317 in *The Decalogue and Its Cultural Influence*. Edited by Dominik Markl. Sheffield: Sheffield Phoenix, 2013.

Beer, Georg. *Exodus*. Tübingen: Mohr Siebeck, 1939.

Berry, Wendell. *The Need to Be Whole: Patriotism and the History of Prejudice*. Berkeley: Shoemaker and Company, 2022.

Biddle, Mark E. *Deuteronomy: Smyth & Helwys Bible Commentary*. Macon, GA: Smyth & Helwys, 2003.

Blake, William. "The Everlasting Gospel." Pages 518–25 in *The Complete Poetry and Prose of William Blake*. Edited by David V. Erdman. New York: Doubleday, 1988.

Block, Daniel I. "The Decalogue in the Hebrew Scriptures." Pages 1–27 in *The Decalogue through the Centuries: From the Hebrew Scriptures to Benedict XVI*. Edited by Jeffrey P. Greenman and Timothy Larsen. Louisville: Westminster John Knox, 2012.

Bloom, Alan. *The Closing of the American Mind*. New York: Simon & Schuster, 1988.

Bockmuehl, Markus. "'Keeping It Holy': Old Testament Commandment and New Testament Faith." Pages 95–124 in *I Am the LORD Your God: Christian Reflections on the*

Ten Commandments. Edited by Carl E. Braaten and Christopher R. Seitz. Grand Rapids: Eerdmans, 2005.

Bok, Sissela. *Lying: Moral Choice in Public and Private Life*. 2nd ed. New York: Vintage Books, 1999.

Bonaventure. *St. Bonaventure's Collations on the Ten Commandments*. Translated by Paul J. Spaeth. New York: Franciscan Institute, 1995.

Bono. *Surrender: 40 Songs, One Story*. New York: Alfred A. Knopf, 2022.

Bottigheimer, Ruth. *The Bible for Children: From the Age of Gutenberg to the Present*. New Haven: Yale University Press, 2014.

Bownde, Nicholas. *The Doctrine of the Sabbath Plainely Layde Forth, and Soundly Proued by Testimonies Both of Holy Scripture, and also of olde and new ecclesiasticall writers*. Early English Books Online 2. https://tinyurl.com/32keucr8.

Boyarin, Daniel. *Carnal Israel: Reading Sex in Talmudic Culture*. Berkeley: University of California Press, 1995.

———. *The Jewish Gospels: The Story of the Jewish Christ*. New York: New Press, 2012.

———. "Women's Bodies and the Rise of the Rabbis: The Case of Sotah." Pages 88–100 in *Jews and Gender: The Challenge to Hierarchy*. Studies in Contemporary Jewry 16. Edited by Jonathan Frankel. Oxford: Oxford University Press, 2000.

Boyle, Gregory. *Barking to the Choir: The Power of Radical Kinship*. New York: Simon & Schuster, 2017.

Breasted, James Henry. *The Dawn of Conscience*. New York: Charles Scribner's Sons, 1933.

Breed, Brennan. *Nomadic Text: A Theory of Biblical Reception History*. Bloomington: Indiana University Press, 2014.

Brenner, Athalya. "An Afterword: The Decalogue—Am I an Addressee?" Pages 255–58 in *A Feminist Companion to Exodus–Deuteronomy*. Edited by Athalya Brenner. Sheffield: Sheffield Academic Press, 1994.

Brown, Jeannine K., and Kyle Roberts. *Matthew*. Grand Rapids: Eerdmans, 2018.

Brown, William P., ed. *The Ten Commandments: The Reciprocity of Faithfulness*. Library of Theological Ethics. Louisville: Westminster John Knox, 2004.

Bruckner, James K. "On the One Hand . . . On the Other Hand: The Twofold Meaning of the Law against Covetousness." Pages 97–118 in *To Hear and Obey: Essays in Honor of Fredrick Carlson Holmgren*. Edited by Bradley J. Bergfalk and Paul E. Koptak. Chicago: Covenant, 1997.

Brueggemann, Walter. *The Creative Word: Canon as a Model for Biblical Education*. Philadelphia: Fortress, 1982.

———. *Sabbath as Resistance: Saying No to the Culture of Now*. Louisville: Westminster John Knox, 2014.

———. "Truth-Telling as Subversive Obedience." Pages 291–300 in *The Ten Commandments: The Reciprocity of Faithfulness*. Edited by William P. Brown. Library of Theological Ethics. Louisville: Westminster John Knox, 2004.

Buber, Martin. *Moses: The Revelation and the Covenant*. New York: Harper and Row, 1958.

———. "What Are We to Do about the Ten Commandments?" Pages 118–121 in *On the Bible: Eighteen Studies*. Edited by Nahum N. Glatzer. Syracuse: Syracuse University Press, 2000.

Burgess, John P. "Reformed Explication of the Ten Commandments." Pages 78–99 in *The Ten Commandments: The Reciprocity of Faithfulness*. Edited by William P. Brown. Library of Theological Ethics. Louisville: Westminster John Knox, 2004.

Burkitt, F. C. "The Hebrew Papyrus of the Ten Commandments." *JQR* (1903): 392–408.

Burnside, Jonathan P. *God, Justice, and Society: Aspects of Law and Legality in the Bible.* Oxford: Oxford University Press, 2010.

Callahan, Allen Dwight. *The Talking Book: African Americans and the Bible.* New Haven: Yale University Press, 2006.

Calvin, John. *Commentary Upon the Acts of the Apostles.* Edited by Henry Beveridge. Translated by Christopher Fetherstone. www.ccel.org.

———. *Harmony of the Law.* Translated by Charles William Bingham. www.ccel.org.

———. *Institutes of the Christian Religion.* Edited by John T. McNeill. Translated and indexed by Ford Lewis Battles. Philadelphia: Westminster, 1960.

———. *The Year of Jubilee.* Vol. 2 of *Harmony of the Law.* Grand Rapids: Christian Classics Ethereal Library, 1999. https://tinyurl.com/ycfmmrsj.

Carter, Jimmy. *A Full Life: Reflections at Ninety.* New York: Simon & Schuster, 2015.

Carter, Stephen L. *God's Name in Vain: The Wrongs and Rights of Religion in Politics.* New York: Basic Books, 2000.

Castelli, Silvia. "Murder and Murder Prohibition in Josephus." Pages 159–72 in *"You Shall Not Kill": The Prohibition of Killing in Ancient Religions and Cultures.* Edited by J. Cornelius de Vos, Hermut Löhr, and Juliane Ta Van. Göttingen: Vandenhoeck and Ruprecht, 2018.

Childs, Brevard. *The Book of Exodus: A Critical, Theological Commentary.* Philadelphia: Westminster, 1974.

———. *Old Testament Theology in a Canonical Context.* Minneapolis: Augsburg Fortress, 1990.

Christo, Gus George. *St. John Chrysostom on Repentance and Almsgiving.* Fathers of the Church 96. Washington, DC: Catholic University Press, 1998.

Chung, Youn Ho. *The Sin of the Calf: The Rise of the Bible's Negative Attitude toward the Golden Calf.* LHBOTS 523. New York: Continuum; T&T Clark International, 2010.

Claiborne, Shane. *Rethinking Life: Embracing the Sacredness of Every Person.* Grand Rapids: Zondervan, 2023.

Claiborne, Shane, and Michael Martin. *Beating Guns: Hope for People Who Are Weary of Violence.* Grand Rapids: Brazos, 2019.

Clines, David J. A. "The Ten Commandments: Reading from Left to Right." Pages 26–45 in *Interested Parties: The Ideology of Writers and Readers of the Hebrew Bible.* Edited by David J. A. Clines. Sheffield: Sheffield Phoenix, 2009.

Coffin, F. J. "The Third Commandment." *JBL* 19 (1900): 166–88.

Comer, John Mark. *The Ruthless Elimination of Hurry.* New York: Waterbrook, 2019.

Curry, Michael, with Sara Grace. *Love Is the Way: Holding On to Hope in Troubling Times.* New York: Avery, 2020.

Davidman, Joy. *Smoke on the Mountain: An Interpretation of the Ten Commandments.* Philadelphia: Westminster, 1954.

Dawn, Marva J. *Keeping the Sabbath Wholly: Ceasing, Resting, Embracing, Feasting.* Grand Rapids: Eerdmans, 1989.

Dempster, Murray. "Pacifism in Pentecostalism: The Case of the Assemblies of God." Pages 137–65 in *The Fragmentation of the Church and Its Unity in Peacekeeping.* Edited by Jeffrey Gros and John D. Rempel. Grand Rapids: Eerdmans, 2001.

Derrett, J. Duncan M. *Law in the New Testament.* London: Darton, Longman and Todd, 1970.

DeSalvo, Louise. *Adultery*. Boston: Beacon Press, 1999.

DeYoung, Kevin. *The 10 Commandments: What They Mean, Why They Matter, and Why We Should Obey Them*. Wheaton, IL: Crossway, 2018.

Douglass, Frederick. "Slaveholding Religion and the Christianity of Christ." Pages 102–11 in *African American Religious History: A Documentary Witness*. Edited by Milton C. Sernett. 2nd ed. Durham, NC: Duke University Press, 1999.

Downame, John. *Foure treatises tending to disswade all Christians from foure no lesse hainous then common sinnes; namely, the abuses of swearing, drunkennesse, whoredome, and briberie*. Early English Books Online 2. https://tinyurl.com/4s923uua.

Duff, Nancy J. "The Old Testament in Public: The Ten Commandments, Evolution, and Sabbath Closing Laws." Pages 447–65 in *The Cambridge Companion to the Hebrew Bible/Old Testament*. Edited by Stephen B. Chapman and Marvin A. Sweeney. Cambridge: Cambridge University Press, 2016.

Durham, James. *The Law Unsealed, or, a practical exposition of the Ten Commandments. With a resolution of several momentous questions and cases of conscience*. Early English Books Online. https://tinyurl.com/phfsuw6v.

Durham, John I. *Exodus*. Word Biblical Commentary. Grand Rapids: Zondervan Academic, 1990.

Early Christian Fathers. Edited by Cyril Richardson. Library of Christian Classics 1:230. Philadelphia: Westminster, 1953.

Eire, Carlos M. N. *War against the Idols: The Reformation of Worship from Erasmus to Calvin*. London: Cambridge University Press, 1986.

Ellul, Jacques. *Humiliation of the Word*. Grand Rapids: Eerdmans, 1985.

Erickson, Amy. *Jonah: Introduction and Commentary*. Grand Rapids: Eerdmans, 2021.

Evans, Craig A. "The Decalogue in the New Testament." Pages 29–46 in *The Decalogue through the Centuries: From the Hebrew Scriptures to Benedict XVI*. Edited by Jeffrey P. Greenman and Timothy Larsen. Louisville: Westminster John Knox, 2012.

Farkas, József. *Bench Marks*. Translated by John R. Bodo. Richmond, VA: John Knox, 1969.

Fein, Leonard. "I Was Young, and I Have Also Grown Older." Pages 65–71 in *Broken Tablets: Restoring the Ten Commandments and Ourselves*. Edited by Rachel S. Mikva. Woodstock, VT: Jewish Lights, 1999.

Fowl, Stephen E. *Idolatry*. Waco, TX: Baylor University Press, 2019.

Fox, Emmet. *The Ten Commandments: The Master Key to Life*. New York: Harper and Row, 1953.

Frank, Bruno. "Honor Thy Father and Thy Mother." Pages 181–225 in *The Ten Commandments: Ten Short Novels of Hitler's War against the Moral Code*. Edited by Armin L. Robinson. New York: Simon & Schuster, 1944.

Freedman, David Noel. *The Nine Commandments: Uncovering a Hidden Pattern of Crime and Punishment in the Hebrew Bible*. New York: Doubleday, 2000.

Freeman, M. D. A. "The Law and Sexual Deviation." Pages 376–440 in *Sexual Deviation*. Edited by Ismond Rosen. Oxford: Oxford University Press, 1979.

Fuchs-Kreimer, Nancy. "Thou Shalt Not Take the Name." Pages 31–39 in *Broken Tablets: Restoring the Ten Commandments and Ourselves*. Edited by Rachel S. Mikva. Woodstock, VT: Jewish Lights, 1999.

Gaiman, Neil. *American Gods: A Novel*. New York: William Morrow, 2001.

Gamble, Eugenia Anne. *Words of Love: A Healing Journey with the Ten Commandments*. Louisville: Westminster John Knox, 2022.

Gellar, Laura. "Competing Values." Pages 115–22 in *Broken Tablets: Restoring the Ten Commandments and Ourselves*. Edited by Rachel S. Mikva. Woodstock, VT: Jewish Lights, 1999.

Gerstenberger, Erhard S. *Leviticus*. OTL Commentary Series. Louisville: Westminster John Knox, 1996.

Ginzberg, Louis, and David Stern. *Legends of the Jews*. Vols. 1–2. Translated by Henrietta Szold and Paul Radin. Philadelphia: Jewish Publication Society, 2003.

Girard, René. *I See Satan Fall Like Lightning*. Translated by James G. Williams. Maryknoll, NY: Orbis Books, 2001.

Gnuse, Robert Karl. *You Shall Not Steal: Community and Property in the Biblical Tradition*. Eugene, OR: Wipf & Stock, 1985.

Green, Ian. "The Dissemination of the Decalogue in English and Lay Responses to Its Promotion in Early Modern English Protestantism." Pages 171–89 in *The Decalogue and Its Cultural Influence*. Edited by Dominik Markl. Sheffield: Sheffield Phoenix, 2013.

Greenberg, Moshe. "The Decalogue Tradition Critically Examined." Translated by In Other Words [Moshav Shorashim]. Pages 83–119 in *The Ten Commandments in History and Tradition*. Edited by Ben-Zion Segal. English version edited by Gershon Levi. Jerusalem: Magnes, 1990.

Greenman, Jeffrey P. "Lancelot Andrewes." Pages 149–68 in *The Decalogue through the Centuries: From the Hebrew Scriptures to Benedict XVI*. Edited by Jeffrey P. Greenman and Timothy Larsen. Louisville: Westminster John Knox, 2012.

Greenspoon, Leonard. "Do Not Covet: Is It a Feeling or an Action?" TheTorah.com. 2018. https://tinyurl.com/y7sjzy7c.

Guendelsberger, Emily. *On the Clock: What Low Wage Work Did to Me and How It Drives America Insane*. New York: Little, Brown and Company, 2019.

Haggerty, Brian A. *Out of the House of Slavery: On the Meaning of the Ten Commandments*. New York: Paulist, 1978.

Halbertal, Moshe, and Avishai Margalit. *Idolatry*. Translated by Naomi Goldblum. Cambridge, MA: Harvard University Press, 1992.

Halevi, Judah. *The Kuzari (Kitab Al Khazari): An Argument for the Faith of Israel*. Translated by Hartwig Hirschfeld. New York: Schocken Books, 1964.

Hallo, William W. *The Context of Scripture: Canonical Compositions from the Biblical World*. Vols. 1–2. Leiden: Brill, 2002.

Harline, Craig. *Sunday: A History of the First Day from Babylonia to the Super Bowl*. New Haven: Yale University Press, 2011.

Harrelson, Walter. "Karl Barth on the Decalogue." *Sciences Religieuses* 6 (1976–77): 229–40.

———. *The Ten Commandments and Human Rights*. Philadelphia: Fortress, 1980.

Hart, David Bentley. "God or Nothingness." Pages 55–76 in *I Am the LORD Your God: Christian Reflections on the Ten Commandments*. Edited by Carl E. Braaten and Christopher R. Seitz. Grand Rapids: Eerdmans, 2005.

Hauerwas, Stanley M., and William H. Willimon. *The Truth about God: The Ten Commandments in Christian Life*. Nashville: Abingdon, 1999.

Hauptman, Judith. "A New Interpretation of the 39 Forbidden Sabbath Labors." Pages 323–37 in *The Faces of Torah: Studies in the Texts and Contexts of Ancient Judaism in Honor of Steven Fraade*. Edited by Christine Hayes, Michael Novick, and Michal Bar-Asher Siegal. Supplements to the Journal of Ancient Judaism 22. Gottingen: Vandenhoeck and Ruprecht, 2017.

Hawthorne, Nathaniel. *The Scarlet Letter*. Minneapolis: Lerner, 2014.
Hazony, David. *The Ten Commandments: How Our Most Ancient Moral Text Can Renew Modern Life*. New York: Scribner, 2010.
Hedges, Chris. *Losing Moses on the Freeway: The Ten Commandments in America*. New York: Free Press, 2005.
Henry, Matthew. *A Commentary on the Whole Bible*. Vol. 1, *Genesis to Deuteronomy*. Old Tappan, NJ: Fleming H. Revell, 1970.
Hersey, Tricia. *Rest Is Resistance: A Manifesto*. New York: Little, Brown, and Spark, 2022.
Heschel, Abraham Joshua. *The Sabbath*. New York: Farrer, Straus and Giroux, 2005.
Heth, William A., and Gordon J. Wenham. *Jesus and Divorce: The Problem with the Evangelical Consensus*. Nashville: Nelson, 1985.
Hill, Andrew, and John Walton. *A Survey of the Old Testament*. 3rd ed. Grand Rapids: Zondervan Academic, 2009.
Hillers, Delbert. "Ritual Progression of the Ark and Ps 132." *CBQ* 30 (January 1968): 48–55.
Hogue, Timothy S. *The Ten Commandments: Monuments of Memory, Belief, and Interpretation*. Cambridge: Cambridge University Press, 2023.
Hooper, John. *Early Writings Comprising the Declaration of Christ and His Office, Answer to Bishop Gardner, Ten Commandments, Sermons on Jonas, Funeral Sermon*. Edited by Samuel Carr for the Parker Society. Cambridge: Cambridge University Press, 1843.
Horton, Michael S. *The Law of Perfect Freedom*. Chicago: Moody, 1993.
Huffmon, Herbert B. "The Fundamental Code Illustrated: The Third Commandment." Pages 205–12 in *The Ten Commandments: The Reciprocity of Faithfulness*. Edited by William P. Brown. Library of Theological Ethics. Louisville: Westminster John Knox, 2004.
Hurston, Zora Neale. *Moses, Man of the Mountain*. New York: Harper Perennial, 1991.
Hütter, Reinhard. "The Twofold Center of Lutheran Ethics: Christian Freedom and God's Commandments." Pages 31–54 in *The Promise of Lutheran Ethics*. Edited by Karen L. Bloomquist and John R. Stumme. Minneapolis: Fortress, 1998.
Imes, Carmen Joy. *Bearing God's Name: Why Sinai Still Matters*. Downers Grove, IL: IVP Academic, 2019.
———. *Bearing YHWH's Name at Sinai: A Reexamination of the Name Command of the Decalogue*. University Park, PA: Eisenbrauns, 2018.
Jackson, Melissa A. "Trickster Matriarchs: Lot's Daughters, Rebekah, Leah, Rachel, Tamar." Pages 41–66 in *Comedy and Feminist Interpretation of the Hebrew Bible: A Subversive Collaboration*. Oxford: Oxford University Press, 2012.
Jacobs, A. J. *The Year of Living Biblically: One Man's Humble Quest to Follow the Bible as Literally as Possible*. New York: Simon & Schuster, 2007.
Jacobsen, Anders-Christian. "The Prohibition of Killing in the Ethics of the Church Fathers." Pages 257–69 in *"You Shall Not Kill": The Prohibition of Killing in Ancient Religions and Cultures*. Edited by J. Cornelius de Vos, Hermut Löhr, and Juliane Ta Van. Göttingen: Vandenhoeck and Ruprecht, 2018.
Johnston, Kenneth R. "Blake's *America*, the Prophecy That Failed: William Blake (1757–1827)." Pages 307–32 in *Unusual Suspects: Pitt's Reign of Alarm and the Lost Generation of the 1790s*. Oxford: Oxford University Press, 2013.
Johnston, Robert M. "The Rabbinic Sabbath." Pages 70–91 in *The Sabbath in Scripture and History*. Edited by Kenneth A. Strand. Washington, DC: Review and Herald, 1982.
Kant, Immanuel. *The Doctrine of Virtue*. New York: Harper & Row, 1964.

Keil, Carl Friedrich, and F. Delitzsch. *Biblical Commentary on the Books of Samuel*. Translated by James Martin. Edinburgh: T&T Clark, 1868.

Keller, Timothy. *Counterfeit Gods: The Empty Promises of Money, Sex, and Power, and the Only Hope That Matters*. New York: Penguin Random House, 2009.

Kirkpatrick, A. F. *The Second Book of Samuel*. Cambridge: Cambridge University Press, 1880.

Knight, George W., III. "Can a Christian Go to War?" *Christianity Today*, November 21, 1975. 4–7.

Knobel, Peter S. "Sacred Boundaries." Pages 91–96 in *Broken Tablets: Restoring the Ten Commandments and Ourselves*. Edited by Rachel S. Mikva. Woodstock, VT: Jewish Lights, 1999.

Knust, Jennifer. "Can an Adulteress Save Jesus? The *Pericope Adulterae*, Feminist Interpretation, and the Limits of Narrative Agency." In *The Bible and Feminism: Remapping the Field*. Edited by Yvonne Sherwood. Oxford: Oxford University Press, 2017. https://doi.org/10.1093/oso/9780198722618.001.0001.

Knust, Jennifer, and Tommy Wasserman. *To Cast the First Stone: The Transmission of a Gospel Story*. Princeton: Princeton University Press, 2018.

Kratz, Reinhard Gregor. "Der Dekalog im Exodusbuch." *VT* 44 (1994): 205–38.

Kugel, James L. *The Bible as It Was*. Cambridge, MA: Belknap Press, 1997.

Kushner, Aviya. *The Grammar of God: A Journey into the Words and Worlds of the Bible*. New York: Spiegel & Grau, 2015.

Lamb, David T. *Prostitutes and Polygamists: A Look at Love, Old Testament Style*. Grand Rapids: Zondervan, 2015.

Lambert, W. G. "Dingir.šà.dib.ba Incantations." *JNES* 33 (1974): 296–97.

Larsen, Timothy. "Christina Rossetti." Pages 181–96 in *The Decalogue through the Centuries: From the Hebrew Scriptures to Benedict XVI*. Edited by Jeffrey P. Greenman and Timothy Larsen. Louisville: Westminster John Knox, 2012.

Lauer, Gerhard. "The Law and the Artist in the Age of Extremes: On Thomas Mann's *Das Gesetz*." Pages 318–32 in *The Decalogue and Its Cultural Influence*. Edited by Dominik Markl. Sheffield: Sheffield Phoenix, 2013.

Lawson, Annette. *Adultery: An Analysis of Love and Betrayal*. New York: Basic Books, 1988.

Lee, Daniel D. "The First and Fifth Commandments: Confucian Family-Centricity in Asian American Hermeneutics." Presented at the Institute for Biblical Research. November 2024.

Leitenberg, Milton. "Deaths in Wars and Conflicts in the 20th Century." Cornell University Peace Studies Program Occasional Paper #29. 3rd ed. 2006.

Létourneau, Anne. "Bathing Beauty: Concealment of Bathsheba's Rape and Counter-Power in 2 Sam 11:1–5." Presented at Society of Biblical Literature meeting. Atlanta, GA. November 21, 2015.

Levenson, Jon. *Creation and the Persistence of Evil: The Jewish Drama of Divine Omnipotence*. Princeton: Princeton University Press, 1988.

———. *Israel's Day of Light and Joy: The Origin, Development, and Enduring Meaning of the Jewish Sabbath*. University Park, PA: Eisenbrauns, 2024.

Levine, Amy-Jill. *Sermon on the Mount: A Beginner's Guide to the Kingdom of Heaven*. Nashville: Abingdon, 2020.

Levinson, Bernard. "Deuteronomy: Introduction and Annotations." Pages 356–450 in *The Jewish Study Bible*. Edited by Adele Berlin and Marc Zvi Brettler. New York: Oxford University Press, 2004.

Levy, Richard N. "A Bit of a Thief." Pages 97–108 in *Broken Tablets: Restoring the Ten Commandments and Ourselves*. Edited by Rachel S. Mikva. Woodstock, VT: Jewish Lights, 1999.

Lewis, C. S. *Letters to Malcolm: Chiefly On Prayer*. New York: Harcourt, Brace & World, 1964.

———. "Meditation on the Third Commandment." Pages 196–99 in *God in the Dock: Essays on Theology and Ethics*. Edited by Walter Hooper. Grand Rapids: Eerdmans, 1970.

———. *The Screwtape Letters*. New York: Collier Books, 1982.

Lewis, Theodore J. *The Origin and Character of God: Ancient Israelite Religion through the Lens of Divinity*. Oxford: Oxford University Press, 2020.

Lockshin, Martin. *Rashbam's Commentary on Exodus: An Annotated Translation*. Atlanta: Scholars Press, 1997.

Lohfink, Norbert. "The Decalogue in Deuteronomy 5." Pages 248–64 in *Theology of the Pentateuch: Themes of the Priestly Narrative and Deuteronomy*. Translated by Linda M. Maloney. Minneapolis: Fortress, 1994.

Long, D. Stephen. "John Wesley." Pages 169–80 in *The Decalogue through the Centuries: From the Hebrew Scriptures to Benedict XVI*. Edited by Jeffrey P. Greenman and Timothy Larsen. Louisville: Westminster John Knox, 2012.

Long, Tom S., and Allen Pote. *Are We There Yet?* Carol Stream, IL: Hope, 2005.

Luther, Martin. *Luther's Large Catechism with Study Questions*. Edited by F. Samuel Janzow. St. Louis: Concordia, 1978.

MacDonald, Nathan. "Recasting the Golden Calf: The Imaginative Potential of the Old Testament's Portrayal of Idolatry." Pages 22–39 in *Idolatry: False Worship in the Bible, Early Judaism and Christianity*. Edited by Stephen C. Barton. New York: Continuum, 2007.

Maimonides. *The Commandments: Sefer ha-Mitzvoth of Maimonides*. Edited by Charles Chavel. London: Soncino, 1976.

Mandell, Alice. "Aaron's Body as a Ritual Vessel in the Exodus Tabernacle Building Narrative." Pages 159–81 in *New Perspectives on Ritual in the Biblical World*. Edited by Laura Quick and Melissa Ramos. London: T&T Clark, 2022.

Mann, Jacob. *The Jews in Egypt and in Palestine under the Fatimid Caliphs*. Oxford: Oxford University Press, 1920.

Mann, Thomas. "Thou Shalt Have No Other Gods Before Me." Translated by George R. Marek. Pages 3–70 in *The Ten Commandments: Ten Short Novels of Hitler's War against the Moral Code*. Edited by Armin L. Robinson. New York: Simon & Schuster, 1944.

Markschies, Christoph. *God's Body: Jewish, Christian, and Pagan Images of God*. Translated by Alexander Johannes Edmonds. Waco, TX: Baylor University Press, 2019.

McCarthy, Dennis J., SJ. *Treaty and Covenant: A Study in Form in the Ancient Oriental Documents and in the Old Testament*. Rome: Biblical Institute Press, 1981.

McCaulley, Esau. *Reading While Black: African American Biblical Interpretation as an Exercise in Hope*. Downers Grove, IL: IVP Press, 2020.

McKelvey, Douglas. "A Liturgy for Those Who Covet the Latest Technology." Pages 160–61 in *Every Moment Holy*. Nashville: Rabbit Room, 2017.

McRoberts, Justin. *Sacred Strides: The Journey to Belovedness in Work and Rest*. Nashville: Nelson, 2023.

Melanchthon, Philipp. *Melanchthon on Christian Doctrine: Loci communes 1555*. Translated and edited by Clyde L. Manschreck. Grand Rapids: Baker, 1965.

Mendenhall, George E. "Ancient Oriental and Biblical Law." *Biblical Archeology* 17 (1954): 25–46.

Merritt, Jonathan. *Learning to Speak God from Scratch: Why Sacred Words Are Vanishing—and How We Can Revive Them*. New York: Convergent, 2018.

Mettinger, Tryggve. *In Search of God: The Meaning and Message of the Everlasting Names*. Translated by Frederick H. Cryer. Philadelphia: Fortress, 1988.

Midrash Rabbah Numbers. Translated by Judah Slotki. London: Soncino, 1983.

Mikva, Rachel S., ed. *Broken Tablets: Restoring the Ten Commandments and Ourselves*. Woodstock, VT: Jewish Lights, 1999.

Milgrom, Jacob. *The JPS Torah Commentary: Numbers*. Philadelphia: Jewish Publication Society, 2003.

Miller, Patrick D. *Deuteronomy: Interpretation; A Bible Commentary for Teaching and Preaching*. Louisville: Westminster John Knox, 2011.

———. "Rethinking the First Article of the Creed." *Theology Today* 61 (2005): 499–508.

———. *The Ten Commandments*. Louisville: Westminster John Knox, 2009.

Moore, Russell. "Abuse and the Third Commandment." *Christianity Today* 66 (July/August 2022): 36.

Moran, William L. "The Conclusion of the Decalogue (Ex 20,17 = Dt 5,21)." *CBQ* 29 (October 1967): 543–54.

———. "The Scandal of the 'Great Sin' at Ugarit." *JNES* 18 (1959): 280–81.

Moyle, Marsh. *Rumors of a Better Country: Searching for Trust and Community in a Time of Moral Outrage*. London: Inter-Varsity Press, 2023.

Nelson, Zed. "Up in Arms." *Time*, July 6, 1998. 36.

Nicholls, Rachel. *Walking on the Water: Reading Mt. 14:22–23 in the Light of Its* Wirkungsgeschichte. Leiden: Brill, 2008.

Niditch, Susan. *A Prelude to Biblical Folklore: Underdogs and Tricksters*. Urbana: University of Illinois Press, 2000.

Nielsen, Eduard. *The Ten Commandments in New Perspective: A Traditio-historical Approach*. Translated by David J. Bourke. London: SCM, 1968.

Norton, Mary Beth. *Founding Mothers and Fathers: Gendered Power and the Forming of American Society*. New York: A. A. Knopf, 1996.

Oluwole, David Bamidele. "Sexual Sin, Punishment and Saving Grace: A Study of the Yoruba Penal Practices in the Light of John 8:1–11." *Ogbomoso Journal of Theology* 22 (2017): 101–17.

Origen. *Homilies on Genesis and Exodus*. Translated by Ronald E. Heine. Washington, DC: Catholic University of America Press, 1982.

Osgood, Kelsey. "Why Your 'Digital Shabbat' Will Fail." *Wired*, April 15, 2022.

Palmer, Earl. *Old Law New Life: The Ten Commandments and New Testament Faith*. Nashville: Abingdon, 1984.

Perel, Esther. *The State of Affairs: Rethinking Infidelity*. New York: HarperCollins, 2017.

Phillips, Anthony. "The Decalogue: Ancient Israel's Criminal Law." Pages 2–24 in *Essays on Biblical Law*. JSOTSup 344. Sheffield: Sheffield Academic Press, 2002.

Philo. *The Works of Philo: Complete and Unabridged*. Translated by C. D. Yonge. Peabody, MA: Hendrickson, 2006.

Pinsky, Mark I. *The Gospel according to the Simpsons, Bigger and Possibly Even Better! Edition*. Louisville: Westminster John Knox, 2007.

Plaskow, Judith. *Standing Again at Sinai: Judaism from a Feminist Perspective*. New York: HarperCollins, 1991.

Rabast, Karlheinz. *Das Apodiktische Recht im Deuteronomium und im Heiligkeitsgesetz*. Berlin-Hermsdorf: Heimatdienstverlag, 1949.

Rabinowitz, Jacob J. "The 'Great Sin' in Ancient Egyptian Marriage Contracts." *JNES* 18 (1959): 73.

Rad, Gerhard von. *Old Testament Theology*. Vol. 1. Translated by D. M. G. Stalker. New York: Harper & Row, 1962.

Radner, Ephraim. "Taking the Lord's Name in Vain." Pages 77–94 in *I Am the LORD Your God: Christian Reflections on the Ten Commandments*. Edited by Carl E. Braaten and Christopher R. Seitz. Grand Rapids: Eerdmans, 2005.

Rashbam. *Rashbam's Commentary on Exodus: An Annotated Translation*. Edited and translated by Marty Lockshin. Atlanta: Scholars Press, 1997.

Ratzaby, Yehudah. "The Ten Commandments in Spanish and Yemenite Liturgical Poetry." Translated by Ora Viskind. Pages 363–81 in *The Ten Commandments in History and Tradition*. Edited by Ben-Zion Segal. English version edited by Gershon Levi. Jerusalem: Magnes, 1990.

Resines, Luis. "American Catechisms of the Sixteenth Century." Pages 232–57 in *The Decalogue and Its Cultural Influence*. Edited by Dominik Markl. Sheffield: Sheffield Phoenix, 2013.

Reventlow, Henning Graf. *Gebot und Predigt im Dekalog*. Gütersloh: Gütersloher Verlagshaus Gerd Mohn, 1962.

Robinson, Armin L., ed. *The Ten Commandments: Ten Short Novels of Hitler's War against the Moral Code*. New York: Simon & Schuster, 1944.

Robinson, Marilynne. *Gilead*. New York: Picador, 2004.

Rofé, Alexander. "The Tenth Commandment in the Light of Four Deuteronomic Laws." Translated by Arnold Schwartz. Pages 45–65 in *The Ten Commandments in History and Tradition*. Edited by Ben-Zion Segal. English version edited by Gershon Levi. Magnes: Jerusalem, 1990.

Rolheiser, Ronald. *The Holy Longing: The Search for a Christian Spirituality*. New York: Doubleday, 1999.

Romains, Jules. "Thou Shalt Not Kill." Pages 226–72 in *The Ten Commandments: Ten Short Novels of Hitler's War against the Moral Code*. Edited by Armin L. Robinson. New York: Simon & Schuster, 1944.

Sacks, Jonathan. *The Great Partnership: Science, Religion, and the Search for Meaning*. New York: Schocken, 2011.

Sandt, Huub van de, and David Flusser. *The Didache: Its Jewish Sources and Its Place in Early Judaism and Christianity*. Minneapolis: Fortress, 2002.

Sarfatti, Gad B. "The Tablets of the Law as a Symbol of Judaism." Pages 383–418 in *The Ten Commandments in History and Tradition*. Edited by Ben-Zion Segal. English version edited by Gershon Levi. Jerusalem: Magnes, 1990.

Sarna, Nahum M. *The JPS Torah Commentary: Exodus*. Philadelphia: Jewish Publication Society, 2003.

Schaeffer, Edith. *Lifelines: The Ten Commandments for Today*. Westchester, IL: Crossway, 1982.

Schipper, Jeremy. *Denmark Vesey's Bible: The Thwarted Revolt That Put Slavery and Scripture on Trial*. Princeton: Princeton University Press, 2022.
Schnocks, Johannes. "When God Commands Killing: Reflections on Execution and Human Sacrifice in the Old Testament." Pages 100–124 in *"You Shall Not Kill": The Prohibition of Killing in Ancient Cultures and Religions*. Edited by J. Cornelius de Vos, Helmut Löhr, and Juliane Ta Van. Göttingen: Vandenhoeck & Ruprecht, 2018.
Scholz, Suzanne. *Sacred Witness: Rape in the Hebrew Bible*. Minneapolis: Fortress, 2010.
Schwartz, Saundra. "From Bedroom to Courtroom: The Adultery Type-Scene and the Acts of Andrew." Pages 267–311 in *Mapping Gender in Ancient Religious Discourse*. Edited by Todd Penner and Caroline Vander Stichele. Biblical Interpretation Series 84. Leiden: Brill, 2007.
Seitz, Christopher R. "The Ten Commandments: Positive and Natural Law and the Covenants Old and New—Christian Use of the Decalogue and Moral Law." Pages 18–39 in *I Am the LORD Your God: Christian Reflections on the Ten Commandments*. Edited by Carl E. Braaten and Christopher R. Seitz. Grand Rapids: Eerdmans, 2005.
Sekulow, Jay A., and Francis J. Manion. "The Supreme Court and the Ten Commandments: Compounding the Establishment Clause Confusion." *William & Mary Bill of Rights Journal* 33 (2005). https://tinyurl.com/5f4663xs.
Shaik, Martin van. *The Harp in the Middle Ages: The Symbolism of a Musical Instrument*. Amsterdam: Rodopi, 2005.
Sheinfeld, Shayna. "The Old Gods Are Fighting Back: Mono- and Polytheistic Tensions in Battlestar Galactica and Jewish Biblical Interpretation." *Journal for Interdisciplinary Biblical Studies* 3 (summer 2021): 1–19.
Shepherd, Scott. *The Last Commandment*. New York: Mysterious Press, 2021.
Shulevitz, Judith. *The Sabbath World: Glimpses of a Different Order of Time*. New York: Random House, 2010.
Shusterman, Neal. *Scythe*. New York: Simon and Schuster, 2016.
Sleeth, Matthew. *24/6: A Prescription for a Healthier, Happier Life*. Carol Stream, IL: Tyndale House, 2012.
Smith, Lesley J. *The Ten Commandments: Interpreting the Bible in the Medieval World*. Leiden: Brill, 2014.
Sommer, Benjamin D. *The Bodies of God and the World of Ancient Israel*. Cambridge: Cambridge University Press, 2009.
Stamm, Johann Jacob, with M. E. Andrew. *The Ten Commandments in Recent Research*. London: SCM, 1967.
Stulac, Daniel J. D. *Gift of the Grotesque: A Christological Companion to the Book of Judges*. Eugene, OR: Cascade, 2022.
Supreme Court of the United States. *U.S. Reports: Stone v. Graham, 449 U.S. 39*. 1980. Periodical. https://www.loc.gov/item/usrep449039/.
Svebakken, Hans. *Philo of Alexandria's Exposition on the Tenth Commandment*. Atlanta: Society of Biblical Literature, 2012.
Swenson, Kristin. *A Most Peculiar Book: The Inherent Strangeness of the Bible*. New York: Oxford Academic, 2021. https://doi.org/10.1093/oso/9780190651732.003.0012.
Swoboda, A. J. *Subversive Sabbath: The Surprising Power of Rest in a Nonstop World*. Grand Rapids: Brazos, 2018.
Talese, Gay. *Honor Thy Father*. New York: Harper Perennial, 2009.
———. *Thy Neighbor's Wife*. New York: Ivy Books, 1981.

Thomas, Keith. "The Puritans and Adultery: The Act of 1650 Reconsidered." Pages 257–82 in *Puritans and Revolutionaries: Essays in Seventeenth Century History Presented to Christopher Hill*. Edited by Donald Pennington and Keith Thomas. Oxford: Clarendon Press, 1978.

Thomas, Rhondda Robinson. *Claiming Exodus: A Cultural History of Afro-Atlantic Identity, 1774–1903*. Waco, TX: Baylor University Press, 2013.

Toorn, Karel van der. *Sin and Sanction in Israel and Mesopotamia: A Comparative Study*. Assen: Van Gorcum, 1985.

Torrance, Thomas. *The Beatitudes and the Decalogue*. London: Skeffington and Son, 1992.

Trainum, James L. *How the Police Generate False Confessions: An Inside Look at the Interrogation Room*. Lanham, MD: Rowman & Littlefield, 2016.

Trible, Phyllis. *Texts of Terror: Literary-Feminist Readings of Biblical Narratives*. Minneapolis: Fortress, 2022.

Trimm, Charlie. "Honor Your Parents: A Command for Adults." *JETS* 60 (2017): 247–63.

Trueman, Carl R. "John Owen." Pages 135–47 in *The Decalogue through the Centuries: From the Hebrew Scriptures to Benedict XVI*. Edited by Jeffrey P. Greenman and Timothy Larsen. Louisville: Westminster John Knox, 2012.

Turner, Philip. "The Ten Commandments in the Church in a Postmodern World." Pages 3–17 in *I Am the LORD Your God: Christian Reflections on the Ten Commandments*. Edited by Carl E. Braaten and Christopher R. Seitz. Grand Rapids: Eerdmans, 2005.

Tyson, Timothy. *The Blood of Emmett Till*. New York: Simon & Schuster, 2017.

Underwood, Richard H. "False Witness: A Lawyer's History of the Law of Perjury." *Arizona Journal of International and Comparative Law* 10 (Fall 1993): 215–52.

Urbach, Ephraim E. "The Role of the Ten Commandments in Jewish Worship." Translated by Gershon Levi. Pages 161–89 in *The Ten Commandments in History and Tradition*. Edited by Ben-Zion Segal, English version edited by Gershon Levi. Jerusalem: Magnes, 1990.

Varden, Helga. "Kant and Lying to the Murderer at the Door . . . One More Time: Kant's Legal Philosophy and Lies to Murderers and Nazis." *Journal of Social Philosophy* 41 (December 2010): 403–21.

Verhey, Allen. "Calvin and the 'Stewardship of Love.'" Pages 157–74 in *The Ten Commandments for Jews, Christians, and Others*. Edited by Roger E. Van Harn. Grand Rapids: Eerdmans, 2007.

Volf, Miraslov, with Linn Tonstad. "Bearing True Witness." Pages 179–93 in *The Ten Commandments for Jews, Christians, and Others*. Edited by Roger E. Van Harn. Grand Rapids: Eerdmans, 2007.

Vom Steeg, Al. *Freedom to Live: A Guide to a Free and Abundant Life as Revealed through the Ten Commandments*. Des Moines, IA: Meredith, 1984.

Vos, J. Cornelius de. "Murder as Sacrilege: Philo of Alexandria on the Prohibition of Killing." Pages 142–58 in *"You Shall Not Kill": The Prohibition of Killing in Ancient Religions and Cultures*. Edited by J. Cornelius de Vos, Hermut Löhr, and Juliane Ta Van. Göttingen: Vandenhoeck and Ruprecht, 2018.

Wall, Robert W. *Reading Hebrews: A Literary and Theological Commentary*. Macon, GA: Smyth & Helwys, 2024.

Wannenwetsch, Bernd. "The Desire of Desire: Commandment and Idolatry in Late Capitalist Societies." Pages 315–30 in *Idolatry: False Worship in the Bible, Early Judaism and Christianity*. Edited by Stephen C. Barton. New York: Continuum, 2007.

———. "You Shall Not Kill—What Does It Take? Why We Need the Other Commandments If We Are to Abstain from Killing." Pages 148–74 in *I Am the LORD Your God: Christian Reflections on the Ten Commandments*. Edited by Carl E. Braaten and Christopher R. Seitz. Grand Rapids: Eerdmans, 2005.

Watson, Thomas. *Body of Divinity: Contained in Sermons upon the Assembly's Catechism*. Grand Rapids: Baker, 1979.

Watts, Isaac. *Divine and Moral Songs for the Use of Children*. London: John Van Voorst, 1848.

Weeks, Stuart. "Man-made Gods? Idolatry in the Old Testament." Pages 7–21 in *Idolatry: False Worship in the Bible, Early Judaism, and Christianity*. Edited by Stephen C. Barton. London: T&T Clark, 2007.

Weiss, Herold. "The Sabbath in the Writings of Josephus." *Journal for the Study of Judaism in the Persian, Hellenistic, and Roman Period* 29 (1998): 363–90.

Wesley, John. "The Unity of the Divine Being." Sermon 114. *The Works of John Wesley*. Vol. 3, *Sermons III (71–114)*. Edited by Albert C. Outler. Nashville: Abingdon, 1986.

Whatley, William. *A pithie, short, and methodicall opening of the Ten commandements*. London: Printed by John Haviland for Thomas Pauier and Leonard Greene, 1622. Early English Books Online. https://tinyurl.com/yc58ervc.

Whitehead, Andrew L. *American Idolatry: How Christian Nationalism Betrays the Gospel and Threatens the Church*. Grand Rapids: Brazos, 2023.

Wierzbicka, Anna. *What Did Jesus Mean? Explaining the Sermon on the Mount and the Parables in Simple and Universal Human Concepts*. Oxford: Oxford University Press, 2001.

Wilf, Steven "The Ten Commandments and the Problem of Legal Transplants in Contemporary America." Pages 354–70 in *The Decalogue and Its Cultural Influence*. Edited by Dominik Markl. Sheffield: Sheffield Phoenix, 2013.

Williamson, Clark M. *A Guest in the House of Israel: Post-Holocaust Church Theology*. Louisville: Westminster John Knox, 1993.

Willis, Jonathan. *The Reformation of the Decalogue: Religious Identity and the Ten Commandments in England, c. 1485–1625*. Cambridge: Cambridge University Press, 2017.

Wirzba, Norman. *Living the Sabbath: Discovering the Rhythms of Rest and Delight*. Grand Rapids: Brazos, 2006.

Wojtyła, Karol (Pope John Paul II). *Love and Responsibility*. Translated by H. T. Willetts. San Francisco: Ignatius Press, 1993.

Wolf, Arnold Jacob. "Ten More Words." Pages 133–36 in *Broken Tablets: Restoring the Ten Commandments and Ourselves*. Edited by Rachel S. Mikva. Woodstock, VT: Jewish Lights, 1999.

Wright, Christopher J. H. *God's People in God's Land: Family, Land, and Property in the Old Testament*. Grand Rapids: Eerdmans, 1990.

———. *Old Testament Ethics for the People of God*. Downers Grove, IL: InterVarsity Press, 2004.

Wright, Melanie J. *Moses in America: The Cultural Uses of Biblical Narrative*. Oxford: Oxford University Press, 2003.

Zimmerli, Walther. *I Am Yahweh*. Translated by Douglas W. Stott. Edited by Walter Brueggemann. Atlanta: John Knox, 1982.

INDEX OF AUTHORS

INDEX OF SUBJECTS

INDEX OF SCRIPTURE

Old Testament

Genesis

Exodus